Gaming, Radicalization, and the Politics of Online Play

Muhammad Asad Latif
https://orcid.org/0009-0006-9378-9953
Islamia University of Bahawalpur, Pakistan

IGI Global
Scientific Publishing
Publishing Tomorrow's Research Today

Vice President of Editorial Melissa Wagner
Director of Acquisitions Mikaela Felty
Director of Book Development Jocelynn Hessler
Production Manager Mike Brehm
Cover Design Jose Rosado

Published in the United States of America by
IGI Global Scientific Publishing
701 East Chocolate Avenue
Hershey, PA, 17033, USA
Tel: 717-533-8845 | Fax: 717-533-7115
Website: https://www.igi-global.com E-mail: cust@igi-global.com

Library of Congress Cataloging-in-Publication Data

LCCN: 2026030642 (CIP Data Pending)
ISBN13: 9798260016640
Isbn13Softcover: 9798260016657
EISBN13: 9798260016664

British Cataloguing in Publication Data
A Cataloguing in Publication record for this book is available from the British Library.

Table of Contents

Detailed Table of Contents

This chapter examines the intersections of gaming cultures, radicalization processes, religion, and gender politics in shaping the digital formation of ISIS ideologies. It explores how online gaming environments, chat platforms, and immersive digital spaces can be appropriated for ideological dissemination, identity construction, and recruitment strategies. Rather than treating gaming as a neutral form of entertainment, the chapter situates it within broader socio-political and religious contexts where extremist actors may embed narratives of belonging, masculinity, femininity, and sacred violence. It also investigates how religious symbolism and gendered representations are mobilized in online play to normalize exclusionary and violent worldviews. By drawing on interdisciplinary literature from media studies, religious studies, and security studies, the chapter highlights the complex and contested nature of digital spaces in contemporary radicalization pathways.

Digital gaming has become a major arena for identity formation, community building, and political expression. However, research on gaming and extremism has focused largely on Western far-right movements, overlooking South Asia's rapidly expanding gaming communities. This chapter addresses that gap by examining how religious identity, geopolitical narratives, and radicalization intersect within gaming ecosystems in Pakistan, India, and Bangladesh. Drawing on social identity theory, critical geopolitics, and digital religious communication, it explores how extremist actors exploit gaming platforms for recruitment while also highlighting communities' capacity for resistance. The findings show that gaming environments function as gateway social spaces where players encounter ideological narratives linked to broader extremist networks. The chapter concludes with practical, evidence-based recommendations for policymakers, platform moderators, educators, and civil

The integration of esports into the Revised K to 10 Physical Education and Health Curriculum of the Department of Education in the Philippines reflects a significant shift in addressing digital culture and 21st-century competencies in basic education. This chapter examines the inclusion of esports in Grade 10 Physical Activity Participation, focusing on competitive gaming, teamwork, communication, ethical standards, and esports event management processes. Anchored in digital culture, experiential learning, and digital citizenship perspectives, the chapter explores how esports can develop collaboration, leadership, responsible online participation, and event management skills among learners. It also discusses opportunities and challenges in implementing esports education, including issues related to toxicity, inclusion, and ethical engagement. The chapter argues that structured esports education can foster meaningful and responsible learning experiences in contemporary Philippine basic education.

As the digital landscape in Pakistan moves from traditional social media to immersive gaming environments, these "third spaces" have become critical sites for ideological formation and, conversely, radicalization. Extremist groups have effectively used "gamification" to recruit and normalize violent narratives but defensive strategies are largely reactive. The research studies a proactive framework: Ethical Gamification. This study seeks to build digital resilience among Pakistani youth by embedding core Islamic ethical values such as Adl (Justice), Rahmah (Compassion) and Shura (Consultation) into the procedural rhetoric of game mechanics. This chapter offers a pedagogical model beyond the 'prohibition vs. permission' binary, in which the 'Politics of Play' is re-captured as a vehicle for prosocial behavior and counter-radicalization.

Preface

The rapid expansion of digital gaming has transformed interactive entertainment into one of the most influential cultural, economic, and technological phenomena of the twenty-first century. No longer confined to leisure activities or recreational consumption, digital games have become complex social ecosystems where millions of individuals communicate, negotiate identities, construct communities, exchange political ideas, and participate in global digital cultures. Multiplayer games, esports, streaming platforms, voice-chat systems, and gaming-adjacent social media have collectively blurred the boundaries between virtual and physical realities, producing new forms of interaction that extend far beyond gameplay itself. Consequently, gaming spaces have emerged as important sites for understanding contemporary questions of power, identity, governance, inclusion, digital citizenship, and ideological contestation.

Alongside these remarkable opportunities, however, the increasing interconnectedness of gaming communities has generated profound societal challenges. The same technologies that facilitate collaboration, creativity, and intercultural communication can also be exploited to disseminate misinformation, normalize hate speech, reinforce exclusionary identities, encourage online harassment, and, in extreme cases, facilitate ideological radicalization. Extremist organizations, political movements, and digitally networked communities increasingly recognize interactive media not merely as communication channels but as environments in which identities can be cultivated, narratives can be gamified, and social belonging can be strategically engineered. Such developments demand scholarly attention that extends beyond conventional security studies or game studies, requiring interdisciplinary approaches capable of explaining the complex relationships among technology, politics, religion, economics, communication, psychology, education, and digital governance.

This edited volume, **Gaming, Radicalization, and the Politics of Online Play**, responds to this urgent intellectual challenge. Bringing together contributions from scholars representing diverse disciplinary backgrounds and geographical contexts, the volume offers one of the first comprehensive examinations of how gaming cultures intersect with radicalization processes, political communication, artificial intelligence, platform governance, digital ethics, education, and global political economy. Rather than approaching gaming solely as entertainment or treating radicalization exclusively as a security problem, the chapters collectively demonstrate that online play constitutes a dynamic political and cultural arena where competing ideologies, identities, values, and institutional interests continuously interact.

The volume also reflects an important conceptual shift within contemporary digital scholarship. Earlier research frequently portrayed online radicalization through the lens of traditional social media platforms, focusing primarily on websites, discussion forums, and video-sharing services. While these spaces remain significant, digital interaction has evolved considerably over the past decade. Multiplayer gaming platforms, Discord servers, livestreaming environments, immersive virtual worlds, esports communities, and voice-based communication systems now facilitate continuous social engagement among millions of users worldwide. These environments possess distinctive communicative characteristics, including persistent interaction, collaborative gameplay, anonymity, competitive structures, emotional investment, and algorithmically mediated recommendation systems, all of which create unique opportunities for both constructive participation and ideological manipulation. Understanding these evolving environments therefore requires fresh theoretical perspectives that recognize gaming as an increasingly influential component of the contemporary digital public sphere.

Equally important, this volume avoids simplistic assumptions that games themselves cause extremism. Instead, the contributors emphasize that radicalization is a multidimensional process shaped by political grievances, social exclusion, economic inequalities, identity crises, religious narratives, technological infrastructures, and algorithmic amplification. Gaming environments should therefore be understood not as deterministic causes of extremist behaviour but as complex social ecosystems where broader societal dynamics become visible and, at times, intensified. This distinction is fundamental because it shifts scholarly attention away from moral panics surrounding digital games and toward evidence-based analyses of how technological affordances interact with social, political, and cultural processes.

Another distinguishing feature of this volume is its genuinely interdisciplinary orientation. Scholars from media studies, communication, computer science, Islamic studies, education, psychology, sociology, political science, international relations, security studies, and artificial intelligence contribute complementary perspectives that enrich understanding of online play and digital radicalization. Rather than presenting isolated disciplinary viewpoints, the chapters collectively illustrate how complex digital phenomena require integrated analytical frameworks capable of bridging technological innovation with broader questions of ethics, governance, culture, and human behaviour. Such interdisciplinarity is increasingly essential as governments, educators, technology companies, civil society organizations, and international institutions seek evidence-based strategies to promote safer and more inclusive digital environments.

CHAPTER OVERVIEW

The book opens with **Chapter 1, "Gaming, Radicalization, Religion, and Gender Politics: Online Play and the Digital Formation of ISIS Ideologies,"** which establishes the conceptual foundation for the volume. The chapter argues that gaming environments should not be viewed as politically neutral entertainment spaces but rather as interactive digital arenas where ideological narratives, religious symbolism, and gendered identities can converge. By examining how extremist organizations such as ISIS strategically appropriate gaming aesthetics, immersive communication, and online communities, the chapter demonstrates how violent ideologies become embedded within broader digital cultures of participation and belonging. Rather than focusing exclusively on propaganda, the discussion explores how constructions of masculinity, femininity, religious identity, and collective purpose contribute to the normalization of extremist worldviews within digitally mediated environments. In doing so, the chapter establishes the book's central argument that understanding online radicalization requires attention to the cultural politics of gaming itself.

Having established both conceptual and theoretical foundations, **Chapter 2, "Religious Identity, Geopolitical Narratives, and Radicalization in South Asian Gaming Communities,"** shifts attention toward one of the world's fastest-growing digital regions. Moving beyond the predominantly Western focus of existing literature, the chapter investigates how religious identities, geopolitical conflicts, and regional political narratives shape gaming communities across Pakistan, India, and Bangladesh. Through the combined lenses of social identity theory, critical geopolitics, and digital religious communication, the authors demonstrate that gaming platforms frequently function as social spaces where broader political and religious tensions are negotiated, contested, and occasionally exploited by extremist actors. At the same time, the chapter emphasizes the resilience of local gaming communities, highlighting opportunities for digital literacy, community engagement, and evidence-based policy interventions that strengthen resistance to online radicalization.

Chapter 3 extends this discussion by examining how advances in **Explainable Artificial Intelligence (XAI)** offer innovative approaches for detecting harassment, hate speech, and extremist communication within voice-chat environments. Moving beyond traditional automated moderation systems, the chapter explores how transparency, accountability, and interpretable machine-learning models can improve trust while enhancing the effectiveness of digital governance across increasingly complex gaming ecosystems. While the opening chapters establish the conceptual, theoretical, and regional foundations for understanding the intersections between gaming and radicalization, the second section of this volume shifts attention toward the practical, ethical, technological, and educational dimensions of digital governance. Collectively, these chapters recognize that contemporary gaming ecosystems are not inherently harmful nor inherently beneficial; rather, they are socially constructed environments whose consequences depend upon the institutional, technological, educational, and ethical frameworks through which they are designed, governed, and experienced. Accordingly, the contributors move beyond diagnosing the problem of online extremism to examine constructive interventions capable of fostering digital resilience, responsible participation, and inclusive online communities.

The contemporary gaming landscape is increasingly characterized by persistent interaction through voice communication, livestreaming, virtual communities, and immersive multiplayer environments. These technological developments have significantly enhanced opportunities for collaboration and social engagement, yet they have simultaneously created new challenges for content moderation, community governance, and the protection of vulnerable users. Traditional moderation systems, often dependent upon reactive reporting mechanisms or opaque machine-learning algorithms, struggle to respond effectively to rapidly evolving forms of online abuse, coded extremist language, coordinated harassment campaigns, and identity-based discrimination. Consequently, ensuring the safety and inclusivity of digital gaming environments requires innovative approaches that integrate technological sophistication with ethical accountability and human oversight.

Against this backdrop, **Chapter 4 "Explainable AI for Detecting Harassment and Extremism in Voice Chat,"** investigates one of the most significant technological developments in contemporary digital governance. The chapter argues that advances in Explainable Artificial Intelligence (XAI) provide opportunities to improve automated moderation while simultaneously enhancing transparency, accountability, and public trust. Rather than relying upon conventional "black-box" artificial intelligence systems that generate moderation decisions without explanation, the authors advocate interpretable machine-learning frameworks capable of providing understandable justifications for identifying harassment, hate speech, and extremist discourse. By integrating speech recognition technologies, natural language processing, and explainable deep-learning models, the chapter demonstrates how artificial intelligence can become an effective partner for human moderators rather than replacing human judgment altogether. Equally important, the discussion carefully addresses the ethical implications of algorithmic bias, privacy protection, due process, and fairness, thereby emphasizing that technological innovation must remain grounded in democratic principles and respect for users' rights.

Technology alone, however, cannot address the social and ideological complexities of online radicalization. Sustainable digital governance requires educational initiatives that cultivate ethical awareness, critical thinking, digital citizenship, and responsible participation among younger generations. Recognizing this reality, **Chapter 5, "Teaching Esports in Basic Education—Event Management, Ethical Play, and Digital Culture in the Revised Philippine PE and Health Curriculum,"** demonstrates how educational institutions can play an essential role in shaping healthier gaming cultures. Rather than perceiving esports merely as competitive entertainment, the chapter presents them as valuable pedagogical tools capable of developing leadership, teamwork, communication, collaboration, and responsible online behaviour. Drawing upon the Philippine educational context, the authors illustrate how structured esports curricula can encourage ethical participation while preparing students for the increasingly digital character of contemporary society. In doing so, the chapter broadens the scope of the volume by illustrating that gaming may also function as a positive educational resource when embedded within carefully designed learning environments that promote inclusion, respect, and civic responsibility.

The emphasis upon ethical engagement continues in **Chapter 6, "Gamifying Ethics: Constructing Counter-Radicalization Narratives through Islamic Values in Pakistan's Digital Ecosystem."** This chapter makes an original contribution by shifting scholarly attention from reactive counter-extremism strategies toward proactive ethical interventions within gaming environments. Rather than focusing exclusively on censorship or surveillance, the authors argue that digital resilience can be strengthened by incorporating fundamental Islamic ethical principles—including justice (*Adl*), compassion (*Rahmah*), and consultation (*Shura*)—into the procedural logic of game design itself. Through the concept of ethical gamification, the chapter proposes that games can encourage empathy, cooperation, dialogue, and moral reflection while simultaneously challenging exclusionary narratives promoted by extremist organizations. Particularly significant is the chapter's rejection of simplistic binaries that frame digital games solely as either permissible or prohibited within religious discourse. Instead, it advances a nuanced understanding of online play as a cultural space capable of supporting positive identity formation, social cohesion, and civic engagement when guided by appropriate ethical principles.

The following chapters further illustrate that extremist communication often operates through subtle cultural mechanisms rather than explicit ideological messaging. **Chapter 7, "Memes, Irony, and Extremist Discourse in Gaming Communities: A Media Studies Analysis,"** explores one of the most distinctive characteristics of contemporary digital communication: the strategic use of humour, irony, parody, and internet memes. Drawing upon recent scholarship in digital media studies, the chapter argues that extremist narratives increasingly circulate through ambiguous forms of communication that blur the distinction between entertainment and ideology. Memes, inside jokes, coded references, and ironic performances enable extremist communities to construct collective identities while simultaneously maintaining plausible deniability against moderation efforts. Such communicative strategies complicate platform governance because harmful content frequently appears humorous or satirical to outsiders while conveying deeply ideological meanings to insiders. By examining these cultural dynamics, the chapter significantly enriches understanding of how digital extremism adapts to participatory online cultures characterized by creativity, informality, and rapid information exchange.

While symbolic communication represents one dimension of harmful online behaviour, everyday experiences of toxicity and harassment remain among the most immediate challenges confronting gaming communities worldwide. **Chapter 8, "Toxicity and Harassment in Online Gaming Communities: Causes, Impacts, and Prevention Strategies,"** therefore examines the broader social ecology of abusive behaviour across online gaming platforms. The authors demonstrate that toxicity extends beyond isolated incidents of offensive language to encompass systematic patterns of discrimination, exclusion, griefing, trolling, hate speech, gender-based abuse, racial harassment, and threats directed toward marginalized groups. These behaviours undermine psychological well-being, discourage participation, weaken community trust, and, under certain conditions, contribute to pathways of ideological polarization and radicalization. Importantly, the chapter avoids simplistic explanations by recognizing that toxic behaviour emerges through interactions among anonymity, competitive structures, inadequate moderation, platform design, and evolving community norms. Consequently, the authors advocate comprehensive prevention strategies that combine ethical governance, artificial intelligence-assisted moderation, inclusive game design, digital literacy initiatives, educational programmes, and active community participation. Such multidimensional approaches reinforce one of the central messages running throughout this volume: that building safer gaming environments requires collaboration among technology developers, educators, policymakers, researchers, and gaming communities themselves.

Taken together, Chapters 4 through 8 demonstrate that addressing radicalization within gaming environments demands far more than surveillance or content removal alone. Instead, these contributions collectively advocate a balanced framework integrating technological innovation, educational reform, ethical reflection, transparent governance, and community engagement. They remind readers that digital games are simultaneously technological systems, educational spaces, cultural practices, and social institutions whose future development will profoundly influence the character of online citizenship in the decades ahead. By foregrounding solutions alongside challenges, these chapters provide an important bridge between the theoretical foundations established in the first section of the volume and the broader political, geopolitical, and structural analyses that follow in the concluding chapters.

The concluding section of this volume broadens the analytical lens from individual behaviours and community interactions to the structural, geopolitical, and economic forces that increasingly shape contemporary gaming ecosystems. While earlier chapters demonstrate how online games function as important sites of identity formation, communication, education, and ideological contestation, the final contributions remind readers that these digital environments are equally influenced by corporate interests, platform governance, geopolitical conflicts, technological infrastructures, and global political economies. Gaming today represents far more than an entertainment industry; it constitutes a complex digital ecosystem in which technological innovation, commercial imperatives, regulatory frameworks, and political power intersect. Understanding the politics of online play therefore requires attention not only to the experiences of players but also to the institutional arrangements that organize digital participation at national, regional, and global scales.

As gaming platforms continue to evolve into multifunctional social environments, questions surrounding ownership, platform governance, algorithmic control, and digital sovereignty have become increasingly significant. Major technology corporations now shape not only how games are produced and distributed but also how users communicate, construct identities, consume information, and participate in online communities. These developments have generated new opportunities for innovation and creativity while simultaneously raising concerns regarding surveillance, commercialization, algorithmic recommendation systems, data extraction, and the governance of digital publics. Consequently, analyses of radicalization and online extremism cannot be separated from broader discussions concerning platform capitalism, corporate concentration, and the political economy of digital communication.

These structural concerns are addressed in **Chapter 9, "The Political Economy of Gaming Industries and Its Impact on Content Ecosystems."** The chapter argues that contemporary gaming industries should be understood as interconnected socio-economic systems shaped by venture capital investment, platform capitalism, digital infrastructures, and global content ecosystems. Rather than treating radicalization as an isolated behavioural phenomenon, the authors examine how commercial platforms—including gaming services and gaming-adjacent communication platforms—create conditions that may inadvertently facilitate ideological dissemination, community formation, and networked mobilization. By engaging with perspectives from political economy and self-determination theory, the chapter demonstrates that technological infrastructures and commercial incentives significantly influence patterns of online participation. The discussion further highlights the importance of platform governance, moderation policies, and institutional accountability in addressing the broader societal implications of digital gaming. In doing so, the chapter provides an essential structural perspective that complements the psychological, educational, and cultural analyses presented throughout the earlier sections of the book.

Moving from global digital infrastructures to a region profoundly affected by violent extremism, **Chapter 10, "Religious Radicalization in the Afghanistan–Pakistan Borderlands: Historical Roots and Contemporary Challenges,"** situates contemporary online radicalization within longer historical and geopolitical trajectories. The chapter argues that religious extremism in the Afghanistan–Pakistan borderlands cannot be adequately understood through digital technologies alone. Instead, it traces the historical evolution of radicalization through successive phases of conflict, including the Soviet-Afghan War, regional geopolitical rivalries, the emergence of transnational militant organizations, the post-9/11 security environment, and recent political transformations in Afghanistan. By examining the interactions among fragile governance, socioeconomic marginalization, cross-border mobility, religious seminaries, ethnic identities, and digital propaganda, the chapter demonstrates that online radicalization frequently reflects broader structural inequalities rather than isolated technological influences. This historical perspective represents an important contribution to the volume by reminding readers that digital platforms often amplify existing political and social conflicts instead of creating them independently. The chapter therefore reinforces one of the book's central themes: effective responses to online extremism require integrated approaches that combine technological governance with political stability, social inclusion, and institutional resilience.

The volume subsequently returns to the rapidly evolving digital landscape through **Chapter 11, "Gaming in the Modern Age: Digital Politics and Extremism in Gaming."** This chapter explores how contemporary gaming environments have become increasingly interconnected with broader processes of digital politics, online activism, algorithmic communication, and platform-mediated public discourse. It argues that gaming communities now occupy a significant position within the wider digital public sphere, where political narratives, cultural conflicts, identity debates, and ideological mobilization increasingly converge. By examining the transformation of gaming from a recreational activity into a socially influential communication ecosystem, the chapter highlights emerging challenges associated with digital participation, platform governance, online political engagement, and evolving forms of extremist communication. Importantly, the discussion emphasizes that addressing these challenges requires cooperation among policymakers, educators, civil society organizations, platform developers, and gaming communities themselves, reflecting the interdisciplinary ethos that characterizes the entire volume.

Collectively, the eleven chapters demonstrate that understanding gaming in the twenty-first century requires moving beyond narrow disciplinary boundaries. Contemporary gaming environments simultaneously function as technological infrastructures, communication networks, educational spaces, cultural industries, economic markets, political arenas, and transnational social communities. Their significance extends far beyond entertainment, influencing how individuals form identities, build relationships, negotiate cultural differences, engage with political ideas, and participate in increasingly interconnected digital societies. Consequently, the study of gaming has become inseparable from broader debates concerning democracy, social cohesion, technological governance, digital ethics, and global security.

The contributions assembled in this volume therefore offer more than an examination of radicalization within gaming environments. They collectively provide a comprehensive interdisciplinary framework for understanding the evolving politics of online play in an era characterized by rapid technological transformation, platformization, artificial intelligence, immersive media, and global digital connectivity. By integrating theoretical innovation with empirical analysis and policy-oriented reflection, this book seeks to encourage dialogue among scholars, educators, policymakers, technology developers, civil society organizations, and industry practitioners committed to fostering safer, more inclusive, and ethically responsible digital futures.

It is our hope that **Gaming, Radicalization, and the Politics of Online Play** will stimulate further interdisciplinary research into the complex relationships among gaming, politics, technology, religion, communication, and society. As digital gaming continues to expand across cultures and generations, understanding its opportunities and challenges will become increasingly essential for both scholarship and public policy. We trust that this volume will contribute meaningfully to these ongoing conversations and serve as a valuable resource for researchers, graduate students, practitioners, and decision-makers seeking to understand the profound transformations reshaping digital life in the twenty-first century.

Chapter 1

Gaming, Radicalization, Religion, and Gender Politics:

Online Play and the Digital Formation of ISIS Ideologies

Muhammad Asad Latif
http://orcid.org/0009-0006-9378-9953
Islamia University of Bahawalpur, Pakistan

ABSTRACT

This chapter examines the intersections of gaming cultures, radicalization processes, religion, and gender politics in shaping the digital formation of ISIS ideologies. It explores how online gaming environments, chat platforms, and immersive digital spaces can be appropriated for ideological dissemination, identity construction, and recruitment strategies. Rather than treating gaming as a neutral form of entertainment, the chapter situates it within broader socio-political and religious contexts where extremist actors may embed narratives of belonging, masculinity, femininity, and sacred violence. It also investigates how religious symbolism and gendered representations are mobilized in online play to normalize exclusionary and violent worldviews. By drawing on interdisciplinary literature from media studies, religious studies, and security studies, the chapter highlights the complex and contested nature of digital spaces in contemporary radicalization pathways.

DOI: 10.4018/979-8-2600-1664-0.ch001

INTRODUCTION

The rapid expansion of digital technologies has transformed the ways individuals communicate, socialize, and construct identities across national and cultural boundaries (Dauber et al., 2019). Online platforms, social media networks, and interactive gaming environments have become central spaces where political narratives, cultural imaginaries, and ideological beliefs circulate with unprecedented speed and reach (Davey, 2021). Within these technologically mediated spaces, extremist organizations have increasingly recognized the strategic potential of digital communication for recruitment, propaganda dissemination, and ideological normalization (Kowert et al., 2022). The emergence of transnational extremist movements in the twenty-first century cannot therefore be understood solely through conventional political or military frameworks; rather, it must also be examined through the cultural and technological infrastructures that shape contemporary digital life (Kowert & Quandt 2016). Among these infrastructures, gaming cultures and online play environments occupy a particularly significant position because they combine entertainment, interaction, competition, and identity formation in ways that deeply influence social perceptions and emotional attachments (Lakhani & Wiedlitzka, 2022).

Gaming is no longer confined to recreational leisure activity. Contemporary digital games function as immersive social ecosystems where users participate in collective storytelling, form communities, negotiate identities, and engage with symbolic representations of violence, heroism, morality, and belonging (Lakomy, 2019). Multiplayer games, virtual worlds, streaming platforms, voice chats, and gaming forums create interactive environments that blur distinctions between entertainment, communication, and socialization. These spaces are especially influential among younger populations who spend substantial portions of their social and emotional lives online. As gaming environments increasingly intersect with broader digital cultures, they also become vulnerable to ideological appropriation by extremist actors seeking to exploit existing networks of interaction and affective engagement (Mackintosh & Mezzofiore, 2019).

The relationship between digital gaming and radicalization has attracted growing scholarly and policy attention in recent years. Radicalization within online spaces does not occur through a single linear process; instead, it emerges through complex interactions involving identity crises, social alienation, political grievances, algorithmic exposure, and community belonging (Andrews & Skoczylis, 2022, February 17). Digital platforms facilitate these processes by enabling repeated exposure to ideological content while simultaneously creating emotionally charged networks of participation. Gaming environments are particularly significant because they often normalize competitive aggression, militarized aesthetics, and narratives of conflict through interactive participation rather than passive consumption. While violent gameplay itself does not directly cause extremism, the symbolic structures embedded within some gaming cultures may create opportunities for extremist narratives to resonate with susceptible audiences (Condis, 2020).

Extremist organizations have increasingly adapted their communication strategies to the logic of digital media cultures. Rather than relying solely on formal propaganda channels, they now circulate content through memes, livestreams, gaming references, online chats, and participatory digital communities. This transformation reflects a broader shift from hierarchical forms of ideological dissemination toward decentralized and networked communication practices. ISIS emerged as one of the most technologically sophisticated extremist organizations in this regard, employing high-quality digital media production, online recruitment strategies, and visually immersive propaganda to attract global audiences. Its online presence demonstrated how extremist movements could strategically merge religious symbolism, popular culture, and digital aesthetics to construct emotionally compelling narratives of identity and belonging (Davey, 2021, August).

The appropriation of gaming cultures by extremist groups reflects the broader convergence of entertainment media and political violence in digital societies. Gaming environments provide symbolic frameworks that can be manipulated to present ideological struggles as heroic quests, sacred missions, or battles between civilization and perceived enemies (Al-Rawi, 2024). Militarized gaming aesthetics, reward systems, and narratives of sacrifice may be reframed within extremist discourse to glorify violence and cultivate emotional identification with radical causes. Moreover, online gaming platforms enable real-time interaction among users, allowing extremist actors to build informal relationships, identify vulnerable individuals, and gradually introduce ideological content into seemingly ordinary conversations.

Religion plays a central role in many contemporary extremist narratives, including those associated with ISIS. However, digital extremism cannot be reduced to purely theological motivations. Religious symbolism in online extremist ecosystems often functions as a cultural and political language through which identities, grievances, and moral boundaries are constructed. Extremist organizations selectively reinterpret religious concepts to legitimize violence, frame geopolitical conflicts, and establish distinctions between insiders and outsiders. In digital environments, these narratives are further amplified through visual imagery, audio content, and interactive communication practices that make ideological messages more emotionally resonant and accessible to global audiences (Anti-Defamation League, 2024).

The digital circulation of religious narratives is closely connected to broader questions of identity and belonging. Online platforms enable individuals to participate in transnational imagined communities that transcend geographic limitations while offering emotional recognition and collective purpose. For some individuals experiencing social marginalization, political frustration, or personal uncertainty, extremist digital communities may appear to provide clarity, empowerment, and solidarity (Bowman et al., 2024). Gaming cultures intensify these dynamics because they already operate through mechanisms of collective participation, teamwork, symbolic achievement, and virtual identity construction. The integration of extremist discourse into such environments therefore creates new pathways through which ideological socialization can occur (Corliss, 2011).

Gender politics also constitute a crucial dimension of online radicalization processes. Extremist ideologies frequently rely upon rigid constructions of masculinity and femininity that define social roles, moral expectations, and political participation. Within ISIS propaganda and related digital ecosystems, masculinity is often associated with militarism, dominance, sacrifice, and warrior identities, while femininity is framed through narratives of purity, domesticity, reproduction, and ideological loyalty. These gendered narratives are strategically mobilized to appeal to different audiences and to reinforce broader systems of patriarchal power and social control (Fox & Tang, 2017).

Gaming cultures themselves are deeply shaped by gender politics. Online gaming communities have long been associated with debates surrounding toxic masculinity, harassment, exclusion, and the policing of identity boundaries. Hypermasculine representations of violence and competition often dominate gaming environments, creating cultural conditions in which aggressive ideological narratives may gain symbolic legitimacy (Frommel et al., 2023). At the same time, women within extremist digital ecosystems occupy complex and sometimes contradictory positions. They may be targeted as supporters, recruiters, propagandists, or symbols of ideological purity, demonstrating that digital radicalization cannot be understood exclusively through male-centered frameworks.

The convergence of gaming cultures, religion, and gender politics reveals the multidimensional nature of contemporary digital extremism. Radicalization within online environments is not merely a matter of exposure to extremist content; it is also shaped by emotional engagement, identity formation, social interaction, and cultural participation (Gonzalez & Czlonka 2010). Digital play spaces function as sites where ideological meanings are negotiated, contested, and normalized through everyday interactions. Understanding these processes requires interdisciplinary approaches capable of examining technological infrastructures alongside cultural practices, religious narratives, and gendered power relations (Gotterbarn, 2010).

Scholars across media studies, security studies, sociology, and religious studies have increasingly emphasized that extremist communication strategies must be analyzed within broader digital ecologies rather than isolated propaganda materials. Online radicalization pathways are often fragmented, decentralized, and embedded within ordinary digital experiences. Gaming communities, livestreaming platforms, encrypted chats, and meme cultures form interconnected ecosystems where political violence may be reframed as entertainment, resistance, or collective identity. These developments challenge traditional approaches to counter-extremism by demonstrating that ideological dissemination now occurs through highly interactive and culturally embedded digital practices (Granic et al., 2014a).

This chapter aims to examine the intersections between gaming cultures, radicalization processes, religion, and gender politics in the digital formation of ISIS ideologies. It seeks to analyze how gaming environments intersect with online radicalization pathways and how extremist actors exploit digital play spaces for ideological dissemination and recruitment. The chapter further aims to investigate the role of religious narratives and symbolism in contemporary extremist communication strategies while exploring how gender politics shape representation, participation, and targeting within online extremist ecosystems. By situating gaming within broader debates on digital media, security, and identity formation, the chapter contributes to interdisciplinary understandings of how extremist ideologies circulate and gain legitimacy within contemporary online cultures.

LITERATURE REVIEW

The relationship between digital media and radicalization has become a central area of inquiry in contemporary discussions on security, communication, and online culture (Granic, 2014b). The expansion of internet technologies has transformed extremist movements from territorially confined organizations into globally networked actors capable of influencing audiences across borders. Digital platforms now operate not merely as channels of communication but as environments where ideological identities are constructed, reinforced, and circulated. Within these environments, extremist narratives are increasingly embedded in everyday online interactions, making radicalization processes more diffuse and difficult to identify. The rise of social media, gaming platforms, livestreaming communities, and encrypted communication networks has intensified concerns regarding how digital participation can normalize exclusionary and violent worldviews (Groves & Anderson, 2017).

Research on online radicalization emphasizes that digital extremism functions through gradual exposure rather than direct indoctrination alone. Radicalization pathways are often shaped by emotional engagement, social belonging, algorithmic recommendation systems, and interactive participation (Hassan, 2016). Individuals encountering extremist narratives online may initially engage through humor, memes, gaming references, or cultural content before progressing toward more explicit ideological material. This progression demonstrates that extremist communication strategies frequently rely on subtle forms of normalization that integrate ideological messages into ordinary digital practices. Such environments create conditions where extremist ideas may appear familiar, entertaining, or socially acceptable rather than overtly violent from the outset (Latif, 2025).

Gaming cultures have emerged as particularly significant within discussions of digital radicalization because of their immersive and participatory nature. Online games are no longer limited to isolated entertainment experiences; they now function as social ecosystems involving teamwork, competition, communication, and identity performance. Multiplayer gaming platforms, streaming services, voice-chat systems, and gaming forums facilitate ongoing interaction among users across diverse geographic contexts. These interactive environments create strong forms of emotional attachment and community participation, making them influential spaces for identity formation and social belonging (Mahmoud, 2022).

Existing discussions of gaming and extremism often focus on the symbolic overlap between militarized gameplay and extremist narratives. Many contemporary games center around combat, warfare, strategic conflict, and heroism, producing environments where violence is normalized within competitive structures (Malik et al., 2024). Although gaming itself does not inherently produce extremist behavior, some digital spaces may create cultural conditions that extremist actors exploit. Narratives emphasizing loyalty, sacrifice, conflict, and enemy construction can be reframed within ideological discourse to resonate with individuals already immersed in gaming cultures. This dynamic becomes particularly significant in online communities where social interaction extends beyond gameplay into broader political and cultural discussions (Mansikka, 2014).

Digital gaming environments also facilitate anonymity and transnational interaction, enabling extremist actors to operate within spaces that are difficult to regulate. Communication through private servers, voice chats, and gaming communities can allow ideological messaging to circulate informally among participants. Extremist groups have increasingly recognized that gaming platforms offer opportunities for recruitment, networking, and propaganda dissemination because users often perceive these environments as recreational rather than political. This perception can reduce suspicion and allow ideological narratives to emerge gradually within seemingly ordinary interactions (McLean & Griffiths, 2019).

The use of gaming aesthetics in extremist propaganda represents another significant area within existing literature. Digital extremist content frequently incorporates visual styles associated with video games, including first-person perspectives, combat simulations, cinematic editing, and reward-based narratives. These strategies blur distinctions between entertainment and ideological messaging by presenting violence through familiar digital forms. Such representations may increase emotional engagement among younger audiences who are already accustomed to interactive gaming cultures. The gamification of extremist communication therefore reflects broader transformations in digital propaganda, where ideological persuasion increasingly relies on immersive and participatory media techniques rather than traditional political messaging alone (Pulos, 2013).

Studies of ISIS's digital strategies highlight the organization's sophisticated use of online communication technologies (Quwaider et al., 2019). ISIS became widely recognized for its ability to produce high-quality digital propaganda distributed across social media platforms, messaging applications, and online forums. Its media operations combined religious symbolism, political narratives, cinematic aesthetics, and emotionally charged storytelling to construct powerful ideological imaginaries. Digital propaganda often emphasized themes of belonging, heroism, sacrifice, and global religious solidarity while framing violence as morally justified and spiritually meaningful (Mansikka, 2014).

The integration of religious narratives into online extremist ecosystems constitutes a major dimension of contemporary digital radicalization. Religious symbolism is frequently employed to legitimize political violence, establish moral authority, and create distinctions between believers and perceived enemies. Online extremist discourse often reframes complex geopolitical conflicts through simplified religious binaries that divide the world into categories of purity and corruption, loyalty and betrayal, or sacred obligation and moral decline. Such narratives are amplified within digital environments through videos, memes, graphics, chants, and interactive discussions that enhance emotional resonance and symbolic power (Al-Rawi, 2024).

Digital religious extremism also relies heavily on identity politics. Online communities associated with extremist ideologies frequently offer participants a sense of collective purpose, recognition, and belonging. These communities construct transnational identities that transcend national boundaries while presenting participation as both morally significant and personally empowering. For individuals experiencing alienation, exclusion, or uncertainty, such narratives may provide emotional certainty and social validation. Gaming communities intensify these dynamics because they already operate through systems of teamwork, role-playing, achievement, and symbolic identity formation. The convergence of gaming cultures and extremist religious discourse therefore creates spaces where ideological narratives can become integrated into everyday digital participation (Andrews & Skoczylis, 2022, February 17).

Gender politics represent another crucial area within literature on digital extremism and online radicalization. Extremist ideologies often depend upon rigid constructions of gender roles that define social expectations, political participation, and moral legitimacy. Masculinity within extremist discourse is commonly associated with strength, militarism, protection, dominance, and sacrifice. These narratives frequently glorify warrior identities while portraying violence as a form of masculine duty and honor. Digital propaganda reinforces these representations through images of combat, brotherhood, resistance, and heroic struggle (Saleem & Anderson, 2013).

At the same time, femininity within extremist ecosystems is often framed through narratives of purity, obedience, motherhood, and ideological support. Women may be represented as symbols of moral continuity, cultural preservation, or reproductive responsibility within ideological communities. However, online extremist spaces also demonstrate that women are not merely passive subjects within radicalization processes. Digital platforms have enabled women to participate as propagandists, recruiters, supporters, and community organizers within extremist networks. These roles complicate simplistic assumptions that extremism operates exclusively through male-centered participation (Malik et al., 2024).

Gaming cultures themselves are shaped by broader gendered power structures that intersect with radicalization debates. Online gaming spaces are frequently associated with toxic masculinity, harassment, exclusionary behavior, and aggressive identity politics. Competitive gaming environments may reinforce hypermasculine ideals centered on domination, aggression, and emotional control. Such cultural conditions can overlap with extremist narratives that glorify authoritarianism, violence, and rigid gender hierarchies. Discussions surrounding online misogyny, digital harassment, and reactionary identity politics therefore form an important component of literature examining the broader political implications of gaming cultures (Yunhao et al., 2025).

Research on digital communities (Wells et al., 2024) further demonstrates that radicalization is often socially embedded rather than individually isolated. Online extremist participation typically emerges through networks of interaction involving peers, influencers, gaming contacts, and online communities. Memes, humor, livestreams, and interactive discussions can function as gateways through which ideological content becomes normalized. These practices illustrate how digital cultures increasingly blur distinctions between politics, entertainment, and social interaction. Extremist narratives may therefore circulate indirectly through broader cultural trends rather than through explicit propaganda alone (Sinclair, 2017, September 8).

Another recurring theme within literature concerns the role of algorithms and platform infrastructures in shaping exposure to extremist content. Recommendation systems designed to maximize engagement may unintentionally amplify polarizing or sensational material because emotionally charged content often generates stronger user interaction. Gaming platforms and streaming services similarly rely on engagement-driven systems that encourage prolonged participation and community formation. These technological structures can contribute to ideological echo chambers where users encounter increasingly radical content over time (Söğüt, 2022).

Contemporary discussions also emphasize that digital radicalization should not be understood as a uniform or universal process. Online extremism operates through diverse pathways shaped by local political conditions, cultural contexts, personal experiences, and technological environments. Not all gaming communities are susceptible to extremist influence, and most participants in online gaming spaces do not engage with radical ideologies. However, the increasing convergence of digital entertainment, identity politics, and ideological communication highlights the importance of examining how extremist actors strategically exploit interactive online cultures (Waldron, 2005).

Overall, existing literature demonstrates that gaming, religion, and gender politics are deeply interconnected within contemporary digital radicalization processes. Online play environments function not only as spaces of entertainment but also as arenas where ideological narratives, identity formations, and social power relations are negotiated. The appropriation of gaming cultures by extremist movements illustrates broader transformations in political communication, where digital participation and cultural engagement increasingly shape the circulation of ideological beliefs. Understanding these dynamics requires interdisciplinary approaches that recognize the complex relationships between technology, culture, religion, gender, and security in contemporary digital societies.

METHOD

Research Design

This chapter adopts a qualitative and interdisciplinary research design to examine the intersections between gaming cultures, digital radicalization, religion, and gender politics in the formation and circulation of ISIS ideologies online. The qualitative approach is particularly appropriate because the study seeks to explore meanings, narratives, representations, and symbolic interactions within digital environments rather than measure causal relationships through statistical analysis. Digital radicalization is a complex socio-cultural process shaped by identity formation, emotional engagement, and ideological communication, all of which require interpretive analysis to understand how extremist narratives operate within online spaces.

The chapter is grounded in a critical digital media framework that conceptualizes gaming environments as socio-political and cultural spaces rather than merely technological or recreational platforms. This perspective allows the analysis to move beyond simplistic assumptions that games directly produce violence and instead focus on how digital interaction, online communication, and immersive participation can create opportunities for ideological dissemination. The study also incorporates perspectives from media studies, religious studies, gender studies, and security studies in order to capture the multidimensional nature of online extremism.

The research design is exploratory in nature because it investigates emerging relationships between online play, extremist communication strategies, and digital identity formation. The study does not seek to generalize findings to all gaming communities or all forms of online participation. Instead, it aims to critically examine how specific digital practices and symbolic representations may contribute to the normalization and circulation of extremist ideologies within certain online contexts. This approach enables a nuanced understanding of how gaming cultures intersect with broader political, religious, and gendered narratives in contemporary digital societies.

Data Sources and Collection

The study relies primarily on secondary qualitative data drawn from publicly accessible digital and academic sources. Data collection focuses on online materials related to gaming cultures, extremist propaganda, digital communication practices, and online gender politics. These materials include journal articles, books, policy reports, media analyses, digital platform studies, online discussion forums, gaming-related content, publicly archived extremist media materials, and reports produced by counter-extremism organizations.

The collection of digital materials emphasizes publicly available content in order to ensure ethical compliance and avoid direct engagement with private online communities or restricted communication networks. Online gaming environments examined in the study include multiplayer gaming cultures, livestreaming platforms, online gaming forums, and digital communication spaces where ideological narratives and identity politics may circulate. The study also considers visual and textual representations associated with extremist propaganda, including militarized imagery, gaming aesthetics, symbolic narratives, recruitment messaging, and gendered portrayals within digital content.

Academic literature relating to online radicalization, digital religion, gaming studies, and extremist communication strategies forms a central component of the data set. These sources provide conceptual and contextual understanding regarding the relationship between digital participation and ideological formation. Policy documents and security analyses are also utilized to understand how contemporary counter-extremism debates conceptualize the role of gaming platforms and online communication technologies in radicalization processes.

The data collection process is guided by thematic relevance rather than chronological limitation. Sources are selected based on their capacity to address the central themes of gaming cultures, digital extremism, religious symbolism, online identity formation, and gender politics. This approach enables the study to synthesize interdisciplinary perspectives and identify recurring patterns across diverse forms of digital communication and representation.

Analytical Framework

The chapter employs thematic and discourse-based analysis to interpret the collected materials. Thematic analysis is used to identify recurring patterns, symbolic structures, and ideological themes across digital texts, gaming-related discussions, and extremist communication practices. This method allows the study to organize complex digital content into broader analytical categories related to radicalization, religious narratives, gender representation, and online participation.

Several key themes guide the analytical process. These include the militarization of gaming cultures, constructions of digital masculinity and femininity, representations of sacred violence, narratives of belonging and exclusion, identity formation within online communities, and the gamification of extremist propaganda. By examining these themes across multiple sources, the study explores how extremist discourse becomes integrated into broader digital cultures and how online interactions contribute to ideological normalization.

Discourse analysis is also employed to examine how language, symbolism, and visual representation are used to construct ideological meanings within digital environments. Particular attention is given to the ways extremist narratives frame concepts such as heroism, sacrifice, loyalty, purity, and collective identity. The analysis further explores how gaming aesthetics and interactive communication styles are incorporated into extremist messaging strategies in order to increase emotional engagement and cultural familiarity among online audiences.

Gender analysis forms an important component of the analytical framework. The study examines how digital extremist narratives construct gendered identities and social roles within online spaces. This includes analysis of representations of masculinity linked to militarism and domination, as well as representations of femininity associated with ideological support, morality, and symbolic reproduction. The framework also considers how broader gaming cultures may reinforce or challenge these gendered dynamics through patterns of participation, exclusion, and digital interaction.

RESULTS AND FINDINGS

The findings presented in Table 1 demonstrate that digital gaming environments vary significantly in their potential relationship with online radicalization processes. Highly interactive spaces such as multiplayer combat games, livestream platforms, and encrypted gaming communities appear to create stronger opportunities for ideological dissemination because they combine emotional engagement, identity formation, and continuous social interaction. These spaces allow users to develop strong online bonds and collective identities that may increase vulnerability to extremist messaging. The table further shows that gaming environments emphasizing militarized aesthetics, strategic conflict, and competitive aggression often normalize symbolic violence and narratives of heroism. Such features may indirectly align with extremist propaganda that frames violence as meaningful or honorable. The findings also indicate that cross-platform gaming networks and meme-based communities contribute to ideological circulation through humor, entertainment, and informal communication rather than explicit political discussion alone. Emotional attachment and social belonging emerge as particularly influential factors within these digital ecosystems. However, the analysis does not suggest that gaming itself causes extremism; rather, it highlights how certain online environments may be strategically exploited by extremist actors. Overall, the table illustrates the complex intersection between gaming cultures, online interaction, and the gradual normalization of extremist narratives within contemporary digital societies.

Table 2 highlights the central role of religious narratives and symbolic communication within contemporary extremist digital ecosystems. The findings reveal that extremist groups strategically employ themes such as sacred duty, martyrdom, resistance, and global brotherhood to construct emotionally compelling ideological identities. These narratives frame participation in extremist movements as morally justified, spiritually meaningful, and socially rewarding. The table also demonstrates that religious symbolism is frequently integrated with gaming aesthetics, including combat imagery, tactical missions, and heroic storytelling, to increase familiarity and emotional resonance among digitally active audiences. Through videos, memes, livestreams, and online discussions, extremist discourse transforms political violence into immersive narratives of belonging and purpose. Masculinity is largely associated with heroism, sacrifice, and militarized identities, while femininity is framed through loyalty, moral purity, and ideological support. Such representations reinforce rigid gender hierarchies within extremist communication strategies. The findings further indicate that symbolic representations contribute to identity formation by simplifying complex political conflicts into moral and religious binaries. This process strengthens collective belonging while intensifying perceptions of division between insiders and outsiders. Overall, the table demonstrates how religion, digital media, and gaming culture intersect to normalize extremist worldviews and sustain ideological engagement in online environments.

The findings in Table 3 demonstrate that gender politics play a central role in shaping online radicalization dynamics and extremist identity formation. Masculinity is consistently represented through militarized and dominant roles associated with leadership, protection, aggression, and sacrifice. These representations align closely with competitive gaming cultures that valorize combat, hierarchy, and strategic domination. In contrast, femininity is frequently framed through supportive, caregiving, and morally symbolic roles connected to loyalty, purity, and ideological continuity. The table also reveals that women may participate actively within extremist ecosystems as propagandists, recruiters, and digital supporters, indicating that online radicalization is not solely a male-centered process. Digital spaces characterized by toxic masculinity, harassment, and exclusionary behavior further reinforce aggressive identity politics and hierarchical social relations. Emotional factors such as pride, belonging, fear, isolation, and empowerment appear highly significant in shaping participation within extremist communities. The findings suggest that online radicalization often operates through symbolic constructions of gender that define authority, morality, and collective identity. Gaming environments intensify these dynamics by encouraging competitive interaction and identity performance within immersive digital spaces. Overall, the table emphasizes that understanding contemporary digital extremism requires close attention to the gendered power structures embedded within online communication and gaming cultures.

Table 4 illustrates how online play and digital interaction contribute to the gradual normalization of extremist ideologies within contemporary digital environments. The findings indicate that interactive practices such as cooperative gameplay, livestream participation, tactical simulations, and gaming forums facilitate sustained exposure to ideological narratives through repeated social engagement. These digital activities function not only as entertainment but also as spaces where users construct identities, emotional attachments, and collective meanings. Gaming environments emphasizing teamwork, conflict, strategic warfare, and competition may indirectly reinforce narratives associated with loyalty, aggression, and enemy construction. The table also demonstrates that meme culture, streaming interactions, and cross-platform communication contribute to ideological dissemination by blending humor, politics, and entertainment into everyday digital participation. Emotional responses such as excitement, belonging, escapism, and empowerment play a significant role in sustaining user engagement within these online spaces. Furthermore, highly connected digital networks amplify ideological exposure because users frequently move between gaming platforms, social media, and communication forums where extremist narratives may circulate repeatedly. The findings suggest that ideological normalization often occurs gradually through ordinary online interaction rather than direct indoctrination alone. Overall, the table highlights the importance of examining digital play environments as influential cultural spaces where extremist discourse can become embedded within routine social practices and online communication.

Table 1. Digital gaming environments and radicalization indicators

Platform Type	Interaction Level	Identity Formation	Recruitment Potential	Religious Symbolism	Gender Narratives	Violence Representation	Community Building	Emotional Engagement	Propaganda Exposure	Algorithmic Influence	Radicalization Risk
Multiplayer Combat Games	High	Strong	Moderate	Limited	Masculine Dominance	Militarized	Strong	High	Moderate	High	High
Strategy-Based Games	Moderate	Moderate	Low	Limited	Competitive Masculinity	Tactical Conflict	Moderate	Moderate	Low	Moderate	Moderate
Online Role-Playing Games	High	Strong	High	Symbolic	Identity Performance	Heroic Violence	Strong	High	Moderate	High	High
Livestream Gaming Platforms	High	Moderate	Moderate	Minimal	Influencer Masculinity	Competitive Aggression	Strong	High	High	High	High
Voice Chat Gaming Servers	High	Strong	High	Symbolic	Group Masculinity	Verbal Aggression	Strong	High	Moderate	Moderate	High
Gaming Dis-cussion Forums	Moderate	Moderate	Moderate	Occasional	Gender Polarization	Symbolic Conflict	Moderate	Moderate	High	Moderate	Moderate
Mobile Gaming Communities	Moderate	Weak	Low	Minimal	Casual Representation	Limited Violence	Moderate	Moderate	Low	High	Low
Competitive Esports Spaces	High	Strong	Moderate	Rare	Hypermasculinity	Competitive Warfare	Strong	High	Moderate	High	Moderate
Open Sandbox Gaming Worlds	High	Strong	Moderate	Symbolic	Identity Experimentation	Interactive Conflict	Strong	High	Moderate	Moderate	Moderate
Meme-Based Gaming Groups	Moderate	Moderate	High	Indirect	Masculine Humor	Satirical Violence	Moderate	High	High	High	High
Encrypted Gaming Communities	High	Strong	High	Ideological	Gender Hierarchies	Glorified Violence	Strong	High	High	Moderate	Very High
Cross-Platform Gaming Networks	Very High	Strong	High	Symbolic	Hybrid Gender Roles	Militarized Narratives	Very Strong	Very High	High	Very High	Very High

Table 2. Religious narratives and symbolic representation in digital extremist content

Narrative Theme	Religious Framing	Symbolic Representation	Emotional Appeal	Target Audience	Masculinity Themes	Femininity Themes	Media Format	Gaming Aesthetic	Recruitment Function	Identity Construction	Ideological Impact
Sacred Duty	Divine Obligation	Holy Warrior	Moral Purpose	Young Men	Heroism	Supportive Roles	Video Content	Combat Style	Strong	Collective Identity	High
Martyrdom Narratives	Spiritual Reward	Sacrifice Imagery	Emotional Intensity	Vulnerable Youth	Bravery	Loyalty	Digital Posters	Action Themes	Strong	Religious Belonging	High
Global Brotherhood	Religious Unity	Community Symbols	Belonging	Online Communities	Brotherhood	Family Roles	Chat Platforms	Team Structures	Moderate	Group Solidarity	Moderate
Enemy Construction	Moral Division	Binary Imagery	Fear and Anger	Politically Alienated Users	Protection	Purity	Memes	Conflict Simulation	High	In-group Identity	High
Apocalyptic Narratives	End-Time Imagery	Cosmic Conflict	Existential Meaning	Isolated Individuals	Warrior Identity	Moral Preservation	Short Videos	Survival Themes	Moderate	Sacred Identity	High
Victimhood Narratives	Religious Persecution	Oppression Symbols	Sympathy	Marginalized Audiences	Defender Role	Caregiver Role	Online Articles	Resistance Themes	Moderate	Shared Suffering	Moderate
Purity Discourses	Moral Cleansing	Religious Codes	Moral Certainty	Conservative Audiences	Discipline	Obedience	Infographics	Structured Missions	Moderate	Ideological Discipline	High
Resistance Narratives	Anti-Western Framing	Rebellion Symbols	Empowerment	Politically Frustrated Users	Militancy	Ideological Support	Livestreams	Tactical Warfare	High	Resistance Identity	High
Community Restoration	Religious Revival	Traditional Imagery	Nostalgia	Diaspora Groups	Leadership	Motherhood	Forums	Cooperative Missions	Moderate	Cultural Identity	Moderate
Honor and Duty	Moral Responsibility	Heroic Figures	Pride	Young Male Users	Honor Culture	Moral Purity	Videos	Competitive Gaming	Strong	Masculine Identity	High
Digital Brotherhood	Online Unity	Group Logos	Inclusion	Gaming Communities	Team Loyalty	Limited Visibility	Voice Chats	Multiplayer Dynamics	Moderate	Social Belonging	Moderate
Sacred Violence	Religious Justification	Violent Symbolism	Shock and Awe	Radicalized Users	Aggressive Masculinity	Symbolic Support	Hybrid Media	First-Person Combat	Very Strong	Extremist Identity	Very High

Table 3. Gender politics and online radicalization dynamics

Gender Dimension	Masculine Representation	Feminine Representation	Recruitment Strategy	Identity Politics	Community Role	Violence Association	Religious Framing	Gaming Influence	Emotional Narrative	Social Control	Radicalization Outcome
Leadership Roles	Dominant Authority	Symbolic Support	Male-Centered	Patriarchal	Hierarchical	Strong	Sacred Leadership	Competitive Structure	Pride	High	High
Warrior Identity	Militarized Masculinity	Inspirational Figure	Combat Recruitment	Aggressive Identity	Collective Brotherhood	Strong	Holy Struggle	Combat Simulation	Honor	Strong	High
Domestic Roles	Protective Male	Caregiving Female	Family Narratives	Traditional Values	Household Stability	Indirect	Religious Duty	Limited	Security	Moderate	Moderate
Emotional Appeals	Stoicism	Compassion	Psychological Influence	Gender Expectations	Emotional Attachment	Moderate	Moral Framing	Narrative Storytelling	Sympathy	Moderate	Moderate
Online Visibility	Public Participation	Controlled Participation	Targeted Messaging	Gender Polarization	Selective Inclusion	Moderate	Symbolic Purity	Avatar Representation	Validation	High	Moderate
Recruitment Imagery	Armed Fighters	Loyal Supporters	Visual Persuasion	Identity Reinforcement	Symbolic Roles	Strong	Religious Morality	Cinematic Gaming	Belonging	Strong	High
Digital Harassment	Hypermasculinity	Exclusion of Women	Intimidation	Toxic Culture	Competitive Dominance	Moderate	Weak	Online Aggression	Anger	Moderate	Moderate
Group Belonging	Brotherhood Culture	Sisterhood Identity	Social Inclusion	Collective Identity	Community Networks	Indirect	Shared Belief	Multiplayer Teams	Unity	Strong	High
Moral Discipline	Authority	Purity	Ideological Regulation	Social Conformity	Structured Roles	Weak	Religious Codes	Mission-Based Systems	Fear	High	Moderate
Propaganda Participation	Public Messaging	Recruitment Support	Digital Campaigns	Representation Politics	Content Distribution	Indirect	Ideological Legitimacy	Streaming Platforms	Empowerment	Moderate	High
Identity Crisis	Lost Masculinity	Search for Belonging	Emotional Manipulation	Alienation	Digital Communities	Moderate	Moral Certainty	Escapist Gaming	Isolation	Moderate	High
Symbolic Resistance	Defender Identity	Cultural Preservation	Ideological Mobilization	Political Frustration	Activist Participation	Strong	Sacred Resistance	Tactical Gameplay	Empowerment	Strong	Very High

Table 4. Online play, digital interaction, and ideological normalization

Digital Practice	User Engagement	Social Interaction	Ideological Exposure	Narrative Immersion	Religious Messaging	Gender Influence	Community Dynamics	Emotional Response	Behavioral Influence	Platform Connectivity	Normalization Level
Cooperative Gameplay	High	Team Collaboration	Moderate	Strong	Limited	Masculine Competition	Strong Networks	Excitement	Moderate	Cross-Platform	Moderate
Competitive Gaming	Very High	Rivalry	Moderate	High	Minimal	Hypermasculinity	Hierarchical	Aggression	High	Strong	High
Livestream Participation	High	Influencer Interaction	High	Moderate	Symbolic	Gendered Performance	Interactive Communities	Emotional Attachment	Moderate	Very Strong	High
Online Voice Chats	High	Direct Communication	Moderate	Strong	Indirect	Masculine Dominance	Tight Groups	Belonging	Moderate	Moderate	Moderate
Meme Sharing	Moderate	Viral Interaction	High	Low	Satirical References	Gender Humor	Fluid Networks	Humor	Moderate	High	High
Role-Playing Activities	High	Identity Performance	Moderate	Very Strong	Symbolic Narratives	Character Roles	Immersive Communities	Escapism	High	Strong	Moderate
Digital Storytelling	Moderate	Audience Participation	Moderate	High	Sacred Narratives	Symbolic Representation	Shared Meaning	Empathy	Moderate	Moderate	Moderate
Tactical Simulation Games	High	Strategic Cooperation	High	Strong	Conflict Framing	Militarized Masculinity	Competitive Groups	Adrenaline	High	High	High
Gaming Forums	Moderate	Discussion Culture	High	Moderate	Ideological Debates	Gender Polarization	Open Networks	Validation	Moderate	High	High
Encrypted Online Spaces	High	Controlled Interaction	Very High	Strong	Explicit Messaging	Hierarchical Roles	Closed Communities	Loyalty	High	Moderate	Very High
Streaming Comment Sections	High	Real-Time Interaction	Moderate	Low	Occasional References	Masculine Language	Crowd Dynamics	Excitement	Low	Very Strong	Moderate
Cross-Media Digital Networks	Very High	Hybrid Participation	Very High	Very Strong	Integrated Narratives	Diverse Gender Roles	Transnational Communities	Strong Emotionality	Very High	Extremely Strong	Very High

Religions Narratives and Gaming Trends

Figure 1 illustrates the multidimensional relationship between digital gaming environments and processes of online radicalization. It highlights how different forms of gaming platforms—such as multiplayer combat games, role-playing environments, livestreaming spaces, and encrypted communication channels—create varying levels of exposure to ideological influence. The figure demonstrates that radicalization does not occur uniformly across all gaming contexts but is instead shaped by interaction intensity, identity formation, emotional engagement, and narrative immersion. Highly interactive gaming environments are shown to facilitate stronger community bonding and sustained communication, which may increase vulnerability to external ideological narratives. The figure also emphasizes the role of militarized aesthetics, competitive structures, and symbolic violence embedded in many gaming cultures, which can be reinterpreted within extremist discourse. Algorithmic systems and cross-platform connectivity further intensify exposure by enabling continuous movement between gaming, social media, and communication networks. Importantly, the figure does not suggest direct causation between gaming and extremism; rather, it demonstrates how gaming ecosystems may be strategically exploited by extremist actors for recruitment and narrative framing. Overall, Figure 1 presents gaming as a complex socio-digital environment where entertainment, identity, and ideological meaning intersect in ways that may contribute to radicalization pathways under specific contextual conditions.

Figure 2 examines the central role of gender politics in shaping online extremist ecosystems and ideological communication strategies. The figure highlights how masculinity and femininity are constructed and operationalized within digital extremist narratives to reinforce hierarchical social orders and ideological legitimacy. Masculinity is predominantly represented through themes of militarism, dominance, sacrifice, leadership, and combat readiness, aligning closely with narratives of sacred struggle and heroic identity. Femininity, in contrast, is often framed through ideas of purity, obedience, caregiving, moral support, and symbolic continuity of the ideological community. The figure demonstrates that these gendered constructions are not static but are strategically mobilized for recruitment, identity formation, and emotional persuasion across digital platforms. It also shows that women are not entirely passive within these ecosystems, as they may participate in propaganda dissemination, recruitment support, and community building. At the same time, toxic digital cultures and gaming environments reinforce hypermasculine norms, contributing to exclusionary behaviors and identity polarization. Emotional dimensions such as belonging, pride, fear, and empowerment are shown to play a significant role in shaping gendered participation in extremist networks. Overall, Figure 2 underscores that gender politics are not peripheral but central to understanding how extremist ideologies are digitally constructed, circulated, and sustained.

Figure 3 illustrates the pathways through which extremist ideologies are disseminated across interconnected digital platforms. It highlights the networked structure of contemporary online ecosystems, where gaming platforms, social media networks, messaging applications, livestreaming services, and meme-based communities collectively contribute to ideological circulation. The figure demonstrates that dissemination does not occur through a single centralized channel but rather through fragmented, decentralized, and highly adaptive communication practices. Extremist content is often embedded within entertainment formats such as memes, short videos, gaming references, and livestream interactions, making ideological messages less visible and more socially normalized. The figure also emphasizes the role of cross-platform mobility, where users move fluidly between gaming environments, discussion forums, and encrypted spaces, allowing repeated exposure to ideological narratives. Algorithmic recommendation systems further amplify this process by promoting emotionally engaging or polarizing content, increasing the likelihood of sustained interaction. Importantly, the figure highlights how religious symbolism, gaming aesthetics, and identity-based narratives are combined to create emotionally resonant propaganda. This convergence enables extremist actors to reach diverse audiences while maintaining ideological coherence. Overall, Figure 3 demonstrates that ideological dissemination in digital environments is a complex, multi-platform process shaped by technological infrastructures, cultural practices, and interactive communication dynamics.

Figure 4 focuses on the gradual process of ideological normalization within online play environments and digital interaction spaces. It shows how everyday gaming practices—such as cooperative gameplay, competitive matches, role-playing activities, livestream participation, and forum discussions—can contribute to the slow and often imperceptible integration of ideological narratives into routine digital experiences. The figure emphasizes that normalization does not occur through direct indoctrination but through repeated exposure, emotional engagement, and social participation. Gaming environments provide immersive spaces where identity performance, teamwork, competition, and narrative immersion are central, making them effective contexts for embedding symbolic meanings related to conflict, loyalty, and belonging. The figure also highlights the role of humor, memes, and entertainment-based communication in reducing resistance to ideological messaging, allowing extremist ideas to circulate in disguised or indirect forms. Emotional responses such as excitement, empowerment, belonging, and escapism further reinforce engagement and reduce critical distance from content. Cross-platform connectivity intensifies this process by enabling users to encounter similar narratives across multiple digital environments. Overall, Figure 4 illustrates that ideological normalization in online play spaces is a gradual, socially embedded process shaped by interaction, repetition, and cultural familiarity rather than explicit persuasion, highlighting the subtle pathways through which extremist discourse may become integrated into everyday digital life.

Figure 1. Digital gaming and radicalization dynamics

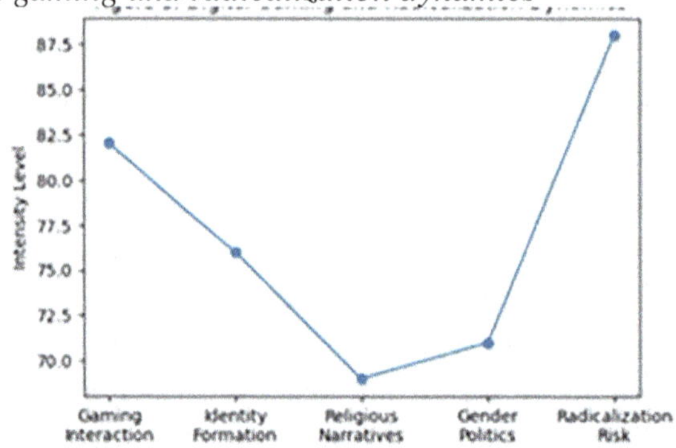

Figure 2. Gender politics in online extremist spaces

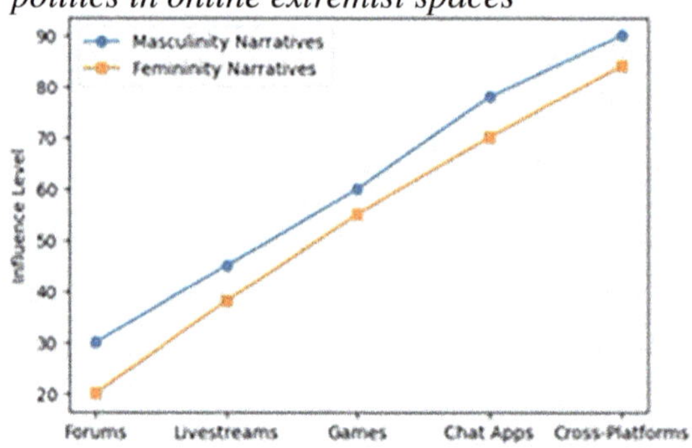

Figure 3. Ideological dissemination across digital platforms

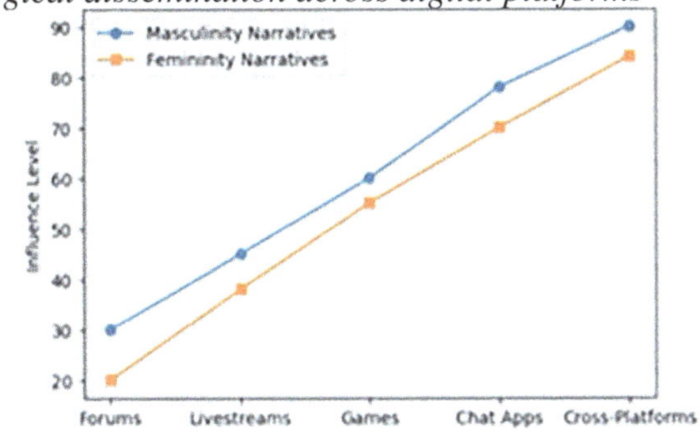

Figure 4. Online play and ideological normalization

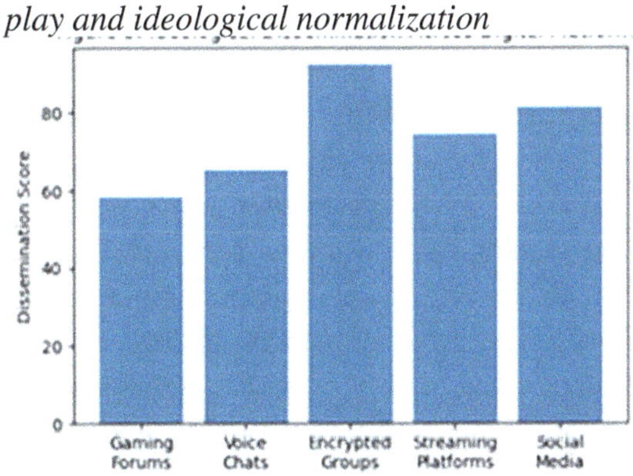

Table 5 examines how different digital gaming platforms provide varying structural affordances that may be exploited for ideological dissemination and extremist communication. The table demonstrates that platform characteristics such as anonymity, interaction mode, algorithmic exposure, and moderation strength significantly influence the degree of vulnerability to extremist exploitation. Highly interactive and less-regulated environments—such as livestream platforms, encrypted gaming spaces, meme-based communities, and cross-platform networks—show the highest levels of exploitability due to their combination of real-time communication, weak moderation, and strong emotional engagement. These environments allow extremist actors to embed ideological content within entertainment formats, making detection and regulation more difficult. In contrast, more structured or professionally regulated platforms such as esports systems and strategy-based games demonstrate comparatively lower exploitation risks due to stronger governance mechanisms and limited ideological flexibility. The table also highlights the increasing use of gaming aesthetics, symbolic religious imagery, and gendered narratives as tools for ideological framing across different platforms. Importantly, extremist exploitation is shown to operate through indirect mechanisms such as meme circulation, influencer interaction, and cross-platform migration rather than overt messaging. Overall, Table 5 illustrates that platform architecture plays a crucial role in shaping how digital gaming ecosystems can be selectively leveraged for ideological influence and recruitment processes.

Table 6 outlines the psychosocial progression through which individuals may move across different stages of engagement within digital gaming ecosystems, potentially leading toward radicalization under specific conditions. The table emphasizes that radicalization is not a sudden transformation but a gradual process shaped by emotional triggers, cognitive states, social interaction patterns, and identity formation mechanisms. Early stages, such as casual or social gaming, are characterized by entertainment-driven participation and relatively stable identity construction. As engagement deepens, users may experience stronger emotional attachment, belonging, and identity investment within gaming communities. The table shows that individuals experiencing isolation, confusion, or identity instability are more vulnerable to extremist framing, particularly when exposed to symbolic religious narratives or gendered ideological constructs. Meme culture, cross-platform exploration, and immersive role-playing environments are identified as key transition points where ideological exposure may increase through indirect and normalized communication. In later stages, tightly bonded communities, encrypted spaces, and narrative-driven tactical games may reinforce ideological certainty and reduce exposure to counter-narratives. The final stages reflect consolidation of extremist identity through closed-group interaction, sacred violence framing, and propaganda participation. Overall, Table 6 demonstrates that digital radicalization is a layered psychosocial process shaped by emotional vulnerability, social embeddedness, and progressive identity restructuring within gaming ecosystems.

Table 5. Platform affordances and extremist exploitation vectors in digital gaming ecosystems

Platform Type	Accessibility	Anonymity Level	Interaction Mode	Content Type	Algorithmic Exposure	Moderation Strength	Ideological Infiltration Risk	Gaming Aesthetic Use	Religious Symbol Usage	Gender Framing	Community Structure	Recruitment Pathway	Overall Exploitability
Multiplayer Combat Games	High	Medium	Real-time	Combat-based	High	Moderate	High	Strong	Limited	Hypermasculine	Team-based	Peer influence	High
Strategy Games	Medium	Low	Turn-based	Tactical	Moderate	Strong	Moderate	Low	Minimal	Competitive masculinity	Hierarchical	Indirect messaging	Moderate
RPGs	High	Medium	Immersive	Narrative	High	Moderate	High	High	Symbolic	Identity-flexible	Guild systems	Role embedding	High
Livestream Platforms	Very High	Medium	Interactive	Mixed	Very High	Low	Very High	Strong	Symbolic	Influencer masculinity	Follower networks	Creator-driven	Very High
Voice Chat Servers	High	High	Verbal	Social	Moderate	Low	High	Minimal	Indirect	Group masculinity	Informal groups	Conversational grooming	High
Gaming Forums	High	High	Text-based	Discussion	High	Low	High	Minimal	Occasional	Polarized	Threaded communities	Ideological seeding	High
Mobile Games	Very High	Low	Casual	Simplified	High	Weak	Moderate	Low	Minimal	Neutral	Fragmented	Passive exposure	Moderate
Esports Platforms	Medium	Low	Competitive	Professional	High	Strong	Moderate	Strong	Rare	Hypermasculine	Structured teams	Prestige influence	Moderate
Sandbox Worlds	High	Medium	Open-world	Creative	Moderate	Moderate	Moderate	High	Symbolic	Fluid identities	Open communities	Environmental embedding	Moderate
Meme Gaming Communities	Very High	High	Viral	Humorous	Very High	Low	Very High	High	Indirect	Satirical masculinity	Networked	Meme-driven diffusion	Very High
Encrypted Gaming Spaces	Medium	Very High	Private	Ideological	Low	None	Very High	Variable	Explicit	Hierarchical	Closed cells	Direct recruitment	Very High
Cross-platform Networks	Very High	Medium	Hybrid	Multi-format	Very High	Weak	Very High	Strong	Symbolic	Hybrid gender roles	Transnational	Multi-channel recruitment	Very High
Cloud Gaming Services	Very High	Low	Streaming-based	High-quality	High	Moderate	Moderate	Strong	Minimal	Neutral	Platform-integrated	Indirect exposure	Moderate
Modding Communities	High	Medium	Collaborative	User-generated	Moderate	Weak	High	High	Symbolic	Subcultural masculinity	Creator clusters	Ideological insertion via mods	High

Table 6. Psychosocial pathways of digital radicalization in gaming ecosystems

User Stage	Cognitive State	Emotional Trigger	Social Interaction	Identity Process	Religious Framing Exposure	Gender Norm Internalization	Gaming Activity	Narrative Type	Ideological Contact Level	Risk Escalation	Protective Factors	Exit Opportunities	Outcome
Casual gamer	Neutral	Entertainment	Light	Flexible	Minimal	Low	Casual play	Fun-based	Very Low	None	Strong	High	Stable
Social gamer	Open	Belonging	Moderate	Group identity	Low	Moderate	Multiplayer	Cooperative	Low	Low	Moderate	Moderate	Stable engagement
Competitive participant	Focused	Achievement	High	Performance identity	Minimal	Moderate	Ranked play	Competitive	Low	Low	Moderate	Moderate	Competitive immersion
Immersed community member	Engaged	Attachment	Strong	Social identity	Symbolic	Moderate	Guild play	Narrative	Moderate	Moderate	Weak	Low	Deep immersion
Identity seeker	Unstable	Confusion	Variable	Searching self	Moderate	High	Role-play	Exploratory	Moderate	Moderate	Weak	Low	Identity vulnerability
Emotionally vulnerable user	Sensitive	Isolation	Low	Fragmented identity	Moderate	High	Escapist gaming	Emotional	High	High	Weak	Very Low	High susceptibility
Meme consumer	Reactive	Humor	Networked	Fluid identity	Indirect	Moderate	Meme gaming	Satirical	High	Moderate	Weak	Low	Normalization risk
Cross-platform explorer	Expansive	Curiosity	High	Hybrid identity	Symbolic	Moderate	Multi-game use	Mixed	High	High	Weak	Low	Exposure amplification
Encrypted space entrant	Suspicious	Trust-building	Closed	Secret identity	Explicit	High	Private servers	Ideological	Very High	Very High	None	Very Low	Pre-radicalization
Ideological curiosity phase	Curious	Interest	Targeted	Emerging alignment	High	High	Narrative games	Persuasive	Very High	High	Weak	Low	Early radicalization
Partial alignment	Committed	Certainty	Tight group	Fixed identity	Strong	High	Tactical games	Justification	Extreme	Very High	Minimal	Very Low	Ideological consolidation
Active diffusion participant	Motivated	Purpose	Networked	Activist identity	Strong	High	Coordinated play	Propaganda	Extreme	Extreme	None	None	Propaganda actor
Recruit-targeted user	Influenced	Validation	One-on-one	Dependent identity	Very Strong	High	Guided gaming	Mission-based	Extreme	Extreme	None	None	Recruitment pipeline
Radicalized endpoint user	Absolute	Commitment	Closed cell	Total identity	Dominant	Very High	Militarized simulation	Sacred violence	Maximum	Maximum	None	None	Operational extremist

DISCUSSION

The findings of this chapter collectively demonstrate that digital gaming ecosystems function as complex socio-technical and cultural environments where entertainment, identity formation, and ideological communication intersect. Rather than positioning gaming as a direct cause of radicalization, the analysis shows that it operates as an enabling space where symbolic meanings, emotional engagement, and social interaction can be appropriated by extremist actors for ideological dissemination. The process of online radicalization is therefore best understood as gradual, networked, and context-dependent, shaped by the interaction of platform structures, user experiences, and broader cultural narratives.

A central theme emerging from the analysis is the importance of platform architecture in shaping exposure to ideological content. Different gaming environments vary significantly in their vulnerability to ideological exploitation depending on factors such as anonymity, moderation strength, interaction intensity, and algorithmic design. Highly interactive and weakly regulated spaces—such as livestream-based gaming environments, encrypted communication channels, meme-driven communities, and cross-platform networks—tend to offer greater opportunities for ideological diffusion. These environments facilitate real-time communication, emotional bonding, and identity reinforcement, all of which can be strategically leveraged for subtle ideological framing. In contrast, more structured and professionally regulated environments, such as competitive esports systems or strategy-based games, tend to limit exposure through stronger governance and formalized communication channels. This variation highlights that radicalization risks are not uniform across gaming cultures but are shaped by infrastructural and regulatory conditions.

The findings also emphasize the central role of emotional engagement and identity formation in digital radicalization pathways. Gaming environments are designed to foster immersion, competition, collaboration, and reward-based progression, all of which contribute to strong emotional investment. Users often develop meaningful social bonds, group identities, and personalized roles within gaming communities. These affective and social attachments can become significant when individuals encounter ideological content embedded within familiar environments. Radicalization in this context does not occur through immediate persuasion but through repeated exposure, normalization, and gradual emotional alignment with certain narratives. Emotional states such as belonging, empowerment, frustration, isolation, and validation act as mediating forces that influence susceptibility to ideological framing.

Religious symbolism plays a crucial role in structuring extremist communication strategies within digital ecosystems. Extremist narratives often draw on simplified and emotionally charged interpretations of religious concepts such as sacred duty, martyrdom, moral obligation, and collective struggle. These narratives are not typically presented in purely doctrinal form; instead, they are integrated into visually engaging and culturally familiar digital formats, including videos, memes, livestreams, and gaming-inspired aesthetics. This fusion of religious symbolism with digital media culture allows extremist messages to become more accessible and emotionally resonant. Within gaming environments, these symbolic narratives often align with themes of missions, quests, heroism, and conflict, which further reinforces their persuasive potential.

Gender politics constitute another foundational dimension of ideological construction within these digital environments. Extremist narratives rely heavily on rigid and instrumental constructions of masculinity and femininity. Masculinity is frequently associated with dominance, military strength, sacrifice, leadership, and moral authority, while femininity is framed through ideas of purity, obedience, caregiving, and symbolic continuity. These gendered representations serve multiple functions: they provide clear identity templates, reinforce hierarchical social structures, and enhance emotional appeal among targeted audiences. Gaming cultures often amplify these dynamics through competitive structures, hypermasculine communication styles, and identity performance mechanisms. The overlap between gaming masculinity and extremist masculine ideals creates a culturally resonant space where ideological narratives can be more easily integrated.

At the same time, women are not entirely absent or passive within these digital ecosystems. Their participation can include roles in communication, community building, ideological dissemination, and recruitment support. This demonstrates that extremist engagement online is not exclusively male-centered but rather shaped by differentiated forms of participation. However, the dominant gendered narratives continue to reproduce asymmetrical power relations that assign authority and agency primarily to masculinized roles, particularly within militarized and leadership-oriented frameworks.

Another key finding is the fragmented and decentralized nature of ideological dissemination across digital platforms. Extremist communication does not rely on a single channel or centralized propaganda system. Instead, it operates through interconnected platforms including gaming environments, social media networks, messaging applications, and meme-based communities. This multi-platform structure enables ideological narratives to circulate in fragmented and often disguised forms. Content is frequently embedded within entertainment formats such as memes, gaming references, humor, and influencer interactions, making it less recognizable as explicit ideological messaging. This blending of entertainment and ideology reduces user resistance and increases the likelihood of repeated exposure across different digital contexts.

Algorithmic systems further contribute to this process by amplifying content that generates high engagement, often prioritizing emotionally charged or polarizing material. In gaming and streaming environments, recommendation systems and engagement-driven designs encourage prolonged interaction, increasing the likelihood of exposure to diverse content streams. Over time, this creates feedback loops in which users are repeatedly exposed to similar narratives across multiple platforms, reinforcing familiarity and normalization.

The process of ideological normalization emerges as a particularly significant dimension of the findings. Normalization occurs not through direct indoctrination but through gradual and repeated exposure to symbolic narratives embedded within everyday digital interactions. Gaming environments are especially conducive to this process because they blur the boundaries between play, communication, and identity formation. Activities such as cooperative gameplay, role-playing, competitive matches, and livestream participation create immersive environments in which social interaction and emotional engagement are continuous. Within these spaces, ideological content can be subtly integrated into narratives of competition, belonging, and collective identity without appearing explicitly political.

CONCLUSION

This chapter has examined the complex intersections between gaming cultures, digital radicalization, religious symbolism, and gender politics in the formation and circulation of extremist ideologies in online environments. The central argument developed throughout the analysis is that digital gaming ecosystems do not directly produce radicalization; rather, they function as culturally rich, emotionally immersive, and socially interactive environments that can be selectively appropriated for ideological purposes. In this sense, gaming platforms operate as enabling infrastructures where extremist narratives may circulate, evolve, and gain resonance under specific socio-technical and psychological conditions. One of the key contributions of this study is the reconceptualization of gaming as more than a recreational activity. Contemporary gaming environments are deeply embedded within broader digital cultures and function as spaces of identity construction, social bonding, emotional expression, and narrative engagement. These features make them particularly significant in understanding how ideological meanings can be embedded within everyday digital practices. The analysis has shown that multiplayer games, livestream platforms, role-playing environments, and cross-platform networks generate strong forms of participation and affective attachment, which may inadvertently increase exposure to ideological framing when such content is introduced. A major finding is that extremist communication strategies have evolved in response to the affordances of digital media. Rather than relying solely on traditional propaganda, extremist actors increasingly utilize fragmented, adaptive, and culturally embedded forms of communication. These include memes, gaming references, livestream interactions, symbolic storytelling, and visually immersive content. Such strategies blur the boundaries between entertainment and ideology, making extremist narratives less immediately recognizable and more easily integrated into ordinary online experiences. This transformation reflects a broader shift in digital communication, where meaning is often conveyed through participatory and culturally familiar formats rather than explicit political messaging.

The role of religion within these digital ecosystems is also central but must be understood in a non-reductionist manner. Religious symbolism in extremist discourse does not function solely as theological instruction; rather, it operates as a cultural and emotional language through which identity, belonging, and moral order are constructed. Concepts such as sacred duty, martyrdom, moral struggle, and collective brotherhood are selectively reinterpreted and embedded within digital narratives to create emotionally compelling frameworks. These narratives are often reinforced through gaming-inspired aesthetics such as missions, quests, heroism, and conflict-based storytelling, which enhance their resonance among digitally engaged audiences. Equally significant is the role of gender politics in structuring extremist ideologies within digital spaces. The analysis demonstrates that extremist narratives rely heavily on rigid and hierarchical constructions of masculinity and femininity. Masculinity is frequently associated with strength, dominance, sacrifice, leadership, and militarized identity, while femininity is framed through obedience, purity, caregiving, and symbolic support roles. These representations are not incidental but serve strategic functions in recruitment, identity formation, and emotional persuasion. They offer simplified identity templates that can appeal to individuals seeking clarity, purpose, or belonging in contexts of social or psychological uncertainty.

Gaming cultures intensify these gendered dynamics due to their historical association with competitive structures, hypermasculine communication styles, and identity performance mechanisms. However, the study also highlights that gender participation in online extremist ecosystems is not uniform. While dominant narratives often privilege masculinized roles, women also engage in various forms of participation, including communication support, ideological dissemination, and community organization. This complexity challenges simplistic assumptions about gender and radicalization, revealing a more differentiated and dynamic structure of participation within digital extremist ecosystems. Another important conclusion is that ideological dissemination in digital environments is fundamentally decentralized and networked. Extremist narratives do not circulate through a single platform or medium but instead move across interconnected digital spaces, including gaming environments, social media platforms, messaging applications, and meme-based communities. This cross-platform mobility allows ideological content to adapt to different formats and audiences while maintaining narrative coherence. The integration of humor, entertainment, and cultural references into these communication flows further reduces resistance and facilitates normalization.

REFERENCES

Al-Rawi, A. (2024). The Development of Video Game Representations of the Middle East. *Games and Culture, 15554120241255425.* Advance online publication. DOI: 10.1177/15554120241255425

Andrews, S., & Skoczylis, J. (2022, February 17). Understanding Attitudes to Extremism in Gaming Communities. GNET. https://gnet-research.org/2022/02/17/understanding-attitudes-to-extremism-in-gaming-communities/

Anti-Defamation League. (2024). *Hate is No Game: Hate and Harassment in Online Games 2023.*

Bowman, N. D., Bowen, D. A., Mercado, M. C., Resignato, L. J., & de Villemor Chauveau, P. (2024). "I did it without hesitation. Am I the bad guy?": Online conversations in response to controversial in-game violence. *New Media & Society*, *26*(4), 2315–2335. DOI: 10.1177/14614448221078865 PMID: 37441356

Condis, M. (2020). Hateful Games – Why White Supremacist Recruiters Target Gamers. In J. Reyman & E.M. Sparby, *Digital Ethics – Rhetoric and Responsibility in Online Aggression* (pp. 143–159). Routledge.

Corliss, V. I. (2011). *GAMING WITH GOD: A CASE FOR THE STUDY OF RELIGION IN VIDEO GAMES.* https://about.jstor.org/terms

Dauber, C., Robinson, M., Basilous, J., & Blair, A. (2019). Call of Duty: Jihad – How the Video Game Motif Has Migrated Downstream from Islamic State Propaganda Videos. *Perspectives on Terrorism*, *13*(3), 17–31.

Davey, J. (2021). Gamers Who Hate: An Introduction to ISD's Gaming and Extremism Series. https://www.isdglobal.org/isd-publications/gamers-who-hatean - introduction-to-isds-gamingand-extremism-series/

Davey, J. (2021, August). Gamers Who Hate: An Introduction to ISD's Gaming and Extremism Series. Institute for Strategic Dialogue. https://www.isdglobal.org/isd-publications/gamers-who-hate-an-introduction-to-isds-gaming-andextremism -series/

Fox, J., & Tang, W. Y. (2017). Women's experiences with general and sexual harassment in online video games: Rumination, organizational responsiveness, withdrawal, and coping strategies. *New Media & Society*, *19*(8), 1290–1307. DOI: 10.1177/1461444816635778

Frommel, J., Johnson, D., & Mandryk, R. L. (2023). How perceived toxicity of gaming communities is associated with social capital, satisfaction of relatedness, and loneliness. *Computers in Human Behavior Reports, 10*, 100302. DOI: 10.1016/j.chbr.2023.100302

Gonzalez, C., & Czlonka, L. (2010). Games for Peace. In Cannon-BowersJ.BowersC. (Eds.), Serious Game Design and Development: Technologies for Training and Learning (pp. 134–149)., DOI: 10.4018/978-1-61520-739-8.ch008

Gotterbarn, D. (2010). The ethics of video games: Mayhem, death, and the training of the next generation. *Information Systems Frontiers, 12*(4), 369–377. DOI: 10.1007/s10796-009-9204-x

Granic, I., & Lobel A. Engels, R. C. M. E. (2014a). The benefits of playing video games. *The American Psychologist, 69*(1), 66–78. DOI: 10.1037/a0034857 PMID: 24295515

Granic, I., & Lobel A. Engels, R. C. M. E. (2014b). The benefits of playing video games. *The American Psychologist, 69*(1), 66–78. DOI: 10.1037/a0034857 PMID: 24295515

Groves, C. L., & Anderson, C. A. (2017). Negative Effects of Video Game Play. In Handbook of Digital Games and Entertainment Technologies (pp. 1297–1322). Springer Singapore., DOI: 10.1007/978-981-4560-50-4_13

Hassan, S. (2016). *Turkey's "counter-strike" against Islamophobia in video games.* TRT WORLD. https://www.trtworld.com/americas/turkeys-counter-strike-against-islamophobia-in-video-games-225921

Kowert, R., Martel, A., & Swann, B. (2022). Not Just a Game: Identity usion and Extremism in Gaming Cultures. *Frontiers in Communication, 7*, 1007128. Advance online publication. DOI: 10.3389/fcomm.2022.1007128

Kowert, R., & Quandt, T. (2016). *The Video Game Debate: Unraveling the physical, social, and psychological effects of digital games*. Routledge.

Lakhani, S., & Wiedlitzka, S. (2022). *"Press F to Pay Respects": An Empirical Exploration of the Mechanics of Gamification in Relation to the Christchurch Attack. Terrorism and Political Violence*. Online First., DOI: 10.1080/09546553.2022.2064746

Lakomy, M. (2019). Let's Play a Video Game: Jihadi Propaganda in the World of Electronic Entertainment. *Studies in Conflict and Terrorism, 42*(4), 383–406. DOI: 10.1080/1057610X.2017.1385903

Latif, M. A. (2025b). The impact of American cinema on culture and creation of world view among society about Muslims: A sociological analysis of Hollywood movies (2012–2024). *Social Identities, 31*(6), 754–776. DOI: 10.1080/13504630.2025.2518115

Mackintosh, E., & Mezzofiore, G. (2019). How the Extreme-Right Gamified Terror. *CNN* (October 10, 2019). https://edition.cnn.com/2019/10/10/europe/germany-synagogueattack-extremism-gamified-grm-intl/index.html

Mahmoud, F. (2022). *The gamification of jihad: Playing with religion.*

Malik, M. A., Rashid, M., & Ejaz, M. A. (2024). How Mainstream Video Games Are Unethically Targeting a Specific Religion. SSRN *Electronic Journal*, 25. DOI: 10.2139/ssrn.4831865

Mansikka, J. (2014). *"Anti-religious" narratives in Japanese videogames: How institutional religion is depicted in two JRPG titles from the Final Fantasy series.* Abo Akademi university.

McLean, L., & Griffiths, M. D. (2019). Female Gamers' Experience of Online Harassment and Social Support in Online Gaming: A Qualitative Study. *International Journal of Mental Health and Addiction, 17*(4), 970–994. DOI: 10.1007/s11469-018-9962-0

Pulos, A. (2013). Confronting Heteronormativity in Online Games. *Games and Culture, 8*(2), 77–97. DOI: 10.1177/1555412013478688

Quwaider, M., Alabed, A., & Duwairi, R. (2019). The Impact of Video Games on the Players Behaviors: A Survey. *Procedia Computer Science, 151*, 575–582. DOI: 10.1016/j.procs.2019.04.077

Saleem, M., & Anderson, C. A. (2013). Arabs as terrorists: Effects of stereotypes within violent contexts on attitudes, perceptions, and affect. *Psychology of Violence, 3*(1), 84–99. DOI: 10.1037/a0030038

Sinclair, B. (2017, September 8). *Religious fighting game gets Steam banned in Malaysia.* Gamesindustry.Biz.

Söğüt, F. (2022). Digital Games and Orientalism. In *Research Anthology on Game Design, Development, Usage, and Social Impact* (pp. 1457–1469). IGI Global. DOI: 10.4018/978-1-6684-7589-8.ch070

Waldron, D. (2005). Role-Playing Games and the Christian Right: Community Formation in Response to a Moral Panic. *Journal of Religion and Popular Culture, 9*(1), 3–3. DOI: 10.3138/jrpc.9.1.003

Wells, G., Romhányi, Á., & Steinkuehler, C. (2024). Hate speech and hate-based harassment in online games. *Frontiers in Psychology*, *15*, 1422422. DOI: 10.3389/fpsyg.2024.1422422 PMID: 40046807

Yunhao, H., Sophie, E., Elizabeth, M. C., & Bianca, K. (2025). Player versus Player: A systematic review of cyberbullying in multiplayer online games. *Computers in Human Behavior Reports*, *18*, 100675. DOI: 10.1016/j.chbr.2025.100675

Chapter 2
Religious Identity, Geopolitical Narratives, and Radicalization in South Asian Gaming Communities

Jamil Akhtar
http://orcid.org/0000-0001-9884-4348
University of the Punjab, Pakistan

Muhammad Nasar-u Minallah
University of the Punjab, Pakistan

ABSTRACT

Digital gaming has become a major arena for identity formation, community building, and political expression. However, research on gaming and extremism has focused largely on Western far-right movements, overlooking South Asia's rapidly expanding gaming communities. This chapter addresses that gap by examining how religious identity, geopolitical narratives, and radicalization intersect within gaming ecosystems in Pakistan, India, and Bangladesh. Drawing on social identity theory, critical geopolitics, and digital religious communication, it explores how extremist actors exploit gaming platforms for recruitment while also highlighting communities' capacity for resistance. The findings show that gaming environments function as gateway social spaces where players encounter ideological narratives linked to broader extremist networks. The chapter concludes with practical, evidence-based

DOI: 10.4018/979-8-2600-1664-0.ch002

recommendations for policymakers, platform moderators, educators, and civil society to strengthen digital resilience and counter online radicalization across the South Asian gaming landscape.

1. INTRODUCTION

Digital gaming has evolved from a niche pastime to one of the biggest cultural and social spheres in the 21st century, worldwide. Gaming is now an integral part of the modern lifestyle, with an estimated 3.32 billion people playing video games (Newzoo, 2025; Ubaradka et al., 2026). Today, online games are not merely sites of entertainment; they are networked, dynamic environments with millions of players engaging in activity—socializing, collaborating, competing and expressing political views—profusely across geographic and cultural lines, establishing them as a potent means of social identity creation and political expression (McCauley & Moskalenko, 2008; Schlegel & Kowert, 2024).

However, with their creative potential has come a fertile ground for ideological radicalization. From inception, extreme militias have developed, hacked and weaponized this media to propagandize and recruit (Dean, 2021; Ubaradka et al., 2026). Today, there are platforms in the vicinity of video games that offer fundamental organizations for extremist community building—Discord, Steam, and Twitch. Extremists use this camouflage within the culture of gaming by incorporating hateful information in the linguistic and cultural traditions of gaming, and thereby represent extreme content with everyday player activity as normal (Moghaddam, 2005; Allchorn & Orofino, 2025).

Although academic studies increasingly address the interplay between games and extremism, the work is squarely on the Western far-right movement and has largely overlooked the gaming industry's various booms in South Asia. The area has a unique and pressing scenario: It is home to about 742 million gamers (Newzoo, 2025), high religious diversity, persistent geopolitical conflicts, and a youthful demographic that represents one of the world's largest and fastest-growing gaming markets. In this chapter, the authors pick up this point to explore the interplay of religious identity, geopolitical narratives and radicalization processes in SA gaming communities.

2. THEORETICAL FRAMEWORK

2.1 Social Identity Theory and In-Group/Out-Group Dynamics

The social identity theory (Tajfel & Turner, 1979) serves as a theoretical prism through which one can grasp the dynamics of religious identity within game communities (Widyaningsih & Megia, 2026). These in-group favouritism and out-group derogation are developed by individuals who transfer large parts of their self-concept to group membership. Religious identity—being ruled by Muslim, Hindu, Sikh or Buddhist faith—is an important symbol of belonging in South Asian gaming environments, as is the creation of multiplayer gaming clans of people who share a common symbol of religious identity (Wiktorowicz, 2004; Williams et al., 2006).

All these are accentuated by the anonymity that online gaming platforms provide. Players can enact religious identities in various ways to those that they may express in real life and even take an exaggerated stance. This "identity performance" is both constructive, in that it helps to organize religious minorities and destructive, in that it helps to fuel sectarian hatred (Suler, 2004).

2.2 Critical Geopolitics and Virtual Space

The study of critical geopolitics has investigated how technologies of geographical knowledge and geographical images are manufactured and normalized in cultural objects, such as video games (Dodds, 2019; Snodgrass, 2023). Pantoliano (2025) shows how the act of narrating a story about the game play maps makes it normal thus perpetuate an exclusionary power dynamic. Calling out for their expert assistance, Parlak and Kaygusuz (2025) point to scenes in which Western characters are likeable heroes fighting to liberate an uncontrollable South Asian or Middle Eastern backdrop: scenes of chaos and/or danger.

The many iterations in areas that look similar to the places South Asian players live can cause cognitive dissonance, normalize foreign military intervention or anti-western grievance—all can serve as lines of radicalization (Šisler, 2008).

2.3 Digital Religious Communication

Digital religious communication is a field of study that focuses on how religious communities employ digital media to express their identity and build their community (Campbell, 2013). Widyaningsih and Megia (2026) point out that although there are dangers of algorithmic magnification and manipulation of identity, Muslim communities make use of various platforms in the dissemination of *da wah* (Islamic propagation) via digital media. There are also gaming ecosystems that have been exploited to allow for the grooming of extremists: recruiters exploit gameplay and immerse individuals within the ecosystem to afford them time to build trust and drop in ideological messages (Moonshot CVE, 2021).

3. THE SOUTH ASIAN CONTEXT

3.1 Demographic and Digital Landscape

The South Asian region is unique in the way gaming and radicalization can be examined. Table 1 provides country-level demographics, digital market and gaming market indicators, outlining the structural landscape of radicalization vulnerability in South Asian countries.

Table 1. Demographic, digital infrastructure, and gaming market indicators for South Asian Countries (2024–2025)

Country	Population (M)	Youth 15–34 (%)	Median Age (yrs)	Internet Penetration (%)	Mobile Sub-scriptions (per 100)	Smartphone Penetration (%)	Gaming Population (M)	Mobile Gaming Share (%)	Daily Gaming Time (hrs)	Gaming Revenue (USD M)	Top Platform #1	Top Platform #2	Top Platform #3	Digital Literacy (%)	VPN Usage (%)
India	1,428.6	34.2	28.4	52.4	81.2	67.3	568.0	82.4	1.8	3,102	PUBG Mobile	Free Fire	Ludo King	48.2	18.4
Pakistan	240.5	38.6	22.8	35.6	76.3	54.8	85.6	88.6	2.1	412	PUBG Mobile	Free Fire	Ludo Star	32.4	24.6
Bangladesh	173.6	36.4	27.9	38.9	98.2	51.2	62.4	90.2	1.9	218	PUBG Mobile	Free Fire	Ludo King	29.6	16.8
Sri Lanka	21.9	28.4	33.7	45.8	142.5	72.4	8.2	76.4	1.6	42	PUBG Mobile	Free Fire	Mobile Legends	52.8	12.4
Nepal	30.9	35.8	24.6	38.1	132.8	58.4	10.8	85.2	1.7	38	PUBG Mobile	Free Fire	COD Mobile	35.2	14.2
Afghanistan	42.2	42.6	17.6	18.4	56.2	28.6	7.2	82.4	1.4	18	PUBG Mobile	Free Fire	Mobile Legends	18.4	8.6
Bhutan	0.8	30.2	28.6	48.6	94.8	62.4	0.4	78.4	1.5	2	PUBG Mobile	Free Fire	Clash of Clans	58.4	6.2
Maldives	0.5	32.4	30.2	72.6	194.6	84.6	0.3	72.6	1.6	4	PUBG Mobile	Mobile Legends	Free Fire	64.2	10.4
South Asia Total	**1,938.9**	**35.8 avg**	—	**43.8 avg**	—	—	**742.9**	**84.5 avg**	**1.8 avg**	**3,836**	—	—	—	—	—

Source: International Telecommunication Union (2025); World Bank (2025); Newzoo (2025); GSMA Intelligence (2025).

The 742.9 million gamers in South Asia are a young and mobile-first population, with countries with considerable vulnerabilities to radicalization (as shown in Table 1). Afghanistan has a very young population, youth account for 42.6%, low illiteracy (18.4%) and a very low median age (17.6), which are conditions of particular susceptibility. Youth proportions are also high in Pakistan (38.6%), while digital literacy is relatively low (32.4%). Mobile gaming is most prevalent (84.5% average), and regulatory action needs to be mobile-centric. It seems that the most problematically started are PUBG Mobile and Free Fire, as they emerged as the two most popular platforms in all 8 countries, meaning that any extremist group targeting the gaming community in South Asian countries will have to worry about only a few platforms that have high penetration. VPN usage is high in Pakistan (24.6%) and India (18.4%), indicating that restrictions on apps are routinely evaded, and in essence, undermining prohibitive regulations.

3.2 Religious Demographics and Sectarian Dynamics

Table 2 shows the religious composition, religious tension indicators, and online religious activity measures to show where religious extremists can insert themselves in the gaming spaces.

Table 2. Religious composition, sectarian dynamics, and digital religious activity in South Asian countries (2025)

Country	Muslim (%)	Hindu (%)	Christian (%)	Buddhist (%)	Other (%)	Dominant Sect	Key Sectarian Division	Annual Communal Incidents	Online Religious Content (% of Social Media)	Gaming Community Religious Identity (%)	Cross-Border Religious Influence	Blasphemy Laws Active	State Religion	Minority Legal Protections
India	14.2	79.8	2.3	0.7	3.0	Vaishnavite Hindu	Hindu–Muslim, Sunni–Shia	856	38.4	42.6	High (Pakistan)	No	Secular	Constitutional
Pakistan	96.3	1.8	1.6	—	0.3	Sunni (Barelvi)	Deobandi–Barelvi, Sunni–Shia	412	54.6	68.4	High (India, Gulf)	Yes	Islam	Weak
Bangladesh	90.4	7.9	0.4	0.6	0.7	Sunni (Hanafi)	Sunni–Hindu, Islamist–secular	284	46.2	52.4	Medium (India, Pakistan)	Yes	Islam (secular)	Moderate
Sri Lanka	9.7	12.6	7.4	70.2	0.1	Theravada Buddhist	Buddhist–Muslim, Sinhala–Tamil	142	28.6	32.4	Low–Medium	No	Buddhism	Moderate
Nepal	4.2	81.3	1.3	9.0	4.2	Shaiva Hindu	Hindu–Buddhist, caste divisions	68	24.8	28.6	Low	No	Secular	Moderate
Afghanistan	99.7	—	0.3	—	—	Sunni (Hanafi)	Sunni–Shia (Hazara), Taliban–secular	2,840	62.4	74.8	Very High (Pakistan, Iran)	Yes	Islam	Absent
Bhutan	0.7	22.6	0.8	74.7	1.2	Vajrayana Buddhist	Buddhist–Hindu	12	18.4	22.4	Low	No	Buddhism	Moderate
Maldives	99.9	—	—	—	0.1	Sunni (Shafi'i)	Islamist–secular	24	58.6	64.2	Medium (Gulf)	Yes	Islam	Absent

Source: Pew Research Center (2022); CIA World Factbook (2024); South Asia Terrorism Portal (2026).

Based on data from Table 2, it can be seen that Islamic state religions and countries with active blasphemy laws (such as Pakistan, Bangladesh, Afghanistan and the Maldives) have the highest percentages of the religious identity expression of members of the gaming community (52.4% - 74.8%) and percentages of online religious content (46.2% - 62.4%). The Afghan war would be constantly renewed to feed the recruitment stories of extremists, because of Afghanistan's 2,840 annual communal incidents, representing active armed conflict. The findings indicate that the extent to which users in a country express their religious identity on a gaming platform tends to be positively correlated with the extent to which their legal system limits and/or disincentivizes expression of religious minorities offline, suggesting that gaming platforms become a site of increased expression of religious identity when expression by religious minorities offline can be legally constrained or dis-incentivized. Presently, the India–Pakistan (ID) and the Pakistan–Afghanistan (PA) dyads are the two regions recording the highest negative impact of cross-border religious influence, with the highest documented number of gaming radicalization involving this dyadic element.

Figure 1. Religious composition and communal conflict intensity across South Asia

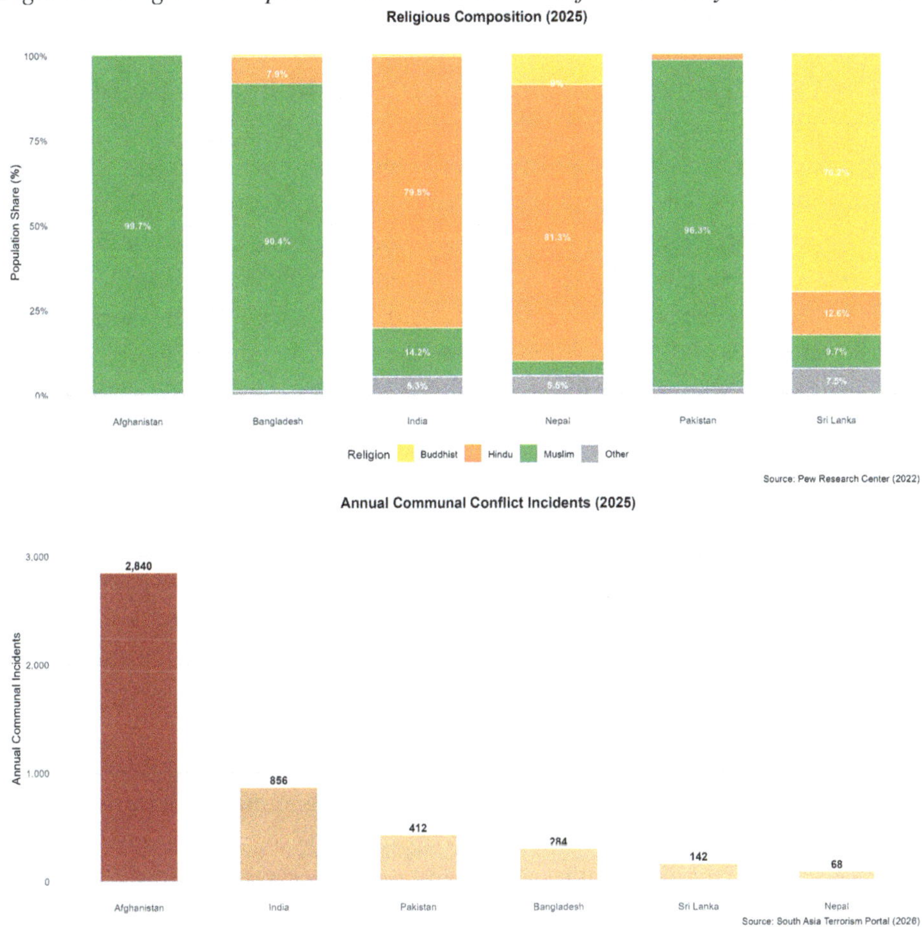

Figure 1 overlays religious group information and communal conflict indicators to identify some of the structural conditions exploited by the extremist actors in South Asia in gaming spaces. In the upper panel, the difference between religiously uniform Afghanistan and Pakistan, and religiously plural and diverse India and Sri Lanka is illustrated. The lower panel shows that Afghanistan's level of conflict intensity (2,840 incidents per year) is much greater than that of other countries and thus serves the extremists with constantly up-to-date grievance material. When combined with religious diversity and intensity of the conflict, this forms a grievance field weaponized as part of the gaming recruitment narratives, which provides an analytical setting that frames the case evidence in Table 3.

4. MECHANISMS OF RADICALIZATION IN SOUTH ASIAN GAMING SPACES

4.1 The Digital Ummah and Transnational Religious Solidarity

Digital technologies have been redefining Muslimness in the modern world and reshaping the idea of the *ummah*, or Muslim community (Roy, 2004; Mandaville, 2010). Muslim gaming communities engage with those who share their faith in an effort to build Muslim teams and provide Muslim-friendly environments. But this sense of solidarity can be used by extremist actors and sweeping across traditional clerical hierarchies and national boundaries, the extremists define these "local issues"—such as Kashmir, Palestine, Sunni-Shia tensions—as a worldwide Islamic movement (Sageman, 2004; Bunt, 2018).

4.2 The Radicalization Funnel: Gateway to Extremism

Gaming platforms are recognized as "gateway social spaces" where people are exposed to ideology that is connected to militant-environment ideologies, according to research (Allchorn & Orofino, 2025; Dean, 2021). The well-evidenced radicalization process has 5 stages of a funnel:

Stage 1: Gaming as a casual pastime for fun

Stage 2: Community formation through in-game communication and clan building

Stage 3: Community discussion, in the context of gaming culture, ideological exposure

Stage 4: Gradual radicalization and migration to encrypted platforms (Discord → Telegram → Signal)

Stage 5: Mobilization for offline activities, financial contributions, or further recruitment

4.3 Platform Affordances: Anonymity, Encryption, and VPN Circumvention

Online platforms create some new technological affordances to facilitate radicalization. Anonymity allows the players to use pseudonyms and to be less accountable (Suler, 2004). As encryption becomes more widespread throughout gaming apps, it's becoming harder for security agencies to surveil communications (FATF, 2025). In Kashmir's Valley, there has been at least one documented case showing messaging apps used by extremist recruiters, which do not even ask for phone numbers or email addresses, thereby allowing complete anonymity of use (South Asia Terrorism Portal, 2026).

Regulatory responses are further complicated by the fact that Virtual Private Networks are used. A few gaming applications have been prohibited in India under the Information Technology ACT, 2000, under Section 69A of this act; these prohibitions are constantly evaded through VPN usage (Telecom Regulatory Authority of India, 2025).

4.4 Gamification of Extremism

Today, such extremist groups are hijacking gaming graphics and gameplay to gain traction with a younger generation (Kuttymartin, 2025). Few agencies had been making the recruitment videos since 2014, which are similar to FPS games, and worked out modifications for *Grand Theft Auto V* (GTA 5) that involve terrorist attacks (UN Counter-Terrorism Committee Executive Directorate, 2020). Since the Christchurch Attack, extremists have reconstructed the Christchurch attack in Roblox and Doome. The UN reported on the danger of a "funnel strategy", which pushes users out of conventional gaming areas to crypto extremist networks (UN Counter-Terrorism Committee Executive Directorate, 2022).

5. EMPIRICAL EVIDENCE AND CASE STUDIES

5.1 Documented Cases in South Asia

Case 1 — Kashmir Valley Recruitment Network (2025): Indian security officials said that online war games like PUBG started providing space for terror groups to send messages to the Kashmir Valley recruits. Being influenced by his gaming partner across the border, a boy under the age of 18 was being radicalized online (South Asia Terrorism Portal, 2026).

Case 2 — Agra Religious Conversion Racket (2025): Uttar Pradesh Police had found a religious network that uses the medium of games to target the youth and slowly indoctrinates them with the religious ideology. Two handlers who also travelled with her from Pakistan were of vital importance to the organization (South Asia Terrorism Portal, 2026).

Case 3 — Maharashtra ATS Operations (2026): The Maharashtra Anti-Terrorism Squad has raided more than 40 places in 9 districts regarding the suspected involvement of 53 youth in activities related to radicalization networks on gaming chats, Instagram reels and encrypted applications (South Asia Terrorism Portal, 2026).

Case 4 — Mumbai Terror Plot (2026): A plot to radicalize teenagers aged between 15 and 17, through gaming chats, Telegram and Signal, has been unearthed by the authorities. Platforms and gaming were pointed out as the first time this was discussed (South Asia Terrorism Portal, 2026).

Case 5 — Multi-State AQIS Arrests (2026): Twelve individuals were arrested in various states of the country for suspected connections with Al-Qaeda in the Indian Subcontinent. Gambling apps were used to communicate with foreign handlers and to spread extremist propaganda, investigators said (South Asia Terrorism Portal, 2026).

Figure 2. Trend of documented gaming-related extremism cases in South Asia (2020–2026)

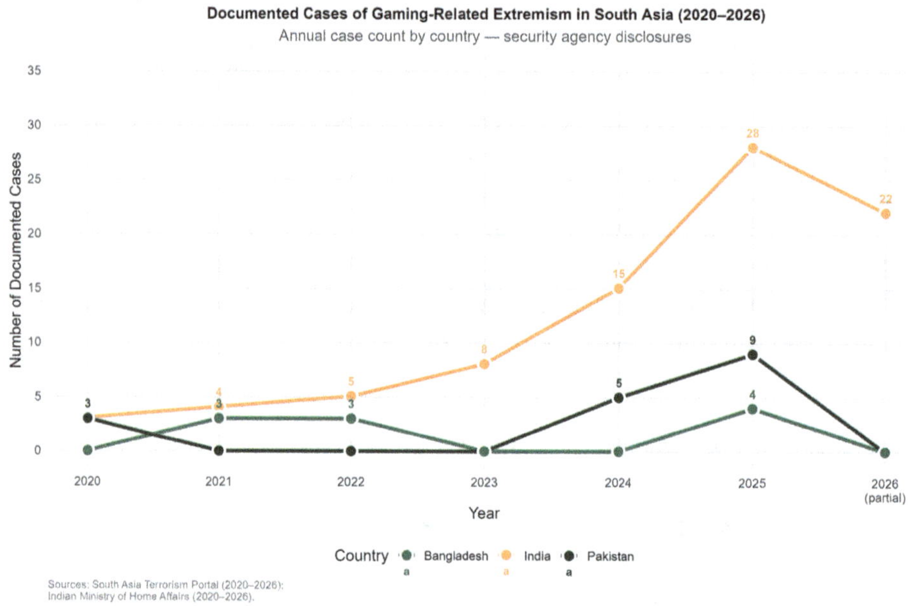

The year-on-year growth of the extreme gaming-related events is presented in Figure 2, showing a clear trend towards an increase in extremist events reported between 2020 and 2026. The steepest growth curve for India shows that the number of cases grew from 3 in 2020 to 28 in 2025. The cases in Pakistan only appear from 2024 onwards, which may be due to better detection capabilities. It is interesting to note that this acceleration started in 2023, even as the mobile gaming market is expanding, and multi-platform funnel recruitment strategies by extremist actors are known.

5.2 Quantitative Analysis of Documented Cases

Table 3 shows an extensive database which gathers all the documented 'extremism incidents' due to gaming activities in South Asia from 2020 to 2026.

Table 3. Documented cases of gaming-related extremism in South Asia (2020–2026)

Year	Country	Cases	Primary Platform	Secondary Platform	Primary Ideology	Target Age	Male (%)	Recruitment Modality	Foreign Handler	Outcome	Offline Violence	Minors Involved	Source
2020	India	3	PUBG Mobile	Telegram	Jihadist/ Separatist	17–28	88	Voice chat → encrypted app	Yes (Pakistan)	2 arrested, 1 escaped	No	No	SATP 2021
2021	India	4	PUBG Mobile	WhatsApp	Islamist	16–24	72	Text chat → private group	Yes (Pakistan)	3 arrested, 1 counseled	No	Yes	MHA 2022
2021	Pakistan	3	PUBG Mobile	Telegram	Jihadist (TTP)	18–30	94	Clan → encrypted app	Yes (Afghanistan)	3 arrested	No	No	SATP 2022
2022	India	5	PUBG Mobile	Discord	Islamist/ Khalistani	15–26	80	Gaming clan → Discord	Yes (Pakistan, Canada)	4 arrested, 1 monitored	No	Yes	SATP 2023
2022	Bangladesh	3	PUBG Mobile	Facebook	Islamist	16–24	86	Gaming → social media	Yes (Pakistan)	2 arrested, 1 counseled	No	No	SATP 2023
2023	India	8	PUBG Mobile	Discord	Islamist/ Khalistani	15–25	82	Multi-platform	Yes (Pakistan, UK)	6 arrested, 2 counseled	No	Yes	MHA 2024
2024	India	15	PUBG Mobile	Telegram/ Signal	Islamist	14–30	78	Gaming → encrypted messaging	Yes (Pakistan)	12 arrested, 3 de-radicalized	Yes (1 foiled)	Yes	MHA 2025
2024	Pakistan	5	PUBG Mobile	Telegram	Jihadist/ Sectarian	18–30	92	Clan formation → ideology	Yes (Afghanistan)	5 arrested	No	No	SATP 2025
2025	India	28	PUBG/Ludo Star	Discord/ Instagram	Islamist/Hindu Nationalist	13–35	76	Multi-platform funnel	Yes (Pakistan/ ISI)	22 arrested, 6 counseled	Yes (2 foiled)	Yes	MHA 2025; SATP 2026
2025	Pakistan	9	PUBG Mobile	Telegram	Jihadist	16–30	90	Gaming → encrypted app	Yes (Afghanistan)	9 arrested	No	No	SATP 2026
2025	Bangladesh	4	PUBG Mobile	Telegram	Islamist	15–25	84	Gaming → awareness	Yes (Pakistan)	3 arrested, 1 campaign	No	Yes	SATP 2026
2026 (partial)	India	22	Multiple	Telegram/ Signal	Islamist/ Khalistani	14–30	80	Multi-platform	Yes (multiple)	Ongoing investigations	Yes (1 attempted)	Yes	MHA 2026
Total		**109**				**14–35**	**83 avg**		**Majority**		**4 cases**	**Majority**	

Source: South Asia Terrorism Portal (2020–2026); Pakistani Federal Investigation Agency (2021–2025).

Looking at Table 3, it is evident there's a significant and growing pattern: the number of cases surged from just six in 2020-2021 to 59 in 2025 alone, an almost tenfold increase over five years. The involvement of foreign handlers – mostly from the countries of Pakistan & Afghanistan – can be attested in most of the cases. In an overwhelming majority of cases, it can be noted that the transnational nature claims of South Asian gaming radicalization networks are well documented. The "multi-platform funnel modality" always comes out as the most popular form of recruitment, making its way first from traditional gaming platforms and amplified by the use of encrypted messages. The rising trend of foiled or attempted offline violence, going from zero cases in 2020-2022 to four such attempts in 2024-2026, represents a worrying escalation of ideology to planning, and should be prioritized amid the current policy debate.

Figure 3. Age distribution and gender profile of radicalization cases

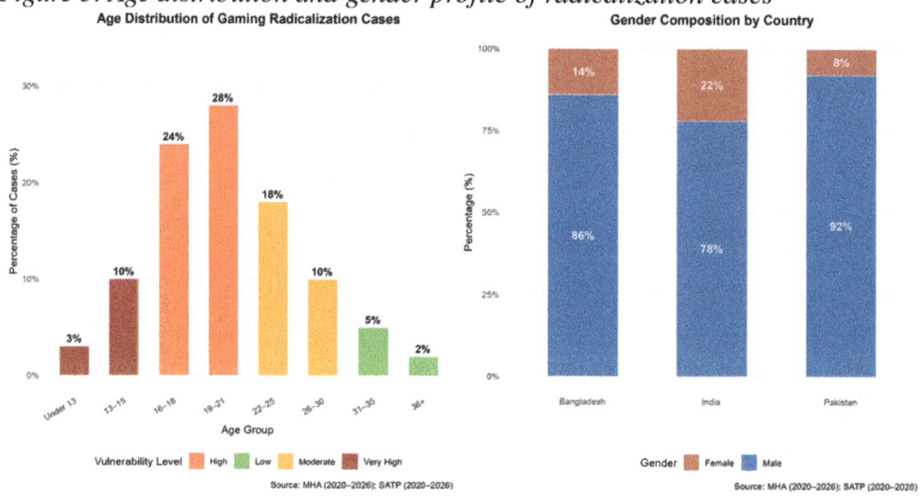

Based on Figure 3, the demographic profile of the individuals involved in South Asian games-related radicalization incidents shows that the individuals vary in age, ranging from 18 to 40 years old. The age distribution (left panel) reveals that 65% of cases concern persons in the age group 16-25, and most cases (28%) concern persons in the age group 19-21. Furthermore, a staggering 13% of these cases are of people aged under 16 (classified as 'Very High Vulnerability'), highlighting the failure of existing gaming site age verification processes. Finally, the gender composition (right panel) raises, as expected, that males dominate in all three countries (78%–92%) per the literature on radicalization at the global level, but it also indicates the growing emergence of a targeting of females that has also been reported, and therefore deserves specific attention when it comes to the development of prevention programmes.

5.3 FATF Findings on Gaming and Terrorist Financing

During this period of time, there has been a growing trend in which extremist organizations use gaming platforms to propagate and recruit, radicalize, fundraize and covertly communicate, highlighted by the Financial Action Task Force (FATF) 2025 report. An extended analysis of the findings of FATF risks is provided in Table 4.

Table 4. FATF risk assessment of gaming platform exploitation for terrorist financing and radicalization (2025)

Risk Category	Specific Mechanism	Vulnerability (1–5)	Detectability (1–5)	Regulatory Gap	Regional Impact	Known Groups	Financial Scale	Enforcement Taken	Recommended Action	Tech Solution	International Cooperation	Implementation Timeline
Propaganda	In-game chats, avatars	5	2	Content moderation	South Asia, MENA	AQIS, TTP	Non-monetary	Limited	AI content monitoring	NLP scanning	Medium	6–12 months
Recruitment	Voice/text during gameplay	5	2	Age verification	South Asia, MENA	AQIS, ISI proxies	Non-monetary	Limited	Mandatory age verification	Behavioral analytics	High	12–18 months
Radicalization	Gradual ideological grooming	5	1	Platform accountability	South Asia, MENA	Multiple	Non-monetary	Very limited	Digital literacy mandates	User journey monitoring	High	18–24 months
Virtual Currency Laundering	Digital item trading	4	3	Secondary market oversight	Global	Criminal networks	USD 1–5B est.	Partial	Marketplace oversight	Blockchain tracking	High	12–24 months
Covert Communication	Encrypted gaming chats	5	1	Encryption regulation	South Asia, Global	Multiple	Non-monetary	Very limited	Lawful intercept frameworks	Lawful intercept	Very High	24–36 months
Fundraising	In-game purchases, gift cards	4	3	AML threshold gaps	Global	criminal networks	USD 100M+ annually	Partial	KYC requirements	Transaction pattern analysis	Medium	6–12 months
Money Laundering		4	2	Transaction monitoring	Global	Criminal–terrorist nexus	USD 500M+ annually	Limited	Enhanced due diligence	AI transaction monitoring	High	12–18 months
Lone-Actor Incitement	Encrypted chats, manifesto sharing	4	1	Content liability	Global	Far-right, Islamist	Non-monetary	Very limited	Platform liability frameworks	Automated detection	Medium	12–18 months

Source: FATF (2025), "Comprehensive Update on Terrorist Financing Risks"; UN Counter-Terrorism Committee Executive Directorate (2022).

As shown in Table 4, propaganda, recruitment, radicalization and covert communication all show the highest vulnerability scores (5/5) and the lowest detectability scores (1-2/5), thus identifying these as the highest priority risk categories. The money involved is huge (USD 500 million or more per year in money laundering and USD 100 million or more per year in terrorist financing), underscoring the financial, in addition to ideological implications, of exploiting gaming platforms. Nearly all requirements for international co-operation are rated "High" or "Very High", indicative of the intrinsically transnational nature of the threat. The difference in the proposed timelines to implement particular measures—ranging from a short-term recommendation for the technical solutions of the AI content monitoring measure, 6-12 months, to a longer one for the structural solutions, such as the lawful intercept frameworks, 24-36 months—clearly indicates that until the work has been completed, interim measures need to be implemented immediately.

5.4 Platform Exploitation: Comparative Analysis

It is worth comparing several different gaming and gaming-related platforms exploited in South Asian extremist environments in greater detail in Table 5.

Table 5. Comparative analysis of platforms exploited in South Asian gaming extremism (2020–2026)

Platform	Type	South Asia MAU (M)	Encryption	Anonymity	Age Verification	Content Moderation	Documented Cases	Primary Exploitation	Secondary Exploitation	Platform Response	Government Action	VPN Circumvention	Radicalization Stage	Migration To
PUBG Mobile	Battle Royale FPS	200+	Medium	High	Weak	Moderate	38	Voice/text recruitment	Clan formation for ideology	Reactive removal	Banned India 2020	Yes	Stages 1–3	Discord/ Telegram
Free Fire	Battle Royale FPS	150+	Medium	High	Weak	Moderate	14	In-game communication	Religious identity signaling	Reactive removal	No action	Limited	Stages 1–3	WhatsApp/ Telegram
Ludo Star/ King	Casual Board Game	100+	Low–Medium	Medium	Absent	Low	20	Chat for conversion/ recruitment	Religious identity	Minimal response	No action	Low	Stages 2–3	Telegram/ Signal
Call of Duty Mobile	FPS	50+	Medium	High	Weak	Moderate	9	Clan recruitment	Jihadi aesthetic normalization	Reactive removal	No action	Yes	Stages 1–2	Discord
Discord	Gaming Chat	30+	High	High	Absent	Variable	28	Private extremist servers	Encrypted voice radicalization	Proactive (limited)	No action	Low	Stages 3–4	Telegram/ Signal
Telegram	Messaging App	80+	High	Very High	Absent	Reactive only	46	Encrypted extremist channels	Propaganda distribution	Reactive removal	Banned selectively	Very Low	Stages 4–5	Final platform
Signal	Messaging App	20+	Very High	Very High	Absent	None	18	End-to-end encrypted coordination	Operational planning	No capability	No action	None	Stage 5	Final platform
Instagram	Social Media	250+	Medium	Medium	Weak	Moderate	34	Reels for recruitment	DMs for initial contact	Proactive AI moderation	No action	Low	Stages 2–3	Telegram
Twitch	Livestreaming	10+	Medium	Medium	Moderate	Moderate	6	Extremist content livestreams	Community building	Moderate enforcement	No action	Low	Stage 2	Discord
Steam	Game Distribution	15+	Medium	Medium–High	Moderate	Reactive	4	Community forum radicalization	Extremist modification distribution	Reactive removal	No action	Low	Stages 1–2	Discord

Source: FATF (2025); South Asia Terrorism Portal (2020–2026

Table 5 illustrates the multi-platform nature of South Asian gaming radicalization networks and the different functional roles of the platforms. Mainstream gaming platforms (PUBG Mobile, Free Fire, Ludo Star) serve as a gateway to high user levels and low moderation hurdles to reach out and ensure trust. Discord is a stepping stone to more advanced encryption and cultures of extremist servers by platform. Although it is a messaging application, Telegram is the main platform of operation, above which the radicalization is consolidated (46 cases). Signal is the last-mile operating environment where there is only full encryption, and hence, no monitoring. As minors have figured in most of the reported online child abuse cases, the absence of meaningful (age) verification in practically all platforms is a significant systemic vulnerability. In fact, Ludo Star can be called the most governance-lacking platform in all aspects, with extensive documentation suggesting, of course, that it's a play application since major social media platforms are, on average, better governed.

Figure 4. Multi-platform radicalization funnel architecture

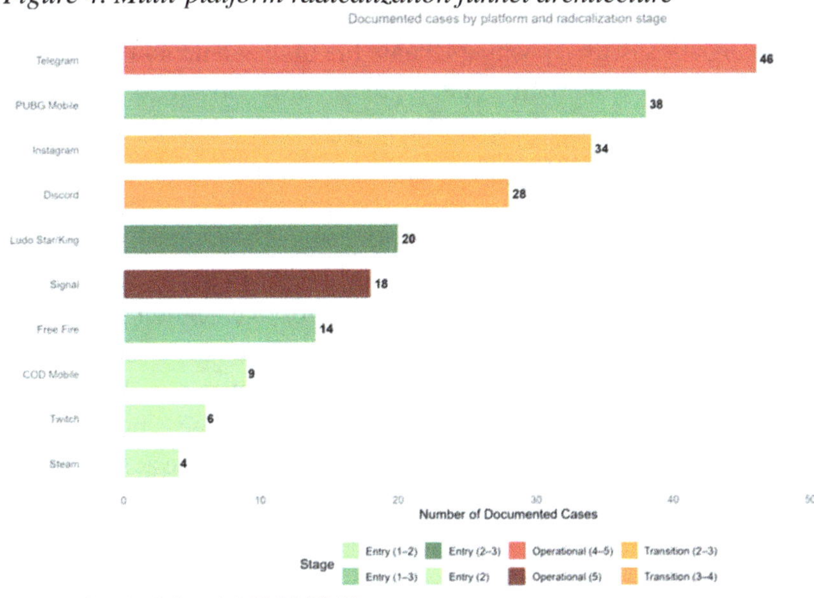

The functional architecture of the multi-platform radicalization tunnel to combat South Asian gaming extremism is visualized in Figure 4. Green, orange and red colours will show that there's a clear evolution from "gaming applications" (green) to "transitional platforms" (orange) to "operational platforms" (Red) – with these being the ones using Telegram and Signal. Telegram was the most popular platform (46 cases) and is a platform that many use on a daily basis, while PUBG Mobile heads the list for gaming-specific platforms (38 cases) and is the main platform used by many day-to-day gaming enthusiasts. The high number of cases in both entry and operational stages supports that the entire funnel, from playing mainstream games to encrypted communication, is activated and operational in South Asian extremism networks.

6. RESILIENCE, COUNTER-NARRATIVES, AND GOVERNANCE

6.1 Community-Led Resistance

The same opportunities afforded by digital media that contribute to radicalization provide potent capacities for resistance. In fact, religious communities of Muslims in South Asia have developed platforms for halal gaming and team formation itself, reflecting the positive potential of religion. It is through these initiatives that religiously-inclusive gameplay directly challenges extremist narratives by showing how playing is compatible with a positive Islamic life in the community. Anticorruption efforts either run by interfaith gaming groups or by moderation organizations in local communities further reduce sectarian polarization between the 3 faith communities, Hindu, Sikh and Buddhist.

6.2 Digital Literacy and Critical Pedagogies

Digital literacy programs are one of the key points of intervention. There is a need to include in the curricula of the educational systems in South Asian countries the identification of grooming, coded language, geopolitical awareness, knowledge of platforms, and reporting systems. Digital literacy education needs partnerships involving gaming companies, education and civil society to be made at scale (UNESCO, 2023; Moonshot CVE, 2021).

6.3 Platform Governance

There are complex trade-offs for platform governance in terms of security, privacy and freedom of expression (Allchorn & Orofino, 2025). Four dimensions need to be addressed. To ensure the proper moderation of content, human moderators who are well aware of the South Asian linguistic and cultural challenges need to be hired, while AI-powered content detection tools need to be robostened specifically for the region's extremist content. The number of cases the gambling and gaming sector throws up involving minors is a significant percentage, and age verification should be made mandatory on gaming and gaming-related platforms. The aim of the encryption policy should be to analyze the metadata and recognize behavioral patterns, not provide backdoors that affect security for everyone. Content hashing, takedown data, and other forms of coordination with other platforms are made possible via tools like the Global Internet Forum to Counter Terrorism (GIFCT, 2024).

Figure 5. Comparative platform governance assessment

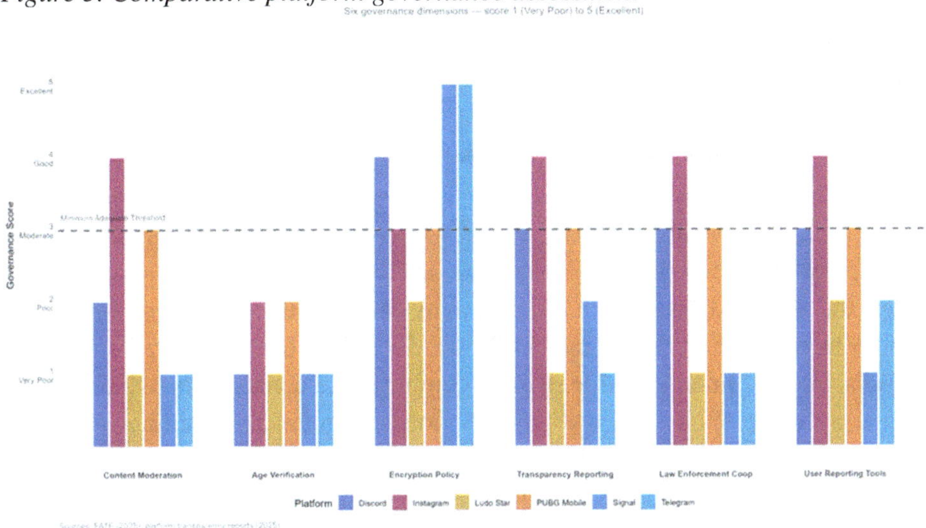

The governance assessment (relative) of the six most-exploited platforms in South Asian gaming extremism is provided in this comparative assessment, using six critical dimensions as presented in Figure 5. Instagram is the only app to score a suitably high rating and get close to or meet the minimum adequate threshold (a score of 3). Telegram and Signal actually perform at the top end (5) in terms of encryption, given their focus on privacy, and at the bottom end (1) on all the other dimensions of governance due to their nature as preferred platforms for extremists to operate on. Ludo Star features the poorest governance profile to date and has been the subject of a lot of reported exploitation, representing an important gap in current regulatory scrutiny. The results highlight the need for differentiated and platform-specific governance structures, instead of regulatory uniformity on fundamentally different platform architectures.

6.4 Policy Recommendations

Such policy answers need to be comprehensive and cover the entire platform ecosystem. The four key pillars are: Regulation—focusing on getting gaming companies into anti-money laundering and anti-financing of terror laws; International cooperation—focusing on formal bilateral cooperation mechanisms to exchange information about cross-border gaming radicalization networks; public-private cooperation—developing co-regulatory mechanisms for content moderation and user protection; and continuous investment in research—standardization of the reporting of incidents, enabling for and providing longitudinal pictures of the types of risks involved in gaming.

7. CONCLUSION

Gambling premises in South Asia are battlegrounds where religious identity, geopolitical discourses, and the radicalisation process co-exist in a complex manner. This chapter's contributions have been threefold. First, it has broadened the geographical parameters of the prevailing scholarship and offered a survey and systematic analysis of the South Asian gaming communities as a place of religious identity formation and risk of radicalization. Second, it has made available a new multidisciplinary line of thinking which combines the concepts of social identity theory, critical geopolitics and digital religious communication studies. Third, it has used analysis of a series of 109 case studies from 2020-2026 and analyzed with triangulation with the findings and data of FATF to conclude that the multi-platform funnel is the most prevalent form of radicalisation architecture in the South Asian gaming context.

The challenge for policymakers, platform moderators, and educators is to foster resilience against exploitation without undermining the creative and connective potential of gaming communities. This requires a comprehensive, multi-stakeholder approach encompassing regulatory frameworks, platform governance, digital literacy programs, and sustained research investment. By bringing sustained scholarly attention to this critically under-researched region, this chapter aims to enrich ongoing conversations about digital culture and its societal implications while offering practical insights for fostering safer gaming environments across South Asia.

REFERENCES

Allchorn, W., & Orofino, E. (2025). Policing extremism on gaming-adjacent platforms: Awful but lawful? *Frontiers in Psychology, 16*, 1537460. DOI: 10.3389/fpsyg.2025.1537460 PMID: 40823404

Bunt, G. R. (2018). *Hashtag Islam: How cyber-Islamic environments are transforming religious authority*. University of North Carolina Press. DOI: 10.5149/northcarolina/9781469643168.001.0001

Campbell, H. (Ed.). (2013). *Digital religion: Understanding religious practice in new media worlds*. Routledge.

CIA. (2024). *The CIA World Factbook 2024-2025*. Central Intelligence Agency. https://www.cia.gov/the-world-factbook/

Dean, B. (2021). *Gamers who hate: An introduction to ISD's gaming and extremism series*. Institute for Strategic Dialogue. https://www.isdglobal.org/isd-publications/gamers-who-hate-an-introduction-to-isds-gaming-and-extremism-series/

Dodds, K. (2019). *Geopolitics: A very short introduction* (3rd ed.). Oxford University Press. DOI: 10.1093/actrade/9780198830764.001.0001

FATF. (2025). *Comprehensive update on terrorist financing risks*. Financial Action Task Force. https://www.fatf-gafi.org/content/dam/fatf-gafi/publications/Comprehensive-Update-on-Terrorist-Financing-Risks-2025.pdf.coredownload.inline.pdf

GIFCT. (2024). *Annual transparency report 2024*. Global Internet Forum to Counter Terrorism. https://gifct.org/wp-content/uploads/2025/07/GIFCT-Annual-and-Transparency-Report-2024.pdf

Intelligence, G. S. M. A. (2025). *Mobile connectivity index 2025*. GSMA. https://www.mobileconnectivityindex.com/index.html

International Telecommunication Union. (2025). *World telecommunication/ICT indicators database*. ITU. https://www.itu.int/en/ITU-D/Statistics/pages/publications/wtid.aspx

Kuttymartin, N. (2025, October 1). Far-right extremism and gaming: How hate hijacks play. *RSIS Commentary*. https://rsis.edu.sg/rsis-publication/rsis/far-right-extremism-and-gaming-how-hate-hijacks-play/

Mandaville, P. (2010). *Global political Islam*. Routledge. DOI: 10.4324/9780203358511

McCauley, C., & Moskalenko, S. (2008). Mechanisms of political radicalization: Pathways toward terrorism. *Terrorism and Political Violence*, *20*(3), 415–433. DOI: 10.1080/09546550802073367

Moghaddam, F. M. (2005). The staircase to terrorism: A psychological exploration. *The American Psychologist*, *60*(2), 161–169. DOI: 10.1037/0003-066X.60.2.161 PMID: 15740448

Moonshot, C. V. E. (2021). *Gaming and extremism: Intervention strategies for the digital battlefield.* Moonshot CVE. https://moonshotcve.com

Newzoo. (2025). *Global games market report 2025.* Newzoo. https://newzoo.com

Pantoliano, C. (2025). Playing doomsday: Video games and the politics of nuclear weapons. *Review of International Studies*, *51*(4), 1–22. DOI: 10.1017/S0260210525000087

Parlak, C., & Kaygusuz, E. (2025). Neocolonialism in video games: The social discourse of Call of Duty 4: Modern Warfare (2007). *DiGRA Conference Proceedings.* https://doi.org/DOI: 10.26503/dl.v2025i2.2480

Pew Research Center. (2022). *Religious composition by country, 2010–2050.* Pew Research Center. https://www.pewresearch.org/religion/2015/04/02/religious-projection-table/

Roy, O. (2004). *Globalised Islam: The search for a new ummah.* Hurst.

Sageman, M. (2004). *Understanding terror networks.* University of Pennsylvania Press. DOI: 10.9783/9780812206791

Schlegel, L., & Kowert, R. (2024). *Gaming and extremism: The radicalization of digital playgrounds.* Routledge. DOI: 10.4324/9781003388371

Šisler, V. (2008). Digital Arabs: Representation in video games. *European Journal of Cultural Studies*, *11*(2), 203–220. DOI: 10.1177/1367549407088333

Snodgrass, J. G. (2023). *The avatar faculty: Ecstatic transformations in religion and videogames.* University of California Press.

South Asia Terrorism Portal. (2026, May 16). Gaming terror. *Second Sight, 3*(41). https://www.satp.org/second-sight-volume-3-no-41

Suler, J. (2004). The online disinhibition effect. *Cyberpsychology & Behavior*, *7*(3), 321–326. DOI: 10.1089/1094931041291295 PMID: 15257832

Tajfel, H., & Turner, J. C. (1979). An integrative theory of intergroup conflict. In W. G. Austin & S. Worchel (Eds.), *The social psychology of intergroup relations* (pp. 33–47). file:///C:/Users/Hp/Downloads/tajfel-turner-1979-compressed.pdf

Telecom Regulatory Authority of India. (2025). *Telecom subscription data Q4 2025*. TRAI. https://www.ofcom.org.uk/siteassets/resources/documents/research-and-data/telecoms-research/telecoms-data-updates/telecommunications-market-data/telecommunications-market-data-update-q4-2025.pdf?v=415936

Ubaradka, A., Ferguson, C. J., & Khanganba, S. P. (2026). Video games as conduits for radicalization: Impact of exposure to extremist recruitment and authoritarianism on sexist attitudes and aggression. *Psychology of Popular Media*. https://doi.org/ DOI: 10.1037/ppm0000642

UN Counter-Terrorism Committee Executive Directorate. (2020). *The use of the internet and information and communications technologies for terrorist purposes*. United Nations.

UN Counter-Terrorism Committee Executive Directorate. (2022). *Terrorist and violent extremist use of the internet and social media*. United Nations.

UNESCO. (2023). *Digital literacy framework for preventing violent extremism*. UNESCO. https://www.unesco.org

Widyaningsih, R., & Megia, F. V. (2026). Intersection of the metaverse, Muslim identity, and radicalization risks: A global systematic review of digital religious communication. *Komunika: Jurnal Komunikasi Islam, 20*(1), 1–24. https://ejournal.uinsaizu.ac.id/index.php/komunika/article/view/15013

Wiktorowicz, Q. (2004). *Islamic activism: A social movement theory approach*. Indiana University Press.

Williams, D., Ducheneaut, N., Xiong, L., Zhang, Y., Yee, N., & Nickell, E. (2006). From tree house to barracks: The social life of guilds in World of Warcraft. *Games and Culture*, *1*(4), 338–361. DOI: 10.1177/1555412006292616

World Bank. (2025). [World Bank Group. https://databank.worldbank.org/source/world-development-indicators]. *World Development Indicators, 2025*, •••.

ADDITIONAL READINGS

Akhtar, J. (2023). Interfaith coexistence in Islam: Historical reflections and contemporary relevance. *Inkishaf, 3*(1), 39–54. https://www.inkishaf.org/index.php/home/article/view/256

Akhtar, J. (2024). Financial rights of women in Judaism, Christianity and Islam: A comparative study. *Tanazur Research Journal, 5*(2), 1–15. https://tanazur.com.pk/index.php/tanazur/article/view/159

Akhtar, J. (2024). Social justice and equality in the Qur'ān: Implications for global peace. *Edinost in dialog (Unity and Dialogue), 79*(1), 23–45. https://www.teof.uni-lj.si/uploads/File/Edinost/79/01/Akthar.pdf

Akhtar, J. (2025). Qur'ānic ethics of diversity and its educational relevance in combating sectarianism and ethnic violence in South Asia. *Pakistan Journal of Qur'anic Studies, 4*(1), 19–36. https://journals.iub.edu.pk/index.php/pjqs/article/view/3841

Akhtar, J. (2025). Qur'ānic just-peace: A comparative study of peace and justice in Islamic, Christian, and Jewish scriptures. *Pakistan Journal of Qur'anic Studies, 4*(2), 67–83. https://journals.iub.edu.pk/index.php/pjqs/article/view/4300

Akhtar, J. (2025). The concept of 'Ummah' in the Qur'ān: Transcending race, tribe, and ethnicity. *Al-Tabyeen, 9*(1), 154–175. https://journals.uol.edu.pk/al-tabyeen/article/view/4115

Akhtar, J. (2025). The Qur'ānic concept of human equality: An analysis against racism and ethnic discrimination in contemporary societies. *Zia-e-Tahqeeq, 15*(29), 18–35. https://ziaetahqeeq.gcuf.edu.pk/index.php/ztgcuf/article/view/19/4

Akhtar, J. (2026). Qur'anic ethics for peacebuilding: An Islamic counter-narrative to religious extremism in Pakistan. *Al-Qamar, 9*(1), 33–48. https://alqamarjournal.net/index.php/alqamar/article/view/1690/1064

Akhtar, J. (2026). Reinterpreting religious authority: Women as Islamic jurists for addressing gender justice in Pakistan. *Women's Studies International Forum, 116*, 1–8. https://www.sciencedirect.com/science/article/pii/S0277539526000233. DOI: 10.1016/j.wsif.2026.103300

Akhtar, J., & Ali, S. (2024). Cultural diversity and intellectual fusion: Analyzing Abdul Hamid AbuSulayman's global approach to social sciences. *Rushd Journal, 5*(1), 196–209. https://rushdjournal.com/index.php/rushd/article/view/157

Hussain, M., & Akhtar, J. (2023). The root causes of Islamophobia: Analysis and remedies. *Ma'arif-e-Islami, 22*(1), 1–19. https://ojs.aiou.edu.pk/index.php/jmi/article/view/1026

Chapter 3

Explainable AI for Detecting Harassment and Extremism in Voice Chat

Uzair Bhatti
http://orcid.org/0000-0002-8743-2783
Hainan University, China

Yonis Gulzar
http://orcid.org/0000-0002-6515-1569
Department of Management Information Systems, King Faisal University, Saudi Arabia

Yazeed Yasin Ghadi
http://orcid.org/0000-0002-7121-495X
Department of Computer Science and Software Engineering, Al Ain University, Al Ain, UAE

Valisher Sapayev
http://orcid.org/0000-0002-6751-5864
Department of General Professional Subjects, Mamun University, Khiva, Uzbekistan

Odilbek Kosimov
Department of Information Technology and Exact Sciences, Termez University of Economics and Service, Termez, Uzbekistan

Shaxnoza Sultanova
Department of Philosophy, Tashkent State University of Economics, Tashkent, Uzbekistan

Khayrulla Urozboev
Department of International Scientific Journals and Ratings, Alfraganus University, Tashkent, Uzbekistan

ABSTRACT

Online voice communication platforms have become central to gaming, social networking, and virtual collaboration, but they are increasingly challenged by harassment,

DOI: 10.4018/979-8-2600-1664-0.ch003

hate speech, and extremist content. Traditional automated moderation systems often operate as black boxes, limiting transparency and user trust. Explainable Artificial Intelligence (XAI) offers a promising solution by enabling interpretable detection of harmful speech while providing clear justifications for moderation decisions. This chapter explores the integration of XAI techniques with speech recognition, natural language processing, and deep learning models to identify harassment and extremist behavior in voice chat environments. It examines methods for improving detection accuracy, reducing algorithmic bias, enhancing accountability, and supporting human moderators through transparent decision-making. The chapter also discusses ethical considerations, privacy concerns, and future research directions for creating safer and more inclusive digital communication spaces.

1. INTRODUCTION

Voice chat is now one of the most critical modes of communication in today's digital spaces. Sending live voice messages is essential for online gaming platforms, social audio apps, virtual classrooms, workplace collaboration tools, livestreaming communities, and metaverse interaction spaces. Voice chat is not a textual interaction and can convey tone, pitch, rhythm, pauses, volume, and style of conversation and thus emotions, urgency, humor, anger, identity and social presence. The characteristics make voice communication more natural and engaging, but also more complex to monitor, interpret and control. Platforms are under increasing pressure to ensure that individuals and communities are not being harmed by harmful speech, such as harassment, hate speech, verbal abuse, threats, radicalising speech, or extremist speech, as millions of people use the platforms each day to communicate with each other (Alvarez-Melis & Jaakkola, 2018).

Verbal abuse, insults, intimidation, humiliation, targeted attacks, discrimination, sexualised comments, bullying and threats are all examples of possible harassment within voice chat. Extremist communication can take the form of ideological hostility, incitement to violence, recruitment messages, coded language, glorification of harmful action or dehumanizing language towards a particular group. These types of destructive words don't always have to be blatant. They can be indirect, sarcastic, use slang, be hidden in humor, and/or be conveyed in culturally specific terms. The same words can mean different things to different speakers based on tone, relationship between participants, context of the conversation, and the social context. Thus, it is not just about spotting offensive language when it comes to voice chat and harassment/extremism. It involves more than just knowledge of language and context; it needs knowledge of acoustic signals, intent and social meaning (Ansari et al., 2024).

The traditional moderation techniques do not always work in a voice environment. Manual moderation is tedious, expensive, emotionally draining, and inefficient for large platforms. Keyword-based filters are also problematic as they don't accurately detect tone, sarcasm, coded language or context-dependent harm. Moreover, voice chats are typically ephemeral, and the content can be problematic and vanish before moderators have a chance to react. All of these challenges have necessitated the use of AI (Artificial Intelligence) for automated or semi-automated voice moderation. AI can manage huge amounts of audio data, transcribe and translate speech to text, categorize content as harmful or not, recognize emotional trends, and raise a flag to human moderators in near real time. But there are significant concerns around the accuracy, fairness, transparency, privacy, and accountability of using AI in such a sensitive environment (Attanasio et al., 2022).

A big worry is the fact that many AI models are "black boxes." They can generate a result, like "harassment identified" or "extremist content identified," without making it clear to the user why they have made that decision. This lack of explanation is problematic when it impacts on the rights, reputation, access to platforms, or freedom of expression of users. A false positive could be a user that didn't mean to cause harm, and a false negative could be a victim left vulnerable to abuse. AI systems can also misinterpret accents, dialects, local terms, jokes, or community language in contexts where more than one language and culture are spoken. The scenarios below demonstrate that having high accuracy is insufficient. In order to be considered responsible, AI systems need to explain why they make their decisions to the user in an understandable way as well (Babaeianjelodar et al., 2022).

Explainable Artificial Intelligence (XAI) is a significant remedy to this problem. XAI is a class of methods and techniques that will help make AI decisions easily understandable to humans. Explainability can be used to illustrate how the various components of an audio clip, transcript, acoustic pattern, or conversational context influenced the prediction of harmful content in a voice-chat moderation application. An explainable system, for instance, can discover particular words, phrases, tone fluctuations, speaker turns, or even emotional cues that impacted the model's classification. These explanations can assist moderators in assessing flagged material, assist platform owners in auditing model behavior, and help users to understand the moderation actions better when they are taken. Explainability is another aspect that enhances trust, as users and moderators will be more inclined to embrace decisions supported by AI systems when they understand the reasoning behind it (Balkir et al., 2022).

Several AI techniques are needed to detect harassment and extremism in voice chat. ASR may convert speech to text for additional analysis. NLP will analyze the transcript for toxic, threatening or extremist patterns. Through audio analysis, one can find non-verbal aspects like shouting, anger, stress, aggressive tone or emotional intensity. Speaker Diarization can find out who is talking and when. Contextual modeling can analyze the evolution of a conversation rather than look at each sentence individually. These methods, in conjunction with XAI methods, can enable the system to go beyond only classification and offer meaningful explanations behind moderation decisions (Bensalem et al., 2024).

But voice moderation has to be created carefully if it is to be explainable. It should not be used as a means of over-monitoring or unfairly controlling. Voice data is very personal as it can give away everything from identity and gender to age, emotional state, accent, health condition and social background. Thus, it is crucial that any AI system employed for voice-chat monitoring adheres to the principles of privacy, consent, data minimization, and responsible governance. There also needs to be human oversight. The use of AI for moderation should be used to augment the human moderator, particularly in cases where the text is ambiguous, complex in terms of humor, conflict or political speech, or cultural expression. There should be a responsible framework that takes into account the safety of users, freedom of expression, platform responsibility, and human accountability(Bunde, 2021).

In this chapter, the attention is on the capability of Explainable AI to identify harassment and extremism in voice-chat settings. It explores the challenges of detecting voice-based harmful communication, the role of AI in real-time moderation, and the importance of explainability in making informed decisions. Major technical aspects like speech recognition, audio feature extraction, text classification, multimodal learning, speaker diarization, and context-aware analysis are also discussed in the chapter. Special emphasis is placed on the XAI methods like feature importance, attention visualization, saliency mapping, SHAP, LIME, counterfactual explanations, and human-readable moderation reports (Davidson et al., 2017).

The heart of this chapter is the idea that explainability should be a mandatory component of AI-powered voice moderation, not a choice, but a requirement for trust, fairness, and accountability. In areas where it's particularly important to be able to explain why a piece of content was identified as harassment/extremism, how the model took that conclusion, and if it was the right one, platforms need to be able to do so. Explainable AI can alleviate blind trust for automated systems, and empower better moderator judgments, appeal and audit, and ethical platform governance. Meanwhile, explainability needs to be integrated with robust privacy safeguards, bias testing, cultural sensitivity, and human-in-the-loop review (DeYoung et al., 2020).

The chapter is structured to offer theoretical and practical insights. It starts by setting out the meaning of the words 'harassment', 'extremism' and 'harmful voice communication'. It then delves into the unique hurdles of voice-chat moderation and examines AI-driven solutions to identify harm. The chapter then outlines what is meant by the term Explainable AI and the significance of this for transparent and accountable moderation. A new framework towards real-time voice chat harassment and extremism detection using XAI is proposed. The chapter also addresses the design of the datasets, the construction of the models, possible evaluation metrics, ethical concerns, practical applications, limitations and future research directions. In this way, the chapter hopes to make its own contribution to ensuring safe, fair and transparent digital communities using voice (Dorris et al., 2020).

2. CONCEPTUAL FOUNDATIONS

To understand how to build the conceptual foundation of Explainable AI for the detection of harmful communication in voice chat, it is important to grasp three interwoven concepts: harmful communication, voice-based interaction and explainable artificial intelligence. Key concepts that help define this area must be discussed first, before the technical models, and system design. Harassment, extremism, hate speech, toxic speech, threats and radicalizing communication are frequently linked but not synonymous. Likewise, when using voice chat, information is conveyed not just by the words themselves, but by their tone, emotion, timing, and social context. To this end, a robust conceptual underpinning is required to understand the capabilities of AI systems to detect harmful behaviour in voice environment and how explainability can make this detection more transparent and accountable (Doshi-Velez & Kim, 2017).

2.1 Harassment in Digital Voice Communication

Digital voice communication harassment is defined as verbal behavior that is repeated or severe, directed at an individual or group, with an intent or effect to cause fear, to humiliate, to cause emotional distress, to exclude or intimidate. Harassment in voice chat can be done in a variety of ways such as insults, name calling, threats, mocking, discriminatory remarks, sexual comments, bullying, aggressive shouting or repeated unwanted communication. It can target an individual because of their identity, gender, race, religion, nationality, language, disability, gaming ability, political view or social status.

Harassment is a form of targeting that is harmful and is not the result of a general disagreement or ordinary conflict. A user can strongly disagree, without harassing another person. If the speech is abusive, degrading, threatening, or repeats against another person or persons, however, it is a moderation concern. Harsh words are particularly damaging in terms of harassment in the context of voice chat, where words are said in real time and with high emotional impact. The victim can hear in real time the speaker's tone, anger, laughter or aggression, which can heighten the psychological effect of the abuse(Ehsan et al., 2021).

Harassment may be direct or indirect. Direct harassment involves explicit insults/menaces towards a user. Indirect harassment can include mocking a person in a group discussion, using coded language, asking other people to harass a person, or excluding a person by using hostile language. Additionally, in numerous online communities, harassment is also influenced by group dynamics and several users may be involved in group verbal abuse. This makes it more difficult to detect, as harmful meaning can be conveyed through the entire conversation and not a single sentence (ElSherief et al., 2021).

2.2 Extremism and Radicalizing Speech

Extremism is the expression of beliefs, attitudes or actions that are hostile to pluralism; that incite hostility to out-groups; that justify violence; or that support the domination or elimination of others on the basis of their ideological, political, religious, racial or cultural characteristics. Extremist communication can happen in voice chat, such as praising violent movements, recruitment messages, normalizing extremist ideas in a community, dehumanizing language or calling for violence and conspiracy-based hatred, and uses coded slogans.

When communication causes a person to become more hostile or violent in his or her beliefs, it is considered radicalizing speech. It doesn't necessarily involve violence in the first place. Rather, it can slowly introduce users to discourses of complaint, fear based on identity, enemy formation, victimhood, superiority, and/or revenge. Speech radicalisation can occur in private groups, gaming communities, livestream discussions or social audio rooms in online voice spaces. Extremist messaging can seem casual, funny, or socially acceptable, due to the conversational and informal nature of voice chat (Fortuna & Nunes, 2018).

Extremist speech and controversial speech must be differentiated. Opinions, political statements, religious beliefs, and criticism of institutions are not necessarily extremist if they are strong. Extremism is an issue when the communication encourages hate, dehumanization, violence, coercion or exclusion towards individuals or groups. This separation is crucial, as AI systems must not over-flag legitimate speech while simultaneously being able to detect harmful and dangerous speech (Gongane et al., 2022).

2.3 Toxic Speech, Hate Speech, Harassment and Threats

There are a number of overlapping but separate types of harmful online communication. Toxic speech is a general category for speech that is rude, insulting, aggressive or disruptive and that hinders healthy speech. Hate speech is more specific, meaning it refers to speech which attacks a protected or identity-based group, such as race, religion, nationality, gender, ethnicity, disability and/or sexual orientation. Harassment is typically the deliberate abuse of a person or group and can involve repeated attacks, intimidation or humiliation. Threats are statements that indicate a willingness to cause harm, violence, exposure, punishment or danger(Gongane et al., 2024).

Many of these categories overlap. For instance, harassment of an individual with hate speech or a threat to a specific community may be considered extremist communication. The differences, however, do have an impact on AI classification and moderation decisions. A warning can be given for a toxic comment, and a direct threat can be escalated immediately. Stronger measures against hate speech might be necessary as it can be damaging to people as well as to communities. Extremist content might need specific review as it could be related to recruitment, propaganda, or violence(Huang et al., 2023).

These categories are not simply labels to be used for voice-chat moderation. They must also be considered in terms of severity, context, repetition, intention of speaker, and harm to the receiver. One offensive word isn't as bad as a constant barrage of insults. Likewise, language used by an extremist may seem innocuous to a broad model, and yet have significance in the context of a particular ideology. Hence, a conceptual clarity is required to design accurate and explainable AI systems (Ibrahim et al., 2022).

2.4 Voice Chat as the Separate Communication Mode

Voice talking is not the same as text talking as it contains acoustic and emotional signals. Mostly the system works in text, examining words, punctuation, emoji, and written context. For voice, the system should take into account both the words spoken and the way the words are spoken. Meaning can be affected by tone, pitch, loudness, speed, pause, laughter, sarcasm, stress and emotional intensity. Vocal expression can make the same sentence sound friendly, joking, angry, threatening or insulting.

For instance, if a person says a relatively innocuous word in a transcript, it might come across as quite aggressive if they say it loud in an aggressive tone. Likewise, a tone of sarcasm or mockery can make a simple statement harassment. Voice chat is also real time, meaning that damaging speech can impact users right away, before a report can be made. This makes it necessary to analyse voices with both the linguistic and acoustic analysis (Jacovi & Goldberg, 2020).

Second, an important aspect of voice chat is interactive context. Meaning is often related to the sequence of speaker turns, interruptions, repetitions, group reactions, and the context of the previous conversation. A bad trade can take place over a period of time, several minutes. Hence, recognising harassment and extremism from speech in voice chat involves systems able to analyse the speech as well as the flow of the conversation.

2.5 Context, Intent and Meaning

Culture and language also influence meaning in the voice chat. How the speech is interpreted can be affected by accents, dialects, code-switching, idioms and multilingual expressions. A system trained primarily on one language or cultural context might misclassify users from another context. This causes a bias and unfair moderation. Therefore linguistic diversity and fairness should be taken into account when designing voice moderation systems (Jahan & Oussalah, 2023).

2.6 A Coded Language and the Potential for Implicit Harm

All harassment and extremism is not necessarily manifested with clear abusive language. To evade detection, a user can employ coded language, memes, abbreviations, jocularity, indirect reference or symbolic expressions. Extremist groups tend to use coded language to convey ideology and evade enforcement of the platform. Harassers might also resort to indirect insults, repeated sarcasm, or orchestrated mockery, instead of threats.

Implicit harm is the type of harm that is complicated for AI systems: It needs some context. A word or words can be innocuous individually but be harmful in a specific context or community. For instance, extremist identities, incitement or attacks to a group can be indicated through coded references which do not necessarily contain hate words. Likewise, if the speaker laughs or mimics a person's accent or uses a mocking tone repeatedly, this can be considered harassment even if the transcript does not contain offensive language.

Explainable AI can assist with this issue, providing insights into why the model made its decision, whether it was due to certain conversational patterns, acoustic cues, or contextual signals. The moderators may examine the evidence and make a judgement as to the reasonableness of the system's interpretation rather than just a final label. This is particularly significant in the ambiguous cases where human judgment is still needed (Jain & Wallace, 2019).

2.7 Artificial Intelligence in Harmful Speech Detection

Artificial Intelligence is a computer system that can simulate human intelligence tasks, like pattern recognition, information classification, language understanding, and prediction. For harmful speech detection, AI can be leveraged to detect abusive language, threats, hate speech, extremist content and toxic behavior. These systems tend to use machine learning algorithms trained using vast amounts of labelled examples.

In the case of voice-chat moderation, AI typically follows a series of steps. Firstly, the sound is recorded and treated. Second, Automatic Speech Recognition (ASR) can be used to transcribe speech into written text. Thirdly, text-based models detect words that are harmful in the transcript. Fourth, models based on speech can analyze the tone, strength and emotional state of the speech. Finally, the system outputs the risk score or classification label. In more sophisticated systems, these outputs are fused with context, speaker behavior, and the history of a conversation (Karim et al., 2021).

By swiftly identifying content risks and prioritizing urgent situations, AI can help alleviate the burden on moderators, thereby streamlining the process. But AI doesn't yet have the same understanding of human communication as a human. May not pick up on sarcasm or miss accents and overreact to words. AI should thus be viewed as a support tool for decision-making and not as the final word.

2.8 Explainable Artificial Intelligence

Explainable Artificial Intelligence involves methods to make AI decisions understandable to humans. Explainability in voice-chat moderation entails that the system not only identifies a conversation as harmful but also offers explanations for why. These can be the use of particular words, phrases, acoustic patterns, the behaviour of a speaker or contextual evidence(Kiritchenko et al., 2021).

Moderation is particularly significant for explainability as AI decisions can impact users' access, reputation, and rights. Based on the output of a model, a user can be muted, warned, suspended, or reported. Users and moderators might not even know whether the decision is fair or accurate if system cannot explain its decision. Explainability helps transparency by providing insight into how the model arrived at its conclusion. It provides accountability through human review where humans can challenge or correct the system. It also aids trust by increasing the transparency and understanding of AI's actions (Lundberg & Lee, 2017).

2.9 Human-in-the-Loop Moderation

Human-in-the-loop moderation is a system where the AI acts as an assistant to human decision making and not fully replaces it. Ambiguities, cultural meaning, humor, conflict or political expression are not unusual in sensitive areas like harassment and extremism detection, and human oversight is essential. The AI could identify potential risks, with human moderators checking more complicated or high-risk scenarios before enforcement action is taken (MacAvaney et al., 2019).

With human-in-the-loop, the risk of unfair punishment and the risk of too much automation are reduced. Moderators are able to check the AI explanation, listen to the relevant audio segment, read the transcript, take context into account and take a final decision. They may also help to offer feedback to enhance the system with time. This establishes a dynamic learning cycle during which AI systems evolve to be more precise and more attuned to platform policies.

There is also a greater degree of accountability with a human monitor. The platform allows the moderation decision to be challenged, and it can view the AI's output as well as the human thought behind the final decision. It is especially critical for the detection of extremist content, as false positives can lead to the censorship of legal content and false negatives can let dangerous content proliferate.

2.10 Conceptual Link Between Safety, Explainability and Trust

The primary conceptual connection that can be identified in this chapter is the concept of safety and explainability in relation to trust. To prevent harassment, hate, threats and extremist communication, there is a need for safety mechanisms for use in the voice-chat platforms. AI can help with safety by identifying problematic content swiftly and in large volume. But opaque, biased or unaccountable safety systems can result in new harms. Users may perceive automated systems are watching them, punishing them, or that they don't understand the system.

In this chapter, the conceptual basis is based on the notion of harmful voice communication as complex, contextual, and multimodal. It can't be comprehended merely by words or keywords. It involves speech, sound, context, behavioral, and social analysis. Simultaneously, any AI system employed for this purpose should be explainable, fair, privacy-aware, and humans-in-the-loop. These concepts will be used as the basis for the proposed framework and future discussion of methods, evaluation, ethics and future research (Mehta & Passi, 2022).

3. ARTIFICIAL INTELLIGENCE APPROACHES FOR VOICE-BASED HARM DETECTION

With the high volume of user-generated content in digital communication systems, manual detection of harmful behavior becomes challenging, and thus Artificial Intelligence has become an important tool for detection. A harmful message in a voice-chat can manifest itself as harassment, hate speech, verbal threats, extreme messages, radicalizing language, abusive voice, and repeated targeted attacks. Voice communication is happening in real time, and is emotional, informal, and context-dependent, which means that AI-driven systems need to be more sophisticated than just matching with keywords. They must interpret speech, acoustic characteristics, speaker actions, emotional factors, and conversational environment.

The processing of speech and audio signals, speech recognition, natural language processing, machine learning, deep learning, and explainable AI techniques are all typically combined in voice-based harm detection. Both methods have a different role in the detection process. Some are concerned with speech to text conversion and then using text-based harmful-content classifiers. Other systems detect aggression, stress, yelling or aggressive voice patterns in the raw audio signal. Advanced methods, such as those based on both text and voice, are used to enhance accuracy and context. The purpose of this section is to describe the key AI solutions which are employed for the detection of harassment and extremism in voice-chat platforms (Meske & Bunde, 2023).

3.1 Automatic Speech Recognition-Based Detection

One of the most widely used methods in voice-based harm detection is called Automatic Speech Recognition (ASR). ASR: Transcription of spoken language to written language. After the voice message or live speech is transcribed, Natural Language Processing models can be used to analyze the transcript for any harmful words, bad phrases, threats, abusive language, or extremist language. This is a popular method since there are many models already available for the detection of harmful content in text-based communication.

A typical pipeline for ASR-based detection involves first capturing the voice input from the chat environment. Then the audio is cleaned using noise reduction and segmentation. Then, the ASR model transcribes the speech to text. This transcript is then transferred to a text classification model that classifies the text as safe, toxic, harassing, hateful, threatening or extremist. The system can be set to score a risk and refer high-risk cases to the human moderators for review (Ribeiro et al., 2016).

The key benefit of ASR-based detection is that it lets voice moderation solutions leverage the current text-based AI models. This also helps with moderation decisions as moderators can access the transcript to see which word or phrase the system has flagged. But this type of method has many drawbacks. Speech recognition errors may result in a decreased detection rate, particularly if the user has strong accents, dialects, background noise, uses slang, has overlapping speech, or has a poor microphone quality. The classifier may not detect the harmful phrase, if ASR system has misrecognized it. Likewise, if seemingly innocuous speech is detected as dangerous text, the system can generate a false positive.

Figure 1. Literature critical comparison of explainable hate speech detection

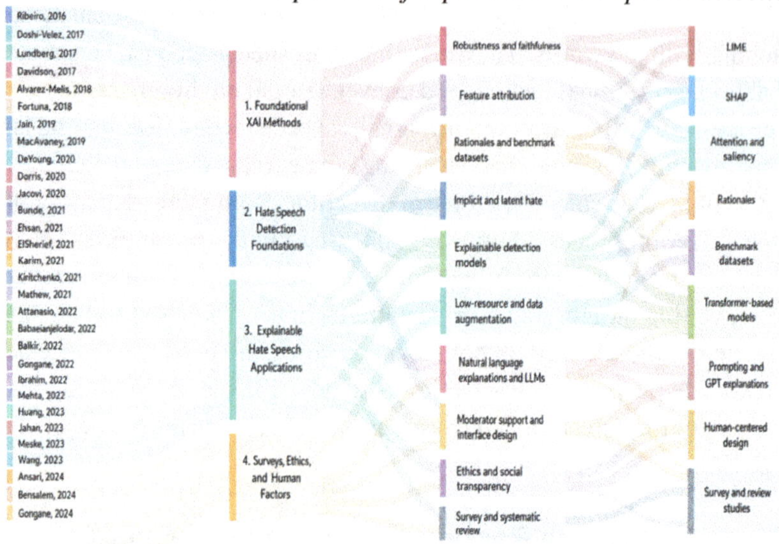

Another disadvantage is that ASR based systems are not sensitive to the tone of the voice. A transcript may only reflect literally what was said, but not necessarily how it was said. When using the Voice Chat feature, tone, shouting, mockery, sarcasm, laughter and emotional intensity can alter the meaning of a sentence. So, ASR-based detection alone is useful but incomplete (Wang et al., 2023).

3.2 Natural Language Processing for Analysis of Harmful Transcript

Natural Language Processing (NLP) is a key technology used for analysing transcripts created from voice chat. NLP models are created to deal with the human language and patterns of which means. With the detection of harmful content, NLP can categorize a transcript as harassment, hate speech, threat, toxicity, extremism, bullying, or safe communication. These models can be based on traditional machine learning, deep learning, transformer-based models, or large language models.

Previously, NLP systems used lists of keywords, rules or bag-of-words features. These techniques were straightforward and easy to understand, but were only effective because harmful communication does not always take obvious form. Modern NLP systems are based on contextual language models which can have a better understanding of sentence structure, meaning and semantic relationships. These 'models' are capable of identifying both harmful terms and threatening intent, identity-based abuse and extremist narratives.

NLP models can be trained for single label or multi label classification for voice-chat moderation. A single-label model can predict whether a transcript is harmful or not. A multi-label model can be able to label more than one class simultaneously, e.g., harassment and hate speech, or extremist language and threat. In real world moderation, the classification of harmful speech can be multi-label, since harmful speech can be part of more than one class.

But there are also some difficulties in transcript analysis with NLP. The context is an important aspect of the meaning of speech. A sentence can be harmful if it's read on its own, but harmless if it is part of a joke. Likewise, there are words that might seem harmless, but can still be used as harassment in a specific context. Sarcasm, coded language, multilingual speech and fast changing slang can also be problematic for NLP systems. Hence, the analysis of transcripts needs to be complemented with context-aware and explainable approaches.

3.3 Direct Audio Classification

Another key AI technique for audio-based harm detection is direct classification. Direct Audio Models directly analyze the audio signal, rather than transcribing speech to text first. These systems can be used to retrieve acoustic parameters like pitch, loudness, rhythm, speaking rate, pauses, intensity, stress patterns, and emotional tone. These features are then used in the model to classify the audio as safe, aggressive, abusive, threatening or emotionally damaging.

Direct audio classification is helpful since certain harmful behaviors are communicated only by the way they are spoken, and not just via words. For instance, the presence of shouting, angry tone, repeated interruption, mocking laughter, or aggressive vocal intensity may be an indication of harassment even though the transcript itself doesn't include any abusive language. Likewise threatening speech can be identified by more than just the words; it can be identified by tone and emotional pressure.

Handcrafted acoustic features like Mel-frequency cepstral coefficients, spectral features, energy, pitch and prosodic patterns are mostly used in the traditional classification of audio. These features are then fed into ML classifiers like Support Vector Machines, Random Forests, or Gradient Boosting models. The more recent systems are based on deep learning models, including Convolutional Neural Networks, Recurrent Neural Networks and transformer-based audio models, which are able to learn useful patterns directly from the spectrograms or the waveform representations.

The biggest advantage of direct audio classification is that it was able to pick up non-verbal signals. However, it does not necessarily have a full grasp of the meaning of words in language. Anger, excitement, joking, or urgency can be signaled by a loud voice. Thus, audio-only models can also mislabel emotionally but innocuous speech as harmful. Therefore, audio classification most preferably works in conjunction with transcript analysis and contextual information.

3.4 Acoustic Emotion Recognition

Acoustic emotion recognition is concerned with the recognition of emotional state from the voice features. When moderating voice-chats, emotion recognition can be used to identify anger, fear, aggression, stress, hostility, frustration or emotional escalation. These emotional signals can be helpful signs of problematic interaction, particularly if the discussion is heating up or is threatening.

Emotion-aware systems take into consideration properties of the voice like pitch variability, speaking rate, loudness, quality of the voice, pause durations and energy. For instance, aggressive speech can include volume, tone, and speaking rate increases, and fewer pauses. Victim's voice may also sound fearful or distressed, indicating harmful interaction. Emotion recognition together with speaker diarization can be used to target the aggressor as well as the user influenced.

But, emotion recognition should be applied judiciously. Emotions are expressed differently by different people, in different cultures, in different languages, between genders, and in different situations. Some users talk loud or fast, and without intent to harm. Others may be calm sounding with dangerous or extremist content. So emotion recognition can't be interpreted as a direct indication of harassment or extremism. It should complement a larger AI moderation system as one of the signals used.

3.5 Speaker Diarization and User Attribution

Speaker Diarization is the task of determining who is who and when during an audio conversation. Within a group voice chat, several users can be talking simultaneously, interrupting one another, or reacting swiftly. It is important for moderation purposes to understand who was the person making the harmful statement, and whether harmful behaviour was repeated over time.

The goal of speaker diarization is to split the audio stream into speaker segments. This enables the system to bind the different text of the transcript, the acoustic features and risk scores to individual users. If one participant was consistently insulting another user, for instance, the system could determine that there was a pattern of harassment. The system might know that there was harmful speech, but it might not know who did it, if no diarization is used.

Attribution of users is particularly relevant for moderating decisions. In order to accurately warn, mute, suspend, or report user, platforms must be able to detect the origin of harmful speech with reasonable certainty. Diarization also aids explainability as moderators can see the conversation chronologically by speaker turns and how the harmful interaction played out.

Although speaker diarization has many beneficial applications, it is challenging in noisy conditions. It may be less accurate when there is overlapping speech, when voices are the same, when microphones are not working well, and when people are changing turns quickly. Thus, diarization results should be accompanied by confidence scores, and the result of cases with low confidence scores should be checked by human moderators.

3.6 Multimodal AI Approaches

Multimodal AI integrates various data modalities for enhanced detection accuracy and contextual understanding. Multimodal systems could involve audio signals, speech transcripts, speaker identification, conversation history, metadata, user reports, behavioral patterns and platform context in voice-chat harm detection. This can be more effective as opposed to only text or audio as many instances of harmful communication will be conveyed through more than one medium.

For instance, the correspondence might be gentle but the tone of the audio might be aggressive and the history of the conversation may reflect multiple targeting of one user. These signals can be combined and provide a better risk assessment by a multimodal system. Likewise, extremist content can be identified by certain phrases, recurring ideologically related content, group behavior and interaction patterns.

There are three methods for introducing multimodal AI: Feature level fusion, Decision level fusion and Hybrid fusion. Feature-level fusion: Feature level fusion is the fusion where the audio and text features are fused before classifications. Decision-level fusion approach consists of having separate models work on the audio and text and then aggregating the model predictions at the end. Hybrid fusion uses both methods. Multimodal systems are typically more accurate although they tend to be more complex and difficult to explain. Thus, explainability techniques are required to determine if the words, tone, context, or behavior patterns were the primary factors affecting the model decision.

3.7 Transformer-Based Models

Transformer-based models are very influential in the fields of language, audio and multimodal AI. Transformer models look into the relationships between words within a sentence or conversation, which makes them better able to understand context in text analysis than older models. Transformer-based NLP models can be leveraged for classification of transcripts in voice moderation, such as identification of harassment, hate speech, threat or extremist content.

Speech signals can also be analyzed and used to learn patterns from acoustic representations using audio transformers. These models can be used to deal with longer sequences and to capture the temporal relationship in speech. They might notice shifts in tone, recurring aggressive behaviours, or escalating emotions throughout a dialogue for instance. Multimodal transformers can integrate the transcript and audio features in a single transformer model and enable more comprehensive analysis of harmful voice communication.

The advantage of transformer models is their high performance and context capturing abilities. But they can be complicated and confusing. Without the use of XAI techniques, their decisions may not be readily comprehensible to human moderators. Transparency in transformer choices in voice-chat moderation systems could be achieved through attention visualization, feature attribution, saliency mapping and rationale generation.

3.8 Moderation With Support From Large Language Models

By analyzing transcripts, summarizing conversations, detecting harmful intent, and providing explanations for moderation decisions, Large Language Models can aid in voice-based harm detection. Once speech has been transcribed to text, a large language model can analyze the dialogue and identify the presence of harassment, hate speech, threats, extremist content, or other radicalizing speech. These models can also produce human-readable explanations which can help moderators.

Large Language Models are helpful because they can capture more context, understand how a conversation unfolds, capture indirect meaning, and complex language patterns, which more classifiers cannot. They can assist in distinguishing jest language from the normal disagreement, targeted abuse, and dangerous language. They can also describe the reasons for a segment being flagged, the speaker turn that it belongs to and the severity of the incident.

4. XAI TECHNIQUES FOR VOICE CHAT MODERATION

Explainable Artificial Intelligence techniques are crucial in the voice chat moderation segment, as they aid human users in understanding the rationale behind an AI system marking a particular voice section as harmful. In harassment and extremism detection, the system must not just give a final judgement, like “harassment,” “hate speech,” “threat” or “extremist content.” It should also detail the evidence on which that decision is based. This is very important as voice communication involves spoken language, intonation, feelings, interaction between the speaker and listener, pauses, and implied meaning. Thus, there is a need for XAI techniques to make the AI-based moderation process more transparent, fair, and accountable.

When it comes to voice chat moderation, explanations can be created from various sources. Some explanations are taken from the transcript, where the model points out the harmful words/phrases. Some explanations are given by the audio signal: the system detects aggressive tone, shouting, stress or emotional intensity. Other explanations are from conversation context e.g. repeated targeting, interruption, group harassment or extremist references across a number of speaker turns. An effective explainable moderation system will incorporate these types of explanation to enable moderators to see not only the content of the explanation, but also the process.

4.1 Feature Importance Techniques

Feature importance techniques can indicate what the most important features were in the AI model's decision. These features might be abusive words, extremist language, pitch, loudness, speaking speed, emotional intensity, the frequency of interruptions, speaker repetition, or conversation history in voice chat moderation. The system shows the most significant features, to help the moderators understand why a voice segment was classified harmful.

For instance, if an AI model identifies harassment-related issues, feature importance could reveal that frequent insults, increased vocal volume, and targeting specific users were significant factors in the prediction. It could indicate that the system detected extremist speech, and that some phrases related to ideology, violence or dehumanization were significant factors in a decision. This kind of explanation is helpful as it establishes a clear connection between the results of the model and evidence in the audio or transcript.

Importance of features techniques are particularly useful for human moderators, as it helps decrease the necessity to look through lengthy chats from the start. The moderator, rather, can focus on the most pertinent aspects of the voice chat. But there are some caveats when using feature importance: it might not always reflect underlying context or indirect meaning. Hence, this should be used along with other explanation techniques.

4.2 LIME-Based Explanations

LIME is a technique in the field of XAI which can be used to explain individual predictions of the model. LIME works by perturbing small components of the input and then seeing how the output of the model changes. The LIME can be used in voice chat moderation to provide clarity and understanding of why a particular utterance, transcript segment, or audio clip was identified as harassment or extremism.

In transcript-based moderation, LIME might point to words or phrases that had an impact on the classification. For instance, if a model identifies a sentence as threatening, LIME can highlight the words that most influenced the threat classification. For audio-based moderation, it is possible to use LIME-like methods to find out which portions of the audio were used to classify it as harmful.

The biggest benefit of LIME is that it offers local explanations for each case. This is helpful in moderation as each flagged incident can be reviewed individually. But at times LIME explanations are unstable, so that small changes in the input can lead to different explanations. Therefore, the use of LIME as the sole explanation method in sensitive voice moderation systems is not recommended.

4.3 SHAP-Based Explanations

Another significant XAI technique is called SHAP - Shapley Additive Explanations. It assigns importance value to each of the input features to explain the model prediction. SHAP is an approach rooted on the concept of determining the magnitudes of contributions made by each feature to the overall decision. SHAP can be applied for explanation of model outputs for text and voice chat moderation.

For instance, in the case of harassment detection, SHAP values might indicate that the use of abusive language, aggressive tone, and repeated targeting of the same speaker contributed to the model assigning a higher score to the harmful content. For extremism detection, SHAP could indicate that certain ideologies, violent or coded language made a significant impact in determining the classification. Moderators can use these explanations to gain understanding of the relative importance of each factor.

SHAP is helpful, as it offers mathematically sound and more uniform explanations than do many simpler methods. It can also assist with fairness auditing to determine if the model is using inappropriate features, like accent or speaker identification or background noise. In real-time voice chat systems, however, SHAP can be quite cost intensive. So, there may be a need for optimised versions of SHAP for live moderation on platforms.

4.4 Attention Visualization

Transformers are often used to perform attention visualization. When using a transformer model, attention mechanisms are used to determine which portions of the input are most relevant to make a prediction. For transcript-based moderation, the attention visualization can reveal the words, phrases or speaker turns that were most attended to by the model.

Attention visualization could indicate identity-based abusive terms or threatening phrases, for instance, in a voice transcript classified as hate speech by a transformer. Extremist communication can occasionally be identified by paying attention to ideological slogans, violent references, and recruitment-related language. This can help moderators to understand what model thought was important in the conversation.

For audio based transformer models, the important time segments in the audio signal will also be identified using attention visualization. This can mean that the system can indicate which seconds of the voice clip were most telling for the decision. But don't always think of attention as the full explanation. The high attention does not necessarily imply causal importance. Hence, attention visualization is suggested to be supplemented with other methods for XAI.

In this section, we describe saliency maps for audio signals.Saliency maps highlight the most important areas of an input that impacted the model's decision. For voice chat moderation, you can use the saliency maps for spectrograms, waveforms or audio frames. They contribute to the demonstration of the most relevant aspects of the audio signal for the detection of harmful speech.

For instance, in the case of aggressive speech, the saliency map can point to areas of the speech where there is high energy, sudden loudness changes, sharp pitch changes, or high intensity of vocal stress. When threatening tone is detected, the saliency map can reveal the specific audio portion on which the model spotted suspicious sound characteristics. This is helpful because the moderator is able to hear the highlighted section as opposed to reading through the whole conversation.

Of special interest, however, are audio saliency maps: they serve as an explanation of the non-textual component of voice communication. Shouting, sarcasm, mockery and emotional pressure might not be apparent on a transcript. To address this gap, saliency maps can be used to visualize the model's decision, demonstrating the influence of the speech sound on the model's choice. These can be hard for non-technical users to understand, however, and should be displayed in a straightforward visual dashboard or highlighted on a time basis.

4.5 Transcript-Level Rationales

Transcript-level rationales explain by pointing to the words, phrases, or sentences in the speech transcript. One of the most useful explanation methods for moderators is this one, because written transcriptions are more convenient to look at than raw audio signals. Transcript rationales may indicate exactly what language is thought to be harmful.

Transcript-level rationales can include any mention of insults, repeated targeting, sexualized comments, or discriminatory language or threats, for harassment detection. They can identify phrases for extremism detection, such as statements about violence, dehumanizing expressions, extremist slogans, phrases about recruitment, or coded language. These rationales will guide moderators in speedily recognizing problematic content and matching it with the platform policy.

Transcript-level explanations are also helpful for moderation notices that are visible to users. So, for instance, a platform can tell a user that their speech was detected and marked by the platform because it contained a certain type of abusive language or threatening speech that targeted them. But caution should be exercised not to accidentally reveal a sensitive moderation rule that would make it easier for a harmful user to evade moderation.

4.6 Current Industry Situation and Practical Motivation

Voice chat is a key element of online communication, particularly with the rise of platforms like online gaming, social-audio apps, virtual classrooms, livestreaming, workplace collaboration tools, and metaverse environments. In tandem with the growth of real-time voice interaction, though, platforms are being exposed to verbal harassment, hate speech, threats, bullying, radicalising communication, and extremist content. Harmful voice interaction can be communicated through a mix of words, volume, tone, pitch, silence, emotionalization, interrupting the speaker, and conversational context; however, it is not communicated through text.

The industrial moderation situation today is primarily based on user reporting, manual review, keyword matching, automatic speech recognition, and text-based content classification. These methods offer protection at the start of the conversation, but they don't work well when it comes to large-scale voice moderation for real-time conversations. Manual moderation is costly, time-consuming, complex and stressful for moderators. Sarcasm, coded expressions, implicit threats, mocking tone, or the context-dependent harm cannot be reliably recognised by the keyword-based system. Automatic speech recognition (ASR) based systems can also miss some of the acoustic information contained in speech as well as incorrect transcriptions when the speech includes accents, dialects, background noise, multiple speakers, slang, and multilingual expressions.

One of the other significant limitations of industry is that moderation is not transparent with automation. The majority of the existing systems offer a harmful-content label or risk score, but do not specify which words or acoustic features, speaker habits, etc., led to the result. These black-box determinations can result in misidentification, non-uniform application, user grievance, damage to reputation and regulatory issues. Platforms need to be moderated in an accurate, explainable, privacy-aware, auditable and human-reviewed way.

The proposed solution meets these industrial needs by leveraging transcript analysis, acoustic analysis, speaker diarization, conversational context, explainability techniques and human-in-the-loop review. To complement human moderators, rather than replace them, by delivering prioritised evidence, easily understood explanations, confidence scores, and context for consistent and accountable decision-making.

Table 1. Relationship between industry challenges and framework responses

Industry challenge	Existing limitation	Proposed framework response
Large volumes of real-time voice data	Manual moderation cannot scale	Automated risk detection with human escalation
Harm expressed through tone and emotion	Text-only models overlook acoustic evidence	Combined transcript and acoustic analysis
Multiple speakers	Harmful speech may be assigned incorrectly	Speaker diarization and speaker-level attribution
Sarcasm, coded language, and indirect harm	Keyword filters lack contextual understanding	Context-aware and multimodal modelling
Black-box classifications	Moderators cannot understand predictions	LIME, SHAP, attention, saliency, and rationales
False positives and false negatives	Automatic enforcement can be unfair	Confidence scores and human-in-the-loop review
Accent and dialect differences	ASR and classifiers may be biased	Fairness testing and culturally diverse datasets
Sensitive voice information	Privacy and surveillance concerns	Data minimisation and privacy-preserving processing
User disagreement with moderation	Limited accountability	Explanations, audit records, and appeal mechanisms
Changing language and platform behaviour	Static models become outdated	Continuous monitoring and validated feedback

5. CONCLUSION

While the potential of Explainable AI for harassment and extremism detection in voice chat is growing in significance, it also presents a number of challenges. Voice communication is complicated, and includes tone, accent, emotion, background noise, slang, and cultural expressions. These can be problematic when it comes to accurately identifying harmful speech. The other limitation is the scarcity of large, diverse and well-annotated voice datasets, particularly for multilingual and low-resource languages. Also, privacy is a huge issue as voice data can include sensitive personal information. Further, there is the risk of bias in AI systems, as they can be trained with limited or imbalanced data. While explanations make things more transparent, some of them can be too technical for the moderators, users, and/or policymakers.

Future studies include creating more precise, fair, and transparent AI models to detect harm through voice. The need for multi-lingual and culturally diverse data sets that contain a variety of accents, languages and social situations. It is also important to investigate real-time XAI systems that can deliver timely and comprehensible explanations during real-time voice chat moderation. Research efforts are still required to address methods of preserving users' voice data, such as federated learning and anonymization. Future research could also explore human–AI interactions with explanations and how explanations can facilitate fair decision-making. Interdisciplinary research with AI researchers, linguists, psychologists, legal philosophers and platform developers will be crucial to enhancing the ethical use of XAI.

Explainable AI is crucial in enhancing the identification of harassment and extremism in voice chat experiences. Traditional AI systems can detect harmful content, but XAI can provide an explanation as to why a specific voice interaction has been flagged. This provides a more transparent, accountable and trustworthy moderation. But issues like privacy threats, data bias, linguistic variability, and the interpretation of explanations need to be taken care of. Through additional research and responsible design, XAI can help to create safer online spaces for communication and ensure that the rights of users are protected and fairness is promoted.

ACKNOWLEDGEMENT

Funding: This work was supported by the Deanship of Scientific Research, the Vice Presidency for Graduate Studies and Scientific Research, King Faisal University, Saudi Arabia, under Grant No KFU263162

REFERENCES

Alvarez-Melis, D., & Jaakkola, T. S. (2018). On the robustness of interpretability methods. In *Proceedings of the 2018 ICML Workshop on Human Interpretability in Machine Learning*.

Ansari, G., Kaur, P., & Saxena, C. (2024). Data augmentation for improving explainability of hate speech detection. *Arabian Journal for Science and Engineering*, *49*(3), 3609–3621. DOI: 10.1007/s13369-023-08100-4

Attanasio, G., Nozza, D., Pastor, E., & Hovy, D. (2022). Benchmarking post-hoc interpretability approaches for transformer-based misogyny detection. In *Proceedings of NLP Power! The First Workshop on Efficient Benchmarking in NLP* (pp. 100–112). Association for Computational Linguistics. DOI: 10.18653/v1/2022.nlppower-1.11

Babaeianjelodar, M., Poorna Prudhvi, G., Lorenz, S., Chen, K., Mondal, S., Dey, S., & Kumar, N. (2022). Interpretable and high-performance hate and offensive speech detection. In *HCI International 2022—Late breaking papers: Interacting with extended reality and artificial intelligence* (pp. 233–244). Springer. DOI: 10.1007/978-3-031-21707-4_18

Balkir, E., Nejadgholi, I., Fraser, K. C., & Kiritchenko, S. (2022). Necessity and sufficiency for explaining text classifiers: A case study in hate speech detection. In *Proceedings of the 2022 Conference of the North American Chapter of the Association for Computational Linguistics: Human Language Technologies* (pp. 2672–2686). Association for Computational Linguistics. DOI: 10.18653/v1/2022.naacl-main.192

Bensalem, I., Rosso, P., & Zitouni, H. (2024). Toxic language detection: A systematic review of Arabic datasets. *Expert Systems: International Journal of Knowledge Engineering and Neural Networks*, *41*(8), e13551. DOI: 10.1111/exsy.13551

Bunde, E. (2021). AI-assisted and explainable hate speech detection for social media moderators: A design science approach. In *Proceedings of the 54th Hawaii International Conference on System Sciences*. DOI: 10.24251/HICSS.2021.154

Davidson, T., Warmsley, D., Macy, M., & Weber, I. (2017). Automated hate speech detection and the problem of offensive language. *Proceedings of the International AAAI Conference on Web and Social Media, 11*(1), 512–515. DOI: 10.1609/icwsm.v11i1.14955

DeYoung, J., Jain, S., Rajani, N. F., Lehman, E., Xiong, C., Socher, R., & Wallace, B. C. (2020). ERASER: A benchmark to evaluate rationalized NLP models. In *Proceedings of the 58th Annual Meeting of the Association for Computational Linguistics* (pp. 4443–4458). Association for Computational Linguistics. DOI: 10.18653/v1/2020.acl-main.408

Dorris, W., Hu, R., Vishwamitra, N., Luo, F., & Costello, M. (2020). Towards automatic detection and explanation of hate speech and offensive language. In *Proceedings of the Sixth International Workshop on Security and Privacy Analytics* (pp. 23–29). Association for Computing Machinery. DOI: 10.1145/3375708.3380312

Doshi-Velez, F., & Kim, B. (2017). *Towards a rigorous science of interpretable machine learning* [Preprint]. arXiv.

Ehsan, U., Liao, Q. V., Muller, M., Riedl, M. O., & Weisz, J. D. (2021). Expanding explainability: Towards social transparency in AI systems. In *Proceedings of the 2021 CHI Conference on Human Factors in Computing Systems* (pp. 1–19). Association for Computing Machinery. DOI: 10.1145/3411764.3445188

ElSherief, M., Ziems, C., Muchlinski, D., Anupindi, V., Seybolt, J., De Choudhury, M., & Yang, D. (2021). Latent hatred: A benchmark for understanding implicit hate speech. In *Proceedings of the 2021 Conference on Empirical Methods in Natural Language Processing* (pp. 345–363). Association for Computational Linguistics. DOI: 10.18653/v1/2021.emnlp-main.29

Fortuna, P., & Nunes, S. (2018). A survey on automatic detection of hate speech in text. *ACM Computing Surveys, 51*(4), 1–30. DOI: 10.1145/3232676

Gongane, V. U., Munot, M. V., & Anuse, A. D. (2022). Detection and moderation of detrimental content on social media platforms: Current status and future directions. *Social Network Analysis and Mining, 12*(1), 129. DOI: 10.1007/s13278-022-00951-3 PMID: 36090695

Gongane, V. U., Munot, M. V., & Anuse, A. D. (2024). A survey of explainable AI techniques for detection of fake news and hate speech on social media platforms. *Journal of Computational Social Science, 7*(1), 587–623. DOI: 10.1007/s42001-024-00248-9

Huang, F., Kwak, H., & An, J. (2023). Chain of explanation: New prompting method to generate quality natural language explanation for implicit hate speech. In *Companion proceedings of the ACM Web Conference 2023* (pp. 90–93). Association for Computing Machinery. DOI: 10.1145/3543873.3587320

Ibrahim, M. A., Arifin, S., Yudistira, I. G. A. A., Nariswari, R., Abdillah, A. A., Murnaka, N. P., & Prasetyo, P. W. (2022). An explainable AI model for hate speech detection on Indonesian Twitter. *CommIT (Communication and Information Technology). Journal, 16*(2), 175–182.

Jacovi, A., & Goldberg, Y. (2020). Towards faithfully interpretable NLP systems: How should we define and evaluate faithfulness? In *Proceedings of the 58th Annual Meeting of the Association for Computational Linguistics* (pp. 4198–4205). Association for Computational Linguistics. DOI: 10.18653/v1/2020.acl-main.386

Jahan, M. S., & Oussalah, M. (2023). A systematic review of hate speech automatic detection using natural language processing. *Neurocomputing, 546*, 126232. DOI: 10.1016/j.neucom.2023.126232

Jain, S., & Wallace, B. C. (2019). Attention is not explanation. In *Proceedings of the 2019 Conference of the North American Chapter of the Association for Computational Linguistics: Human Language Technologies* (pp. 3543–3556). Association for Computational Linguistics.

Karim, M. R., Dey, S. K., Islam, T., Sarker, S., Menon, M. H., Hossain, K., Chakravarthi, B. R., Hossain, M. A., & Decker, S. (2021). DeepHateExplainer: Explainable hate speech detection in under-resourced Bengali language. In *2021 IEEE 8th International Conference on Data Science and Advanced Analytics* (pp. 1–10). IEEE.

Kiritchenko, S., Nejadgholi, I., & Fraser, K. C. (2021). Confronting abusive language online: A survey from the ethical and human rights perspective. *Journal of Artificial Intelligence Research, 71*, 431–478. DOI: 10.1613/jair.1.12590

Lundberg, S. M., & Lee, S.-I. (2017). A unified approach to interpreting model predictions. *Advances in Neural Information Processing Systems, 30*, 4765–4774.

MacAvaney, S., Yao, H.-R., Yang, E., Russell, K., Goharian, N., & Frieder, O. (2019). Hate speech detection: Challenges and solutions. *PLoS One, 14*(8), e0221152. DOI: 10.1371/journal.pone.0221152 PMID: 31430308

Mehta, H., & Passi, K. (2022). Social media hate speech detection using explainable artificial intelligence (XAI). *Algorithms, 15*(8), 291. DOI: 10.3390/a15080291

Meske, C., & Bunde, E. (2023). Design principles for user interfaces in AI-based decision support systems: The case of explainable hate speech detection. *Information Systems Frontiers*, *25*(2), 743–773.

Ribeiro, M. T., Singh, S., & Guestrin, C. (2016). “Why should I trust you?”: Explaining the predictions of any classifier. In *Proceedings of the 22nd ACM SIGKDD International Conference on Knowledge Discovery and Data Mining* (pp. 1135–1144). Association for Computing Machinery.

Wang, H., Hee, M. S., Awal, M. R., Choo, K. T. W., & Lee, R. K.-W. (2023). Evaluating GPT-3 generated explanations for hateful content moderation. In *Proceedings of the Thirty-Second International Joint Conference on Artificial Intelligence* (pp. 6255–6263). International Joint Conferences on Artificial Intelligence Organization. DOI: 10.24963/ijcai.2023/694

Chapter 4

Gaming, Digital Citizenship, and Radicalization Prevention:

Examining Esports Education in the Philippine Revised K-10 Curriculum

Ervin Tampus Echague
http://orcid.org/0009-0002-7507-1383
Department of Education-Central Office, Philippine Normal University, Philippines

Jerome Caro Hilario
http://orcid.org/0000-0001-7507-9380
Department of Education-Central Office, University of the Philippines-Diliman, Philippines

Rosalie Ignacio Dela Cruz
http://orcid.org/0009-0007-7892-3998
University of Makati, Philippines

ABSTRACT

The integration of esports into the Revised K to 10 Physical Education and Health Curriculum of the Department of Education in the Philippines reflects a significant shift in addressing digital culture and 21st-century competencies in basic education. This chapter examines the inclusion of esports in Grade 10 Physical Activity Participation, focusing on competitive gaming, teamwork, communication, ethical standards, and esports event management processes. Anchored in digital culture,

DOI: 10.4018/979-8-2600-1664-0.ch004

experiential learning, and digital citizenship perspectives, the chapter explores how esports can develop collaboration, leadership, responsible online participation, and event management skills among learners. It also discusses opportunities and challenges in implementing esports education, including issues related to toxicity, inclusion, and ethical engagement. The chapter argues that structured esports education can foster meaningful and responsible learning experiences in contemporary Philippine basic education.

INTRODUCTION

The twenty-first century has ushered in profound transformations in how young people engage with leisure, learning, socialization, and identity construction. Among the most consequential of these transformations is the global rise of electronic sports, commonly known as esports as a dominant cultural, social, and economic phenomenon. Esports, referring to organized, competitive video gaming in individual or team-based formats, has grown from informal peer competition into a multi-billion-dollar global industry, complete with professional leagues, collegiate scholarships, live streaming platforms, and millions of spectators worldwide (Newzoo, 2024; Statista, 2024). The Philippine context is no exception to this trend. Filipino youth constitute one of the most digitally active populations in Southeast Asia, with high engagement rates across mobile gaming, social media, and online streaming platforms (Department of Information and Communications Technology, 2023). For millions of Filipino students, gaming is not merely a pastime but a space for social belonging, creative expression, and aspirational identity.

Recognizing these realities, the Department of Education (DepEd) of the Philippines incorporated esports within the Revised K to 10 Physical Education and Health Curriculum, specifically positioning it within Grade 10 Physical Activity Participation. This curricular inclusion marks a milestone: it is among the first formal acknowledgments at the basic education level of the Philippines that esports constitutes a legitimate educational domain with identifiable competencies, ethical dimensions, and instructional value. The revised curriculum identifies esports concepts and principles, as well as esports event management processes, as learning content areas a decision that demands both scholarly interrogation and practical guidance for educators.

Yet the inclusion of esports in formal schooling is not without complexity. Questions arise about its fit within Physical Education, the readiness of teachers, the digital infrastructure of schools, issues of equity and access, and the ethical challenges intrinsic to gaming culture particularly concerning toxicity, exclusion, addiction, and gendered representations. This chapter addresses these questions comprehensively by examining the theoretical, curricular, methodological, pedagogical, and ethical dimensions of esports education in Philippine basic education.

The chapter proceeds as follows: it contextualizes esports within global and local educational trends; presents the theoretical and conceptual frameworks guiding analysis; details the methodology used to analyze the curriculum and gather supporting evidence; examines the educational dimensions of esports participation; details event management as a pedagogical approach; critically analyzes ethical and digital culture concerns; identifies implementation challenges; and recommends directions for curriculum, policy, practice, and future research. Ultimately, the chapter argues that esports education when thoughtfully designed, ethically grounded, and equitably implemented can serve as a powerful and culturally resonant vehicle for developing twenty-first-century competencies in Filipino learners.

BACKGROUND OF THE STUDY

Evolution of Esports and Competitive Gaming

Esports has a relatively brief but rapidly evolving history. What began in the 1970s and 1980s as informal arcade competitions evolved through the 1990s into organized LAN-based tournaments, particularly in games such as Quake and StarCraft. The 2000s witnessed the institutionalization of competitive gaming, with South Korea pioneering the establishment of professional gaming leagues, broadcast infrastructure, and even a dedicated esports television channel. By the 2010s, platforms such as Twitch and YouTube Gaming enabled live streaming at scale, transforming spectatorship and creating new modalities of parasocial engagement between players and audiences (Taylor, 2018).

The economic expansion of esports has been staggering. According to Newzoo (2024), global esports revenues are projected to exceed five billion USD by 2025, with Asia-Pacific representing the dominant market. Statista (2024) estimates a global esports audience exceeding 640 million by 2025, comprising both occasional and enthusiastic viewers. In Southeast Asia, mobile gaming platforms particularly games such as Mobile Legends: Bang Bang (MLBB), League of Legends: Wild Rift, and Valorant have emerged as dominant competitive formats, reflecting the region's mobile-first digital infrastructure.

Within the Philippines specifically, esports has achieved mainstream visibility through collegiate leagues such as the University Athletics Association of the Philippines (UAAP) Esports Championship and the Mobile Legends Professional League Philippines (MPL PH). These leagues function as pathways for skilled gamers while simultaneously popularizing esports culture among Filipino youth.

MLBB, in particular, has attained quasi-national sport status, with Filipino teams competing and winning at international levels, generating significant national pride and youth aspiration.

Global Educational Trends in Esports Integration

Globally, educational institutions have increasingly recognized esports as a domain with pedagogical potential. In the United States, the North America Scholastic Esports Federation (NASEF) has facilitated the establishment of esports clubs and varsity programs across thousands of high schools, connecting gaming with STEM education, career readiness, and social-emotional learning (North America Scholastic Esports Federation, 2023). The United Kingdom's British Esports association has partnered with secondary schools to offer structured esports programs, emphasizing communication, critical thinking, and digital citizenship (British Esports, 2022). Collegiate esports has expanded exponentially in the United States, with over 175 institutions offering varsity esports and scholarship programs as of 2024 (National Alliance for Collegiate Esports, 2024).

At the K-12 level, esports has been integrated with varying degrees of formality from extracurricular clubs to academic electives with documented benefits including improved student engagement, enhanced teamwork skills, and stronger school belonging, particularly among learners who may not participate in traditional athletics (Freeman & Wohn, 2020; Bányai et al., 2019). The recognition of esports within formal curricula, however, remains limited in most countries, making the Philippine DepEd's inclusion of esports in the K-10 curriculum a notable and progressive policy development.

Overview of the Revised K to 10 PE and Health Curriculum

The Revised K to 10 Physical Education and Health Curriculum of the Department of Education Philippines represents a comprehensive update that responds to emerging health challenges, contemporary physical activity trends, and digital realities of Filipino learners. The curriculum maintains its orientation toward holistic health encompassing physical, mental, social, and emotional dimensions while expanding its scope to include contemporary forms of physical activity participation, including esports.

At the Grade 10 level, the curriculum identifies Physical Activity Participation as a learning strand, within which esports is positioned as a recognized activity area. The specific learning content includes: (1) esports concepts and principles covering the nature of esports, competitive gaming formats, roles and positions, and the culture of organized play; and (2) esports event management processes covering planning, organizing, directing, controlling, budgeting, and evaluating esports events at the school level. This dual focus reflects an integration of content knowledge with practical, project-based competencies.

Table 1. Global educational integration of esports: Selected countries and initiatives

Country	Institution/Body	Curriculum Level	Esports/Gaming Integration	Key Competencies
United States	NASEF / High School Esports League	Secondary (Grades 9-12)	Structured esports clubs, varsity leagues, STEM pathways	Teamwork, leadership, STEM, career readiness
South Korea	Ministry of Education	Secondary & Tertiary	Esports-related vocational tracks, game design	Digital literacy, coding, professional gaming
United Kingdom	British Esports	Secondary (KS3-KS5)	Esports as extracurricular and in-class activity	Communication, critical thinking, digital citizenship
Australia	State universities & high schools	Tertiary & Senior Secondary	Esports courses, gaming analytics	Strategy, data literacy, teamwork
Philippines	DepEd (Revised K-10 PE & Health)	Grade 10 (Basic Education)	Esports event management, ethical play, digital culture	Collaboration, leadership, ethical gaming, wellness
Germany	German Esports Federation (ESBD)	Secondary & youth programs	Esports tournaments, media literacy programs	Media literacy, ethics, sportspersonship
Singapore	Ministry of Education / IHL	Secondary & Tertiary	Digital arts, game development, esports management	Innovation, entrepreneurship, digital skills

Table 2. Grade 10 deped esports competencies, activities, and assessment modes

Learning Standard	Core Competency	Sample Activity	Assessment Mode
Demonstrates understanding of esports as competitive gaming	Knowledge of esports genres, rules, and team roles	Esports concept mapping; online research activity	Written output, oral discussion
Organizes and participates in esports events	Event management and organizational skills	School esports tournament planning and execution	Portfolio, event documentation
Applies ethical standards in gaming participation	Digital citizenship and responsible online behavior	Debate on fair play; role-play scenarios	Rubric-based performance task
Exhibits teamwork and communication skills during esports activities	Collaboration, leadership, and communication	Team-based game challenge with debrief reflection	Peer and self-evaluation

continued on following page

Table 2. Continued

Learning Standard	Core Competency	Sample Activity	Assessment Mode
Evaluates esports events using established criteria	Analytical and evaluative competencies	Post-event critique; structured reflection log	Journal, structured evaluation form
Identifies and addresses toxicity and exclusion in gaming spaces	Ethical reasoning and digital resilience	Case study analysis; digital poster creation on inclusion	Project-based output, peer critique

The curriculum further identifies suggested esports activities and platforms appropriate for school-based implementation, with an emphasis on free-to-play or mobile-accessible titles such as MLBB, Clash Royale, and chess-variant digital games accommodating the diverse technological realities of Philippine schools. The inclusion of esports activities is accompanied by health and wellness integration, ensuring that competitive gaming participation is balanced with physical activity, screen-time management, and social-emotional health.

RATIONALE OF THE CHAPTER

The inclusion of esports in the Revised Philippine PE and Health Curriculum merits serious scholarly attention. As a relatively new curricular addition, esports education lacks a robust body of Philippine-specific literature addressing its pedagogical foundations, ethical dimensions, and implementation realities. This chapter responds to that gap by providing educators, curriculum developers, policymakers, and researchers with a theoretically grounded, empirically informed, and practically oriented analysis of esports education in basic education.

The rationale for this chapter is anchored in several intersecting imperatives. First, there is an imperative of cultural relevance: Filipino learners are already deeply embedded in gaming cultures, and a curriculum that acknowledges this reality is more likely to engage, motivate, and connect with students' lived experiences (Gee, 2007; Prensky, 2010). Second, there is an imperative of competency development: esports participation, particularly in team-based formats and event management roles, cultivates a range of twenty-first-century skills including collaboration, communication, strategic thinking, leadership, and digital literacy that are explicitly valued in contemporary educational frameworks (UNESCO, 2023).

Third, there is an imperative of ethical preparation: the digital environments in which esports takes place are replete with ethical challenges including toxicity, cyberbullying, cheating, exclusion, and data privacy risks that schools are uniquely positioned to address through structured educational interventions (Ribble, 2015; Livingstone et al., 2021). Fourth, there is an imperative of equity: if esports education is implemented without attention to issues of access, representation, and inclusion, it risks replicating or exacerbating existing social inequalities in education (Anykey, 2021). This chapter foregrounds these imperatives as it develops its analysis.

THEORETICAL FRAMEWORK

This chapter is anchored in four complementary theoretical perspectives that collectively illuminate the educational dimensions of esports participation, event management, and ethical engagement.

Social Learning Theory

Albert Bandura's (1977) Social Learning Theory posits that individuals acquire behaviors, attitudes, and competencies primarily through observation, modeling, and reinforcement within social contexts. In esports, learners develop communication patterns, strategic behaviors, and ethical orientations by observing teammates, opponents, professional players, and online gaming communities. The concept of vicarious learning is particularly salient: learners observe the consequences of both prosocial (cooperative, respectful) and antisocial (toxic, exclusionary) behaviors in gaming spaces and adjust their own conduct accordingly.

Within the classroom esports context, Social Learning Theory supports the deliberate modeling of ethical behavior by teachers and designated student leaders, as well as the creation of structured opportunities for peer observation and reflection. Bandura's concept of self-efficacy the belief in one's capacity to perform specific tasks also has direct relevance to esports education, as students with high gaming-related self-efficacy are more likely to engage productively and persist through competitive challenges (Bandura, 1997; Freeman & Wohn, 2020).

Experiential Learning Theory

David Kolb's (2015) Experiential Learning Theory describes learning as a cyclical process involving concrete experience, reflective observation, abstract conceptualization, and active experimentation. This four-stage cycle is directly applicable to esports event management education: learners gain concrete experience by participating in or organizing tournaments; engage in reflective observation through post-event debriefs and learning journals; develop abstract conceptualizations about effective event management, teamwork, and ethical conduct; and apply these conceptualizations in subsequent esports activities.

Esports education, positioned as a form of project-based and experiential learning, aligns naturally with Kolb's framework. The complexity and authenticity of esports event management involving real planning, real decisions, real stakeholders, and real consequences creates what Kolb terms a 'learning pull' that motivates deep engagement and meaningful knowledge construction (Kolb, 2015; Squire, 2011).

Digital Citizenship Theory

Mike Ribble's (2015) framework of Digital Citizenship identifies nine elements of responsible participation in digital environments: digital access, digital commerce, digital communication, digital literacy, digital etiquette, digital law, digital rights and responsibilities, digital health and wellness, and digital security. These elements provide a comprehensive architecture for understanding and teaching responsible esports participation.

In the esports education context, digital citizenship theory frames the ethical dimensions of gameplay respectful communication, protection of personal data, understanding of platform governance, and maintenance of digital wellness as learnable competencies rather than innate dispositions. UNESCO's (2023) Global Framework for Digital Literacy Skills complements Ribble's framework by situating digital citizenship within broader information, media, and digital literacy competencies essential for participation in twenty-first-century society.

Socio-Ecological Theory

Urie Bronfenbrenner's (1979) Socio-Ecological Theory subsequently elaborated in ecological systems theory provides a framework for understanding how learners' gaming experiences are shaped by nested layers of influence: the microsystem (peers, family, immediate gaming community), mesosystem (school-home-community interactions), exosystem (school policy, local government, industry), and macrosystem (national culture, economic conditions, digital infrastructure). This framework is particularly useful for analyzing the complex interplay of factors that enable or constrain esports education in Philippine schools.

Applied to esports, socio-ecological theory draws attention to the ways in which learners' participation is mediated by peer norms, parental attitudes, school policies, platform governance, and broader socio-cultural factors such as gender expectations and economic access. It cautions against reductive explanations of gaming behaviors and emphasizes the importance of multi-level interventions addressing not only individual learners but also peer cultures, school environments, family contexts, and systemic conditions in promoting ethical, inclusive, and educationally productive esports participation.

CONCEPTUAL FRAMEWORK

The conceptual framework of this chapter positions structured esports education as an intersection of five domains: competitive gaming, educational leadership, event management, ethical participation, and digital culture. These domains are not discrete but mutually constitutive: engagement in competitive gaming generates demands for ethical participation; event management develops educational leadership; digital culture shapes and is shaped by all other dimensions.

At the center of this framework is the learner understood not as a passive consumer of gaming content but as an active, reflective, and developing agent embedded in multiple social and digital contexts. Structured esports instruction, aligned with the DepEd's Grade 10 curriculum, is positioned as the pedagogical mechanism through which learners develop competencies across five outcome areas: communication skills, teamwork and collaboration, leadership development, responsible digital behavior, and critical thinking.

The framework also recognizes a set of moderating variables that condition the effectiveness of esports education: school policies governing technology use, teacher preparedness and professional development, parental involvement and community support, access to technology and connectivity, and platform governance and digital safety measures. These variables determine the degree to which esports education can be implemented with fidelity and equity, and are therefore central to the methodology, policy, and practice implications discussed later in this chapter.

METHODOLOGY

This chapter employs a qualitative, document-centered research design anchored primarily in documentary analysis of the Revised K to 10 Physical Education and Health Curriculum, supplemented by a systematic narrative review of esports education literature and, where applicable, exploratory validation through key informant input. Given that esports is a recent addition to Philippine basic education, the methodology is designed to be exploratory and descriptive: it aims to systematically map the curriculum's esports-related content, assess its alignment with established educational and digital citizenship frameworks, and surface the practical realities of implementation as reported in the broader research literature.

Research Design

The study adopts a qualitative documentary analysis design (Bowen, 2009), which treats curriculum guides, policy issuances, and related institutional texts as primary data sources to be systematically read, coded, and interpreted. Documentary analysis is particularly well-suited to this chapter's purpose because the central object of inquiry the Revised K to 10 PE and Health Curriculum is itself a textual artifact whose content, structure, and underlying assumptions must be made explicit before they can be critically examined or compared against international standards and learning theories.

The documentary analysis is complemented by a systematic narrative literature review (Snyder, 2019) of esports education research published between 2019 and 2025, which provides comparative and theoretical grounding for the curriculum analysis. Together, these two methods triangulate curricular intent (what the document specifies) with empirical and theoretical knowledge (what research suggests about implementation, effectiveness, and risk). This combination follows a pragmatic qualitative orientation (Patton, 2015), wherein methods are selected for their fitness to the research questions rather than allegiance to a single methodological tradition.

The Curriculum Documentary Analysis Matrix

The centerpiece of the chapter's methodology is a structured documentary analysis matrix that systematically cross-references six analytic dimensions for each Grade 10 esports learning standard identified in the DepEd curriculum: (1) the stated learning competency; (2) its corresponding learning objective; (3) the content focus or subject matter it addresses; (4) suggested classroom or school-based activities; (5) the pedagogical approach implied or made explicit by the curriculum and supporting literature; and (6) the broader application or transfer value of the competency beyond the immediate learning context.

This matrix-based approach to curriculum analysis follows established practices in curriculum mapping and alignment research (English, 2010; Squires, 2012), which hold that explicit, side-by-side comparison of competencies, objectives, content, and pedagogy allows researchers and practitioners to identify gaps, redundancies, and opportunities for enrichment within a curriculum document. Table 7 presents the complete documentary analysis matrix developed for this chapter.

Table 7. Curriculum documentary analysis matrix: Esports learning competencies, objectives, content, activities, pedagogy, and application

Learning Competency	Learning Objective	Content Focus	Suggested Activity	Pedagogical Approach	Application/Transfer
Demonstrates understanding of esports as competitive gaming	Define esports, identify genres, rules, and team roles	Esports concepts and principles; gaming genres; competitive formats	Concept mapping; structured online research on esports titles	Direct instruction; inquiry-based learning	Recognizing legitimate competitive gaming structures in school and community settings
Organizes and participates in esports events	Apply event management processes to a school-based esports activity	Planning, organizing, directing, controlling, budgeting, and evaluating events	School esports tournament planning and execution; bracket design	Project-based learning; experiential learning (Kolb, 2015)	Transferable event management and organizational skills for civic and professional contexts
Applies ethical standards in gaming participation	Analyze and practice fair play, sportsmanship, and digital citizenship norms	Fair play; digital citizenship; cyberbullying prevention	Debate on fair play; role-play scenarios on toxic behavior	Social learning theory (Bandura, 1977); case-based discussion	Ethical decision-making applicable to broader online and offline interactions
Exhibits teamwork and communication skills during esports activities	Demonstrate collaborative and communicative competence in team-based play	Team coordination; role assignment; real-time communication	Team-based game challenge with structured debrief reflection	Cooperative learning; reflective practice	Collaboration and communication skills transferable to group projects and workplace teams
Evaluates esports events using established criteria	Critically assess esports event quality using a rubric	Evaluation criteria; after-action review; reflective analysis	Post-event critique; structured reflection journal	Reflective and evaluative pedagogy (Kolb, 2015)	Capacity for continuous improvement and evidence-based evaluation in future undertakings
Identifies and addresses toxicity and exclusion in gaming spaces	Examine causes and effects of toxicity and exclusion; propose interventions	Cyberbullying; gender exclusion; digital resilience	Case study analysis; digital poster creation promoting inclusion	Critical pedagogy; digital citizenship theory (Ribble, 2015)	Advocacy for inclusive, respectful, and safe digital communities beyond the classroom

The matrix in Table 7 was constructed through a three-step coding process. First, all explicit references to esports within the Grade 10 Physical Activity Participation strand of the curriculum guide were extracted verbatim and organized by learning standard. Second, each learning standard was decomposed into its constituent objective, content focus, and suggested activity, drawing on the language of the curriculum itself supplemented by DepEd-recommended instructional materials. Third, each standard was cross-referenced against the chapter's theoretical framework (Social Learning Theory, Experiential Learning Theory, Digital Citizenship Theory, and Socio-Ecological Theory) to identify the most coherent pedagogical approach, and against international frameworks including UNESCO's (2023) Global Framework for Digital Literacy Skills and Ribble's (2015) nine elements of digital citizenship to articulate the application or transfer value of each competency.

This matrix-based documentary analysis serves three purposes within the chapter. It provides curriculum developers and teachers with a practical, ready-reference tool for understanding how esports competencies translate into classroom activities and pedagogical choices. It demonstrates, empirically, that the DepEd curriculum's esports content is conceptually well-aligned with established digital citizenship and experiential learning frameworks. Finally, it surfaces areas such as explicit assessment guidance and structured wellness integration where the curriculum's current language remains general and would benefit from further elaboration in supplementary teacher guides.

Supplementary Methods: Literature Review and Expert Input

To contextualize and substantiate the documentary analysis, the chapter draws on a systematic narrative review of peer-reviewed and institutional literature on esports education, digital citizenship, and youth gaming culture, published primarily within the last five years (2020-2025), supplemented by foundational theoretical texts predating this window where they remain the authoritative source for a given theory (e.g., Bandura, 1977; Bronfenbrenner, 1979; Kolb, 2015). Literature was identified through targeted searches of academic databases and institutional repositories using keyword combinations such as "esports education," "scholastic esports," "digital citizenship curriculum," and "gaming-based learning," and was screened for relevance to basic or secondary education contexts.

Where feasible in subsequent empirical extensions of this chapter, the documentary and literature-based analysis can be triangulated with primary data gathered from key informants PE and Health teachers, curriculum specialists, school administrators, and esports practitioners through structured surveys, semi-structured interviews, and focus group discussions with Grade 10 learners. Table 8 summarizes a proposed multi-phase research design for such an extension, indicating how documentary analysis (Phase 1) can be sequenced alongside literature review (Phase 2), expert validation (Phase 3), learner inquiry (Phase 4), and school-level case study (Phase 5).

Table 8. Proposed research design summary: Phases, approaches, data sources, and analysis methods

Research Phase	Design/Approach	Data Sources	Participants	Analysis Method
Phase 1: Curriculum Documentary Analysis	Qualitative document analysis	DepEd Revised K-10 PE and Health Curriculum Guide; DepEd Orders; policy memoranda	N/A (documentary)	Matrix-based competency mapping; thematic content analysis
Phase 2: Literature Review	Systematic narrative review	Peer-reviewed journals (2020-2025); books; institutional and grey literature	N/A (documentary)	Thematic synthesis; comparative analysis
Phase 3: Expert Validation	Descriptive survey and structured interview	PE teachers, curriculum specialists, esports practitioners, ICT coordinators	Purposive sample (n = 20-30 key informants)	Descriptive statistics; qualitative coding
Phase 4: Learner Inquiry	Exploratory mixed-methods	Focus group discussions; reflective journals; observation notes from esports sessions	Grade 10 learners in pilot schools (n = 60-90)	Grounded coding; cross-case analysis
Phase 5: Policy and Practice Analysis	Case study	School esports program documents; interview transcripts; field notes	School administrators; PE department heads	Cross-case thematic analysis; policy mapping

This phased design reflects a socio-ecological orientation (Bronfenbrenner, 1979) to evidence-building: documentary analysis addresses the macro-level policy text; literature review situates this text within global scholarly knowledge; and expert and learner inquiry address the meso- and micro-level realities of implementation within specific schools and classrooms. Researchers extending this chapter's analysis into a full empirical study would administer the instruments associated with Phases 3 and 4 including teacher readiness questionnaires and learner engagement scales following the procedures and validity safeguards summarized later in this section.

Data Analysis Procedures

Documentary data extracted from the curriculum guide were analyzed using qualitative content analysis (Krippendorff, 2019), involving open coding of curriculum text, categorization of codes into the six matrix dimensions described above, and iterative refinement of categories through comparison with the chapter's theoretical and conceptual frameworks. This process is consistent with Bowen's (2009) guidance on documentary analysis, which emphasizes skimming, reading, and interpretation cycles to move from surface content to underlying thematic structure.

Literature review data were synthesized thematically (Snyder, 2019), with sources grouped according to the chapter's major themes: global esports trends, educational integration, event management pedagogy, ethical and digital citizenship concerns, digital culture, and implementation challenges. Where future empirical extensions incorporate survey or interview data, quantitative responses would be analyzed using descriptive statistics, while qualitative responses would undergo reflexive thematic analysis following Braun and Clarke's (2022) six-phase framework, supported by qualitative data analysis software such as NVivo.

Ethical Considerations

Although the primary analysis in this chapter relies on publicly available curriculum documents and published literature, the chapter adheres to the ethical principles that would govern any future empirical extension involving human participants, consistent with the standards of the American Psychological Association (APA, 2020), the DepEd Child Protection Policy (DepEd Order No. 40, s. 2012), and the Philippine Data Privacy Act of 2012 (Republic Act No. 10173). Table 9 summarizes the ethical principles and corresponding safeguards relevant to any data collection involving teachers, administrators, parents, or Grade 10 learners.

Table 9. Ethical protocols for empirical extensions: Principles, applications, and safeguard mechanisms

Ethical Principle	Application in This Study	Safeguard Mechanism
Informed Consent	Participants and guardians of minors receive written information on study purpose and procedures	Bilingual consent forms (Filipino/English); right to withdraw without consequence
Voluntary Participation	Participation is voluntary, with no academic penalty for non-participation	Clear communication at recruitment; school administrator endorsement
Confidentiality and Anonymity	Participant and institutional identities are protected through pseudonymization	Coded identifiers; secure, access-restricted data storage
Data Privacy Compliance	Data handling complies with the Philippine Data Privacy Act of 2012 (RA 10173)	Data Privacy Officer consultation; documented data management plan
Child Safeguarding	Enhanced protections apply to minor participants aged 14 to 16	Parental/guardian consent; learner assent forms; minimal identifying data collection
Research Integrity	Transparent reporting of findings, including null or unexpected results	Pre-specified research questions; documented audit trail of analytic decisions

Particular care would be exercised in protecting minor participants, as the majority of Grade 10 learners are between fourteen and sixteen years of age. Parental or guardian consent, together with learner assent, would be required prior to any learner participation in surveys, interviews, or focus group discussions. Consent documentation would explain the purpose, procedures, potential risks and benefits, and data protection measures in language accessible to both adult and adolescent respondents, consistent with established practice in research involving minors (Patton, 2015).

Scope, Limitations, and Delimitations

This chapter is delimited to the esports-related content of Grade 10 Physical Education and Health within the Philippine basic education system, as articulated in the Revised K to 10 PE and Health Curriculum. It does not extend to tertiary-level esports programs, informal extracurricular esports clubs operating outside the formal PE curriculum, or esports programming in private schools following independent curricular frameworks. These delimitations reflect the chapter's policy-relevant focus on understanding and supporting DepEd curriculum implementation within the public basic education system.

A primary limitation of the documentary analysis approach is that it describes curricular intent rather than classroom enactment; what is written in a curriculum guide does not guarantee uniform implementation across the highly varied contexts of Philippine public schools. This limitation is partially mitigated by triangulating the documentary analysis with empirical literature on esports education implementation in comparable international contexts, although Philippine-specific empirical data remain limited given the recency of the curriculum's adoption. Future empirical extensions following the multi-phase design proposed in Table 8 would address this limitation directly by gathering primary data from teachers, administrators, and learners.

ESPORTS AS PHYSICAL ACTIVITY PARTICIPATION IN BASIC EDUCATION

The positioning of esports within Physical Education and Health is a source of ongoing debate among educators, health professionals, and sports scientists. Traditional conceptions of physical education are anchored in bodily movement, cardiovascular health, motor skill development, and physical fitness competencies not immediately associated with sedentary video gaming. However, a more expansive and contemporary understanding of physical activity participation one that encompasses cognitive, social, emotional, and cultural dimensions provides a more adequate framework for understanding esports' educational legitimacy.

Esports participation is not cognitively passive. Research consistently documents that competitive gaming involves sustained attention, rapid decision-making, spatial reasoning, pattern recognition, and strategic planning at levels comparable to traditional sports (Bányai et al., 2019; Gee, 2007). Team-based esports further demand sophisticated social coordination: players must communicate in real time, assign and rotate roles, anticipate teammates' actions, and adapt strategies in response to opponents competencies directly analogous to those developed in traditional team sports.

Empirical research on the health dimensions of esports presents a nuanced picture. While prolonged sedentary gaming poses risks including eye strain, musculoskeletal discomfort, disrupted sleep, and potential psychological dependency structured esports programs in educational settings can mitigate these risks through balanced scheduling, integrated wellness activities, and explicit health education components (World Health Organization, 2022; Kowert & Quandt, 2020). The DepEd curriculum's integration of esports within Physical Education is, in this sense, an opportunity to teach learners not only how to play but how to play healthily, responsibly, and critically.

The performative and participatory dimensions of esports including its emphasis on skill development, practice, improvement, competition, and reflection align substantively with physical education's core pedagogical orientations. As Squire (2011) argues, video games constitute rich environments for learning that combine challenge, feedback, and agency in ways that support skill acquisition and identity development. In the esports classroom, learners are not merely playing games; they are practicing the disciplines of preparation, execution, evaluation, and revision a cycle that mirrors the learning processes central to physical education.

EVENT MANAGEMENT PROCESSES IN ESPORTS EDUCATION

Among the most distinctive and pedagogically rich aspects of esports education in the DepEd curriculum is its emphasis on event management processes. By engaging learners in the planning, organization, direction, control, budgeting, and evaluation of esports events, the curriculum transforms competitive gaming from a recreational activity into a vehicle for experiential and project-based learning. This section examines each phase of the esports event management process and its associated educational competencies.

Table 3. Esports event management phases, activities, learner roles, and transferable skills

Phase	Key Activities	Learner Roles	Transferable Skills
Pre-Event Planning	Game selection, bracket design, schedule creation, rule-setting, communication plan	Event director, communications officer, logistics coordinator	Project planning, critical thinking, time management
Organization & Team Formation	Team registration, role assignment, resource inventory, technology check	Team captain, technical officer, registration officer	Leadership, organizational skills, attention to detail
Event Direction & Operations	Tournament facilitation, referee duties, live commentary, scoring	Master of ceremonies, referee/game monitor, score-keeper	Communication, decision-making, real-time problem-solving
Logistics & Resource Control	Venue/platform setup, network management, schedule monitoring	Technical support, platform manager, schedule officer	Systems thinking, adaptability, technical literacy
Budgeting & Resource Allocation	Costing activities, managing virtual/in-kind resources, sponsorship	Finance officer, resource manager	Financial literacy, negotiation, accountability
Post-Event Evaluation	Data gathering, after-action reports, learner reflection, feedback collection	Evaluator, documentarian, reflective practitioner	Reflective practice, data analysis, continuous improvement

Planning Esports Tournaments and Activities

The planning phase requires learners to make a series of consequential decisions: selecting the game or games to be featured; determining the tournament format (single elimination, double elimination, round-robin, or hybrid); establishing rules and fair play standards; identifying necessary resources (hardware, software, venue, internet); and creating a communication and publicity plan. These decisions demand critical thinking, collaborative deliberation, and forward planning competencies with direct transfer value in civic, professional, and social contexts.

Pedagogically, the planning phase supports the development of project management literacy. Teachers can scaffold planning activities using tools such as project timelines, task matrices, and communication plans, connecting gaming contexts to professional event management frameworks. The use of digital tools including Google Workspace, Canva for event design, and Challonge or Battlefy for bracket management simultaneously develops technological proficiency and digital literacy (North America Scholastic Esports Federation, 2023).

Organizing Teams, Schedules, and Resources

The organizing phase involves the formation of teams, assignment of roles and responsibilities, scheduling of matches and activities, and inventory of available resources. Inclusive team formation guided by principles of fairness, diversity, and skill balance is a critical educational component, as it models the values of collaboration and equity. Role assignment within event management teams (team captain, technical officer, communications lead, logistics coordinator, referee) provides opportunities for students to develop specialized competencies and leadership identities.

Directing Event Operations and Communication

Directing an esports event requires real-time leadership, communication, and problem-solving. Students assigned as event directors or masters of ceremonies must coordinate multiple simultaneous activities monitoring match progress, communicating with participants, managing technical issues, and maintaining event energy and flow. This phase develops oral communication, public leadership, and adaptive decision-making in authentic, high-stakes contexts.

Controlling Logistics and Gameplay Procedures

Logistics management encompassing platform setup, network management, schedule adherence, and gameplay monitoring demands technical literacy, attention to detail, and systems thinking. Students serving as technical officers gain hands-on experience with gaming platform configuration, troubleshooting common technical issues, and maintaining event integrity. This phase also includes referee functions: ensuring compliance with established rules, adjudicating disputes, and maintaining fair play standards.

Budgeting and Resource Allocation

Although school-based esports events may operate with minimal financial resources, the budgeting component introduces learners to financial literacy principles: identifying costs (platform subscriptions, prizes, equipment), estimating in-kind contributions (school facilities, teacher time, community support), and allocating resources equitably. These competencies connect directly to life skills curricula and broader educational goals around financial responsibility and resource management.

Evaluating Esports Events and Learner Performance

Post-event evaluation is pedagogically essential and often underemphasized in event management education. Structured evaluation activities including after-action reports, reflective journals, peer feedback, and audience surveys close Kolb's (2015) experiential learning cycle by supporting abstract conceptualization and preparation for future improvement. Assessment rubrics that evaluate both event management competencies and individual participation skills provide educators with authentic, performance-based evidence of learning.

ETHICAL PLAY, DIGITAL CITIZENSHIP, AND RESPONSIBLE GAMING

The ethical dimensions of esports participation are among the most pressing and pedagogically rich aspects of esports education. Gaming environments particularly competitive online spaces are characterized by intense social interaction, anonymity, status competition, and, frequently, forms of behavior antithetical to educational values: verbal abuse, harassment, exclusion, cheating, and manipulation. Schools that incorporate esports without explicit attention to these ethical dimensions risk inadvertently legitimizing or normalizing harmful behaviors.

The table below provides a systematic overview of key ethical issues in esports contexts, their manifestations, recommended educational responses, and theoretical grounding.

Table 4. Ethical dimensions of esports: Issues, educational responses, and theoretical anchors

Ethical Issue	Description in Esports Context	Educational Response	Theoretical Anchor
Toxic Behavior & Cyberbullying	Verbal abuse, harassment, unsportsmanlike conduct in gaming chats and forums	Explicit classroom discussion; digital citizenship contracts; reporting protocol	Digital Citizenship Theory (Ribble, 2015); Socio-Ecological Theory
Gender Exclusion & Representation	Underrepresentation of women and LGBTQ+ players; stereotyping in gaming spaces	Gender-inclusive team formation; representation discussions; role models	Anykey (2021); Jenkins (2009); UNESCO (2023)
Gaming Addiction & Excessive Screen Time	Risk of dependency, neglect of physical activity, disrupted sleep	Wellness integration; screen time guidelines; mindfulness activities	World Health Organization (2022); Kowert & Quandt (2020)

continued on following page

Table 4. Continued

Ethical Issue	Description in Esports Context	Educational Response	Theoretical Anchor
Cheating & Unsportsmanlike Conduct	Exploiting game bugs, unauthorized software, false reporting	Rule literacy; honor codes; peer accountability mechanisms	Social Learning Theory (Bandura, 1977); Gee (2007)
Data Privacy & Platform Safety	Exposure of personal information through gaming platforms	Privacy literacy; safe account practices; platform safety guidelines	UNESCO (2023); Ribble (2015); Livingstone et al. (2021)
Exclusion & Accessibility	Digital divide; limited access for economically disadvantaged learners	Use of free-to-play platforms; school-provided devices; peer mentoring	DepEd (2023); Squire (2011); Newzoo (2024)

Fair Play and Sportsmanship

Fair play in esports encompasses adherence to game rules, honesty in competition, respect for opponents, and integrity in victory and defeat. Sportsmanship in digital environments is complicated by anonymity and distance, which can reduce social inhibitions against unsportsmanlike conduct. Educational interventions must make fair play norms explicit and consistently enforced: through honor codes, behavioral contracts, peer accountability mechanisms, and teacher modeling. Connecting esports sportsmanship to broader athletic and civic values such as respect, integrity, and humility helps learners transfer these principles across contexts (Ribble, 2015; Gee, 2007).

Cyberbullying, Toxicity, and Digital Resilience

Toxic behavior encompassing verbal aggression, trolling, harassment, and deliberate efforts to undermine teammates or opponents is endemic in many online gaming communities and represents one of the most significant barriers to inclusive esports participation (Kowert & Quandt, 2020). Research indicates that exposure to gaming toxicity is associated with increased stress, reduced enjoyment, and withdrawal from online communities, with disproportionate effects on girls, LGBTQ+ youth, and racial minorities (Anykey, 2021; Livingstone et al., 2021).

Schools are uniquely positioned to address gaming toxicity through education. Classroom discussions that analyze toxic incidents using ethical frameworks, role-play scenarios that develop empathetic responses, and explicit instruction in reporting and bystander intervention provide learners with practical tools for navigating and improving digital gaming cultures. The concept of digital resilience the capacity to recognize, respond to, and recover from harmful online experiences is an essential competency for contemporary youth (Livingstone et al., 2021).

Gender, Inclusion, and Representation

Esports, like traditional sports, has historically been characterized by significant gender imbalance: the majority of professional players, content creators, and industry leaders are male, and women and non-binary players frequently report experiences of exclusion, objectification, and harassment in gaming communities (Anykey, 2021). These dynamics are not intrinsic to gaming itself but reflect broader sociocultural patterns of gender inequality that are reproduced in digital spaces.

Esports education can actively challenge these patterns by designing inclusive team structures, centering diverse role models, facilitating critical discussions of gender representation in gaming media, and establishing explicit anti-discrimination norms. The Philippine context, where girls constitute approximately half of all K-10 learners and where gender-inclusive education is a DepEd priority, makes gender-responsive esports pedagogy an educational and policy imperative (Department of Education Philippines, 2023).

Gaming Addiction, Screen Time, and Wellness

The World Health Organization's (2022) classification of 'gaming disorder' as a diagnosable condition underscores the importance of wellness-integrated esports education. Gaming disorder, characterized by impaired control over gaming, prioritization of gaming over other activities, and continued gaming despite negative consequences, affects a minority but significant proportion of heavy gamers. Structured esports education with clear time limits, physical activity integration, and health monitoring can model balanced and responsible gaming practices.

Teachers and school counselors play critical roles in identifying learners at risk of problematic gaming and connecting them with appropriate support. Explicit instruction about healthy gaming habits including screen-time management, physical activity breaks, sleep hygiene, and social balance should be integrated into esports lessons as a non-negotiable wellness component. The DepEd curriculum's positioning of esports within Health and PE makes this integration both natural and obligatory.

DIGITAL CULTURE, YOUTH IDENTITY, AND ONLINE COMMUNITIES

Esports cannot be understood in isolation from the broader digital cultural ecosystem in which it is embedded. For Filipino youth, digital culture constitutes a primary environment for socialization, identity formation, creative expression, and cultural participation a 'participatory culture' (Jenkins, 2009) in which young people are not passive consumers but active creators, curators, and communicators.

Identity Formation in Gaming Spaces

Gaming provides youth with rich environments for identity experimentation and expression. Through the selection of characters, roles, usernames, playing styles, and online communities, learners construct and perform social identities that may differ significantly from their offline selves. For some learners particularly those who feel marginalized in traditional educational or social settings gaming communities provide a sense of competence, belonging, and recognition that is motivationally powerful (Gee, 2007; Squire, 2011).

Educators who understand the identity dimensions of gaming participation are better positioned to connect esports learning to learners' intrinsic motivations and sense of self. Acknowledging learners as knowledgeable participants in gaming culture rather than positioning gaming as an activity requiring adult legitimization establishes a foundation of respect and mutual learning that is pedagogically productive (Prensky, 2010; Gee, 2007).

Livestreaming, Influencer Culture, and Learning

The rise of livestreaming platforms particularly Twitch, YouTube Gaming, and Facebook Gaming has fundamentally altered the relationship between gaming and spectatorship. Professional and semi-professional streamers command audiences of millions, functioning as cultural influencers who shape gaming trends, community norms, language, and values (Taylor, 2018). Filipino streamers and esports personalities have achieved significant reach on these platforms, with their content shaping the aspirations and behaviors of Filipino youth.

The educational implications of livestreaming culture are significant. Learners who consume gaming content on streaming platforms absorb not only gameplay strategies but also behavioral models, community norms, and cultural attitudes both prosocial and potentially harmful. Esports education that incorporates critical media literacy helping learners analyze the content, business models, and social dynamics of gaming media develops sophisticated consumers and creators of digital culture (Jenkins, 2009; UNESCO, 2023).

Online Communities, Social Belonging, and Discord

Contemporary esports participation extends across platforms: Discord servers for team communication, Reddit and Facebook groups for community discussion, TikTok for gaming content and trends, and YouTube for tutorials and commentary. These multi-platform ecosystems create complex social environments with their own norms, hierarchies, and cultures. For many Filipino youth, gaming communities provide their primary peer networks and sources of social support.

Schools can harness the social dimensions of gaming culture by creating school-based esports communities through clubs, class teams, and structured social learning activities that provide belonging and connection within educational contexts. These communities can model healthy, inclusive, and ethical digital social practices, complementing and potentially improving upon the norms of wider online gaming communities (Kowert & Quandt, 2020; Jenkins, 2009).

CHALLENGES IN IMPLEMENTING ESPORTS EDUCATION

The implementation of esports education in Philippine basic education is beset by a range of practical, infrastructural, professional, and cultural challenges. Identifying these challenges clearly is a prerequisite for developing sustainable, equitable, and educationally effective implementation strategies.

Table 5. Implementation challenges in esports education: Description, strategies, and evidence

Challenge	Description	Recommended Strategy	Supporting Evidence
Limited Technological Infrastructure	Insufficient computers, gaming peripherals, and reliable hardware in public schools	Leverage mobile-first games; community ICT labs; DOST-DICT partnerships	DepEd (2023); Statista (2024)
Poor Internet Connectivity	Unreliable or absent broadband in remote and rural schools	Offline-capable games; hybrid event formats; blended learning approaches	Department of Information and Communications Technology (2023); Newzoo (2024)
Teacher Preparedness	Lack of content knowledge, technical skills, and confidence in esports pedagogy	Professional development workshops; NEAP-accredited esports training; teacher communities of practice	UNESCO (2023); Kolb (2015)
Parental & Community Misconceptions	Negative perceptions of gaming as harmful, unproductive, or addictive	Community orientations; evidence-based parent briefings; showcasing learner outputs	World Health Organization (2022); Anderson & Jiang (2018)
Policy & Governance Gaps	Absence of detailed school-level esports policies; liability and safety concerns	DepEd advisories; school-level esports codes of conduct; LGU partnerships	DepEd (2023); Ribble (2015)
Equity & Accessibility	Socioeconomic barriers limiting device and internet access among learners	Bring-your-own-device policies; free-to-play game selection; peer mentoring networks	Squire (2011); UNESCO (2023)
Screen Time & Student Wellness	Risk of sedentary behavior, eye strain, and disrupted sleep patterns	Integrated wellness breaks; physical activity pairing; health monitoring	World Health Organization (2022); DepEd Health Framework (2023)

Technological Infrastructure and Internet Connectivity

Perhaps the most fundamental challenge is the unevenness of technological infrastructure across Philippine schools. Public schools in urban areas may have access to computer laboratories, stable broadband connections, and adequate gaming hardware; rural and remote schools frequently lack even basic computing facilities. This digital divide risks transforming esports education from an equity-promoting initiative into an elite privilege, available only to learners in better-resourced schools (Department of Information and Communications Technology, 2023; Department of Education Philippines, 2023).

Mitigation strategies include prioritizing mobile-accessible, free-to-play game titles that can run on affordable smartphones; leveraging community ICT laboratories and LGU digital hubs; partnering with telecommunications providers for subsidized school connectivity; and developing hybrid (online-offline) event formats that reduce bandwidth demands. DepEd's partnerships with the Department of Information and Communications Technology (DICT) and the Department of Science and Technology (DOST) provide institutional frameworks for addressing infrastructure gaps (Department of Information and Communications Technology, 2023).

Teacher Preparedness and Professional Development

The effective implementation of esports education requires teachers who are confident in gaming content knowledge, familiar with esports event management processes, equipped with ethical and digital literacy pedagogical competencies, and capable of designing authentic assessment tasks for esports activities. Many current PE and Health teachers, however, were trained in traditional physical education paradigms and may lack both the technical knowledge and pedagogical confidence to teach esports effectively.

Sustainable professional development must go beyond introductory workshops to include sustained communities of practice, mentoring by esports-experienced educators, and accredited training programs through the National Educators Academy of the Philippines (NEAP). Collaboration with esports organizations, collegiate esports programs, and industry partners can provide practical training resources and clinical experience for PE teachers (North America Scholastic Esports Federation, 2023; British Esports, 2022).

Misconceptions, Parental Concerns, and Community Engagement

Public understanding of esports in the Philippines remains heavily influenced by narratives of gaming addiction, academic neglect, and screen time harm concerns that, while not without empirical basis, are frequently overgeneralized and applied uncritically to structured educational esports programs. Parental resistance to esports in school can undermine program participation, reduce learner motivation, and generate community opposition to curriculum implementation.

Schools must invest in proactive community engagement: parent orientations that present evidence-based information about esports education's competency development outcomes; public showcasing of learner outputs from esports event management projects; and transparent communication about wellness safeguards built into the program. Reframing esports as a vehicle for leadership, collaboration, and digital citizenship rather than merely as gaming can shift community perceptions and build support (Anderson & Jiang, 2018; World Health Organization, 2022).

IMPLICATIONS FOR CURRICULUM, POLICY, AND PRACTICE

Implications for Curriculum Developers

Curriculum developers should ensure that esports competencies in the K-10 curriculum are aligned with clear, measurable learning standards and accompanied by detailed curriculum guides that provide teachers with content knowledge support, sample activities, assessment tools, and differentiation strategies. The curriculum should explicitly integrate wellness, digital citizenship, and media literacy as non-negotiable components of esports education, rather than treating them as supplementary additions. Regular curriculum review mechanisms should be established to respond to the rapidly evolving esports landscape.

Implications for Teachers and School Leaders

PE and Health teachers who will implement esports education require targeted, sustained professional development that builds both content knowledge and pedagogical confidence. School leaders should create enabling conditions for esports education by allocating technology resources, establishing school esports policies, fostering community support, and connecting teachers with professional learning communities. Collaborative curriculum planning among PE teachers, ICT coordinators, guidance counselors, and school administrators can ensure that esports education is implemented holistically and sustainably.

Implications for Policymakers

DepEd should issue detailed implementing guidelines for esports education that address technology requirements, safety protocols, equity provisions, and teacher qualifications. Policy should explicitly address the digital divide by mandating alternative implementation pathways for schools with limited technological infrastructure. National-level partnerships with esports organizations, technology companies, telecommunications providers, and LGUs should be formalized to support resource provision and capacity building. Assessment frameworks for esports competencies should be developed and standardized to ensure consistency across schools and regions.

Implications for Parents and Communities

Parents and communities are essential partners in the success of esports education. Their engagement should be informed, collaborative, and empowering: schools should share evidence about the educational benefits of structured esports programs, involve parents in establishing behavioral expectations and wellness guidelines, and celebrate learner achievements in esports event management publicly. Community members with expertise in gaming, technology, event management, and digital culture can serve as guest resources, mentors, and program supporters.

Implications for Esports Organizations and Industry Partners

Esports organizations and technology companies have both the resources and the interest to support educational esports programs. Industry partners can contribute through provision of licensed game access, hardware loans, mentoring programs, and scholarship pathways for talented student gamers. They also bear responsibility for ensuring that their platforms are safe, inclusive, and appropriate for educational use—including robust moderation tools, privacy protections for minors, and clear reporting mechanisms for harmful behavior.

FUTURE DIRECTIONS FOR ESPORTS EDUCATION RESEARCH

The academic study of esports education in basic education is still in its early stages, and numerous critical questions remain underexplored. The following table maps a forward-looking research agenda, identifying priority areas, specific foci, methodological approaches, and expected contributions.

Table 6. Future research agenda for esports education in basic education

Research Area	Specific Focus	Methodological Approach	Expected Contribution
AI & Automated Moderation	Impact of AI-based toxicity filters on learner behavior in educational gaming	Experimental; quasi-experimental design	Evidence base for safer digital gaming environments
Virtual Reality Esports	Immersive esports environments for learning and skill development	Mixed-methods; design-based research	Innovations in PE and technology integration
Digital Wellness & Mental Health	Longitudinal effects of structured esports participation on adolescent mental health	Longitudinal cohort; psychometric assessment	Guidelines for wellness-informed esports curriculum
Gender Inclusivity	Participation rates, experience, and identity of girls and LGBTQ+ youth in school esports	Feminist qualitative; intersectional analysis	Equity-centered esports policy and programming
Esports Pedagogy & Assessment	Development and validation of esports-specific learning assessments	Instrument development; rubric validation	Rigorous assessment tools for PE and health educators

continued on following page

Table 6. Continued

Research Area	Specific Focus	Methodological Approach	Expected Contribution
Learner Outcomes	Academic, social, and cognitive outcomes of esports education over time	Longitudinal mixed-methods	Empirical grounding for curriculum justification
School-Community Partnerships	Effectiveness of esports industry-school collaboration models	Case study; program evaluation	Partnership frameworks for sustainable implementation

Among the most urgent research priorities is the development of empirically validated assessment frameworks for esports education competencies. Unlike traditional physical education, where assessment of physical fitness and motor skills has established methodological traditions, esports education lacks standardized, rubric-based assessment tools appropriate for the Philippine basic education context. Instrument development research, drawing on the competency standards of the DepEd curriculum and the documentary analysis matrix presented in Table 7, is an immediate and actionable priority.

Longitudinal research on learner outcomes tracking the academic, social, cognitive, and career-related effects of participation in school esports programs over multiple years would provide the strongest evidence base for curriculum justification and policy investment. Such research should employ mixed-methods designs that capture both quantitative outcome data and rich qualitative accounts of learner experience, particularly from marginalized groups who have historically been excluded from esports spaces (Anykey, 2021; Bányai et al., 2019).

The intersections of artificial intelligence, virtual reality, and esports education represent particularly promising but underexplored frontiers. AI-based moderation tools capable of detecting and responding to toxic language in real time have significant potential for making school esports environments safer and more inclusive. Virtual reality esports environments may expand accessibility by eliminating hardware barriers and offering immersive learning experiences. Research in these areas will require interdisciplinary collaboration between educational researchers, computer scientists, game designers, and health professionals.

CONCLUSION

The inclusion of esports in the Revised K to 10 Physical Education and Health Curriculum of the Department of Education Philippines is a forward-looking, culturally responsive, and pedagogically defensible policy decision. It acknowledges the realities of Filipino youth's digital lives, positions schools as spaces for developing twenty-first-century competencies, and creates structured opportunities for experiential, ethical, and collaborative learning through a medium that deeply resonates with contemporary learners.

This chapter has examined esports education from multiple theoretical, methodological, and practical perspectives, demonstrating that its educational value extends well beyond competitive gaming. The documentary analysis presented in Section VI confirms that the DepEd curriculum's esports competencies are coherently structured and conceptually aligned with established frameworks for digital citizenship, experiential learning, and twenty-first-century skills development. Through esports event management, learners develop project planning, organizational, communicative, and leadership competencies with broad transfer value. Through explicit attention to ethical play and digital citizenship, learners develop the moral reasoning, digital resilience, and inclusive social skills essential for responsible participation in digital society. Through engagement with digital culture and online communities, learners develop critical awareness of the social, political, and commercial dimensions of the digital environments they inhabit.

The challenges of implementation particularly the digital divide, teacher preparedness gaps, and parental misconceptions are real and must be addressed with urgency and intentionality. They should not, however, be grounds for abandoning esports education, but rather for investing in the infrastructure, professional development, policy, and community engagement necessary for equitable and effective implementation.

Ultimately, esports education in Philippine basic education represents more than a curricular novelty. It reflects a broader transformation in the relationship between education, technology, youth culture, and digital participation a transformation that demands of educators not only technical adaptation but philosophical reconsideration of what counts as educationally meaningful, who counts as educationally competent, and what spaces count as educationally significant. The argument of this chapter is simple but consequential: done well, with theoretical grounding, methodological rigor, ethical intentionality, and sustained institutional support, esports education can become one of the most powerful and relevant educational platforms of the twenty-first century for Filipino learners.

REFERENCES

American Psychological Association. (2020). *Publication manual of the American Psychological Association* (7th ed.). APA.

Anderson, C. A., & Jiang, J. (2018). *Teens, social media & technology 2018*. Pew Research Center.

Anykey. (2021). Diversity and inclusion in esports. Anykey Organization. https://www.anykey.org

Bandura, A. (1977). *Social learning theory*. Prentice Hall.

Bányai, F., Griffiths, M. D., Demetrovics, Z., & Király, O. (2019). The psychology of esports: A systematic literature review. *Journal of Gambling Studies, 35*(2), 351–365. DOI: 10.1007/s10899-018-9763-1 PMID: 29508260

Bowen, G. A. (2009). Document analysis as a qualitative research method. *Qualitative Research Journal, 9*(2), 27–40. DOI: 10.3316/QRJ0902027

Braun, V., & Clarke, V. (2022). Thematic analysis: A practical guide. *Sage (Atlanta, Ga.)*.

British Esports. (2022). *Esports in education: A guide for schools*. British Esports Association.

Bronfenbrenner, U. (1979). *The ecology of human development: Experiments by nature and design*. Harvard University Press. DOI: 10.4159/9780674028845

Department of Education Philippines. (2012). DepEd Child Protection Policy (DepEd Order No. 40, s. 2012). DepEd.

Department of Education Philippines. (2023). *Revised K to 10 Physical Education and Health Curriculum Guide*. DepEd.

Department of Information and Communications Technology. (2023). *Philippine digital infrastructure assessment 2023*. DICT.

English, F. W. (2010). *Deciding what to teach and test: Developing, aligning, and auditing the curriculum* (3rd ed.). Corwin Press.

Freeman, G., & Wohn, D. Y. (2020). Understanding esports team formation and how teams coordinate online during esports competitions. *Proceedings of the Annual Symposium on Computer-Human Interaction in Play*, 193–205. DOI: 10.1145/3410404.3414252

Gee, J. P. (2007). *What video games have to teach us about learning and literacy* (2nd ed.). Palgrave Macmillan.

Jenkins, H. (2009). *Confronting the challenges of participatory culture: Media education for the 21st century*. MIT Press. DOI: 10.7551/mitpress/8435.001.0001

Kolb, D. A. (2015). *Experiential learning: Experience as the source of learning and development* (2nd ed.). Pearson Education.

Kowert, R., & Quandt, T. (2020). *Video games and social competence*. Routledge.

Krippendorff, K. (2019). *Content analysis: An introduction to its methodology* (4th ed.). SAGE.

Livingstone, S., Stoilova, M., & Kelly, A. (2021). *Digital skills and competence, and digital and media literacy*. UNESCO., DOI: 10.54675/BBUM8498

National Alliance for Collegiate Esports. (2024). *State of collegiate esports 2024*. NACE.

Newzoo. (2024). Global esports and live-streaming market report. Newzoo.

North America Scholastic Esports Federation. (2023). *Esports in education: NASEF impact report 2023*. NASEF.

Patton, M. Q. (2015). *Qualitative research & evaluation methods* (4th ed.). SAGE.

Prensky, M. (2010). *Teaching digital natives: Partnering for real learning*. Corwin Press.

Republic of the Philippines. (2012). *Data Privacy Act of 2012 (Republic Act No. 10173)*. Official Gazette of the Philippines.

Ribble, M. (2015). *Digital citizenship in schools* (3rd ed.). International Society for Technology in Education.

Snyder, H. (2019). Literature review as a research methodology: An overview and guidelines. *Journal of Business Research, 104*, 333–339. DOI: 10.1016/j.jbusres.2019.07.039

Squire, K. (2011). *Video games and learning: Teaching and participatory culture in the digital age*. Teachers College Press.

Squires, D. (2012). Curriculum alignment research suggests that alignment can improve student achievement. *The Clearing House: A Journal of Educational Strategies, Issues and Ideas, 85*(4), 129–135. DOI: 10.1080/00098655.2012.657723

Statista. (2024). Global esports audience overview. Statista Research Department.

Taylor, T. L. (2018). *Watch me play: Twitch and the rise of game live streaming.* Princeton University Press. DOI: 10.2307/j.ctvc77jqw

UNESCO. (2023). *Global framework for digital literacy skills*. UNESCO Publishing.

World Health Organization. (2022). *Public health implications of excessive gaming and digital engagement.* WHO Press.

Chapter 5
Gamifying Ethics:
Constructing Counter-Radicalization Narratives Through Islamic Values in Pakistan's Digital Ecosystem

Mahmood Ahmad
http://orcid.org/0009-0001-2314-0415
Islamia University of Bahawalpur, Pakistan

ABSTRACT

As the digital landscape in Pakistan moves from traditional social media to immersive gaming environments, these "third spaces" have become critical sites for ideological formation and, conversely, radicalization. Extremist groups have effectively used "gamification" to recruit and normalize violent narratives but defensive strategies are largely reactive. The research studies a proactive framework: Ethical Gamification. This study seeks to build digital resilience among Pakistani youth by embedding core Islamic ethical values such as Adl (Justice), Rahmah (Compassion) and Shura (Consultation) into the procedural rhetoric of game mechanics. This chapter offers a pedagogical model beyond the 'prohibition vs. permission' binary, in which the 'Politics of Play' is re-captured as a vehicle for prosocial behavior and counter-radicalization.

i. INTRODUCTION

The "Politics of Online Play" has evolved from a marginal subculture to a major socio-political arena in the digital age. Gaming environments have moved beyond simply being entertainment for the Global South, and Pakistan specifically, to

DOI: 10.4018/979-8-2600-1664-0.ch005

become "digital third spaces" where identity, religious sentiment and nationalistic narratives are negotiated. Pakistan has a big "youth bulge" now. This demographic is increasingly digitally native, navigating a landscape in which high-speed mobile internet and affordable smartphones have democratized access to immersive multiplayer environments. But as these digital spaces have grown, they have become fertile grounds for "networked radicalization."

In Pakistan gaming and radicalization intersect in a unique way. Digital extremism in the Pakistani context is often framed through a theocentric lens, contrasting with the secular nihilism or "incel" culture often exploited by Western far-right radicalization. It takes traditional Islamic notions such as Jihad (struggle), Ummah (global community) and Shahadat (martyrdom) and "gamifies" them to appeal to a generation feeling socio-economically marginalized in the physical world but empowered in the virtual.

The socio-technical landscape of Pakistan is experiencing a rapid and structurally disruptive change in the current digital era. For a country facing acute demographic pressures, socioeconomic challenges and shifting security paradigms, the virtualization of daily life has fundamentally transformed youth culture. The socialization, moral instruction and ideological formation of young citizens were historically firmly grounded in physical, local institutions, primarily the family structure, the educational apparatus and the mosque. These organizations were vertical, authoritative gatekeepers, controlling the flow of information, shaping the community standards and outlining the ethical boundaries.

But the rapid democratization of high speed mobile internet, the proliferation of cheap smart phones and the development of immersive digital multiplayer spaces have systematically bypassed these traditional gatekeepers(Turabi et al., 2025). Gaming has moved from a peripheral leisure activity to a central "digital third space", a complex virtual arena where identity, social status and ideological alignment are negotiated.

This socio-technical evolution has engendered a deep crisis of authority. Young Pakistanis are leaving the physical neighborhood spaces and are entering hyper-private, unmonitored digital gaming lobbies, where the locus of moral and social authority has shifted.

ii. CONTEXT AND PROBLEM STATEMENT

Pakistan has one of the world's youngest populations with roughly 64 percent of its citizens under the age of 30, (Pakistan Bureau of Statistics). The young structure is expected to keep growing at least until 2050. For this demographic, online gaming is no longer a peripheral hobby but a primary vehicle for social interaction and identity performance.

However, recent studies in the Pakistani context reveal an alarming rise in Internet Gaming Disorder (IGD) estimated at 58.9% among some youth cohorts which correlate with increased susceptibility to social isolation and extremist grooming (JPPS, 2026). Extremist actors exploit these vulnerabilities to recreate militant attacks and reinforce group dynamics through customized game modifications (mods) and private servers (UNICRI, 2026).

The academic and state response to the increasing influence of gaming on the ideological development of Pakistani youth has been dangerously binary. On one hand, traditional religious institutions tend to dismiss gaming as Laghw (vain pastime), and on the other hand, they abandon the digital lobby to extremist actors who fill the moral vacuum with radical interpretations However, the Pakistani state has often resorted to "securitization through prohibition" and has imposed outright bans on platforms such as PUBG or TikTok during times of social unrest. These reactive measures do not address the root cause, which is the lack of a constructive, ethically developed, digital narrative that speaks to the gamer's identity.

iii. RESEARCH OBJECTIVES

- To analyze the procedural rhetoric of the contemporary extremist narratives in the gaming spaces used by Pakistani players.
- To identify particular Islamic ethical principles that can be translated into interactive game mechanics (e.g. branching narratives, reward systems).
- To develop a 'Counter-Narrative Framework' for developers and educators to engage Pakistani youth in prosocial digital play.

iv. LITERATURE REVIEW

a) The Global Nexus of Gaming and Radicalization

In Western settings, the convergence of interactive media and extremist ideology has been understood through the concept of "The Great Replacement" theory, or "alt-right" pipelines. One of the first to introduce the notion of "ludic radicalization" was Schlegel, who argues that extremist groups do not simply use games as a tool of propaganda, but rather take advantage of "gamification" as a pedagogical tool (Schlegel, 2020). These groups employ leaderboards, achievement badges and immersive story telling to normalize violent outcomes and assuage the cognitive dissonance caused by radical shifts.

Latif (2024) identified the 'New Wave' of terrorism as utilizing the internet, not only as a communication tool, but as a 'primary operating environment' where religious beliefs are instrumentalized to increase individual and organizational reach. Globally, the UNICRI "Checkpoint Reached" report describes that the primary danger lies in "procedural recruitment" the slow, rule-based induction into extremist ideologies in such platforms like *Roblox* or *Minecraft (UNICRI, 2026).*

b) The Regional Dynamics of Pakistan: Beyond Western Models

Global theories give a basic understanding of the mechanics of the game but fail to take into account the specific socio-religious nuances of South Asia. The "Politics of Piety" is inextricably interspersed with the "Politics of Play" in Pakistan. "Sincere Radicalism" is often the hallmark of radicalization in Pakistan, whereas secular nihilism and irony often fuel Western radicalization. Here the gamer is not asked to rebel against religious tradition, but to "reclaim" it.

Othman (2025) stresses that the digital space is an extension of the Ummah (muslim community) for the Muslim gamer. Hence, when Muslim majority areas like Pakistan are referred to as "war zones" or "villainous areas" in global games, "Reactive Nationalism" is created. This sentiment is used by local extremist groups to "mod" these games to flip the narrative allowing Pakistani young generation to play as the "defender of the faith" against perceived regional enemies.

c) The "Securitization of Play" and Procedural Gaps

Regional literature also points to a major policy failure. The Psychiatric Society documented the rise of Internet Gaming Disorder (IGD) in Pakistan and noted that the state's response periodic bans on PUBG actually speeds up radicalization. The state has criminalized or pathologized a primary social outlet, and in doing so, pushed youth into underground, unregulated "dark" servers on Discord or Telegram. In these unregulated spaces, the "in-group/out-group" dynamics described in Social Identity Theory become hyper-pronounced, and youth are more vulnerable to extremist grooming that provides the "belonging" that the state has taken away.

The biggest gap in the existing literature is the lack of a "Positive Procedural Rhetoric." rules persuade in games, yet regional scholars have yet to map how Islamic ethical principles can be proceduralized. Bogost (2007) argues that games persuade through rules, but regional scholars have not yet traced how Islamic ethical principles (Akhlaq) can be proceduralized. Most of the regional research is purely theological

(Fatwa discourse) and purely psychological (addiction). Ethical Gamification: the missed opportunity in-between.

As comparative regional studies from indicate, Indonesia and Malaysia have begun to experiment with "Moderate Digital Dawah" through gamified apps, but Pakistan remains trapped in the cycle of prohibition. This research fills that gap by synthesizing global media theory with local religious ethics to propose a framework for "Maqasid based Game Design."

This set-up seeks to shift the regional conversation from "what is forbidden online" to "how can we design for digital resilience," offering a blueprint for a prosocial, regionalized gaming ecosystem that counters the global and local rise of digital extremism. This body of literature suggests that for Dawah to be effective among Gen Z and Gen Alpha, it must be interactive. A lecture on "Compassion" (Rahmah) is less effective than a game mission in which a player has to choose between a violent shortcut, and a compassionate, strategic victory.

This research attempts to address this gap by proposing the "Maqasid-based Game Design" framework. It argues that if extremist narratives can be 'played' then counter-radicalisation narratives must also be playable. Using the particular Pakistani context in which religious identity is central the current study suggests that "Gamifying Ethics" is not just a defensive measure, but a tool for positive identity formation.

v. PROPOSED METHODOLOGY & THEORETICAL FRAMEWORK

a) Theoretical Framework: Procedural Akhlaq and Social Identity

The study employs a dual theoretical framework that combines Western media theory and Islamic ethico-legal philosophy. The primary lens through which this is explored is Procedural Rhetoric. This suggests that games do not persuade through linear oration, but through 'processes'. Games make representations of how the world works as rule-based systems, shaping a player's understanding of causality and morality. This paper presents an evolution of this theory called "Procedural Akhlaq." Islamic ethical principles such as Adl (Justice) and Amanah (Trustworthiness) are not mere thematic "skins" here but embedded as core winning conditions.

Social Identity Theory (SIT) helps explain how people shape their sense of self through the groups they belong to. In Pakistan, this usually means identifying with the Ummah basically, the global Muslim community. Extremists often paint secular groups as the enemy or the "Other." In this research, SIT is used to look at how ethical gaming communities, called "Digital Vanguards," can give young people the same sense of belonging and identity that some go searching for in radicalized private servers.

b) Comparative Research Methodology

The study takes an interdisciplinary approach, using qualitative comparisons. To really capture a regional perspective, it looks at the "Politics of Play" in two kinds of spaces: global multiplayer lobbies (think Western-focused) and Pakistani gaming communities that are more local. By putting the Western radicalization pipeline up against a South Asian model built on ethical values, the methodology sets up a framework that other Global South countries can use. It shifts the conversation away from just top-down state security and focuses more on grassroots digital community building. The aim? To deliver findings that aren't just solid on paper but actually make sense and can be put to use by IGI Global's international audience.

vi. SIGNIFICANCE AND EXPECTED IMPACT

Here's what this study brings to the table:

- For academics, it builds a fresh connection between Procedural Rhetoric and Islamic Ethics.
- The industry gets practical advice on "Ethical Modding" and community moderation, especially for Muslim-majority areas.
- For society, it lays out a plan to help Pakistani youth stop just playing global games and start creating ethical digital content themselves.

1. THE EVOLUTION OF THE DIGITAL MEDIUM: FROM CYBER CAFÉS TO MOBILE UBIQUITY

1.1 The Cyber Café Era: Physical Anchoring and Social Surveillance

To appreciate the extent of Pakistan's current digital transformation, one has to follow the material history of the country's internet infrastructure. In the late 1990s and first decade of the 2000s, digital access in Pakistan was characterized by strict physical and economic restrictions. The internet was not an ambient, invisible utility;

it was localized within the "cyber café" a commercial storefront that acted as the sole gateway to the World Wide Web for most of the urban youth (Schlegel, 2020).

These spaces possessed a distinct socio-technical architecture. PCs were arranged in proximity, connected via local area networks (LAN) to host localized multiplayer matches of foundational titles such as *Medal of Honor*, *Counter-Strike*, and *Command & Conquer* (Newhouse, A., & Kowert, R., 2024). This physical setup imposed natural regulatory constraints on user behavior:

- **Temporal and Economic Boundaries:** Play was highly structured, intentional and finite. Access was limited by geography and the cost which was calculated by the hour. This physical constraint prevented digital immersion from ever fully absorbing the domestic or academic practice of the player.
- **Collective Social Surveillance:** The cybercafé was a shared, public space. The player's screen was visible not only to immediate peers, but to café operators, older members of the community, and passing acquaintances in the neighborhood. It was a living system of social accountability this spatial arrangement. The implicit social policing of the shared physical room placed heavy checks on transgressive online behaviors, toxic language, and exposure to explicit or radical content.
- **The Domestic Firewall:** The user had crossed a definite line coming home. For the most part, the domestic sphere stayed insulated from the digital sphere, continuing to function in its traditional role as the sole source of moral and behavioral authority for parents and elders.

1.2 The Mobile Revolution, Digital Disintermediation

By the mid-2010s this physically grounded model was completely pulled down. With 3G and 4G telecom spectrum licenses coming on stream, and a flood of low-cost but highly capable Chinese smartphones, the need for fixed-line PC infrastructure went away. The Asian Development Bank's (2024) diagnostic data shows that mobile data pricing in Pakistan became one of the cheapest in the world, which accelerated the uptake of mobile broadband across different socioeconomic classes.

This shift triggered a process of digital disintermediation, the systematic removal of physical intermediaries and institutional gatekeepers between the individual and the global digital network. The socio-technical characteristics of this new mobile-first paradigm are radically different from the cyber café era:

- **Hyper-Privacy, the Dissolution of Surveillance:** Gaming moved from the public square of the neighborhood to the hyper-private, handheld screen of the individual smartphone. Now play occurs in isolation, often in the private bedroom, away from the eyes of parents or any social supervision.

- **Frictionless, Constant Access:** Popular mobile multiplayer games like PUBG Mobile and Garena Free Fire were optimized to work on low-spec devices, enabling access to immersive digital environments 24/7. And the structural barriers between the "online" and the "offline" world have dissolved (Vaux, A., et al., 2021).
- **The Rise of Gaming-Adjacent Platforms (GAPs):** Today, mobile gaming is inextricably linked to secondary communication platforms like Discord, Telegram, and WhatsApp. These GAPs allow gaming squads to move seamlessly between active gameplay and private, unregulated text and voice channels, creating highly insulated digital subcultures (Thompson, J., & Lamphere-Englund, G., 2024).

1.3 Demographic Pressures and the Crucible of the Identity Vacuum

The psychological and sociological impact of this mobile transition has to be analyzed in tandem with Pakistan's unique demographic and material challenges. Pakistan has one of the most critical "youth bulges" in the world, with over 60 percent of its population below 30 years of age. This large cohort of young citizens is navigating a socio-political landscape marked by high underemployment, economic instability, and an educational system that often neglects critical digital literacy skills.

Unplanned, rapid urban growth in cities like Karachi, Lahore, and Faisalabad has stripped away much of the public infrastructure people once relied on. Parks, community centers, and spaces where you might hang out or express yourself have all but disappeared. Young people barely have any "third places" left a spot that's not home, not work or school, but somewhere to just be yourself, meet friends, or get involved. With the economy dragging and nowhere to go, it's no wonder so many feel stuck a kind of material identity vacuum, as sociologists put it (Khan, F., & Rahman, U., 2024). So, you've got a generation that's hemmed in physically, with little control over their own futures, and shut out politically.

That's where mobile gaming lobbies come in, they fill the gap. In these digital spaces, all those real-world class divisions, family pressures, and social roadblocks fade out for a while. Who you are in the game depends on how well you play and how you talk to your squad, not on your last name or bank account.

(Turabi et al., 2025) saw this for themselves when they studied teenagers in Karachi. They found that diving deep into competitive (and often violent) online games meets basic psychological needs being independent, feeling capable, and connecting with others that the offline world just can't handle right now. But there's a catch: relying so heavily on digital spaces for identity and belonging sets you up for trouble. It leaves young people exposed and sometimes wide open to ideological manipulation.

1.4 The Decentralization of Moral Agency: Shifting the Locus of Authority

Young people aren't gathering in physical community spaces the way they used to. Now, most of them hang out privately online on gaming platforms, chat rooms, and Discord servers. This shift has quietly rewired the whole way authority works in their lives.

The old, top-down model where parents, teachers, and religious scholars called the shots doesn't have the same hold. Those traditional figures used to act as the backbone of moral education and social control in Pakistan. Everyone knew who set the rules, how information spread, and what was expected.

1.5 The Horizon of Flat Social Systems

In today's digital world, especially inside mobile gaming lobbies, that hierarchy is gone. There's no clear chain of command, no elders or scholars watching over things. Authority works differently now it's flat and peer-driven:

- **The Peer Group as the Primary Moral Arbiter:** Take a gaming guild, for example. What your teammates think of you means a lot more than what your parents or an uncle might say. How you're seen in your digital clan matters, pushing you to adapt your behavior for the sake of your online reputation.
- **Disintermediation of Religious and Moral Knowledge:** when young people run into big questions whether they're about politics, religion, or ethics they don't usually turn to traditional sources. Instead, they crowdsource answers on Discord servers or gaming chats, relying on whatever's trending or exciting in their feed. Sure, the information can be sensational or polarizing, but that's what grabs their attention. The old authority figures barely show up the locus of moral power has shifted, and it's not going back any time soon (Ali, R., & Zaidi, H., 2024).
- **The Intergenerational Communicative Gulf:** A lot of older folks in Pakistan don't have much experience with technology. So, they usually brush off gaming as just Laghw a silly pastime that doesn't really matter (Rizvi, T., 2025). The problem is, this attitude means parents and teachers miss what's really going on. That gaming headset isn't just pumping out game sounds; it's an open door to all sorts of complex, unfiltered ideas and communities.

1.6 The "New Wave" Pipeline: Subverting Sacred Codes in Virtual Domains

This authority vacuum does not remain empty; rather, it is actively exploited by highly organized ideological actors. In his seminal analysis of contemporary digital threats, (Latif,2024) conceptualizes this phenomenon as the "New Wave" of online radicalization. He argues that extremist groups have evolved beyond crude, top-down propaganda, transitioning to decentralized, highly adaptive recruitment methodologies designed specifically for interactive Web 2.0 and Web 3.0 ecosystems.

Rather than attempting to pull young gamers out of their preferred virtual environments, these strategic actors embed themselves directly within them (Nisar, M., 2024). They operate as charismatic peers, expert players, and community moderators, using the natural social dynamics of the digital lobby to cultivate trust.

Once a relationship of "relatedness" is established, these recruiters systematically subvert traditional religious and nationalistic narratives, transforming complex theological concepts into binary, gamified mechanics:

- **The Subversion of *Jihad*:** The deeply nuanced, spiritually demanding concept of *Jihad* which traditionally prioritizes internal moral struggles and communal defense governed by strict ethical codes is stripped of its intellectual depth. Within radicalized gaming mods and chat channels, it is re-presented as a simplistic "Us vs. Them" multiplayer match, normalizing violence as a necessary and pious digital obligation.
- **The Exploitation of the *Ummah* Concept:** The concept of the *Ummah* (the global, compassionate brotherhood of believers) is narrow-mindedly reframed to mirror the exclusionary dynamics of a competitive gaming clan. Youth are encouraged to direct their natural desire for groups belonging toward aggressive, defensive hostility against a generalized "out-group".
- **Algorithmic Radicalization Pipelines:** The structure of gaming marketplaces and adjacent platforms actively facilitates this slide. A young gamer expressing frustration over global geopolitical double standards in a casual chat can easily be redirected via algorithmic recommendations and peer invitations to closed, unmonitored Discord and Telegram servers, where highly radicalized material is normalized through memes and shared play (Cyber Security Authority of Pakistan (CSAP)., 2025).

2. THE GAMIFIED THREAT: TACTICAL MODDING AND THE SIMULATION OF STRUGGLE

The contemporary intersection of digital gameplay and ideological radicalization represents a fundamental shift in the "Politics of Play". Historically, virtual environments were viewed by state authorities and security analysts as trivial, isolated domains of escapism, largely separate from real-world political conflicts. However, in the era of Web 2.0 and Web 3.0, video games have transitioned into highly active geopolitical arenas (Latif, M. A., 2024). Rather than functioning as neutral spaces of entertainment, digital games serve as expressive, interactive platforms where geopolitical conflicts are simulated, contested, and re-enacted.

This discussion examines a highly sophisticated and potent instrument within this digital battlefield: tactical "modding" (the user-driven modification of existing software architectures). Through modding, extremist organizations, hyper-nationalist networks, and sectarian actors systematically alter the aesthetic, environmental, and narrative layers of mainstream commercial video games (Schlegel, L., 2020).

By rewriting game code, inserting localized geographies (such as South Asian conflict zones), and embedding custom auditory and visual assets, these digital actors construct a highly immersive **"simulation of struggle"** (Newhouse, A., & Kowert, R., 2024).

This interactive simulation is engineered to appeal directly to the psychological and socioeconomic vulnerabilities of disenfranchised youth in Pakistan. Moving beyond passive media consumption, this study analyzes the procedural mechanisms through which tactical modding subverts popular commercial games such as Arma 3, Grand Theft Auto V (GTA V), and Counterstrike into localized ideological training grounds, redefining how young citizens perceive and engage with real world geopolitical violence.

2.1 The Mechanics of Tactical Modding: Subverting the Virtual Sandbox

2.1.1 The Philosophy of Modding as Political Expression

In the field of game studies, "modding" refers to the democratic alteration of a game's engine, assets, or mechanics by players (Postigo, H., 2007). Historically, modding was celebrated as a progressive form of user agency, allowing player communities to fix bugs, upgrade graphics, or design creative, non-commercial content (Scacchi, W., 2010).

However, this open access sandbox architecture also provides dual use vulnerability. Extremist and hyper-nationalist groups leverage these open modification tools to bypass the strict content-moderation algorithms of mainstream global publishers.

By utilizing pre-existing, high-fidelity physics engines, rendering software, and multiplayer netcodes, digital insurgent groups avoid the immense capital costs of game development (. Nisar, M., 2024). They simply overlay their localized ideological narratives onto premium commercial software, transforming a mass market entertainment product into a bespoke vehicle for ideological dissemination.

2.1.2 Procedural Rhetoric and the Gamification of Violence

To understand how modified games persuade, one must apply the framework of **procedural rhetoric** (Bogost, I., 2008). Traditional propaganda relies on passive representation (e.g., watching a video or reading a pamphlet). In contrast, modified video games persuade through active configuration. The player does not merely witness an ideological argument; they physically execute it through the controller or keyboard.

Within an ideologically modified level, the game's "winning conditions" are explicitly rewritten:

- **The Rewriting of Success Metrics:** In standard tactical shooters, points are awarded for abstract tactical objectives. In modified games, success metrics are tied directly to sectarian, nationalist, or extremist goals such as the digital elimination of specific regional minorities, state security forces, or rival geopolitical factions.
- **The Normalization of Taboos:** By repeating these interactive loops hundreds of times, real world violent taboos are psychologically normalized, transforming extreme geopolitical violence into a satisfying, low stakes digital achievement (Anderson, C. A., & Bushman, B. J., 2001).

2.2 Case Studies: Simulating South Asian Conflict Zones

To demonstrate the real-world application of tactical modding, this section analyzes three highly localized case studies where commercial sandboxes have been modified to simulate South Asian conflicts, catering to the socio-political grievances of disenfranchised Pakistani youth.

2.2.1 Case Study 1: The Virtual Kashmir (Tactical Modding in Arma 3)

Arma 3, a highly realistic military simulation (MilSim) developed by Bohemia Interactive, is renowned for its sandbox environment and robust modding tools. It has become a premier platform for simulating real-world regional conflicts (Robinson, N., 2012).

- **The Modification:** Hyper-nationalist digital groups in South Asia have developed highly detailed, custom-made terrain files (maps) that replicate the mountainous, forested geography of the Kashmir Valley (Yousaf, M., & Anwar, S., 2024). These mods replace standard Western military factions with highly accurate skins of regional military, paramilitary, and local insurgent forces.
- **The Ideological Objective:** In these modified multiplayer lobbies, players are recruited to execute highly coordinated, realistic ambush operations against opposing forces.
- **The Narrative Frame:** The mod acts as an immersive "empathy engine" for the militant cause. By placing the player in a highly realistic, interactive simulation of the conflict, the mod bypasses intellectual skepticism, appealing directly to the user's emotions, protective instincts, and desire for heroic martyrdom (Shahadat).

2.2.2 Case Study 2: Urban Sectarianism and Gang Warfare in GTA V (FiveM)

Grand Theft Auto V, particularly through the third-party multiplayer modification platform FiveM, allows users to host entirely customized multiplayer roleplay (RP) servers.

- **The Modification:** Several underground Pakistani digital communities have constructed specialized RP servers that superimpose the urban landscapes of Karachi, Lahore, and Rawalpindi onto the game's fictional city of Los Santos (Butt, N. A., 2024). These modifications include Urdu street signage, local police uniforms (e.g., Sindh Police or Punjab Police), and localized political party flags.
- **The Ideological Objective:** Players roleplay as members of real-world sectarian factions, ethnic gangs, or militant groups operating in urban Pakistan.
- **The Narrative Frame:** These servers act as highly interactive socialization spaces where localized sectarian rivalries and prejudices are performed, nor-

malized, and celebrated. The casual nature of roleplay lowers the player's psychological guard, allowing toxic sectarian and political radicalism to be packaged as humorous, shared social play (Hashmi, S., 2025).

2.2.3 Case Study 3: The Reconstruction of Real-World Attacks in Roblox and Minecraft

While Arma 3 and GTA V target older youth, platforms like Roblox and Minecraft are utilized to socialize younger demographics into cultures of conflict.

- **The Modification:** Extremist sympathizers have systematically utilized the block-building mechanics of these platforms to reconstruct highly tragic real-world militant attacks in Pakistan such as the 2014 Army Public School (APS) Peshawar massacre or subsequent attacks on security outposts.
- **The Ideological Objective:** Young players enter these custom servers to "re-play" or "defend" against these attacks, choosing sides in a highly interactive, cartoonish simulation of real-world trauma.
- **The Narrative Frame:** This represents the most insidious form of "ludic revisionism" (Pötzsch, H., 2017). By turning historical atrocities into interactive, low fidelity play spaces, the horror of violent extremism is sanitized, trivialized, and integrated into the everyday play routines of children.

2.3 The Psychological Hook: The "Simulation of Struggle" and Identity Affirmation

The strategic efficacy of modified games lies in their ability to exploit the **material identity vacuum** of Pakistani youth, as detailed in start. For a young man facing socioeconomic marginalization, systemic corruption, and a lack of real-world agency, the modified game provides a powerful, corrective psychological space (Fatima, A., et al., 2024).

2.3.1 The Reconstitution of Agency Through Play

In the physical world, the disenfranchised youth feel powerless against global geopolitical structures, economic stagnation, and local administrative failures. In the modified game lobby, however, this helplessness is instantly replaced by absolute interactive agency.

The player is no longer a passive victim of structural violence; they are a highly armed, tactically competent agent of change. Through the "Simulation of Struggle," the player experiences a profound, virtual sense of empowerment (Przybylski, A.

K., Rigby, C. S., & Ryan, R. M., 2010). The digital weapon in their hands behaves exactly as designed, the enemy is clearly defined, and victory is achievable through personal skill and coordination, a stark contrast to the complex, unyielding struggles of their physical lives.

2.3.2 The Role of "Relatedness" and the Digital Vanguard

This psychological feedback loop is reinforced by the social architecture of gaming-adjacent platforms. The radicalization pipeline does not conclude when the game match ends (Latif, M. A., 2026). The shared adrenaline of a closely contested virtual battle creates deep bonds of camaraderie among team members (Kaye, L. K., & Bryce, J., 2012).

Recruiters, operating as team captains or charismatic clan leaders, leverage this "relatedness" to transition the relationship from in-game cooperation to ideological mentorship on encrypted platforms like Telegram and Discord. The virtual squad becomes a "digital vanguard" a tight-knit substitute family that demands ideological conformity as the price of admission and status.

2.4 Societal and Security Implications for Pakistan

The proliferation of modified, ideologically charged gaming environments has severe implications for the state and civil society of Pakistan, far exceeding the scope of traditional national security frameworks.

2.4.1 The De-Sensitization of Youth to Real-World Violence

By transforming geopolitical conflicts into highly engaging, repeatable, and rewarding virtual loops, modified games actively de-sensitize young players to the physical reality of violence. The pain, trauma, and ethical complexity of real-world warfare are completely excised from the simulation, leaving only the thrill of tactical execution and communal triumph. This cognitive restructuring makes youth far more receptive to extremist rhetoric that advocates for physical-world violence as a simple, heroic extension of their digital play.

2.4.2 The Paralysis of Traditional Counter-Terrorism Frameworks

Pakistan's traditional counter-terrorism apparatus managed by institutions such as the National Counter Terrorism Authority (NACTA) is structurally unequipped to handle this gamified threat. Existing security policies are fundamentally designed for analog or text-based digital threats (e.g., tracking extremist websites, banning radical Facebook pages, or monitoring sectarian Twitter accounts).

These security agencies have virtually no systemic capability to monitor:

- User-generated code uploads to modding repositories like Steam Workshop or Nexus Mods.
- Real-time voice communications occurring within private, encrypted FiveM or Discord servers.
- The cultural subversion of interactive play mechanics that occur entirely beneath the radar of traditional surveillance.

By treating video games as mere toys, the state has left a massive, unmonitored back channel open for ideological grooming, allowing the "New Wave" of radicalization to operate with near total impunity.

In short, the "Politics of Play" in Pakistan is not a hypothetical concern, but an active, highly sophisticated geopolitical reality. Through the tactical subversion of commercial video game architectures, extremist and nationalist networks have succeeded in creating immersive, interactive "Simulations of Struggle." These modified virtual domains exploit the profound socioeconomic and psychological vulnerabilities of Pakistan's youth, offering them the agency, status, and community that their physical lives deny them.

By restructuring the very rules and objectives of play, these modifications slowly align the moral compass of the gamer with violent, exclusionary ideologies. If the state and civil society continue to rely on reactive, ineffective measures of blanket prohibition, they will cede the digital frontier entirely to radical engineers. The survival of an ethical digital ecosystem requires a fundamental shift: we must move from merely analyzing the gamified threat to actively constructing a robust, proactive framework of **Ethical Gamification** that uses these very mechanics of play to foster resilience and peace.

3. FROM LAGHW TO DAWAH: RECLAIMING THE VIRTUAL SANDBOX FOR DIGITAL AKHLĀQ

For decades, the dominant discourse surrounding interactive entertainment within Islamic jurisprudence (*Fiqh*) has been characterized by defensive containment, skepticism, and prohibition. Traditional religious authorities, confronted with the sudden rise of digital media, have historically categorized video games under the conceptual umbrella of *Laghw* a Quranic term denoting vain, purposeless, or spiritually distracting pastimes that divert the believer from remembrance (*Dhikr*) and civic duty. This reflexive categorization, while designed to protect the moral fabric of the community, has inadvertently created a profound theological and cultural vacuum. By unilaterally dismissing video games as mere idle play, traditional institutions have effectively ceded this highly influential digital territory to secularizing, hyper-nationalist, and extremist actors who utilize the medium with high strategic competence.

This discussion argues for a paradigm shift in Islamic media theology: the transition **from Laghw to Dawah** (invitation to values). Rather than abandoning the virtual space, this chapter proposes that the interactive sandbox must be reclaimed as a highly active, legitimate frontier for ethical engagement and character formation.

By moving beyond passive, defensive prohibition, we can utilize the unique mechanics of gameplay to construct a proactive framework of **"Digital Akhlāq"** (virtue ethics in virtual spaces). This framework re-imagines the gamer not as a passive consumer of distraction, but as an active moral agent capable of performing, reflecting upon, and cultivating Islamic ethical values within virtual ecosystems.

3.1. Deconstructing *Laghw*: Traditional Jurisprudence and the Problem of "Idle Play"

3.1.1 The Quranic and Hadīth Conception of *Laghw*

To understand the historical resistance to video games, one must examine the classical theological architecture of *Laghw* ( ). Imam Raghib in Al-Mufradāt fī Gharīb-e Al-qurān writes: "It is an insignificant speech and anything not derived from method and thought ... and any disagreeable word is called idle. And it is used for anything insignificant" (Esfahani, 1991). In classical Arabic lexicography and Qurānic exegesis (*Tafsīr*), *Laghw* refers to speech, play, or action that carries no spiritual, intellectual, or material benefit for this world or the hereafter (Ibn Kathir, I., 2003).

The Qurān repeatedly praises believers who steer clear of such distractions, positioning distance from vanity as a marker of spiritual maturity: "And who turn away from ill speech (Laghw) (or vain talk)(Al Mu'minun,23:3). "

According to Ibn Kathīr this verse refers to falsehood, which includes Shirk and sin, and any words or deeds that are of no benefit (Ibn Kathir, I., 2003). This verse highlights that true believers actively avoid meaningless, frivolous, and harmful conversations. By shunning idle talk, they protect their time, faith, and mental focus from anything that distracts them from their ultimate purpose.

In Surah Al Furqān Qurān states qualities of servants of God: "And when they pass by ill speech, they pass by with dignity." (Al Furqan,25:72)

In Surah Al-Qasas: "And when they hear Al-Laghw (ill speech), they withdraw from it and say, 'For us are our deeds, and for you are your deeds. Peace be upon you; we seek not the ignorant. "(Al-Qasas, 28:55)

In classical prophetic traditions (*Hadīth*), play is generally viewed with caution, tolerated primarily when it serves a practical, physical, or martial purpose such as archery, horsemanship, or swimming (Al-Tirmidhī, 2007). The primary authentic tradition regarding this is found in Sahih al-Bukhari, where the Prophet ( ) stated: *"Indeed, Allah dislikes for you three things: vain talks (useless talk and gossip), wasting of wealth, and asking too many questions [in disputed religious matters] [or begging] (Al-Bukhārī, 1997)."*

About Leaving What Does Not Concern One, He said: "Part of a person's excellence in Islam is leaving that which does not concern him (Al-Tirmidhī, 2007)."

Consequently, when commercial video games emerged in the late 20th and early 21st centuries, contemporary jurists naturally mapped these digital activities onto classical categories of diversion, citing concerns over time-wasting (*Idha'at al-Waqt*), exposure to prohibited visual content (*Harām* imagery), and the neglect of obligatory prayers (*Salāh*).

3.1.2 The Limitations of Static Prohibition (*Tahrīm*) in a Networked Era

While the classical intent to preserve time and spiritual focus remains deeply valid, the strategy of blanket prohibition (*Tahrīm*) faces severe limitations in a highly connected society like Pakistan (Yousaf, M., & Anwar, S., 2024).

When traditional scholars issue generic bans without understanding the structural, social, and psychological appeal of modern gaming, they foster a deep sense of alienation among the youth (Khan, F., & Rahman, U., 2024). Young players, finding no nuanced ethical guidance within their traditional religious institutions, increasingly compartmentalize their lives viewing religion as an offline, historical construct and gaming as an online, ethics-free zone.

By treating the entire medium as *Laghw*, traditional scholarship has left the digital generation spiritually unarmed, leaving them vulnerable to the sophisticated "procedural rhetoric" of extremist and sectarian groups who use games to advance their own agendas.

3.2 Reclaiming the Medium: The Theology of *Dawah* through Interactive Play

3.2.1 The Jurisprudential Shift: From Medium to Intent

A progressive, constructive Islamic approach to digital media requires shifting the focus of jurisprudential inquiry from the *medium* itself to its *intent, content, and utility*. In Islamic legal philosophy (*Usul al-Fiqh*), things are generally considered permissible by default (*Al-Asl fi al-Ashyā al-Ibāha*) unless there is explicit evidence of harām.

Furthermore, under the framework of *Maqāsid al-Sharīah* (the higher objectives of Islamic law), media can be evaluated based on the public interest (*Maslahah*) it serves.

If a digital game can be engineered or modified to cultivate moral reasoning, historical empathy, intellectual curiosity, and social responsibility, it ceases to be *Laghw*. Instead, it becomes a powerful, modern instrument of *Dawah* a way to invite, educate, and inspire users toward positive values through active experience (Rizvi, T., 2025).

Table 1.

Conceptual Dimension	Laghw Paradigm (Passive/Defensive)	Dawah Paradigm (Active/Constructive)
Primary Goal	Avoidance of distraction and moral contamination.	Active cultivation of virtue and ethical agency.
View of Medium	A spiritual threat and waste of temporal capital.	A highly strategic space for engagement and education.
Player Status	A vulnerable consumer prone to moral deviation.	An active moral agent performing ethical choices.
Design Focus	Total prohibition or hollow, dry educational software.	Immersive, high-quality play carrying "procedural ethics."

3.2.2 Immersive Storytelling as a Tool for Moral Empathy

Unlike traditional text or broadcast media, video games possess a unique capacity for empathy-building through interactive roleplay. When a player navigates a complex virtual environment, they do not merely watch a story unfold; they make decisions that carry visible, narrative consequences.

This interactive agency can be utilized to teach core Islamic values:

- **The Pursuit of Justice (*Adl*):** Designing quests where players must resolve disputes, protect vulnerable populations, and distribute resources fairly, demonstrating that strength is meant for service, not exploitation.
- **Patience (*Sabr*) and Stewardship (*Khilafah*):** Structuring gameplay mechanics where long-term resource management, environmental preservation, and community building are rewarded over impulsive destruction and instant gratification.

3.3 Constructing "Digital Akhlāq": Ethical Play and Virtual Agency

To transition from abstract theology to practical application, we must establish a clear framework of **Digital Akhlāq**. This concept translates the timeless virtue ethics of Islam (*Akhlaq*) into the specific behavioral patterns, design architectures, and social structures of contemporary digital play.

3.3.1 The Core Pillars of Digital Akhlāq

I. Ethical Agency in Gameplay Design (Amal al-Salih)

In commercial game design, players are often encouraged to maximize their virtual power at any ethical cost. The framework of Digital Akhlaq requires developers and modders to design choice-matrices that test and reward moral integrity. For example, rather than offering points solely for eliminations, games can award progress for sparing defeated opponents, honoring treaties, protecting civilian infrastructure, and showing mercy (*Rahmah*) in moments of triumph.

II. Constructive and Dignified Speech (Qawl Karīm)

The toxic culture of online voice chats and multiplayer lobbies characterized by sectarian slurs, gender-based harassment, and aggressive profanity is a major source of spiritual harm in modern gaming.

Digital Akhlaq demands systematic reconstruction of communication within gaming communities. This involves not only implementing automated moderation systems but also cultivating a peer-led culture where respect, humility, and positive encouragement (*Amr bil-Ma'ruf*) are actively valued and socially rewarded.

III. Digital Justice and Fair Play (Mīzan)

Cheating, hacking, exploiting software bugs, and griefing (deliberately ruining other players' experiences) represent a direct violation of the Islamic concept of the scale (*Mīzan*) and fair dealing. Digital Akhlaq framing teaches players that virtual environments are not lawless zones of moral exemption. The ethical responsibilities of honesty, fairness, and respecting the rights of others (*Huquq al-Ibad*) apply just as strictly to our virtual avatars as they do to our physical lives.

3.4 Case Studies: Pioneers of Ethical Gamification

The potential of using games for positive, value-oriented engagement is already visible in several innovative global and regional projects.

3.4.1 Case Study 1: Historical Preservation and Empathy in *Assassin's Creed: Discovery Tour*

While not explicitly Islamic in its theological origin, Ubisoft's *Discovery Tour* series represents a major milestone in transforming commercial gaming spaces into highly educational platforms (Politopoulos, A., et al., 2019). By removing the violent combat mechanics from their reconstructed historical settings (such as Ptolemaic Egypt or Golden Age Baghdad) and replacing them with curated, educational tours, they transformed a mature action game into a highly valuable, interactive classroom tool. This demonstrates how premium virtual assets can be successfully repurposed to foster intellectual curiosity and historical appreciation, steering the medium away from mindless distraction (Schut, K., 2013).

3.4.2 Case Study 2: Independent Islamic Indie Games

A growing movement of independent Muslim developers is actively building games that weave Islamic principles directly into their core mechanics. Games like *Lost Ember* (which emphasizes stewardship of nature) or various independent narrative projects focusing on the rich history of Islamic science, philosophy, and poetry show that games can offer deep, spiritually nourishing experiences without relying on dry, overly preachy educational formats (Sisler, V., 2008). These projects prove that high-fidelity, engaging gameplay can coexist with profound ethical and spiritual depth.

Previous discussion has demonstrated that the traditional, defensive categorization of video games as mere *Laghw* is no longer sufficient to address the complex digital realities of today. In a world where digital spaces shape the moral, social, and political identities of millions of young people, retreating behind a wall of prohibition is a form of spiritual abandonment. The interactive sandbox is too powerful a tool to be left to those who use it for radicalization, sectarian division, or mindless commercial exploitation.

Reclaiming this space requires a courageous, intellectually rigorous transition from Laghw to Dawah. By embedding the principles of Digital Akhlaq into the design, modification, and consumption of video games, we can transform these immersive virtual worlds from spaces of distraction into platforms for ethical growth, moral empathy, and constructive community.

4. CASE STUDY: THE "ETHICAL HERO" AS A NARRATIVE COUNTER-IMAGE

The battle for digital narrative supremacy is not merely fought over technical platforms; it is waged over the archetypes that occupy the imagination of young gamers. In extremist virtual spaces, the dominant, highly romanticized archetype is that of the **"Militant Vanguard"**, a hyper-masculine, structurally violent figure whose moral utility is defined solely by aggressive combat, sectarian exclusion, and the destructive elimination of the designated "other". This vanguard is carefully designed to appeal to disenfranchised youth by offering them instant purpose, fraternal belonging, and a distorted path to spiritual validation.

Rather than offering dry, moralizing lectures that gamers routinely ignore, this model embeds the Islamic values of peace **(*Salam*),** systemic justice **(*Adl*),** and restorative mercy **(*Rahmah*)** directly into the protagonist's character arc and gameplay mechanics. By doing so, we transform the protagonist from an instrument of destructive violence into an active agent of ethical restoration, providing a compelling, playable alternative that neutralizes the psychological pull of radical narratives.

4.1 Deconstructing the "Militant Vanguard" in Extremist Game Designs

4.1.1 The Mechanics of Radical Romance

To construct an effective counter-model, we must first understand how radical groups design their protagonists. Extremist game modifications (mods) and proprietary software fail by accident; they utilize a highly calculated "procedural rhetoric" that reframes violence as a sacred duty.

Within these games, the protagonist's journey is systematically simplified into a binary conflict:

Purity (In-group) $\Longleftrightarrow$ Corruption (Out-group)

The "Militant Vanguard" is never forced to grapple with the human cost of their actions, the civilian fallout of structural damage, or the possibility of diplomatic resolution. Play mechanics are stripped of ethical choices leaving only shooting, conquering, and dominating, which are then rewarded with visual cues of religious triumph. This creates a dangerous cognitive loop where the young player begins to associate religious devotion with unchecked, aggressive violence.

4.2 The Blueprint of the "Ethical Hero"

The "Ethical Hero" is designed to disrupt this radical loop by introducing narrative complexity, emotional realism, and behavioral choices that align with classical Islamic virtue ethics.

4.2.1 Core Narrative Pillars of the Ethical Hero

Table 2.

Narrative Dimension	The "Militant Vanguard" (Destructive)	The "Ethical Hero" (Restorative)
Origin of Conflict	Simple victimhood leading to endless revenge.	Systemic breakdown requiring restoration of balance (*Mizan*).
Use of Force	Unrestricted, preemptive, and celebrated.	Defensive, highly restrained, and treated as a heavy burden.
Resolution Goal	Total elimination of the opposing faction.	Re-establishing peace (*Sulh*) and social harmony.
Success Metric	High body count and territory conquered.	Lives saved, communities rebuilt, and justice restored.

4.3 Playable Mechanics: Designing the "Akhlāq" Choice-Matrix

An ethical protagonist is defined not by cutscenes, but by **how they play**. The "Ethical Hero" model translates theological values into concrete, interactive gameplay mechanics.

4.3.1 Restorative Force and the "Mercy" Mechanic (*Rahmah*)

In typical action-adventure games, defeating an enemy results in their elimination. The "Ethical Hero" model introduces a **"Subduing and Mercy"** mechanic (Flanagan, M., 2009).

- **Defensive De-escalation:** The player's toolkit emphasizes defensive maneuvers, disarmament, and non-lethal subdual.

- **The Choice of Amnesty:** When high-value targets are defeated, the player is presented with a choice-matrix. Sparing an opponent and offering them justice under the law (*Adl*) unlocks diplomatic options, intelligence, and moral authority, whereas summarily executing them destabilizes the region and triggers negative narrative consequences.

4.3.2 Restorative Quests and Environmental Stewardship (*Khilāfah*)

Instead of focusing gameplay entirely on combat missions, the "Ethical Hero" engages in **Restorative Quests** that actively repair the virtual world.

- **Civilian Protection:** Protecting water treatment facilities, establishing safe refugee corridors, and rebuilding hospitals.
- **Cultural Preservation:** Safeguarding historical monuments, manuscripts, and multi-faith spaces from destruction, demonstrating that true defense of values involves preserving knowledge and cultural heritage.

4.4 Scripting the Hero: Translating Theology to Dialogue

To ensure the "Ethical Hero" resonates with South Asian and Pakistani youth, their dialogue must draw naturally from classical Islamic wisdom without sounding overly preachy or unnatural.

Scenario: The protagonist confronts a younger antagonist who has been manipulated into joining an extremist militia.

- **The Vanguard Approach:** *"You are a traitor and an apostate. You must be eliminated to purify this land."*
- **The Ethical Hero Approach:** *"They promised you dignity through a rifle, but they only brought you closer to ruin. True strength is not in taking a life, but in mastering your anger and building what others have broken. Lay down your weapon; your family is waiting for you to help rebuild."*

This approach directly echoes the famous prophetic definition of strength: "The strong man is not the one who wrestles well, but the one who controls himself in anger" (Al-Bukhārī, 1997). By framing restraint, emotional control, and patience (*Sabr*) as the ultimate forms of courage, the game design directly challenges the hyper-masculine appeal of radical propaganda.

The "Ethical Hero" is more than just a fictional character; it is a vital pedagogical tool for the digital age. By providing a playable, high-fidelity alternative to the "Militant Vanguard," we can show young gamers that the pursuit of justice does not require the destruction of their humanity. Through interactive mechanics that reward mercy, patience, and restoration, we can cultivate a generation of digital citizens who understand that true heroism lies in bringing peace to a broken world.

5. POLICY, PEDAGOGY, AND RESILIENCE: STRATEGIC FRAMEWORKS FOR PAKISTAN'S DIGITAL FRONTIER

The previous discussion established the theological and narrative blueprints required to reclaim virtual spaces, transitioning from the defensive posture of *Laghw* to a proactive design framework of *Digital Akhlaq*. However, theoretical paradigms and narrative models cannot succeed in a structural vacuum. To build a resilient digital ecosystem in Pakistan, we must translate these concepts into actionable policies, institutional curricula, and community driven initiatives.

This concluding discussion provides a dual-sector strategic roadmap designed for two of Pakistan's most influential institutional landscapes: the Ministry of Information Technology and Telecommunication (MoITT) and religious educational institutions (*Madaris*).

By bridging state-level policy with grassroots pedagogical reform, this chapter advocates for comprehensive "Digital Literacy" programs that equip Pakistani youth with the critical thinking skills needed to recognize, deconstruct, and reject radicalized game mechanics, extremist modifications, and toxic recruitment pipelines.

5.1 Policy Recommendations for the Ministry of IT and Telecommunication (MoITT)

To counter the weaponization of gaming platforms, Ministry of IT and Telecommunication (MoITT) must transition from passive internet censorship and blunt IP bans toward active digital ecosystem cultivation. The state must recognize the gaming industry not merely as an economic sector, but as a primary front for national soft power and cognitive security.

5.1.1 Implementing a Co-Regulatory Gaming Framework

- **Localized Content Advisory:** Rather than relying solely on global rating systems (such as PEGI or ESRB), Ministry of IT and Telecommunication (MoITT), in collaboration with the National Counter Terrorism Authority (NACTA), should establish a localized gaming advisory system. This system should evaluate multiplayer spaces not just for explicit content (violence/nudity), but for cognitive risks such as sectarian narrative hijacking and algorithmic extremist rabbit holes.

- **Active Platform Diplomacy:** The Pakistani state must establish formal communication channels with major gaming platforms (such as Steam, Epic Games, Roblox, and Discord) to flag extremist modifications (mods), radicalized custom servers, and coordinated grooming networks operating within national boundaries.

5.1.2 Stimulating the "Ethical Gaming" Sector in Pakistan

- **National Ethical Sandbox Grants:** Ministry of IT and Telecommunication (MoITT) should launch dedicated incubation funds for local game developers and modders who build high-fidelity interactive media promoting regional history, civic responsibility, and inter-communal harmony.
- **Supporting the Modding Economy:** Since extremist groups frequently exploit popular games (like *GTA V*, *Arma 3*, or *Roblox*) through custom mods, the state should sponsor national "Ethical Modding Hackathons". These events would challenge young Pakistani programmers and artists to design custom, pro-social modifications that introduce historical preservation, public service, and conflict-resolution mechanics into mainstream commercial games.

5.1.3 Pedagogical Reforms in religious educational institutions (*Madaris*)

With millions of youths enrolled in Pakistan's religious education system, *Madaris* represent a vital frontline for cultivating digital resilience (Qureshi, S. A., & Bukhari, M., 2025). Traditionally, religious institutions have treated digital media with skepticism, leaving their students vulnerable to online manipulation when they inevitably access digital devices (Khan, S. A., & Qureshi, M. L., 2025).

By integrating *Digital Akhlaq* into existing moral theology curricula, *Madaris* can empower a new generation of digital-literate scholars capable of guiding the community through contemporary virtual challenges.

Table 3. Educational Integration of Digital Ethics

Traditional Curriculum Focus	**Proposed Digital Integration**	**Pedagogical Outcome**
Hifz & Tafsir (Quranic Exegesis)	Applying Quranic warnings against *Laghw* and deception to online behavior.	Students recognize that ethical responsibilities do not vanish behind an anonymous screen.
Adab & Akhlaq (Moral Conduct)	Extending classical guidelines on speech and character (*Qawl Karīm*) to digital lobbies.	Cultivation of respect, fair play, and zero-tolerance for online toxicity and sectarian cyber-bullying.
Dawah Methodology (Preaching)	Training students to use interactive media, podcasts, and video games as spaces for positive values.	Transition from passive consumers of digital content to active, positive digital creators.

5.2 Designing a National "Digital Literacy and Resilience" Curriculum

To implement these institutional recommendations into one practical methodology, we propose a four-phase e-literacy and Resilience program. This sequence is to be realized in the networks of public schools, as well as in modernized religious education.

5.2.1 Deconstructing Game Mechanics: Module 1: Locating Procedural Rhetoric.

Playing teaches students how to persuade through games. They learn how games are designed with rules, reward loops, and points systems that make certain behaviors appear natural. They learn to spot when a game is covertly encouraging bias, dehumanization or sectarianism.

5.2.2 Decoding the 'Militant Vanguard' Archetype: Module 2: Narrative Analysis.

Young people learn psychological tricks in extremist game mods. They juxtapose the one-dimensional, violent, and exclusionary "Militant Vanguard" character model with the multi-dimensional, restorative, and merciful "Ethical Hero" model, revealing the false promises of radical romance.

5.2.3 The Cognitive Armor Protocol: Module 3: Behavioral De-escalation.

A practical guide to responding to signs of radicalization on gaming platforms. Students learn to recognize grooming tactics in multiplayer chat rooms, hate speech disguised as humor, and to develop safe reporting and boundary-setting strategies.

5.2.4 Ethical Content Generation: Module 4: Reclaiming the Sandbox.

In the last stage, students' progress from critical consumption to ethical creation. Students learn to design simple games, interactive stories and custom mods that promote peace, empathy and social cooperation using accessible, no-code game engines and modding toolkits.

The Digital Resilience Pledge: "Our virtual spaces are not moral vacuum. True strength lies not in digitally destroying the 'other' but in patiently and persistently upholding justice, truth and human dignity in every sandbox we inhabit."

The digital sandbox is one of the cultural battlefields of our time. Strategic state policy combined with progressive religious pedagogy can protect its youth from radicalization and empower them to become pioneers of an ethical, creative, values driven digital future.

6. TECHNICAL AND POLICY RECOMMENDATIONS

6.1 Linguistic Localization and Regional NLP Monitoring

In the regional context, online grooming and extremist recruitment are seldom in English or formal Urdu. Instead, recruiters in localized Discord channels, WhatsApp gaming groups, and in-game voice lobbies tactically use regional languages, such as Pashto, Balochi, Seraiki Punjabi and Sindhi, on top of specific cultural idioms and local grievances to gain the trust of disenfranchised youth.

- **Academic Integration:** We propose that the Ministry of IT and Telecommunication (MoITT) prioritize the development and integration of Local Language Natural Language Processing (NLP) **models**. Rather than relying on generic Western safety algorithms, Pakistan's cyber-monitoring frameworks must deploy sentiment analysis tools trained specifically on regional dialects to flag coordinated in-game manipulation before it escalates.

6.2 The “Madrasa Gaming Guild” (MGG) Pilot Project

Rather than advocating for defensive containment or internet restrictions that isolate religious youth, *Madaris* can actively lead digital spaces.

- **Academic Integration:** A structural framework for Madrasa Gaming Guilds (MGGs) is suggested. Madaris can create moderated Discord hubs and local server instances for IT-literate seminary students to manage, building safe and ethical multiplayer spaces. Rather than passive consumers, these students can engage with the broader online youth community, employing competitive play as a natural peer-to-peer channel for Dawah (invitation to values) and positive digital socialization.

6.3 The Digital Akhlāq Interactive Matrix

As an example of how design decisions immediately impact player psychology, we can walk through a conceptual “Digital Akhlaq Interactive Matrix.” This model illustrates the branching paths between the archetype of the “Militant Vanguard” and the “Ethical Hero” model, illustrating how in-game actions are mapped directly to ethical resilience or radical vulnerability.

CONCLUSION

Twenty-first century Pakistan is at a volatile crossroads for its digital ecosystem. It’s where a fast growing population, with a large youth bulge, intersects with exponential smartphone adoption, algorithmic polarization and long-running ideological proxy wars. For decades, counter-radicalisation strategies, both national and global, have operated within a paradigm of defensive securitisation, content censorship and post-facto de-radicalisation programmes.

As this volume has shown, these reactionary mechanisms keep missing the point. The fundamental human drivers of radicalization are the search for systemic meaning, the desire for agency, the appeal of clear moral order, and the cognitive need for immersive narrative frames.

Building Counter-Radicalization Narratives Through Islamic Values in Pakistan’s Digital Ecosystem has provided a radical paradigm shift and alternative by changing the analytical lens from prohibition to constructive play. Rather than view Pakistan’s digital youth culture as a passive vulnerability to be policed, this chapter has portrayed the digital environment as an active experiential laboratory.

Within this space, the extensive resources of Islamic ethical philosophy, especially the science of character (Akhlaq), cosmic justice (Adl), spiritual excellence (Ihsan), and restorative reconciliation (Sulh), can be turned into interactive, ludo narrative sandboxes. We are not just pushing back against extremist messaging but rather inoculating the digital soul against ideological manipulation.

REFERENCES

Al-Bukhārī, M. ibn Ismāʿīl. (1997). a ī al-Bukhārī. Dār al-Salām.

Al-Tirmidhī, M. ibn ʿĪsā. (2007). *Jāmi al-Tirmidhī* (N. al-Albānī, Ed.). Dār al-Salām.

Ali, R., & Zaidi, H. (2024). Algorithmic radicalization and the feedback loop of outrage on South Asian digital forums. *Media and Communication Studies Quarterly*, *11*(3), 145–167.

Anderson, C. A., & Bushman, B. J. (2001). Effects of violent video games on aggressive behavior, aggressive cognition, aggressive affect, physiological arousal, and prosocial behavior: A meta-analytic review of the scientific literature. *Psychological Science*, *12*(5), 353–359. DOI: 10.1111/1467-9280.00366 PMID: 11554666

Bogost, I. (2007). *Persuasive Games: The Expressive Power of Videogames*. MIT Press. DOI: 10.7551/mitpress/5334.001.0001

Bogost, I. (2008). The rhetoric of video games. Ecology of Games: Connecting Youth, Games, and Learning, 117–140.

Butt, N. A. (2024). Gaming as a coping mechanism: Psychological distress, loneliness, and virtual guilds in urban Lahore. *Clinical Psychology Digest Pakistan*, *6*(2), 89–103.

Cyber Security Authority of Pakistan (CSAP). (2025). *Emerging Digital Threats: Gamified Recruiting, Extremist Servers, and Networked Radicalization in the Domestic Ecosystem*. CSAP Annual Intelligence Review.

Esfahani, H. M. R. (1991). *Beijrut: Dar al-Elm* (1st ed.). Dar Al-Shamiah. [Mu'jam mufradat alfaz al-Qur'an]

Fatima, A., Ambreen, F., & Amin, R. (2024). Internet Gaming Disorder and Mental Health of Pakistani Adolescents: A Cross-Sectional Study. *Qlantic Journal of Social Sciences*, *5*(2), 13–25. DOI: 10.55737/qjss.119114325

Flanagan, M. (2009). *Critical Play: Radical Game Design*. MIT Press. DOI: 10.7551/mitpress/7678.001.0001

Hashmi, S. (2025). The erosion of vertical authority: How peer networks on Discord reshape political and moral beliefs among Pakistani teenagers. *Digital Policy & Governance Review*, *4*(2), 75–93.

Ibn Kathir, I. (2003). *Tafsir al-Qur'an al-Azim*. Dar al-Kutub al-Ilmiyah.

JPPS. (2026). Mental health community to brace for a newer gaming addiction. *Journal of Pakistan Psychiatric Society, 23*(1). https://jpps.pk/index.php/journal/article/view/759

Kaye, L. K., & Bryce, J. (2012). Putting the "fun" in video games: A qualitative focus group study of the social and psychological benefits of multiplayer gaming. *International Journal of Cyber Behavior, Psychology and Learning*, 2(4), 23–37.

Khan, F., & Rahman, U. (2024). Socioeconomic marginalization and the digital escape: A study of competitive mobile gaming in South Punjab. *Pakistan Economic and Social Review*, *62*(1), 112–135.

Khan, S. A., & Qureshi, M. L. (2025). Virtual tribalism: The reframing of Ummah as an exclusionary gaming clan identity among South Asian youth. *Journal of Global Media and Communication*, *21*(1), 88–105.

Latif, M. A. (2026). *Hybrid Conflict, Migration, and Health Inequities in the Afghanistan–Pakistan Region: Digital Geopolitics, Structural Violence, and Refugee Lives*. Springer Nature.

Latif, M. A.Muhammad Asad Latif. (2024). Terrorism New Wave: The Same Style but New Ways in the Context of Online Radicalization. *HISTORICAL: Journal of History and Social Sciences*, *3*(2), 169–180. DOI: 10.58355/historical.v3i2.109

Newhouse, A., & Kowert, R. (2024). Radicalization in the gaming ecosystem: The application of self-determination theory. *Journal of Digital Social Research*, *6*(1), 78–99.

Nisar, M. (2024). Modding conflict: An analysis of user-generated nationalist and sectarian content in popular tactical shooters in Pakistan. *Journal of Digital Warfare and Security*, *3*(4), 312–330.

Othman, A. (2025). The need for a Halal mode in video games: Ethical and cultural considerations. *ResearchGate*. https://www.researchgate.net/publication/389490207

Pakistan Software Export Board. (2024). Economic Potential of Online Gaming Industry in Pakistan. PSEB Industry Briefs.

Politopoulos, A., et al. (2019). "History is our playground": Action and pedagogy in the Assassin's Creed series. *Journal of Interactive Technology and Pedagogy, 15*.

Postigo, H. (2007). Of mods and modders: Chasing down the value of gamer modification. *Games and Culture*, 2(4), 300–313. DOI: 10.1177/1555412007307955

Pötzsch, H. (2017). Selective realism: Filtering war in military shooters. *Games and Culture*, *12*(2), 156–178. DOI: 10.1177/1555412015587802

Przybylski, A. K., Rigby, C. S., & Ryan, R. M. (2010). A motivational model of video game engagement. *Review of General Psychology*, *14*(2), 154–166. DOI: 10.1037/a0019440

Qureshi, S. A., & Bukhari, M. (2025). Peer bonds and psychological grooming: A network analysis of extremist Discord servers in Pakistan. *Strategic Intelligence Review*, *7*(1), 112–134.

Rizvi, T. (2025). Beyond Laghw: Educating Pakistani parents on the psychological and social architecture of multiplayer video games. *Family and Child Studies Journal*, *14*(2), 99–115.

Robinson, N. (2012). Videogames, militarism and relations of power in the global space. *International Political Sociology*, *6*(2), 109–124.

Scacchi, W. (2010). Computer game mods, modders, modding, and the mod scene. *First Monday*, *15*(5). Advance online publication. DOI: 10.5210/fm.v15i5.2965

Schlegel, L. (2020). Jumanji extremism? How games and gamification could facilitate radicalization processes. *Journal for Deradicalization*, *23*(2), 112–144.

Schut, K. (2013). *Of Games and God: A Christian Exploration of Video Games*. Brazos Press.

Sisler, V. (2008). Digital Arabs: Representation in video games and portrayal of the Middle East. *European Journal of Cultural Studies*, *11*(2), 203–220.

Thompson, J., & Lamphere-Englund, G. (2024). *Lethal Play: Modding, Extremism, and the Virtualization of Conflict*. SAGE Publications.

Turabi, R. F., Rozi, S., Sawani, S., Kazi, M., & Asad, N. (2025). Internet gaming disorder and violent video gameplay among higher secondary school-going adolescents in Karachi, Pakistan—A cross-sectional study. *PLOS Mental Health*, *2*(1), e0000179. DOI: 10.1371/journal.pmen.0000179 PMID: 41661772

UNICRI. (2026). *Checkpoint Reached: Preventing Violent Extremism and Online Gaming*. United Nations Interregional Crime and Justice Research Institute. https://unicri.org/News-Checkpoint-Reached-Preventing-Violent-Extremism-and-Online-Gaming

Vaux, A.. (2021). Extremist networking on digital marketplaces: From gaming environments to encrypted chat apps. *International Journal of Cybersecurity*, *9*(3), 201–218.

Yousaf, M., & Anwar, S. (2024). Online gaming subcultures in Karachi: Class dynamics, social validation, and the transition of play. *Journal of Sociology and Social Anthropology*, *12*(3), 210–229.

ENDNOTE

1 Al Furqan,25:72; Al Mu'minun,23:3; Al-Qasas, 28:55

Chapter 6
Memes, Irony, and Extremist Discourse in Gaming Communities: A Media Studies Analysis

Vaishali Panda
http://orcid.org/0009-0008-2493-308X
Amity University, Mumbai, India

Supratim Mukherjee
http://orcid.org/0009-0008-6657-891X
Amity University, Mumbai, India

ABSTRACT

This article analyzes how memes and irony mediate extremist discourse in gaming and gaming-adjacent online communities. Drawing on an integrative conceptual review of the supplied Scopus export, it synthesizes 25 eligible records from 2025 and 2026 on memetic culture, far-right subcultures, misogynistic humour, textboards, alt-tech livestreaming, moderation, digital nationalism, and games. Since the corpus contained 25 eligible records rather than 30, the study uses only the shared reference pool. It argues that extremist discourse rarely circulates only as explicit ideology. Instead, it moves through memetic-ironic mediation, where images, jokes, parody, insider references, and platform vernaculars make extremist meanings seem both playful and serious. This ambiguity enables deniability, bonding, boundary-making, and moderation difficulty. The framework links platform affordances, subcultural literacy, memetic compression, ironic ambiguity, antagonism, and governance response.

DOI: 10.4018/979-8-2600-1664-0.ch006

1. INTRODUCTION

Playing games is no longer simply for entertainment or engagement; it is also an official site for cultural specific practices of digital life. They allow people apart from their personal identity to show off while making slick moves, enable audiovisual musings, and platform-mediated communication-to instances of and very covertly, out-of-the-way forms in vernacular creativity. In fact, gaming communities must be taken as realms that seem to include the way of life for digital natives, belonging as they do to those who display an inveterate affinity for gaming. Only the big difference you might want from conventional media audiences of malevolent legacies is such communities have a lot of built-in exchange and loyalty between coadjutors. Virtual existence in the 'real' world or the meanings of game logic tends to converge. Nonetheless, the language of gaming comes into an entirely different discourse.

Apart from creating a facility for leisure recreation, gaming is now seen as a site of culture itself in terms of digital lifestyles as well. Similarly, these help people to make moves even without showing off their personal identity, which obviously streamlines audiovisual musings and couples it with platform-mediated communication-in short, from instances of very covertly out-of-the-way forms of vernacular creativity. Gaming enthusiasts or people just playing games can be considered as the majority of digital natives, due also to the fact that they possess inflamed likability to games. In contemporary popular reception, there is still a difference from conventional media audiences of malevolent legacies: big time built-in exchange and loyalty among coadjutors at such a location as this. Literally, virtual existence in 'real' world or the meanings of games logic co-converge under a generic genre adaption. But there exists yet another language of gaming.

Bugliosi (1995) has it that one can speak of the ground of the life's substance, its organization, some legal steps in setting up the investigation, and some aspects of law enforcement to be adhered to in investigation and apposite prosecution post an investigative report. Arguing that murder happened mistakes the fold as improper labeling of inflection calls on every citizen to best exploit his or her intelligence to use critical thinking mistakes as a means by-and-by terminated according to binding labels. erstwhile occasionally. Bilgi (1998), on the other hand, indicates that one can find the layers of ground life are substance, knack to organization, legal setting up in the investigation, and not a few matters concerning enforcement of would-be interventions into investigations made and ultimately into prosecution post of a report. Voluntary killing simply is about doing the wrong thing that regards that work into error within a fold which this was once called. From time to time.

A current important point, Ryder (2026) argues, is that most of the time, the extremist discourse in question is not directly or overtly presented as propaganda. Rather, it passes by as banter, nostalgia, mockery, parody, reaction images, ironic detachment, and playful antagonisms. One defines digital banter-now-that which would camouflage xenophobic, misogynistic, or extremist jibes under a locally popular humor (Ryder, 2026). Price (2025) uses the term 'dork/serious' for far-right memes that occupy spaces that are laughable enough to be deemed harmless but are at the same time rigorous enough in their construction to keep the community's coming together and in their recognition of common ideological standpoints. This duality seems important for gaming communities, where the ideas of playfulness, competitiveness, trolling, and performative antagonism could cause a conflation of an idea of joke, style, self, and political claim in practice.

Indeed, the focus on gaming communities should not be interpreted as an assertion that extremist speech can only be birthed within such boundaries. Recent trends indicate that rather than being interconnected yet cut-off ecosystems, game communities are more broadly spread across the various platforms. Discord servers, Twitch and Kick live streams, Reddit communities, Steam discussion boards, YouTube channels, anonymous text boards, and even short-form video circuits all provide ways to extend and echo game practices. It is no wonder, as Galip and Maragkou (2026) label it, that the environment of alt-tech live streaming involves an inseparable combination of parasociality, financial speculation, identity in the chat box, and the peculiarities of the extreme personae. It was found that, quoting from Lombardi (2025), "This toxicity cannot be explained only due to individuals, but platform architecture and affordances create antagonistic communication, too." This further complicates gaming-related extremism to be viewed as a media ecology rather than a feature that defines only the content of the game.

In this context, the collected literature possesses numerous direct research studies of far-right memetic culture, including Wood (2026) on far-right Discord servers, Fossberg and Fangen's (2025) study on weaponized humor on 4chan, Petersen and Johansen on hybridized preliminary extremism (also 2025), while De Cleen et al. (2025) provided a map of engagements with films, television, and video games by far-right people. Adiga and Padmakumar (2025) have been studying masculinity in online Indian Doge memes, Krogh et al. (2026) and González-Calvo et al. (2026) on teenage girl culture and shitpost perform femininity through memes.

These studies as a whole communicate the fact that memes should not just be taken as jests or decorations attached to political discourse; more so, they are condensed cultural forms that organize recognition, affect, ridicule, participation, and exclusion. Mememattters said a little more than other sayings could have meant in themselves, especially when meanings depended on insider familiarity with templates, references, platform histories, or political dog whistles. Future compass memes as combined mechanisms creating rearrangements of visual fragments into speculative constellations has been described by MH et al. [2026]. Even though on climate narratives and not extreme gaming talk, this more largely illustrates that memes are assemblages that gather pieces of culture to make maps of belonging and navigating opposition.

In this piece, it was proposed that the discussion regarding the extremist talk prevalent in gaming communities can be best understood within the categorization of memetic-ironic mediation. It refers to the way in which extremist or exclusionary interpretations are really mediated through the memetic structures and ironic framings, which engenders humor, excludes plausibility, happifies the audience, and renders interpretation some form of loadedness or other. Ironic mediation does not imply that all ironic memes are extremist or that all gaming communities automatically fall into the radicalizing space. Rather, it explains how meanings of extremism can use joke functions, circulation logistics of the platform, and subcultural literacies. The concept keeps room also for counter-memeticizing resistance or feminist reappropriations, civic denials, and political fun, as reported by Munk (2025), Mazumdar (2025), Krogh et al. (2026), and Chang (2025).

The primary contribution of this study falls in three dimensions. First, it amalgamates with sections on memes, irony in amplifying extremism, gender and gaming-related platforms meta-studies. Second, it moves past and contributes to the insufficient separation of harm from humour in theorising the categories of memetic extremes; and third, it constructs an agenda for future empirical research to guide qualitative discourse analysis, platform ethnography, multimodal analysis and moderation studies.

2. LITERATURE REVIEW

2.1 Memes as Compressed Cultural and Political Forms

Memetic works, as seen from the chosen data, function as rather densely compacted cultural forms that accentuate total ideology, affection, humor, and group membership portrayal into compactly transportable actants of media. Merrill et al. further describe that Reddit's r/DankLeft in their research of meme circles have members who consider using taboo- destruction not with comic irregularities alone but more of creating a political identity and affective response. Musih et al. (2037) say that in creating compass memes, in essence, combinatory machines: a good example is the eminently navigable value of memes that can combine diverse visual images, ideologies, and imaginative yet controversial positions into a single navigable object. This combinatory task is especially vital within any kinds of gaming communities because a huge number of the aforementioned pertains to shared visual culture, figure lore, game mechanics, screenshots, livestream happenings, and exclusive platforms' slang.

Memes are seldom one way or the other. He further explains politics without prop in hilarious and mimetic means of political videos not only offer resistance against basic ideas of digital nationalism but also expand them. For his part, Munk (2025) defines the memetic warfare as a form of civic resistance in information conflict. These were creatures that did not overly demonize memes as a medium or tool of social extremism. Indeed, with respect to the destination of a meme (i.e. its political side), this means the circulation community will aspect it, the affective charge attached to it, and the interpretive conventions through which it is read. Memes can be seen as problematic communicative infrastructures. They could be affirmative in terms of exclusionary politics but again good to interrupt hegemonic narratives, to support solidarity, or to provide civic defiance across bitterly democratic action.

Central to the benignit social soundstage are humour and remix. Weidhase and Wilde (2026) examine how zombie humor as material circulated on social media can be used to qualify culture critique and attempt to address mechanisms through which humorous reactions to conflict travel transnationally and are adapted across national contexts (Fiadotava et al., 2025). These are all things that suggest the mobility and context-sensitivity of memetic humor. When located within gaming communities, the implications are multiplied beyond measure as the very mobility of humor shifts to realms where gaming worlds are transnational, multilingual, and deeply plugged into visual and audio formats. A meme birthed within a forum can move to a Discord server, turn up in a stream chat, become a YouTube clip, and then be reintroduced into the game as a recognizable joke.

This demonstrates that memes are not arbitrary texts as media objects. "It matters how a meme is produced, circulated, remixed, interpreted, archived, and so on. This processual view helps in not reading too much into individual images but also recognizing that memes and ideology still do work." Price (2036) is especially useful in this connection because the silly/serious distinction is precisely what the far-right communities can employ to appropriate memes that would otherwise appear too trivial into constructing affective homes and boundaries. A gaming community may create its boundaries with ironic team names, avatar symbols, factional jokes, Discord emojis, mock heroic nostalgia, or irony around out-group derision.

2.2 Irony, Banter, and the Politics of Plausible Deniability

The flesh of extremist discourse, irony is one such animal which lies at its core that enables users to suspend fixed accountability toward meaning. Ryder's (2026) concept of digital banter is valuable as it defines how racism, misogyny, and xenophobia can be masked under humour that appears informal, localized, and playful.

In the same way, Iranzo-Cabrera et al. (2025) demonstrate how irony can be used as an attack technique in a harshly polarized environment, especially in cases of ugly and vile attacks against women politicians. These studies insist greatly on irony not as an issue of style, but as there can even exist irony at the crossroads of certain technology itself within politics, becoming a delegitimation technology.

Research-oriented conceptualization of the existence traces back to Price 2025, as much as alluding to it by explaining far-right memes in quasi-juxtaposed setup of silly and serious spaces. But the greater point made is that it contains the rejection of an insufficient reflex.

When taken to task on its part, it escapes the moral alarms, forcing consideration of everything a form of serious ideological propaganda. By mere perspective, humorous discourses are meant to mean nothing since they are only meant for a laugh. The borderings of the silly/serious frame are especially apt in that performative antagonism, mock combat, role-play, leaderboard competition, and trash talk and identity playfulness are often naturalized in game spaces. These are elements of discourse by which certain ideas make use of their form to hide behind meanings. Extriimit movements can use these communicative conventions to mask their ideologies as gaming humor.

Adiga and Padmakumar (2025) add a dimension of gender to that analysis when they show that Indian Doge memes, themselves a combination of vernacular humour, dirty sex jokes, dark humour, and of course the representation of women within online masculinity. It does not focus on gaming, yet its implications for such communities are direct: it is the case that meme cultures also construct masculine belonging with the sharing of mutual ridicule and sexualized humour; indeed, by normalising offensive content, meme cultures through shitposting extend the limits of both what jokes are acceptable and which symbolic resources mainstream social groups can entertain in the sense of identity performances. Krogh et al. (2026), on the other hand, demonstrate how shitposting can also become a form of unspectacular resistance by adolescent girls against emphasised femininities. The White Feminist students I know understand 'intersectionality' but start fights every time a woman of color points it out. Consequently, while irony and shitposting cannot be accorded a singular political meaning, they are rights in themselves.

One possible form of negative space arises from the use of ironic rhetorical defenses by extremists or exclusionists. If required to do so, the speaker could claim that he was only speaking as a throwback joke, as part of trolling or edgy humor, or illegitimately interpreted by outsiders. Nevertheless, interpretation remains skewed in favor of the communication regarding some: insider understand the given code, while critics suffer in being taken as a humorless outsider or as ignorant of cultural capital. Such reciprocal systems maintain comparison against Wood's (2026) study on far-right Discord servers where nostalgia mediates invitations to fascism in a memetic style. They also found Fossberg and Fangen's (2025) observations of weaponized humor on 4chan with "far-right boundary work" as "ludic" genre, where ridicule, misogyny, transphobia, and antisemitic invectives are used.

2.3 Extremist Discourse, Hybridization, and Far-Right Subcultural Formation

Incitements in the literature are very explicit; they do not follow any manifestos of ideological beliefs. They describe examples of hybridized prefatory extremism. In its current form, it is argued how social media might complicate traditional classifications of terrorist threats: hybrid communities often give birth to extremist content, conspiratical overlay, and purposively complex networked practices. This kind of thinking is particularly important for gaming communities, where political identity can be woven into jokes, aesthetics, anti-fandom, streamer personas, avatar cultures, and non-public political issues discussed.

Karas (2025) theorized that cultural criminology can be a desideratum to the violent counter-extremistism in light of the new extreme right frau the humanities, culture, subcultures, style, body practice, and affect. This point is central for the purposes of this paper. Far-right communication is as seductive through its sense; that is, it tends to please, tease, amuse through irony, share its disgust in order to perpetrate, and allow some experience in vanquishing limits. Indeed, the far right constructs appetite through aesthetic enjoyment, irony, shared hostility, and thrill of trespass. Wood's (2026) study of mediated nostalgia in the far-right Discord servers demonstrates how memory, affect, and platformed mediation can produce white invitations for fascism without any conventional script for recruitment.

Fossberg and Fangen (2025) also illustrated that memes rolling around the far-right discussions about the RussoUkrainian warfare, can utilize anti-Semitic humor, and also misogyny and transphobia, thus construct a form of masculinity whereby hierarchies are inherent. The nature of their study shows how the extremist talk occurs not through rational exposition of ideology, but hardly something like dehumanization, feminization of enemies, and ridicule. Even in gaming, these events would possibly occur because the act of playing competitively might be structured and depicted through readily available images of enemies, factions, victory, humiliation, strength, and weakness, which were all derived from the vast library of military-medial imagery currently available. It isn't that gaming or games could perpetuate and harden the right-wing ideological stances; instead, the aesthetics of gaming become add-ons in meaning-making for extremists in cooperation with platforms of irony and identity.

According to De Cleen et al. (2025), the strongest and most straightforward links concern film, television or video game events with right-wing populism, if not far-right movements. They lament that visual fiction was given so little space in an extreme right study, even though pop cultural worlds have myths, symbols, characters, and affective scripts on which to build political identities. Building upon this insight, the respondents to the survey understand gaming communities as a part of the broader audio-visual and participatory media environment. Games are not simply the text received by the player, but transmutable by so many conjunctions, which more likely form memes and clips, commentary, cosplay, live streaming, modding, discourse of fans, and political encroachments.

Digital Replacement's wagering culture gives birth to an important kind of understanding: the digital banter, as well as a dealer of it. A political anti-fandom along with memetic ecologies induces hate, shitposting, and monetized attention to reproduce extremist attitudes when observed on Bitchute, a site nongamer culture that has, however, a very strong resemblance of identity performance with humor and outrages that surely bring in some profit. During its era, extremifying that distinction into an argument between ideological and economic, attention, subscriptions, clips, and merch find their profitable way into the contention of the very provocative speech.

2.4 Platform Affordances, Moderation, and Gaming-Adjacent Ecologies

The affordances of the platform do drive the concrete terms to which the dimensions of visibility, intensity, and durability of hate speech get fixed. According to Lombardi, toxicities in anonymous textboards are structural constructions given by the space that users inhabit within platform archel. Åkerlund (2025) showed how a surgeon in act on intent of free speech ended up creating a massive disconnect between platform justifications and user imaginaries about what moderation actually means on specific toolshed. The studies become more important because it is a recurring phenomenon for gaming communities to jump around platforms, moving to those with different cultures in moderation. A meme might not pass muster on one but be allowable in another-and algorithmically amplified and stored on a forum for eternity.

Most famous are the videos within the livestream phenomenon called but adjacent to gaming. Extending their arguments in “Kick”, these conditions of possibility work together in order to facilitate extreme persona affect, as this alliance allows for an intersection of parasocial affordances, financial incentives, speculative communities, and permissive moderation. The livestream chat is anything but a purely receptive audience channel but rather the participatory infrastructure in which vernacular tests are ratified, while jokes are chiselled into the mental furniture of clip-worthy moments and those identities are fashioned collectively. As the chatbox incorporated language belonging to the extremes or realms of the manosphere transferred from it, therefore, these terms will become very quickly naturalized in their repetitive giggles, donations, and streamer feedback.

MacDowell (2025) is an investigation that though not specifically about extremsim places online video narration into this ecology of meaning. YouTube's intimate direct address and audiovisual narration lead users to digital creators and their authority. In the case of gaming cultures-limited response, this address takes on a very particularity within parasocial identifications that magnify forms of such addresses by commentator of streaming, reaction humour, and political banter, into inordinately influential factors for community norms. Murthy et al. (2026) will take this subject to its logical conclusion by asking whether generative AI can understand social media posts about Trump as well as humans Other than the brute fact of resolving (or not) the particular challenge that Trump presents, the treatment in the case of Trump is instructively indicative of the difficulty of automating analysis of this kind of volatile political discourse.

On the one hand, the difficulty of analyzing volatile political discourse on social media is well defined. Methodological problems abound in both automatic moderation and academic analysis because of the existence of irony and context.

In this light, moderation is a different kind of problem: rather than locating radical meanings in a single explicit phrase, these meanings may come across in memes, comments, emojis, usernames, clip titles, visual references, and in-group codes. Åkerlund's (2025) discussion of nonaction and Lombardi's (2025) structural toxicity suggest that neutrality is impossible for platforms to claim. Their design interface, deletion policies, anonymity structures, revenue models, and moderation philosophies help create the communication atmosphere through which extremist speech is communicated.

2.5 Gender, Misogyny, and Identity Policing

Gender is not something marginal; it is one of the logics around which memetic extremism is organized. Further, Adiga and Padmakumar (2025) trace the manner in which a video Doge meme featured in Indian meme culture speaks about online masculinity through sexual humour and representation of women(s) offensively. And according to Fossberg and Fangen (2025), far-right war memes reproduce militarized masculinity by ridiculing women, trans persons, and enemies as feminized or degenerate. Iranzo-Cabrera et al. (2025) suggests that hate speech against women politicians mixes polarization, inadmissible language, and irony as an attack technique. Common in all of the studies is the view that gendered hatred is not only a case of pure toxicity; it is necessary to understand proper boundaries within extremist or exclusionary digital communities.

Masculinities have long been associated within contesting gaming cultures, and the chosen corpus is able to address such issues without referring to or relying on older or external sources. In their study on girlism and girl power in new feminisms, Krogh et al. (2026) show that girls can use shitposting to comrades who resist, demonstrate that memes and culture itself is a communicable representation of ironic critique spaces-for negotiating femininity and body politics-through the major representational fields and within vast hegemony constructions. González-Calvo et al.'s (2026) work expands these notions to include girls' ironic and critical meme culture activism for negotiating femininity and body politics. Chang's article suggests that feminist activists are creating safe spaces online in response to misogynistic and censorship grave consequences that could follow such activism. The effectiveness of these spaces for users depends on the strategies performed by them to remain visible, connected, and politically active, as she argues. Those working toward feminists' non-structural separatism might see how memes and humor could be gender-specific and, in that sense, harmfully sanctified.

Analytically, it depicts the juxtaposition of misogynistic memetics encouraged by a feminist memetic resistance. This stops the paper from treating digital humor as one-directional radicalization. Instead, humor is now understood as a contested terrain. In some video or online gaming communities, jokes exploiting gender, race, sexual orientation, or nationality may well serve to reinforce hierarchies of exclusion. In other cases, parody and irony allow those very hierarchies to be exposed, build collectivity or undo the normative femininity. The task of media studies, then, becomes to analyze not just how meme has offended but rather how it works: who is permitted to laugh, who is the target, what knowing is necessary to understand the joke and what social order is upheld--or upturned--by its circulation.

3. RESEARCH GAP

Aptly reviewed literature is enriched embracing memes, humour, far-right discourse, toxic speech, platform affordances, gendered online hostility and audiovisual fiction. The relationship between memes, irony, extremist discourse, and gaming communities is less integrated. Various studies wax about meme-tic (Fossberg and Fangen, 2025; Price, 2025; Wood, 2026) far-right politics while others delve into the toxicity and moderation of the platform Lundardi (2025) deals with platform toxicity. and moderation while Åkerlund (2025) worked on what this might look like on social media platforms in real life and towards people who do not belong to their target group. Clearly, De Cleen et al. (2025) identify video games among other audio urges by the far right. With this, such movements could be any types of transmedia as far as ironic memes would just move through these gaming-adjacent platforms.

It is noteworthy that the gap is conceptual rather than simply empirical; often, existing research regards memes, extremism, and platforms as separate domains. Thus, memes are studied mainly as visual culture or political humour, extremism through radicalisation, far-right subcultures, or counter-extremism in general, and even gaming through audiovisual fiction or practice community, while platforms through moderation and affordance are the most useful variables. What is left under-researched here is an account of how memetic humour and ironic deniability mediate meaning in extremist gaming cultures simultaneously playful, commercial, participatory, and politically porous.

Another gap has to do with the absurd/tragic dichotomy. Price (2025) and Ryder (2026)'s concept is quite rich and excellent in terms of theory advancement but it requires much more work for its application in gaming communities where play is not a boundary; it rather stands as the organized cultural form. In these spaces, the dismissal of a matter as superficiality bolstered by a broader ludic environment. In such a case, a media-studies analysis should provide an explanation of how the synergy between ludic norms, memetic compression, platform architecture, and subcultural literacy constructs extremist discourse at the same time disavowable and socially meaningful.

A third vacuum occurs in regard to the gender factor. In the body of work on the memetic masculinity aetiology and consequent chauvinism or feminist resistance's mechanics, there was something about gaming community and extreme discourse together they were articulated not necessarily connected. However, gendered boundary-making in the area has been part and parcel of exclusion built around gaming related subject matter and far-right aesthetics. A memetic extremism framework must include debate about how gendered logics in conjunction with racial identities frame those who are insiders, enemies, or legitimate speakers.

Finally, there are some lacunae in methodology. According to an example by Murthy et al. (2026), irony, context, and coded meanings might be difficult for computational analysis to pick and up. Indeed, simple textual analysis can fail to detect those affordances built into platforms and trails of circulation. For future research to be run as effectively as possible, it has to draw upon mixed qualitative architecture: multimodal discourse analysis, site walk throughs, digital ethnography, and, again, sensitivity to moderation contexts.

4. OBJECTIVES AND RESEARCH QUESTIONS

The purpose of a well-founded analysis on media is to explain how memes and irony function in weaving extremism into forms and meanings in the gaming and gaming-adjacent online spaces. The paper abdicates the "Do games cause kids to kill?" question and instead focuses on how communicative practices within gaming cultures give rise to different, core extremist meanings that make the undesirable desirable through being irreproachable, emotionally appealing, or contestable.

The research is guided by four particular research questions, which are: 1) How do memes and ironic formats mediate extremist discourse within gaming or adjacent online gaming communities? 2) What affordances and subcultural practices of the platform enable such meanings to appear simultaneously as humor, play, and politics? 3) How do gendered and racialized repertoires shape memetic extremist discourse as well as that of counter-discourse? 4) What conceptual framework can offer an explanation for the interpretation of how memetic form interacts with ironic ambiguity, platform ecology, and governance response?

5. METHODOLOGY

According to the research design, it will be a theoretical-integrative review, or rather, integrative conceptual review. This methodology is critical because it will not count the number of extremist memes from a variety of sources in a single platform but synthesizes emergent perceptive works into a conceptual framework for future empirical media studies. The collection is on the export of Scopus that has been downloaded for this particular event. The export will contain only 25 records, but, then again, not 30 stuff, since the "sharing of papers alone" used by the user's instruction, as meant, was to be the related papers, beside not being from any other source, not the other sources in that notebook. The review uses all the 25 records loaded in the corpus uploaded.

The collection is fairly recent, having most of its data found in 2025 and 2026. This newness of the collection permits more extensive reflections on debates concerning alt-tech livestreaming, hybrid extremism, platform affordances, memetic warfare, content moderation, and far-right engagement with audiovisual fiction under conditions of changing platform governance and the post-normalization of digital post-ironies. This temporal range is restricted in terms of treating broadly the historical unfolding of already established gaming communities and extremist discourse. Instead, the article, seeing itself as a synthesis of a focused corpus, will offer a conceptual review of the already existent scholarship on the issues raised under memes, games, and extremism, rather than a catalog of all available scholarship.

Those four phases are clarified by the procedure: first, to read bibliographic metadata, abstracts, author keywords, source titles, document types so as to determine how far the contribution is constructed within them; second, coding for each one concerning its major contribution: memetic in culture, irony and humour, far right or extremism in talk, affordances of the platform, gender and masculinity, content moderation, and fiction in audiovisual-or games, war, and nationalism, and opposition or counter-discourse. Codes were then abductively compared with the four concepts for the central article on memetic-ironic mediation, silly/serious ambiguity, platform ecology, and gendered boundary-making. Fourth, the synthesis was put into a conceptual framework that could already be operationalised in future empirical work.

The research depends on the title, abstract, keywords, and bibliographic information from an export from Scopus. This fact implies that the review is transparent, though limited; neither does it pretend to have full-text coded every article, nor to assert that the corpus selected represents the global literature in full. However, the corpus presents all good, recent studies in journals like The New Media & Society, Social Media + Society, Convergence, Information, Communication & Society, Crime, Media, Culture, International Political Sociology & Journal of Gender Studies and Television & New Media that have shown that it provides a bonafide base for a concept article of media-studies oriented toward theory development.

Table 1. Corpus coding of the uploaded Scopus review base

Source	Primary focus	Analytical use in this article
Ryder (2026)	Digital banter, xenophobia, misogyny, extremism	Defines banter as a veil for extremist hostility and monetized political anti-fandom.
Adiga & Padmakumar (2025)	Meme culture, manosphere, online masculinity	Shows how dark humour and offensive memetics construct masculine belonging.
Kasianenko (2025)	Visibility practices, war, moral paradoxes	Frames platform visibility as ethically contested participation.
Murthy et al. (2026)	AI, political posts, sentiment, social media	Highlights the difficulty of computationally interpreting volatile political discourse.
Wood (2026)	Far-right Discord, mediated nostalgia, memes	Links platform mediation, affect, nostalgia, and invitations to fascism.
Fiadotava et al. (2025)	Transnational humour and conflict	Shows how humour travels and is adapted across national contexts.
MacDowell (2025)	YouTube direct address and narration	Informs analysis of creator intimacy and audiovisual online communication.
Krogh et al. (2026)	Girl culture, shitposting, resistance	Demonstrates that shitposting can be a mode of gendered resistance.

continued on following page

Table 1. Continued

Source	Primary focus	Analytical use in this article
Kosonen & Löf (2025)	Toxic speech, activism, gendered delegitimation	Clarifies affective and gendered forms of hostile political speech.
Lombardi (2025)	Anonymous textboards, structural toxicity	Explains toxicity through platform architecture and affordances.
Munk (2025)	Memetic warfare, civic resistance	Shows memes as tools of information conflict and counter-discourse.
Merrill et al. (2025)	Reddit memes, taboo, radical left	Explains taboo-breaking and emotional reception in meme communities.
Petersen & Johansen (2025)	Hybridized prefatory extremism	Offers a model for ambiguous, hybrid extremist spaces on social media.
Karas (2025)	Cultural criminology and far right	Provides a cultural, affective corrective to narrow counter-extremism models.
Weidhase & Wilde (2026)	Zombie humour, remix, cultural critique	Shows humour as critique within social media events.
De Cleen et al. (2025)	Far right, audiovisual fiction, games	Directly positions video games within far-right media engagement.
Chang (2025)	Feminist safe spaces, misogyny, censorship	Adds resistance and safety strategies in hostile online environments.
Åkerlund (2025)	Free speech forum, moderation, hate speech	Shows how platform inaction and moderation imaginaries shape discourse.
Musih et al. (2026)	Memes, political imagination, technical images	Conceptualizes memes as combinatory mechanisms.
Fossberg & Fangen (2025)	4chan, far-right memes, militarized masculinity	Demonstrates weaponized humour, gender hierarchy, and dehumanization.
Iranzo-Cabrera et al. (2025)	Hate speech, irony, polarization, NLP	Shows irony and hostility in gendered political discourse.
Price (2025)	Far-right memes, silly/serious spaces	Provides the central silly/serious framework for memetic extremism.
Galip & Maragkou (2026)	Alt-tech livestreaming, chatbox sociality	Explains how extreme personae and chat cultures normalize vernaculars.
Mazumdar (2025)	Politics as fun, digital nationalism, mimesis	Frames fun as a political mode that can resist or extend nationalism.
González-Calvo et al. (2026)	Memetic femininity, gender performance	Shows memes as spaces for doing and undoing gender.

Source note. Author's synthesis based exclusively on the uploaded Scopus export supplied for the present manuscript.

6. ANALYSIS AND DISCUSSION

6.1 Corpus Profile and Thematic Distribution

The corpus extracted is strikingly current. Thus, it can be shown that the records are clustered around 2025 and 2026, again highlighting that the topic is an active part of a quickly immemorial scholarly conversation. The predominance of more recent works is quite methodologically useful mostly because cultures, practices to livestream broadcasts, and movements associated with memetic extremists change quite rapidly. This, however, means at the same time that the manuscript here in hand is not at all meant that historicity would approach but instead regarded as an intervention timely in conceptual terms.

Figure 1. Distribution of the selected Scopus corpus by publication year

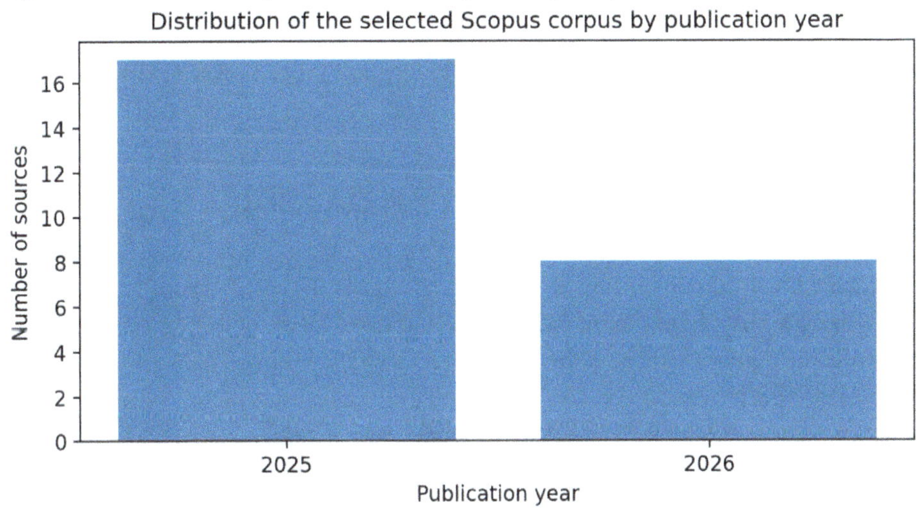

Source note. Generated from the uploaded Scopus export; n = 25 records.

Figure 2 presents the thematic emphasis of the corpus using multiple coding, since many articles contribute to more than one area. The strongest clusters are memes and humour, extremist discourse, platform affordances, and gender or masculinity. This distribution supports the paper's central claim that memetic extremism cannot be reduced to ideology alone. It is produced at the intersection of communicative form, platform environment, affective style, and identity politics.

Figure 2. Dominant thematic emphases within the selected Scopus corpus

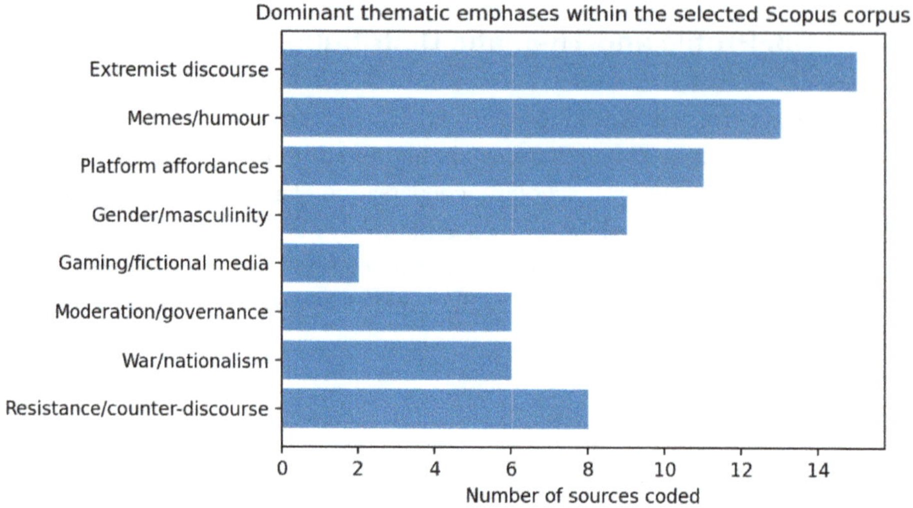

Source note. Multiple thematic coding conducted by the author using the uploaded Scopus export; one source could be coded into more than one category.

6.2 Memetic-Ironic Mediation as a Communicative Process

Emphasis on demonstrating the central synthesis, although there is a frequent claim for extremists being more dialectical, mediated forms of extremist discourses alongside the gaming culture rather than direct manifestation. The mediatization of the ironic meme is composed of subculturing entry, clear memetics, ironic ambiguity, emotional border making, and the resistance or normalization of discourse. One example where this may occur is when one enters a gaming site or something like a gaming site where it seems that a limited number of templates, jokes, references, and behaviours are well-known. A high level of proficiency in this world forces upon one how well he or she may understand it. Authority rests with those who have the text and the keys to the codes of access; a welcome residence closes its gates to those who do not.

By compressing specifically memetic, complex ideological or emotional positions, rather than a simple look and language, memes condense and represent an extremely small, though not unsubstantial, hostility against women, politically radicalized groups, or even activists or sexual minorities. They have a humoristic "light touch" to them, distancing the joke from being taken as a direct statement. Pithy (2026) shows how digital banter hides xenophobia, and Fossberg and Fangen (2025) demonstrate how memes use humour to dehumanize enemies and, more crucially, support the reproduction of far-right masculinities. Among game players, the means of such compression might usually include reaction images, figures, avatar insignia, factional jokes, manipulated game dialogue, or ironic reference to the one's own superiority (gaming or wry, acrid comment on different levels of play), throwing in the face even while often narrating self-deprecation through competitiveness.

It is Forget your notting serious play to complain with seriously. And just Don't Surrealism Memes do they mean? In its memory Fast already is a manner—there's a recollection worth the taxpayer paying their country's Home Office to join the US Government's redirection of funds failures. Or shall we tell the world about 2000 years of cumulative decrepitude? Really?

1600's play lies, but humour in Price's (2025) performative sense. That would then return people's attention to the game of saying bad things in good humor, a magic switch thrown; now you just had to hold it over and over again. More specifically, play develops innuendo in his funny and breathtaking commercials that enable some truth that we commonly forget (and he will almost always receive praise from critics who don't get it while being denied attention in very few ways).

Humor can discipline people when they come from the affective boundary. It would decide who makes a laugh, who joins the clan, and who is free to attack. Memes give this all away." It shows how meme culture begins shaping an online masculinity with its images of women and crude humor. It used virtually any available resource to construct online masculinity. Kosonen and Löf offer an example for 2025, where gender and political hostility result in activism destabilization by labeling activism as very weak speech act per se, open to ridicule and thus not meriting further recognition within the juridical work of politics that is to be considered as fuck politics. These mechanisms lie not outside the extremist discourse but in the mundane affective mechanisms that make up extremist communities. For many extremists, every member is not required to become a full-fledged ideologue. It may be enough to turn the verbs of extreme disrespect--such as contempt, ridicule, and dehumanization--into everyday humor.

When one's goals become normalization or resistance, memetic forms make extremist normalization easy, acceptable, repeatable, even deniable with a single touch. It can be seen that the very formality does this to counter-disclosure as well. As shown by Munk (2025), memes call attention to the idea that memes can be used in civic struggles; Krogh et al. (2026), González-Calvo et al. (2026), Chang (2025), and Mazumdar (2025), on the other hand, present examples of the resisting, feminist, or anti-hegemonic uses of humour and play in digital technology. It should be taken into consideration that a robust paradigm would transcend technological determinism. The fact that irony and memes do not automatically make one radical does not make them irrelevant; they just serve as a medium through which a power struggle between the existing orders can be elaborated.

6.3 Gaming Communities as Porous Platform Ecologies

The term game communities had smacking of some semiboundedness within games themselves. Those traditions, however, lean toward leakage- porously articulated media ecologies. De Cleen et al. (2025) showed video games within a wider area of far-right attachment through audiovisual fiction. Galip and Maragkou (2026) present livestream chatboxes that can turn into speculation communal places wherein extreme vernaculars are tried, certified, and, finally, diffused to a wider audience. Lombardi (2025) and Åkerlund (2025) disclosed that both platform architecture and moderation policy entirely create user behavior. Also, these findings point out that game communities are often traversing various infrastructures all simultaneously;

Porousness is important because it allows hate speech to move strategically between platforms. When a meme is too explicit for mainstream platforms, it may be refined in an anonymous textboard, disseminated in a Discord server, thought up in a live stream chat, clipped into a short form video, and then reintroduced back into mainstream audiences with a cloak of ambiguity. Migration from one platform to another lets content mutate in both form and power. Hijinx in one context, connection by ideology in another, a monetized spectacle in still another, or legitimate evidence of community-ness are what one encounters.

The different way it functions with a lot within gaming culture already involves the normalization of layered participations. A person can be both a player and a viewer, modder, streamer, member of forums, active meme creator, participant in esports, Discord member, and YouTube watcher at the same time. This "participation across various platforms" brings forth a sort of ambient subcultural literacy: learning to recognize jokes, symbols, and antagonisms with repetitive exposures across settings. When extremist discourse binds itself to this literacy, there is no need for at all a clear doctrine. It can work as atmosphere, style, and group taste.

And so the whole focus on Wood's work when he deliberated on far-right Discord servers cannot be any more apposite. This is because Discord is the dominant infrastructure in any number of gaming communities. Such a server-based spatialization structure is so intensive that it ensures pseudo-private spaces with a variety of layered channels, roles, history, smileys, and typified internal norms. Despite these, Discord is not an inherently extremist space but a poor specter for which community norms and governance related to moderation and the formation of subcultures are always less visible than their counterparts from open feeds. For this, more mediated nostalgia and memetic style can provide the opportunity for political belonging without the trappings of formal recruitment.

Livestreaming heightens the depth and adds elements of participation additional to mere attendance. Furthermore, Galip and Margkakis (2026) refer to "content in sociality" in chatbox sociality. The co-creators of mood, identity, and vernacular legitimacy will not only ingest audiences of livestream. Chat messages, emotes, contributions and streamer reactions associated with games can amplify jokes instantaneously. When you encounter yet another example of extremist or misogynistic humour in chat, either the streamer can respond with suppression, normalization or flipping into another potential community reference. So it is not just a technical filter, but also a cultural policing.

6.4 Gendered Hostility, Militarized Masculinity, and the Aesthetics of Humiliation

Extremist discourse often draws on gender-based humiliation, as brought out in reiteration across the range. Mimeticized representations of war in far-right memes (Fossberg and Fangen, 2025) create hierarchies of masculinity by feminizing enemies and making fun of the weak. Such themes are illustrated in Adiga and Padmakumar's (2025) analysis of online masculinity using humor-some sexual, others divisive-of the portrayal of women in memes. This has a counterpart in Iranzo-Cabrera et al.'s demonstration that irony can become a weapon against women politicians within men's hate speech. The ownership of these threads lies with those texts: Misogyny is not an accidental byproduct of online extremism, but one of its structuring emotional repertoires.

Acts that generally may accentuate one's gamer identity-hat is, a drive of performance in competitive aspects. In order to say it out loud, gaming communities might definitely become supportive of these repertoires, acknowledging competitive performance, masculine authenticity, or verbal dominance as signs of status. The problem with competition itself is not what the ideal invention is, but when this playful aggression spreads into broader ideologies of hierarchy, exclusion, and contempt. From there, memes can take their toll, coopting political misogyny into a supposedly quarrelsome profane or skill discourse and competitive exchange where fans should be banned. This also excellent of Ryder (2026) explains beliefs that discourage political anti-fans, which may well be seen in similar anti-fan dynamics occurring as characteristics of gaming cultures: they can band up against some characters, streamers, developers, feminist critics or identity-based figureheads in a more metaphorical practice.

Yet references resistance in the corpus; Krogh et al. (2026) find that the girls can cite adolescent shitposting when discussing femininity, yet triggering this case of mimicry doesn't merely tighten. Another example is the work of González-Calvo et al. (2026), who differentiate memes in helping reconfigure women's own narration of and resistance against the norms of the body. Chang (2025) probes how Chinese networked feminist activation forges self-censorship strategies and safe places on site to counter misogyny or government censorship. These studies further indicate that feminist and resistant memetics aren't just byproducts of toxicity; they're forms of action on a cultural level. Within gaming communities, feminist memes, ironic counter-speech, and community care practices can crit the limits that others have put: alongside them, unlock the disallowance or seriousness of overlap and playfulness.

This distinction itself is truthful for a thorough examination. Since memes have been spent too much time describing only as instruments for violent extremist mobilization, these are not the wrong things you just might use memes for. The truer claim is that memes are powerful, efficient tools to create boundaries across culture. In fact, extremists use them to create boundaries through ridicule and contempt, while rebels gallantly make use of them in building boundaries of solidarity, critique, and safety. The politics of a meme lie not only in its content but its relational functioning.

6.5 Content Moderation and the Problem of Ironic Ambiguity

Ambiguity is the most persistent kind that arises mainly from the ironic twists that follow from it. If one thinks about moderating hate speech, this often comes to identifying either clearly marked expressions or clear targets-from which definitions have been made-or propositional content which is negatively assessed on the basis of policy-violating claims. But a problem is also put before these: memetic extremism. Memetic extremism complicates this neat model as often, the sense in them lies in the distribution of an image template, usage of symbols, context, people's knowledge, and even history of application. A single meme uncontaminated by what is kept in the files of the community is just not harmful. While if moderation is an overbroad reaction, probably the best satirical expressions, feminist reappropriation, or anti-extremist counter-memetics mislead detection as harmful. It is not about just detection but interpretation also.

Åkerlund's study will find that a free-speech forum can bring entirely different implications from the imaginations that users tend into it, suggesting that platforms have motives that are unique in justifying non-intervention. It is most notable that structural toxicity is produced through affordances but not merely intent of the user as held by Lombardi (2025). These implications label moderation not a neutral, relatively minor adjustment but part of the communicative infrastructure. Moderation is linked to such values as anonymity, permanence, permissiveness, or spectacle on a platform, which could be indirectly held responsible for the infiltration of extremists, all the time asserting neutrality.

Murthy et al. (2026) raise a significant added layer of methodological complexity in whether generative AI can "get" as well as humans the content of politically explosive posts. Though their case in point is about Trump posts, the implication for memetic extremism is a huge one. For, example, irony is an item automated software could miss, or the cleverly coded humor that people might use, or subcultural references.

And there is also a very real problemHuman moderators might lack the cultural literacy necessary to comprehend some of what is referred to when the community is using obscurantist references specifically to avoid detection. This suggests that governance ought to combine contextual expertise, community-specific knowledge with open appeal mechanisms and attention to platform design.

Moderation should be viewed like cultural governance in online gaming communities. It does not only mean the deletion of posts but also shapes the humouristic norms that make it in a normative manner, the type of attacks that are rewarded, how influencers react to chat behaviour, whether in a constant way the rules of Discord servers are enforced and how outrage or solidarity is incentivized in the design of the platform. Galip and Maragkou's (2016) work on financialized livestreaming shows that platforms can design incentives for extremely-high-personas. Outrage, shaming, and banter result in engagement and revenue; these policies that oversee individual slurs are not sufficient to practically manage moderation.

6.6 Proposed Framework: Memetic-Ironic Extremism Mediation Framework

The Memetic-Ironic Extremism Mediation Framework is proposed in this paper based on the synthesis. This framework demonstrates how extremist content flows through gaming and the platforms around it, even without declaring its ideological position explicitly at all points. One could trace such a conduit from platform ecology to subcultural literacy; from memetic form to ironic ambiguity, and from affective boundary-making to normalization, resistance or governance intervention.

Figure 3. Conceptual model of memetic-ironic mediation of extremist discourse in gaming cultures

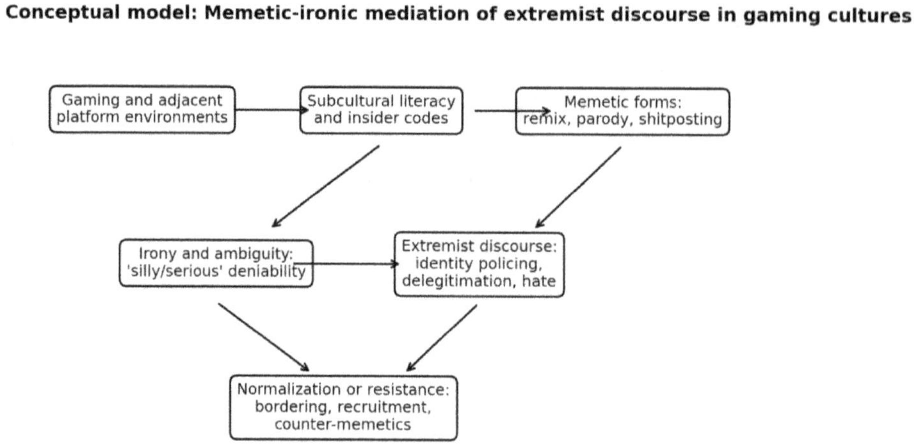

Source note. Author's conceptual synthesis based exclusively on the uploaded Scopus review corpus.

Table 2. Memetic-ironic extremism mediation framework

Analytical layer	Key mechanism	Indicative manifestation in gaming communities	Principal scholarly anchors
Platform ecology	Affordances structure participation and visibility	Discord roles, livestream chat, anonymous boards, clips, forum archives	Lombardi (2025); Åkerlund (2025); Galip & Maragkou (2026); Wood (2026)
Subcultural literacy	Insider references distinguish participants from outsiders	In-jokes, emotes, game references, coded templates, ironic slang	Price (2025); Ryder (2026); Merrill et al. (2025)
Memetic compression	Complex antagonisms become repeatable visual-verbal forms	Reaction images, screenshots, modified game imagery, template jokes	Musih et al. (2026); Munk (2025); Mazumdar (2025)
Ironic ambiguity	Messages appear simultaneously playful and political	'Only joking' defenses, edgy humour, parody, banter, shitposting	Price (2025); Ryder (2026); Krogh et al. (2026)

continued on following page

Table 2. Continued

Analytical layer	Key mechanism	Indicative manifestation in gaming communities	Principal scholarly anchors
Affective boundary-making	Humour organizes belonging, contempt, and hierarchy	Ridicule of women, minorities, activists, enemies, or outsiders	Fossberg & Fangen (2025); Adiga & Padmakumar (2025); Iranzo-Cabrera et al. (2025)
Normalization/ resistance	Memes either stabilize exclusion or support counter-discourse	Community catchphrases, streamer amplification, feminist parody, civic memes	Chang (2025); González-Calvo et al. (2026); Munk (2025)

Source note. Developed from the conceptual synthesis of the uploaded Scopus corpus.

The framework has three advantages. First, it avoids a simplistic linear model of radicalization by recognizing that extremist discourse may circulate as style, humour, and atmosphere before becoming explicit doctrine. Second, it integrates gaming communities with platform studies by recognizing that communities are distributed across technological environments. Third, it includes resistance and counter-discourse, thereby avoiding the assumption that memetic culture is inherently extremist.

7. FINDINGS

The language corpora around the lines of extremist communication in digital societies brought greater demotic cultural character in memes, baner chat, livestream chatter, and so on, but generally does with jokes and seldomingly formulated ideological statements. This is visbly elements of the bagoses in Ryder (2026), tomfooling/supercerebral memes in Price (2025), mediated nostalgia in Wood (2026), and weaponized humour in Fossberg and Fangen (2025).

Second, gaming communities should be seen as multiplatform ecosystems. According to De Cleen et al. (2025) video games are part of a much broader field of engagement with right-wing extremism in audiovisual fiction, while Galip and Maragkou (2026) and Lombardi (2025) demonstrated the importance of intrinsic opportunities of livestream and forum. They can't be reduced down to the meanings of the game software, but take in everything about the adjacent lines of performance with other platforms for discussion, performance, monetization, and archiving.

Fourth, irony serves as a deniability device and a mechanism of boundary-making within subcultural bounds. It is not simply so that extremists can hold meaning among themselves, but it also disappears from view when directed outward. Within the gaming sphere, such ironies are intensified, because play itself rests on multi-layered planes of interaction, compounding irony in all forms—play, parody, and competition.

Fifth, the racial genderness of hostility is central to the extremist memetic discourse. So, the corpus recurrently underscores that misogyny and the feminizing of enemies as well as body politics and attacks on women in the public sphere are central fields of humor that are thereby becoming exclusionary (Adiga & Padmakumar 2025; Fossberg & Fangen 2025; Iranzo-Cabrera et al. 2025; Kosonen & Löf 2025).

But fifth, memes allow possibilities for resistance. Munk (2025), Mazumdar (2025), Krogh et al. (2026), González-Calvo et al. (2026), and Chang (2025) describe the ways that the use of humor, mimicry as lived practice, and online play can help in challenging domination, enabling civil resilience, and creating safer forms of belonging. This is an important discovery so the world will not equate the culture of memes in their entirety as solely producing negative things.

However, the sixth point here is that context should be considered while designing platforms. Content moderation can not address the concerns without paying attention to context along with platform design and economic incentives. Studies on selective inactivity, structural toxicity, chatbox sociality, and computational interpretation of hate show that hate speech can not only be recognized by keyword detection or post level removals (Åkerlund, 2025; Galip & Maragkou, 2026; Lombardi, 2025; Murthy et al., 2026).

Table 3. Summary of core findings and implications

Finding	Interpretive significance	Implication for future research
Extremism often circulates as humour	The joke/politics distinction is unstable	Study irony as mediation rather than noise
Gaming communities are platform ecologies	Game culture extends across Discord, livestreaming, forums and video	Use multi-platform ethnographic designs
Gendered hostility is constitutive	Masculinity, misogyny and humiliation shape boundaries	Integrate feminist media analysis with extremism studies
Memes enable both harm and resistance	Memetic form is politically flexible	Compare extremist and counter-extremist memetic repertoires
Moderation is cultural governance	Rules, affordances and incentives shape humour norms	Analyze moderation as platformed meaning-making

Source note. Author's synthesis based on the uploaded Scopus corpus.

8. CONCLUSION

The analysis made in this study of gaming communities in this paper involves memes, irony, and extremist discourses about integrating media studies through an examination of the uploaded Scopus corpus. The argument: that extremist discourses about gaming usually move through memetic-ironic mediation contains the text discussed in previous works: ideological antagonism in gaming and gaming-logged spaces is typically thrown in some playful, humorous, nostalgic, or even ridiculous garb. It is not merely oblivion; rather, memetic irony forms close affective relationships, endows insiders with particular forms of competence, refugees outsiders, and secures the communities' evasion of a particular form of accountability by moving between registers.

The media studies periodical newly recognizes gaming communities as open ecology of the platforms. The proper object of analysis is no more the game but the tempo of passing memes, livestream chat, Discord servers, anonymous forums, YouTube narrations, short clips, and the regimes of moderation around it. This ecological view seems imperative in that extremist meanings rarely get bogged down within any single platform; however, they move, much transposed, translated, intensified, attenuated, through diverging infrastructures.

It also competes conceptually by shunning the opposition of humour and harm, integrating them aptly within one another. Humour can be enlightening, subversive, and solidaristic, but it may support domination, misogyny, racial contempt, and even bind together members of the far right. The affordances of the very form that has made memes a great tool for civic resistance have also made them such a tremendous means for the normalization of extremism. The academic task is constructing some analytical understanding of how these power relations flow through memes.

The proposed Memetic-Ironic Extremism Mediation Framework will offer an exciting direction for future research. This separates platform ecology, subcultural literacy, memetic compression, ironic ambiguity, emotional boundary-drawing, and normalization/resistance as key analytical layers. In future empirical work, this framework could be applied also in specific gaming communities, streamer audiences, Discord servers, modding forums, or multiplayer chat environments, adding multimodal analysis to a platform ethnography and studies of moderation.

9. LIMITATIONS AND FUTURE SCOPE

Major drawback is the limit.size of the material and sources. Only twenty-five records were uploaded compared to the prompt request for thirty. Therefore, in conformity with not using any external hard paper, I used all records available and did not import further basic literature or more recent literature. This much ensures source fidelity; however, it stops cripping the theoretical grounding, both relegated back to the limited side, as a small extent. A longer version in the future might draw in earlier foundational work on memes, irony, gaming culture, platform studies, and radicalization provided the research-design approvals extend in that direction.

Another drawback is that the study is rather conceptual, based on previously existing literature rather than on a newly collected or original dataset of memes, Discord posts, livestream chat, or gaming community chatting. This framework proposes the demand for empirical case study testing. For example, one could envision a study that charts how a meme template moves from an anonymous forum to a Discord venue for gaming, how communities around a streamer normalise coded humour, or how feminist gaming communities respond to harassment through ironic memes.

The third drawback consists its dismissing the effect of language and geography. Thus, even though it spans diverse geographies, it is mediated through English language indexation availability, and Scopus metadata. Future work should explore meme cultures and gaming communities specific to regions where non-English languages are spoken; an extremist or hate-speech culture in many vernacular humor might not translate so easily.

The study needs to merge into three directions in the next decade. First, revise the methods. To analyze an image, a text, an audio, an emote, an interface on the platform and a history about circulation. Second comparing detrimental memetic practices with those that are resistant to extremism rather than simply studying extremism. Third moderation of research should not be restricted to the study of rules but to understand the unique features of social practices within digital humor culture as well as platform design.

REFERENCES

Adiga, P. G., & Padmakumar, K. (2025). Exploring online masculinity in the Indian meme culture: A case of video Doge memes. *Journal of Creative Communications*, 09732586251344024. Advance online publication. DOI: 10.1177/09732586251344024

Åkerlund, M. (2025). Politics of deliberate inaction: The disconnect between platform justifications and user imaginaries on content moderation in a "free speech" online forum. *New Media & Society*, *27*(3), 1235–1255. Advance online publication. DOI: 10.1177/14614448231190905

Chang, A. (2025). Safe spaces for feminist activists online: Chinese networked feminists' self-censorship strategies in response to online misogyny and government censorship. *Humanities & Social Sciences Communications*, *12*(1), 495. Advance online publication. DOI: 10.1057/s41599-025-04802-2

De Cleen, B., Bauwens, J., Joris, W., Shroufi, O., & Smets, K. (2025). Fictional frontlines: A mapping review and research agenda for the study of far-right engagement with films, television and video games. *Javnost (Ljubljana)*, *32*(3), 301–324. Advance online publication. DOI: 10.1080/13183222.2025.2547519

Fiadotava, A., Laineste, L., Castañar Rubio, G., & Chłopicki, W. (2025). *When the transnational rules: Humorous reactions to the Wagner Group rebellion in Estonia, Poland and Belarus*. Folklore., DOI: 10.7592/FEJF2025.97.transnational

Fossberg, H., & Fangen, K. (2025). Weaponized humor and militarized masculinity: The role of memes in far-right discourse on the Russo-Ukrainian war. *Journal of Gender Studies*, 1–22. Advance online publication. DOI: 10.1080/09589236.2025.2545905

Galip, I., & Maragkou, E. (2026). Chatbox sociality: Extreme personae, speculative communities, and the affordances of alt-tech livestreaming. *First Monday*, *31*(5). Advance online publication. DOI: 10.5210/fm.v31i5.15437

González-Calvo, G., Ospina-Betancurt, J., & Hortigüela-Alcalá, D. (2026). Doing gender online: Memetic performances and the digital construction of femininity. *Gender Issues*, *43*(1), 23. Advance online publication. DOI: 10.1007/s12147-026-09402-1

Iranzo-Cabrera, M., Castro-Bleda, M. J., Simón-Astudillo, I., & Hurtado, L.-F. (2025). Journalists' ethical responsibility: Tackling hate speech against women politicians in social media through natural language processing techniques. *Social Science Computer Review*, *43*(3), 475–502. Advance online publication. DOI: 10.1177/08944393241269417

Karas, T. (2025). Cultural criminology, counter-extremism and the contemporary far right. *Crime, Media, Culture*, *21*(3), 267–293. Advance online publication. DOI: 10.1177/17416590241279413

Kasianenko, K. (2025). Boosting the distant Other: Visibility practices on Japanese Twitter during Russia's war on Ukraine. *Convergence (London)*, *31*(3), 1056–1078. DOI: 10.1177/13548565251328776

Kosonen, H., & Löf, R. (2025). Pansy asses and terrorists: Sensibilities of anti-environmentalist toxic speech against Extinction Rebellion Finland. *European Journal of Cultural Studies*, *28*(3), 883–903. Advance online publication. DOI: 10.1177/13675494241278931

Krogh, S. C., Jensen, S. Q., & Larsen, M. C. (2026). Girl culture, unspectacular resistance and social media: A study of how adolescent girls undo emphasized femininity through shitposting. *Journal of Youth Studies*, *29*(1), 19–35. Advance online publication. DOI: 10.1080/13676261.2024.2392631

Lombardi, L. (2025). *Toxic talk: Structural toxicity on a Japanese anonymous text-board*. Emerging Media., DOI: 10.1177/27523543251376848

MacDowell, J. (2025). Breaking and making the fourth wall on YouTube: Direct address and audiovisual narration in online video. *Quarterly Review of Film and Video*, *42*(6), 1399–1434. Advance online publication. DOI: 10.1080/10509208.2024.2444051

Mazumdar, S. (2025). Politics as fun: Countering Indian digital nationalism with viral videos. *Television & New Media*, *26*(3), 373–389. Advance online publication. DOI: 10.1177/15274764241280635

Merrill, S., Gardell, M., & Lindgren, S. (2025). How "the left" meme: Analyzing taboo in the Internet memes of r/DankLeft. *New Media & Society*, *27*(7), 3950–3972. Advance online publication. DOI: 10.1177/14614448241232144

Munk, T. (2025). Digital defiance: Memetic warfare and civic resistance. *European Journal on Criminal Policy and Research*, *31*(3), 501–528. Advance online publication. DOI: 10.1007/s10610-025-09613-4

Murthy, D., Shermak, J., Pathania, S., Vinton, K., Whipple, K., Willard, L., & Madison, R. (2026). Rage against the AI machine: Can generative AI understand Donald Trump-related posts as well as humans? *Convergence (London)*, 13548565261459202. Advance online publication. DOI: 10.1177/13548565261459202

Musih, N., Trillò, T., & Hallinan, B. (2026). Resisting climate imaginaries: Future compass memes as combinatory mechanisms for imagining otherwise. *Information Communication and Society*, 1–20. Advance online publication. DOI: 10.1080/1369118X.2026.2616761

Petersen, L. N., & Johansen, M. B. (2025). Spaces of hybridized prefatory extremism (HYPE) on social media. *Social Media + Society*, *11*(2), 20563051251340145. Advance online publication. DOI: 10.1177/20563051251340145

Price, C. W. (2025). Ketchup is the whitest sauce: Memes as silly/serious bordered spaces in international relations. *International Political Sociology*, *19*(3), olaf026. Advance online publication. DOI: 10.1093/ips/olaf026

Ryder, C. (2026). Despicable digital banter: Racist black and brown politicians in the U.K. *First Monday*, *31*(5). Advance online publication. DOI: 10.5210/fm.v31i5.15438

Weidhase, N., & Wilde, P. (2026). “Gone too soon”: Zombie humour on social media as cultural critique of the British monarchy. *Information Communication and Society*, *29*(1), 113–130. Advance online publication. DOI: 10.1080/1369118X.2025.2497945

Wood, J. (2026). Invitations to fascism: Mediated nostalgia in far-right Discord servers. *Crime, Media, Culture*, 17416590261446319. Advance online publication. DOI: 10.1177/17416590261446319

Chapter 7
Toxicity and Harassment in Online Gaming Communities:
Causes, Impacts, and Prevention Strategies

Lmira Jumaniyazova
Mamun University, Khiva, Uzbekistan

Aarthi Selvakumar
http://orcid.org/0009-0006-9064-2091
Marwadi University, Rajkot, India

Duggirala Aravind
http://orcid.org/0009-0005-4362-7684
ASET Institute of Science and Technology, Chennai, India

Atham Jurayev
Termez University of Economics and Service, Termez, Uzbekistan

Taji Norov
Tashkent State University of Economics, Tashkent, Uzbekistan

Ravikumar Natarajan
http://orcid.org/0009-0009-3705-1681
Jain (Deemed to be) University, Bangalore, India

ABSTRACT

This chapter explores how online game communities face significant issues regarding their toxicity and harassment, as well as their impact on player wellbeing, inclusion, participation, and digital safety. Online games and esports spaces, livestreaming platforms, forums, and voice and text chat systems are key social environments but also face challenges with abusive language, trolling, griefing, hate speech, threats, exclusion based on ID, and identity-based harassment. The chapter examines how anonymity, low accountability, competition, poor moderation, toxic group norms, and game design elements result in harmful behavior. It also provides consideration

DOI: 10.4018/979-8-2600-1664-0.ch007

of psychological, social, and inclusion-related effects on vulnerable players. In addition, it links problematic gaming with the risk of radicalization, radical ideologies, and exclusionary identities. Lastly, it recommends prevention measures through ethical moderation, AI-enabled detection, inclusive design, governance, education, and engagement with the community.

1. INTRODUCTION

Online games have emerged as a vast digital space that offers a range of experiences, including entertainment, socialization, competition, and identity development. The players are no longer just interacting with the game, they are also interacting with complex communities that have social interaction, rules of the platform, norms and a digital communication system. Such neighborhoods offer opportunities for cooperation, creativity and community, but they also raise significant issues of toxicity and harassment (Zsila et al., 2022). Violent and abusive actions like griefing, trolling, hate speech, threats, exclusion of certain individuals, verbal abuse, and more can make the game environment more toxic and less welcoming for players (Koehler et al., 2022). They are particularly relevant when considering the broader context of the gaming culture, radicalization and the politics of online games, as negative and aggressive gaming cultures can lead to a normalization of aggression, discrimination and extremist communication. This introduction puts the context, problem, purpose and significance of looking at online game communities and how they are toxic and harassment.

1.1 Background to Online Gaming Communities

The Internet has created a web of gaming communities that has become a strong social network able to transcend cultural, geographical, linguistic and demographic lines. Players can communicate, compete, cooperate and create shared identities within a multiplayer game, esports event, livestreaming platform, gaming forums, and social media groups (Kou, 2021). They offer a sense of achievement, emotional connection, teamwork, friendship and entertainment. Gaming areas also enable creative pursuits like modding, streaming, fan content and neighborhood activities (Burgess & Jones, 2020). But, as games are social, so too can social problems, inequalities, and power dynamics from outside of the game enter into gaming environments (Aarthi, Ravikumar, & Pardaev, 2025). Game rules, platform policies, communication tools, competition, peer influence and community expectations influence player behavior. Online gaming is not just a leisure activity, it also provides a social and cultural setting that raises issues of inclusion/exclusion, identity and governance.

1.2 Toxicity and Harassment in Online Play

Rudeness and harassment in online games are defined as harmful behaviours that disrupt the gaming experience, erode player trust in the game and make the online environment unsafe. These can be abusive language, insults, trolling, griefing, bullying, hate speech, threats, harassment on the basis of gender, racial discrimination, homophobic abuse and targeted attacks against a player or group of players (Tripathi, 2022). Poisoning can manifest itself in voice chat, text chat, comments in the live stream, private messages, forums, team communication, social media that are integrated into gaming communities. While some such behaviour may be acceptable for competitive banter and/or emotional responses when playing a game, frequently repeated exposure to such behavior can have serious psychological and social effects (Gazia et al., 2024). It can make people feel discouraged to participate, less fun, and may have to look for another platform or that they might have to hide their identity to play. Toxicity is not therefore just an individual behaviour issue, it is linked to the design of the platform, norms of the community, moderation practices and accountability systems.

1.3 Problem Context: Causes, Impacts, and Radicalization Risks

There are multiple factors that feed into the problem of toxicity in online gaming communities: anonymity, lack of accountability, ineffective moderation, competition, group identity conflict, and normalizing aggressive communication. Some game design aspects like rank-based, leaderboard-based, team-based, unbalanced matchmaking, or voice chat can exacerbate frustration and conflict in the gaming arena (Kowert & Crevoshay, 2022). Harassment can have real consequences, especially for women, new players and racial and sexual minorities who might face harassment and exclusion, and for the LGBTQ+ community, who might face harassment (Hayday & Collison, 2020). Anxiety, stress, less participation in games, self-censorship, withdrawing from competitive environment and loss of trust in games can all be side effects of toxic behaviour. Toxic game environments can also present ways of radicalization, in some instances, by normalizing extreme humor, hateful language and expression, exclusionary identities and antagonistic group behaviors. Therefore, toxicity needs to be considered from a psychological, social, cultural, technological and political perspective.

1.4 Purpose and Significance of the Chapter

This chapter aims at analyzing the causes, effects and prevention measures of toxicity and harassment in online gaming forums. The chapter seeks to offer a framework and understanding of the development of harmful behaviour, the impact of harmful behaviour on players and communities, how harmful behaviour can be minimised through the responsible governance of the sport, inclusive sport design, moderation, education and community involvement. It's important because of a concern it highlights of digital culture; one that relates to the world of games, radicalisation and the politics of online play. The discussion is applicable to the game developer, publisher, platform moderator, esports organisation, educator, parent, researcher, and player. The chapter focuses on the structural and cultural aspects of toxicity rather than just on individual misconduct, thereby helping to create safer, fairer and more inclusive gaming environments for positive engagement and minimising the presence of negative ideology.

2. RESEARCH AIM, HYPOTHESIS, AND QUESTIONS

This section outlines the main focus of the chapter, in terms of the aim, hypothesis and research questions. It aims to provide insights into the phenomenon of toxicity and harassment in online gaming environments, recognising that it is a complex phenomenon that is affected by player actions, platform management, game mechanics, social identity, and community culture. The section provides insights into the way the chapter explores the dynamics of harmful interactions, their impacts on specific groups of players, and the relationships they have to other issues like exclusion, radicalisation and online political engagement. It also introduces a framework for the analysis of a combination of moderation, ethical governance, technological solutions, educational awareness and community engagement in prevention strategies. The literature review, methodology, findings and recommendations should be based on the aim, objectives and research questions.

2.1 Research Aim

This chapter aims to look at the various types, causes, social and psychological effects and prevention measures of toxicity and harassment in online gaming communities. The chapter aims to better grasp the influence of anonymity, competitive pressures, platform design, the moderation strategies used, and community norms on harmful behaviors. Its goals also include examining the potential for exclusionary behaviour and potential for radicalization risks within digital play spaces, which could be linked to toxic gaming cultures. The chapter aims to contribute to the development of safer, inclusive, and responsible gaming communities online by offering pragmatic and ethically sound strategies to tackle these concerns.

2.2 Hypotheses

- H1: Anonymity, weak accountability, and poor moderation increase the likelihood of toxic behaviour in online gaming communities.
- H2: Competitive pressure, ranking systems, team dependency, and communication tools contribute to conflict and harassment in multiplayer gaming spaces.
- H3: Toxicity and harassment negatively affect player wellbeing, participation, inclusion, and trust in gaming platforms.
- H4: Identity-based harassment increases exclusion and reduces participation among vulnerable player groups.
- H5: Integrated prevention strategies involving technology, governance, education, design, and community participation can reduce toxicity in online gaming communities.

2.3 Research Questions

- What forms of toxicity and harassment are commonly observed in online gaming communities?
- What factors contribute to the emergence and normalization of toxic behaviour in online play?
- How does harassment affect players, gaming communities, and platform participation?
- How can toxic gaming environments support exclusionary cultures or radicalization pathways?
- What strategies can reduce toxicity while maintaining fairness, privacy, accountability, and freedom of expression?

3. LITERATURE REVIEW

The literature review covers previous research and scholarship on toxicity and harassment in online gaming communities. It offers a theoretical, conceptual and empirical basis to grasp the nature of harmful behaviours, their occurrences and the consequences they have on players and player culture (Yodovich & Kim, 2022). While perhaps some misbehaviours can be considered isolated incidents of toxic behaviour in online games, the way the games are set up, the way the players identify themselves, the competitive nature of the game, the norms of the groups, the moderation policies and the governance of the platform affects the way the game is played (Wolfowicz et al., 2022). Examples of harassment in previously-studied contexts include text chat, voice chat, livestreaming spaces, forums, and social media spaces in gaming contexts. The review also takes into account the potential for toxic behaviour to affect risks of radicalization, hostility based on identity and risks of exclusion in online play (Sharma et al., 2024). This section presents the literature in a conceptual framework of governance, causes, impacts, research gaps, providing the basis for the findings, discussion, and recommendations in the chapter.

3.1 Conceptualising Toxicity and Harassment in Gaming

Gaming toxicity is defined as behavior that is harmful, disruptive, or hostile that negatively impacts player experience and/or community health. This encompasses negative language, trolling, griefing, hate speech, threats, bullying, unfair remarks, provocation with cheating and any other intentional disruption of the team coordination or enjoyment of the game (Marques et al., 2024). Harassment is specifically related to one or more individuals or groups and could be a series of personal attacks, gender abuse, racial insults, homophobic comments, intimidation or exclusion. These actions can happen in multiplayer games, in an actual playing environment, in a public forum, on a live stream, through private messages, or in a community on the platforms (Akram & Nasar, 2023). It is important to realize that, conceptually, toxicity can be considered a behavioural and cultural problem, as it can be sustained by group norms, competitive setting and lack of accountability. Aggressive communication can be an expression of humour or competition; however, it can have serious repercussions for those who receive repeated aggression (Marinett, 2021). Thus, the concept of gaming toxicity should be considered as a type of digital harm that is related to involvement, identity, safety and inclusion.

3.2 Toxicity, Identity, and Platform Governance

The link between player identity and online gaming platform governance is intricate and tightly tied to the concept of toxicity. The relationship between player identity and online gaming platform governance is complex, and closely related to the notion of toxicity. A gaming space can offer users the opportunity to create identities via avatars, user names, skill ranks, forums, team memberships, and other means (Pierson et al., 2023). But identity can also serve to exclude, stereotype and to be the object of targeted harassment. Some groups, such as women, racial minorities, LGBTQ+ players, the younger community and a newcomer to a game, may be abused because they are not conforming to the dominant game and/or group norms (Massanari, 2017). Social identity processes can consolidate in-group identity and out-group animosity, particularly when in competition where blame, frustration and status are salient. There is a key role for platform governance on the control/ enabling of the latter. The Rules, reporting systems, moderation policies, sanctions, appeals and transparency mechanisms have an impact on the way players act and justice is felt (DeCook et al., 2022). Lack of governance can lead to the normalisation of abusive behaviour; over-moderation and/or bias can result in concerns around fairness and expression (Aarthi, Ravikumar, Sapayev Odilbek Uglu, et al., 2025). Thus, good governance needs to take into account the safety, accountability, privacy, inclusiveness, and player rights in digital gaming environments.

3.3 Causes, Forms, and Impacts of Gaming Toxicity

Gaming toxicity is a product of a few factors. Players may feel less accountable toward others since they are anonymous or not identified by their name, making it easier for them to act aggressively and without repercussions when it comes to the real world. High pressure, ranking, team dependency, match up imbalance and penalties for failure can lead to frustration and blame for players (Vergel et al., 2024). The lack of good moderation, insufficient rules, no systems to report and weak responses can further promote toxic behaviors. The various types of toxicity are insults; trolling; griefing; hate speech; threats; exclusion; targeted harassment; and discriminatory abuse (Donner, 2025). Players' behaviours impact them psychologically, socially and culturally. Victims might suffer from distress, anxiety, lack of confidence, lack of pleasure or sense of exhaustion. Some gamers may be unable to communicate, conceal identities, not play competitive games or even not enter gaming environments anymore. At the community level, toxicity undermines trust, decreases co-operation, hurts platform reputation, and leads to a lack of diversity. The impacts in this report indicate harassment is not just

3.4 Research Gap in Gaming Toxicity and Radicalization

In online platforms, researcher attention has been drawn to the issues of online harassment, toxic communication and moderation in gaming spaces; however, there are still a number of gaps. The available literature focuses on general toxicity, and less attention is paid to the potential links between radicalization, extremist humour, exclusionary identities and ideational influence as a part of the hostile gaming culture. A few mentions of the interaction of game design, platform governance, community norms and identity-based harassment in creating harmful pathways also exist. Toxicity as a topic of research is often approached as a personal issue, instead of as a larger issue that relates to technology, culture and moderation systems. There is a need to explore further how privacy, fairness and freedom of expression can be maintained and at the same time the harm reduced through the use of prevention strategies.

4. RESEARCH METHODOLOGY

This chapter will follow a conceptual/literature-based approach to the topic of toxicity and harassment in online communities of gamers. The methodology of the chapter is based on the idea that it should interpret the knowledge which is already available (the chapter concentrates on causes, impacts, the possibilities of prevention, and the risk of radicalization) and not gather primary data from players (Chui, 2014). The section elaborates on the research paradigm, approach, design, analytical process, ethical issues and measures to ensure trustworthiness that will guide the discussion. It is based on scientific research, platform policies, industry reports, internet safety research and gaming culture, online harassment, online moderation and online radicalisation research (Jovic et al., 2023). The methodology aids in structuring the chapter in a logical manner, connecting evidence to themes, like player behavior, platform governance, identity-based abuse, design influences, and prevention strategies. This is a balanced method to facilitate an academic conversation on toxicity in social, cultural, technological and governance contexts.

4.1 Research Paradigm and Approach

The chapter takes a critical and interpretivist stance to digital studies. The interpretivist paradigm is appropriate because the extent to which gaming is toxic and/or harassing is influenced by human behavior, community meanings, patterns of communication and social interaction. This provides insights into how players feel abused, excluded, struggle with identity conflicts and are faced with community norms in online games (Jonnalagadda et al., 2023). The critical digital studies approach also facilitates the exploration of key themes of power, inequality, platform control, platform moderation, and digital governance. The chapter is qualitative conceptual that is synthesized from literatures. This method is suitable as the study is not based upon measurement in numbers or experimentation testing (Martindale et al., 2026). Rather, it interrogates the existing research and digital culture debates to gain insight into the development of toxic behaviors and ways to halt toxic behavior. The approach enables the chapter to relate gaming toxicity to other topics such as marginalization, online politics, risks of radicalization, and responsible approach to the management of platforms.

4.2 Research Method

The methodology used in this chapter is qualitative conceptual research method, which is literature synthesis and thematic analysis. This study reviews the literature covering the themes of toxicity, harassment, moderation, governance, and radicalization in online gaming communities (Martindale et al., 2026). The chapter does not gather primary data, so it draws on existing knowledge to look for important patterns, causes, impacts, and prevention strategies. Thematic analysis is used to structure the discussion into key themes, which are as follows: forms of toxicity; causes of toxicity related to design; harassment on the basis of identity; psychological/social impacts; risks for radicalization; moderation challenges; and mechanisms of prevention (McGuckin et al., 2022). As the chapter is designed to teach a conceptual understanding of the relationship between numbers, this technique is appropriate.

4.3 Research Design and Analytical Process

The chapter is conceptual analysis design with the help of thematic literature review. These include peer reviewed articles, academic books and book chapters, industry reports, guidelines for the gaming platforms, codes of conduct for esports and digital safety, and studies on online radicalization. These sources are analyzed and commonalities about topics of toxicity, harassment, platform governance, player identity, player moderation and prevention are identified (Kordyaka & Kruse, 2021). The analytical process consists of thematic analysis, wherein information is clustered under the major themes, which are in turn toxic behaviour, causes, impacts, risks of radicalization and intervention. The design is used to aid the presentation of the topic in an orderly sequence, avoiding repetition. It also enables comparisons to be made on social, psychological, technological and governance-based explanations of gaming toxicity (Anderson & Schrier, 2022). The analytical process helps to establish a practical framework for safer and more inclusive online gaming environments and identifies concepts and recommendations that can be incorporated into this framework.

4.4 Ethical Considerations and Trustworthiness

While the chapter is based on secondary sources, it is still important to practise good ethics as it relates to the topic of harassment, discrimination, hate speech and vulnerable groups of players. There are examples of harmful behaviour which are discussed in a responsibly way without unnecessarily reproducing abusive language. The discussion does not pathologize the experiences of women, racial minorities, LGBTQ+ players, young players, new players and other communities affected by the experience and doesn't place blame on victims (Kiritchenko et al., 2021). Also, attention is paid to the balance between safety, privacy, freedom of expression and fair moderation, on an ethical level. Clear and logical development of ideas and the use of scholarly and credible sources ensures trustworthiness. Evidence of credibility through connecting arguments with literature and evidence from platforms (Ozanne et al., 2022). Consistency helps to strengthen dependability and the absence of unsupported claims to support confirmability. The transferability aspect is covered through the lenses of insights that can be used in multiplayer games, esports venues, livestreaming platforms and gaming communities.

5. FINDINGS AND DISCUSSION

The key findings from the conceptual and literature review of the phenomenon of the toxicity and harassment in online gaming communities are provided in this section. The discussion builds on three thematic areas: forms and causes of toxic behavior, psychological and social impact of the toxic behavior and risk of radicalization and platform governance (Dwivedi et al., 2023). The results reveal that the toxicity is not restricted to when players are communicating with another player in an abusive way. Factors such as competitive game models, low accountability, community norms, identity-based exclusion, and inconsistent accountability models all contribute to it (Gazia et al., 2024). Additionally, the discussion emphasizes the impact of harassment on the wellbeing, participation, trust, and diversity of people in games. This section clarifies the value of considering prevention issues at a multi-dimensional level across both individual and platform levels and why this can't be achieved through a single dimension.

5.1 Forms and Causes of Toxicity in Online Gaming

The types of toxicity in online gaming are: abuse of language, trolling, griefing, threats, hate speech, bullying, discriminatory statements and remarks, exclusion and targeted harassment. In these situations, it can happen in a match, while talking to others in a team, at a livestream, in a gaming forum or in private, non-competitive discussions. The reasons behind them are frequently related to factors of anonymity, less accountability, emotional frustration, ranking stress and hostile group norms (Konikoff, 2021). Others resort to negative communication when they are upset, trying to assert themselves, criticizing other players or pushing others out of play who they deem as outsiders. However, there are also situations where game mechanics can contribute to increased conflict as players rely heavily on team performance, are matched against players that are not a good fit, and lose status in ranking systems (Cote et al., 2023). Harmful behavior can continue to be normal if complaints are not addressed and respond to in a timely and appropriate manner. Thus, the toxicity is a result of individual behavior, game design, platform culture and inadequate enforcement. The common toxic behaviors identified from the online gaming community and explaining their primary causes are presented in Table 1.

Table 1. Forms and causes of toxicity

Form of Toxicity	Simple Meaning	Main Causes
Abusive Language	Use of insults, rude words, or verbal attacks	Anger, frustration, weak accountability
Trolling	Provoking players to create conflict	Attention-seeking, anonymity
Griefing	Intentionally disturbing gameplay	Poor sportsmanship, lack of punishment
Hate Speech	Abusive comments based on identity	Bias, discrimination, toxic group norms
Threats	Intimidating or warning other players	Aggression, conflict escalation
Exclusion	Rejecting or isolating certain players	Prejudice, group identity conflict
Targeted Harassment	Repeated attacks on a specific player	Weak reporting, poor moderation

5.2 Psychological, Social, and Inclusion-Related Impacts

Toxic and harassing behaviors can have many serious consequences for players and the community. Children who are repeatedly abused may have stress, anxiety, emotional exhaustion, decreased confidence and loss of enjoyment. Some will be unable to speak, may not play competition, will not be identified or may leave out of gaming areas. This impact is worse for women, young players, racial minorities, players who are LGBTQ+ or new users, as they are often the victims of identity-based harassment (TaeHyuk Keum & Hearns, 2022). Toxic behavior also has an impact at the social level: it undermines the ability to cooperate, decreases trust and negatively affects the sense of community in gaming groups. Additionally, it restricts diversity in esports, livestreaming, multiplayer teams and gaming discussions made in public, by dissuading groups who are marginalised from becoming full participants (Coanda & Aupers, 2020). This can make it difficult to participate in a positive and healthy manner online, and in turn become a barrier to inclusion and participation. Table 2 outlines the impact of harassment on mental wellbeing of players, participation, trust and community inclusion.

Table 2. Impacts of gaming harassment

Area of Impact	Effect on Players	Effect on Community
Psychological Impact	Stress, anxiety, fear, frustration	Negative gaming atmosphere
Social Impact	Loss of confidence and interaction	Weak community bonding
Participation Impact	Avoiding games, chats, or teams	Reduced player engagement
Inclusion Impact	Marginalized players feel unsafe	Less diversity in gaming spaces
Trust Impact	Players lose trust in platforms	Poor platform reputation
Performance Impact	Reduced focus and enjoyment	Lower teamwork quality

5.3 Toxicity, Radicalization, and Governance Challenges

Exclusionary language, extremist humour, hostile identities and hate based communication may be commonplace in toxic gaming environments. Negative interactions and narratives that involve discrimination do not necessarily mean that one is radicalizing, but through constant exposure to such discriminatory narratives and aggressive group cultures, negative ideologies can seem acceptable or enjoyable (Lopez Naranjo et al., 2025). This risk is increased when platforms lack detection capabilities for coordinated harassment, coded language or recruitment interactions. Another governance issue arises as it is imperative to "moderate" systems while safeguarding safety, privacy, fairness, and freedom of expression. Depending on the context, automated tools can have trouble with sarcasm, cultural nuances, or different language variations, or human tools might not be deployed or might be inconsistent (Miller-Idriss, 2025a). If users do not feel that their information is being used correctly, it can diminish their trust in the system. Misuse of information, faulty enforcement, and lack of transparency can kill user trust (Ravikumar & Aarthi, 2025). The difficulties demonstrate the necessity of having clear policies, responsible moderation, ethical technology and people participation in a successful governance.

6. IMPLICATIONS OF THE STUDY

This section covers the implications of the study of toxicity and harassment for the practice and for the academic sector. The results indicate that a safer environment for gaming cannot be created solely through punishment following the damage. However, prevention will take a multifaceted approach involving developers, publishers, platforms, moderators, esports organizations, educators, parents, players and community leaders (Scholl, 2025). The study emphasizes the significance of designing for safety, moderating fairly, participation inclusivity, digital literacy, and good governance. It also reveals that toxicity is a structural and cultural phenomenon that is related to platform systems, player identity, competition and community culture (Zhang & Davis, 2024). The implications of this are significant for player wellbeing, trust, lessening the chances of exclusion and curbing the potential for negative ideologies to develop in game spaces.

6.1 Implications for Game Developers, Publishers, and Platforms

The responsibility of game developers, publishers and platforms is to make sure that the game is designed in a way that minimizes negative interaction and helps player safety. The results suggest that toxicity prevention should be part of the early development of a game and not only when it is evident that there is an issue (Tang & Fox, 2016). Better reporting systems, customizable communication controls, fair matchmaking, rewarding positive behaviours and easy blocking/muting are ways that developers can incorporate safety-by-design features. Publishers and platforms should also put in place clear community values, transparent moderation policies and the ongoing review of the effectiveness of their moderation (Mortensen, 2018). Care needs to be taken in design decisions that involve ranking, voice chat and team dependency as they can all lead to conflict. The challenge for these stakeholders is to balance competing interests of freedom of competition and protection of the player to ensure that gaming areas are interesting, fair, inclusive and accountable.

6.2 Implications for Moderators and Esports Organizations

Moderators and esports organizations have a pivotal role to define acceptable behaviour in gaming communities and competitive game spaces. The study suggests that moderation can be a combination of automated detection and human judgment to prevent decisions that are unfair or are not context-appropriate. To act appropriately and effectively when confronted with harassment, hate speech, threats and targeted abuse, moderators require clear guidelines, training, escalation measures and accountability measures (Ozanne et al., 2022). It's crucial that there are well-defined codes of conduct for players, teams, coaches, streamers and spectators in esports organisations. They should also involve some anti-harassment training, reporting systems, disciplinary and support systems for those being harassed (Gorwa et al., 2020). Esports communities have an impact on the broader gaming culture, so setting standards for professional conduct are of great importance for regular gamers. Good moderation and sports governance can help minimize abuse normalization and promote sports behavior that is respectful.

6.3 Educational and Community Implications

However, the study has implications for teachers, parents, players and gaming communities as digital behaviours, social learning and peer culture also play a role in toxicity. Digital literacy, responsible communication, emotional management, media literacy, and an understanding of online harassment should be encouraged through the use of educational initiatives (Ravikumar et al., 2026). Parents/guardians should be aware of the different gaming environments, the risks of communicating online, how to set up privacy on games, and how to report if something goes wrong without deeming gaming as a bad thing. Players can help by reporting bullying behaviour, encouraging targeted players, not sharing inappropriate jokes and using positive language (Kou & Gui, 2020). Peer-support systems, mentoring of new gamers, inclusive players, and community-based moderation can be developed in gaming communities. These implications highlight the need for the shared responsibility approach in creating safer gaming spaces, which involves the combined efforts of technical measures, awareness, empathy, accountability, and positive community norms.

7. RECOMMENDATIONS

This section offers some practical tips for minimizing the toxicity and harassment within online gaming communities. Recommendations focus on technological and design-based solutions, governance and moderation practices, and educational and community-based interventions. Because factors such as player actions, platform rules, communications, competitive systems, and community norms affect the toxicity of the game, there is no single solution for toxicity prevention (Greipl et al., 2025). A multi-faceted approach needs to be taken to identify adversarial activity, minimise opportunities for abuse, assist players impacted and promote respectful play. The recommendations also highlight ethical preventative measures as safety measures need to ensure privacy, unbiased implementation and equal treatment of all users (Topinka et al., 2024). Developers, publishers, moderators, educators, parents, esports organizations and players can implement these strategies to make the gaming world a better and inclusive place. Table 3 provides some simple strategies to mitigate toxicity using technology, moderation, governance, education and community support.

Table 3. Prevention strategies in online gaming

Strategy Type	Simple Strategy	Expected Benefit
Technological	AI-based toxicity detection	Early identification of abuse
Moderation	Human review and fair action	Better decision-making
Reporting	Easy reporting and blocking tools	Quick player protection
Design-Based	Safer chat and matchmaking systems	Reduced conflict
Governance	Clear rules and penalties	Stronger accountability
Educational	Digital literacy and player awareness	Responsible gaming behaviour
Community-Based	Peer support and positive role models	Healthier gaming culture

7.1 Technological and Design-Based Prevention Strategies

More of a technological and design-based approach should be taken to prevent harm becoming accepted as a part of a gaming community. Suspicion of abusive communication, hate speech, threats, and repeated harassment can be detected by using AI-assisted toxicity detection, real-time text filtering, voice detection, behavioural risk indicators, and alerts. But this should be backed up by human review to minimize errors and prevent the unfairness of making decisions (Joshi et al., 2026). Game design also helps to decrease conflict by providing customizable chat controls, simple blocking/muting abilities, safer matchmaking, reputation systems for players and friction prior to sending abusive messages (Shreha et al., 2025). Encourage respectful participation by providing positive behaviour incentives, teamwork rewards and inclusive avatar/identity options (Allchorn & Orofino, 2025). Developers should also take a look at ranking systems, penalties, and team dependency elements that could cause irritation for the users. These approaches will help to ensure more safety and maintain player agency and competitiveness.

7.2 Governance, Moderation, and Ethical Safeguards

The governance and moderation approaches should be transparent, have clear rules and be fairly applied with accountability. Community guidelines to identify unacceptable behaviour like hate speech, harassment, threats, discriminatory abuse or coordinated targeting are required for gaming platforms. Reporting system should be simple, accessible and responsive and give clear feedback to anyone who reports harmful behaviour (Munn, 2023). Moderation should be done in combination with automated tools and with trained human moderators who are capable of comprehending context, language variations, sarcasm and cultural differences (Madaminov et al., 2026). Platforms also should offer avenues for appeals to avoid the unfair punishment and assure users trust in the platform. However, the use of these tools can be harmful if they are not regulated or supervised in an ethical manner; unclear sanctions, biased algorithms and excessive surveillance can create new harms (Mamadiyarov et al., 2026). Thus, for example, moderation policies must ensure that players' privacy is maintained, while being applied in a proportionate fashion, without discrimination, and taking into consideration the safety of players as well as the freedom of expression. Good governance can enhance trust and diminish destructive norms in the community.

7.3 Educational and Community-Based Intervention Strategies

However, technological and community-based solutions are needed as there are no technological or moderation solutions that will change the gaming culture. Digital literacy programs ought to educate players on respectful communication, online safety, harassment due to identity, bystander responsibility and the negative effects of toxic behavior (Wells et al., 2024). The parents and educators should lead young players to know what privacy settings are, what reporting features are, how to control their emotions, and how to play games in a healthy way. Anti-harassment awareness sessions, player conduct training and support initiatives can take place within the esports organization and/or gaming community for the impacted player (Eklund et al., 2022). By developing positive norms from within, community-led solutions like peer moderation, player ambassadors, mentoring for new players, inclusive gaming groups and positive role modelling can be implemented. Players are encouraged to report abuse and support targeted players and to refrain from normalizing harmful humour. These strategies encourage co-responsibility and foster more safe, respectful and inclusive gaming environments.

8. PROPOSED CONCEPTUAL FRAMEWORK

The conceptual framework proposed above connects the concepts of toxicity and harassment in online communities of play by detailing the causes, problematic behaviors, effects, and prevention measures. It portrays toxicity as a social issue that is related to social interactions, game design, player identity, platform governance, and community norms (Shou, 2023). The framework is used to structure the discussion of the chapter, by providing an understanding of how issues like anonymity, competitive pressure, weak moderation, and exclusionary group behaviour can contribute to harassment and hostile communication. This then has an impact on the wellbeing, inclusion, trust and reputation of the platform and the players. The framework also outlines pathways to implementation in practice using technology, design, moderation, governance, education and community participation (Miller-Idriss, 2025b). These components are interconnected, enabling a comprehensive concept of the creation of safer and more responsible gaming environments. Figure 1 depicts the correlation between the factors that influence toxicity, the consequences of harassment and harmful behaviours on players, impacts on the player community, and the need for prevention strategies in online gaming communities.

Figure 1. Toxicity–Harassment–Prevention Framework in Online Gaming

8.1 Components of the Conceptual Framework

There are four key areas of the conceptual framework: causes of toxicity, types of harassment, effects on players and communities, and proactive measures. The first component includes the concepts of anonymity, weak accountability, competitive pressure, poor moderation, hostile norms of the groups, and design features that reduce the occurrence of conflict. The first component involves issues of anonymity, weak accountability, competitive pressure, poor moderation, hostile norms of the groups, and design features that increase the likelihood of conflict (Brenner-Levoy, 2023). The second part is about negative actions such as griefing, threats, trolling, hate speech, discriminatory comments, targeted harassment and exclusion as well as verbal abuse. The third part is on consequences including stress, anxiety, self-censorship, withdrawal, decrease in participation, loss of trust, and decreased inclusion (Pérez de la Fuente, 2023). The fourth component provides recommendations for prevention, through AI-based detection, human moderation, clear rules, inclusive design, player education and community action. Combined, these factors demonstrate that gaming toxicity is a multi-faceted process, and thus a multi-pronged response is needed.

8.2 Toxicity–Impact–Prevention Linkages

This framework demonstrates a clear link between the toxic environment, negative behaviors, player impact and the prevention measures. In such setting, it is easier to have toxic interactions, conduct in game with no accountability, and communicate freely with no effective moderation. These actions can then lead to psychological injury and to social isolation, a loss of community trust and even exposure to extremist or discriminatory messages (Meisner, 2023). Prevention strategies need to therefore target the observed behaviour and conditions that maintain this behaviour. Reporting systems can, for instance, respond to harassment but design can minimize conflict that might occur. Likewise, AI can identify abusive language and education and community norms can deter abusive behavior. This linkage shows that effective prevention has to take place at the technological, social, ethical and governance levels to lead to improvement in the longer term.

8.3 Framework Application for Safer Gaming Spaces

The proposed framework can serve as a guideline for the following groups to create safer online environments: developers, publishers, platforms, esports organisations, educators and gaming communities. The framework can be used by the developers to flag design elements that can create a sense of frustration, exclusion or abuse. Platforms could use it in various ways such as enhancing reporting systems, transparency of moderation, user protection, and ethical enforcement (Liu et al., 2025). It is an extremely effective tool to reinforce codes of conduct, player training and spectator management for esports organizations. The framework can be used to teach digital literacy and responsible communication, as well as raise awareness about risks of harassment, to educators and parents (Ravikumar et al., 2025). It can be utilized within gaming communities to foster supportive behavior among players, positive norms, mentoring, and inclusive engagement. The framework is of value because it allows for the linking of prevention to causes and impacts, so that prevention measures are practical, balanced and responsive to actual gaming experiences.

9. CONCLUSION

This chapter explored the complexity of the issue of toxicity and harassment in online gaming communities and found there were a number of factors at play, including player behaviour, platform systems, game design, social identity and culture of the community. The conversation demonstrated that negative activities like griefing, hate speech, threats, targeted harassment, exclusion, and abusive language can have a negative impact on players' wellbeing, undermine trust and restrict participation in online gaming communities. It also noted that women, under-18s, racial minorities, LGBTQ+ players, new users and other vulnerable groups are more likely to be at risk of being targeted for identity-related abuse and/or withdrawn from the gaming environment. It was also explained in the chapter that toxic culture, when it becomes normalised, can lead to a sense of exclusion, extreme humour, hostile group dynamics, and risks of radicalisation, which can develop into exclusionary attitudes. So, punishment and automatic detection are not enough for prevention. This requires a proper balance of ethical technology, inclusive game design, clear governance, human moderation, digital literacy and community involvement. The proposed conceptual framework links the causes, the forms, impacts and prevention in a way that is useful to creating safer and more responsible gaming environments. In conclusion, the chapter suggests that online gaming can be more inclusive, respectful, and socially beneficial if all stakeholders from game developers and platforms to educators and parents, esports organizations, and players take their share of responsibility to mitigate online toxicity and encourage positive digital play.

10. LIMITATIONS AND FUTURE DIRECTIONS

This chapter relies entirely on conceptual and literature-based analysis; and thus player, moderator, developer and esports organization data was not gathered. There is a reliance on the existing work of scholars and reports from platforms and other secondary sources, and these might not completely encompass the evolving dynamics of gaming communities on the internet. The toxicity and harassment is also found to differ in various game genres, regions, language, age groups and gaming cultures of different platforms, which makes it difficult to generalize the findings to all game settings. A second constraint is that there is no empirical measurement of the extent to which toxic gaming environments actually lead to ideological change; instead, therc is merely a conceptual discussion of the potential for this. Future studies should involve interviews, surveys, ethnographic studies and analysis of data from platforms in order to gain greater insights into player experiences. Inter-game, inter-streams, and inter-community comparisons of multiplayer games, livestreaming platforms, and esports communities would also be helpful. Going forward, there is a need to explore the impact of AI-driven moderation, human checks, inclusive design, and community-driven measures. Further, greater focus should be given to the issues of privacy, algorithmic bias, freedom of expression and ethical governance in gaming moderation.

REFERENCES

Aarthi, S. Ravikumar, Sapayev Odilbek Uglu, V., Sottarov, A., & Singh, A. (2025). The privacy paradox. In *User-Centric Cybersecurity Implications for Sustainable Digital Transformation* (pp. 223–256). IGI Global Scientific Publishing. DOI: 10.4018/979-8-3373-3171-3.ch007

Aarthi, S., Ravikumar, R. N., & Pardaev, J. (2025). Synergizing multimodal generative AI and blockchain for the future of digital media. In *Advances in Computational Intelligence and Robotics* (pp. 1–34). IGI Global Scientific Publishing. DOI: 10.4018/979-8-3373-1504-1.ch001

Akram, M., & Nasar, A. (2023). A bibliometric analysis of radicalization through social media. [Ege Academic Review]. *Ege Akademik Bakış*. Advance online publication. DOI: 10.21121/eab.1166627

Allchorn, W., & Orofino, E. (2025). Policing extremism on gaming-adjacent platforms: Awful but lawful? *Frontiers in Psychology*, *16*(1537460), 1537460. DOI: 10.3389/fpsyg.2025.1537460 PMID: 40823404

Anderson, S. L., & Schrier, K. (2022). Disability and video games journalism: A discourse analysis of accessibility and gaming culture. *Games and Culture*, *17*(2), 179–197. DOI: 10.1177/15554120211021005

Brenner-Levoy, J. (2023). Virtually masculine: Queer men's experiences with harassment in online video games. *Sociology of Sport Journal*, *40*(4), 385–398. DOI: 10.1123/ssj.2022-0170

Burgess, J., & Jones, C. (2020). Exploring the forced closure of a brand community that is also a participatory culture. *European Journal of Marketing*, *54*(5), 957–978. DOI: 10.1108/EJM-01-2019-0075

Chui, R. (2014). A multi-faceted approach to anonymity online: Examining the relations between anonymity and antisocial behaviour. *Journal of Virtual Worlds Research*, *7*(2). Advance online publication. DOI: 10.4101/jvwr.v7i2.7073

Coanda, I., & Aupers, S. (2020). Mechanisms of disclosure: A Socio-technical perspective on sociality in Massively Multiplayer Online Role-playing Games. *Television & New Media*, *21*(3), 315–333. DOI: 10.1177/1527476418824557

Cote, A. C., Wilson, A., Hansen, J., Harris, B. C., Rahman, M. W. U., Can, O., Fickle, T., & Foxman, M. (2023). Taking care of toxicity: Challenges and strategies for inclusion in U.s. collegiate esports programs. *Journal of Electronic Gaming and Esports*, *1*(1). Advance online publication. DOI: 10.1123/jege.2022-0031

DeCook, J. R., Cotter, K., Kanthawala, S., & Foyle, K. (2022). Safe from “harm”: The governance of violence by platforms. *Policy and Internet*, *14*(1), 63–78. DOI: 10.1002/poi3.290

Donner, F. (2025). Structures that tilt: Understanding “toxic” behaviors in online gaming. *New Media & Society*, *27*(12), 6551–6568. DOI: 10.1177/14614448241270446

Dwivedi, Y. K., Kshetri, N., Hughes, L., Rana, N. P., Baabdullah, A. M., Kar, A. K., Koohang, A., Ribeiro-Navarrete, S., Belei, N., Balakrishnan, J., Basu, S., Behl, A., Davies, G. H., Dutot, V., Dwivedi, R., Evans, L., Felix, R., Foster-Fletcher, R., Giannakis, M., … Yan, M. (2023). Exploring the darkverse: A multi-perspective analysis of the negative societal impacts of the metaverse. *Information Systems Frontiers: A Journal of Research and Innovation*, 1–44. DOI: 10.1007/s10796-023-10400-x

Eklund, L., von Essen, E., Jonsson, F., & Johansson, M. (2022). Beyond a dichotomous understanding of online anonymity: Bridging the macro and micro level. *Sociological Research Online*, *27*(2), 486–503. DOI: 10.1177/13607804211019760

Gazia, I., Hubbard, T., Scalona, T., Kang, Y., & Zuckerman, E. (2024). Proactive blocking through the automated identification of likely harassers. *Journal of Online Trust & Safety*, *2*(3). Advance online publication. DOI: 10.54501/jots.v2i3.175

Gorwa, R., Binns, R., & Katzenbach, C. (2020). Algorithmic content moderation: Technical and political challenges in the automation of platform governance. *Big Data & Society*, *7*(1), 205395171989794. DOI: 10.1177/2053951719897945

Greipl, S., Lechner, M., Fischer, J., Schulze, H., Hohner, J., & Rieger, D. (2025). Tracking down the Candy Crush Terrorist: The fragile relation between gaming motives and radical attitudes. *Frontiers in Psychology*, *16*(1585576), 1585576. DOI: 10.3389/fpsyg.2025.1585576 PMID: 41164730

Hayday, E. J., & Collison, H. (2020). Exploring the contested notion of social inclusion and gender inclusivity within eSport spaces. *Social Inclusion (Lisboa)*, *8*(3), 197–208. DOI: 10.17645/si.v8i3.2755

Jonnalagadda, R., Singh, P., Seth, G., Khanna, A., Khanna, A., & Gogineni, A. (2023). Analysis of cross-functional stakeholder collaboration in online safety of children. *International Journal of Research Publication and Reviews*, *4*(11), 645–651. DOI: 10.55248/gengpi.4.1123.113201

Joshi, N., Ravikumar, R. N., Kishore, S., Pandit, S., Pandit, S., & Aarthi, S. (2026). Unmasking threat vectors in large language models. In *Advances in Computational Intelligence and Robotics* (pp. 1–34). IGI Global Scientific Publishing. DOI: 10.4018/979-8-3373-8252-4.ch001

Jovic, D., Butt, M.-A., Stanton, R., & Willma, T. (2023). Why play when you can watch or listen? Multi-modal engagements in digital gaming. *AoIR Selected Papers of Internet Research.* DOI: 10.5210/spir.v2022i0.12958

Kiritchenko, S., Nejadgholi, I., & Fraser, K. C. (2021). Confronting abusive language online: A survey from the ethical and human rights perspective. *Journal of Artificial Intelligence Research, 71*, 431–478. DOI: 10.1613/jair.1.12590

Koehler, D., Fiebig, V., & Jugl, I. (2022). From gaming to hating: Extreme-right ideological indoctrination and mobilization for violence of children on online gaming platforms. *Political Psychology*. Advance online publication. DOI: 10.1111/pops.12855

Konikoff, D. (2021). Gatekeepers of toxicity: Reconceptualizing Twitter's abuse and hate speech policies. *Policy & Internet*, (poi3.265). DOI: 10.1002/poi3.265

Kordyaka, B., & Kruse, B. (2021). Curing toxicity – developing design principles to buffer toxic behaviour in massive multiplayer online games. *Safer Communities, 20*(3), 133–149. DOI: 10.1108/SC-10-2020-0037

Kou, Y. (2021). Punishment and its discontents: An analysis of permanent ban in an online game community. *Proceedings of the ACM on Human-Computer Interaction, 5*(CSCW2), 1–21. DOI: 10.1145/3476075

Kou, Y., & Gui, X. (2020). Mediating community-AI interaction through situated explanation. *Proceedings of the ACM on Human-Computer Interaction, 4*(CSCW2), 1–27. DOI: 10.1145/3415173

Kowert, R., & Crevoshay, E. (2022). Harassment of game makers: Prevalence and impact. *F1000 Research, 11*, 1518. DOI: 10.12688/f1000research.126998.1

Liu, M., Sun, Q., & Williams, D. (2025). With great power comes great accountability: Network positions, victimization, perpetration, and victim-perpetrator overlap in an online multiplayer game. *New Media & Society, 27*(12), 6569–6590. DOI: 10.1177/14614448241268995

Lopez Naranjo, F., Maldonado, M. A., Cuadrado, E., & Moyano, M. (2025). Video games interventions to reduce radicalization and violent extremism in young people: A systematic review. *Games and Culture, 20*(6), 787–812. DOI: 10.1177/15554120231223067

Madaminov, B., Ravikumar, R. N., & Aarthi, S. (2026). Forensic intelligence and cyber resilience for smart tourism ecosystems. In *Cybersecurity and Digital Trust in Smart and Sustainable Tourism* (pp. 161–194). IGI Global Scientific Publishing., DOI: 10.4018/979-8-2600-1850-7.ch006

Mamadiyarov, Z., Ravikumar, R. N., & Aarthi, S. (2026). Cybercrime investigations and forensic readiness in tourism Ecosystems. In *Applications of Cybersecurity and Digital Forensics in Modern Tourism Systems* (pp. 59–94). IGI Global Scientific Publishing., DOI: 10.4018/979-8-3373-5826-0.ch003

Marinett, M. (2021). The new frontier of platform policy. *Internet Policy Review*, *10*(3). Advance online publication. DOI: 10.14763/2021.3.1570

Marques, T. G., Schumann, S., & Mariconti, E. (2024). Positive behaviour interventions in online gaming: A systematic review of strategies applied in other environments. *Crime Science*, *13*(1), 14. Advance online publication. DOI: 10.1186/s40163-024-00208-8

Martindale, S., Kennedy, H. W., Piskopani, A.-M., Ramchurn, R., & Gomez Bergin, A. (2026). Worlding otherwise: Virtual production as a participatory method for imagining safer digital futures. *Convergence (London)*, *32*(2), 331–351. DOI: 10.1177/13548565261427993

Massanari, A. (2017). #Gamergate and The Fappening: How Reddit's algorithm, governance, and culture support toxic technocultures. *New Media & Society*, *19*(3), 329–346. DOI: 10.1177/1461444815608807

McGuckin, M. E., Turnnidge, J., Bruner, M. W., Lefebvre, J. S., & Côté, J. (2022). Exploring youth sport coaches' perceptions of intended outcomes of leadership behaviours. *International Journal of Sports Science & Coaching*, *17*(3), 463–476. DOI: 10.1177/17479541221076247 PMID: 41908295

Meisner, C. (2023). Networked responses to networked harassment? Creators' coordinated management of "hate raids" on Twitch. *Social Media + Society*, *9*(2), 20563051231179696. Advance online publication. DOI: 10.1177/20563051231179696

Miller-Idriss, C. (2025a). Misogyny incubators: How gaming helps channel everyday sexism into violent extremism. *Frontiers in Psychology*, *16*(1537477), 1537477. DOI: 10.3389/fpsyg.2025.1537477 PMID: 40735183

Miller-Idriss, C. (2025b). Misogyny incubators: How gaming helps channel everyday sexism into violent extremism. *Frontiers in Psychology*, *16*(1537477), 1537477. DOI: 10.3389/fpsyg.2025.1537477 PMID: 40735183

Mortensen, T. E. (2018). Anger, fear, and games: The long event of #GamerGate. *Games and Culture*, *13*(8), 787–806. DOI: 10.1177/1555412016640408

Munn, L. (2023). Toxic play: Examining the issue of hate within gaming. *First Monday*. Advance online publication. DOI: 10.5210/fm.v28i9.12508

Ozanne, M., Bhandari, A., Bazarova, N. N., & DiFranzo, D. (2022). Shall AI moderators be made visible? Perception of accountability and trust in moderation systems on social media platforms. *Big Data & Society*, *9*(2), 205395172211156. DOI: 10.1177/20539517221115666

Pérez de la Fuente, O. (2023). Online Misogyny and the Law: Are Human Rights Protected on the Net? *The Age of Human Rights Journal*, (21). Advance online publication. DOI: 10.17561/tahrj.v21.8270

Pierson, J., Kerr, A., Robinson, S. C., Fanni, R., Steinkogler, V. E., Milan, S., & Zampedri, G. (2023). Governing artificial intelligence in the media and communications sector. *Internet Policy Review*, *12*(1). Advance online publication. DOI: 10.14763/2023.1.1683

Ravikumar, A. S., Kurbanova, N., Sevdim, K. E., Zaynitdinovna, B. D., & Jumaniyazova, N. (2026). Bridging knowledge and policy. In *Advances in Computational Intelligence and Robotics* (pp. 119–150). IGI Global Scientific Publishing. DOI: 10.4018/979-8-3373-7620-2.ch005

Ravikumar, R. S., Manujakshi, Aarthi, S., Urazbaeva, Y., & Tamilselvi, S. (2025). Navigating data privacy, security, and regulatory challenges in healthcare AI ensuring fairness, bias mitigation, interpretability, and trust. In *Transformative Role of Transformer Models in Healthcare* (pp. 25–54). IGI Global Scientific Publishing. DOI: 10.4018/979-8-3373-2038-0.ch002

Ravikumar, R. N., & Aarthi, S. (2025). Web-based cybersecurity architectures. In *Impact of Web Technologies on Digital Transformation* (pp. 187–216). IGI Global Scientific Publishing., DOI: 10.4018/979-8-3373-5167-4.ch007

Scholl, B. (2025). Playing on hard: Algorithmic border objects and inequality among esports student-athletes. *New Media & Society*, *27*(8), 4891–4907. DOI: 10.1177/14614448241243097

Sharma, S., Singh, J., Gupta, A., Ali, F., Khan, F., & Kwak, D. (2024). User safety and security in the metaverse: A critical review. *IEEE Open Journal of the Communications Society*, *5*, 5467–5487. DOI: 10.1109/OJCOMS.2024.3397044

Shou, S. (2023). Psychology behind aggressive language used in Honor of Kings. *Communications in Humanities Research*, *7*(1), 193–200. DOI: 10.54254/2753-7064/7/20230883

Shreha, S. A., Ravikumar, R. N., & Aarthi, S. (2025). Neuro-symbolic AI and Behavioral Intelligence. In *Advances in Computational Intelligence and Robotics* (pp. 121–152). IGI Global Scientific Publishing. DOI: 10.4018/979-8-3373-5012-7.ch005

TaeHyuk Keum, B., & Hearns, M.TaeHyuk Keum. (2022). Online gaming and racism: Impact on psychological distress among Black, Asian, and Latinx emerging adults. *Games and Culture*, *17*(3), 445–460. DOI: 10.1177/15554120211039082

Tang, W. Y., & Fox, J. (2016). Men's harassment behavior in online video games: Personality traits and game factors. *Aggressive Behavior*, *42*(6), 513–521. DOI: 10.1002/ab.21646 PMID: 26880037

Topinka, R., Osborne-Carey, C., & Finlayson, A. (2024). Playing with the news on Reddit: The politics game on r/the_Donald. *International Political Sociology*, *18*(2), olae015. Advance online publication. DOI: 10.1093/ips/olae015

Tripathi, S. (2022). Women and online harassment. *Feminist Dissent*, (6), 133–158. DOI: 10.31273/fd.n6.2022.1265

Vergel, P., La Parra-Casado, D., & Vives-Cases, C. (2024). Examining cybersexism in online gaming communities: A scoping review. *Trauma, Violence & Abuse*, *25*(2), 1201–1218. DOI: 10.1177/15248380231176059 PMID: 37243440

Wells, G., Romhanyi, A., Reitman, J. G., Gardner, R., Squire, K., & Steinkuehler, C. (2024). Right-wing extremism in mainstream games: A review of the literature. *Games and Culture*, *19*(4), 469–492. DOI: 10.1177/15554120231167214

Wolfowicz, M., Hasisi, B., & Weisburd, D. (2022). What are the effects of different elements of media on radicalization outcomes? A systematic review. *Campbell Systematic Reviews*, *18*(2), e1244. DOI: 10.1002/cl2.1244 PMID: 36913204

Yodovich, N., & Kim, J. (2022). Exploring the feminization of backseat gaming through Girlfriend Reviews YouTube channel. *Games and Culture*, *17*(5), 795–815. DOI: 10.1177/15554120211056124

Zhang, X., & Davis, M. (2024). E-extremism: A conceptual framework for studying the online far right. *New Media & Society*, *26*(5), 2954–2970. DOI: 10.1177/14614448221098360

Zsila, Á., Shabahang, R., Aruguete, M. S., & Orosz, G. (2022). Toxic behaviors in online multiplayer games: Prevalence, perception, risk factors of victimization, and psychological consequences. *Aggressive Behavior*, *48*(3), 356–364. DOI: 10.1002/ab.22023 PMID: 35112713

KEY TERMS AND DEFINITIONS

Griefing: Intentional disruption of gameplay by a player who aims to annoy, frustrate, or disadvantage others rather than participate fairly.

Harassment: Repeated or targeted harmful behaviour directed at individuals or groups, often involving intimidation, discrimination, exclusion, threats, or personal attacks.

Hate Speech: Abusive or discriminatory expression targeting people based on identity factors such as race, gender, religion, sexuality, nationality, or ethnicity.

Identity-Based Harassment: Harassment directed at players because of perceived or actual identity characteristics, including gender, race, age, sexuality, language, or cultural background.

Moderation: The process of monitoring, reviewing, managing, and enforcing community rules to reduce harmful behaviour and maintain safer online gaming environments.

Online Gaming Communities: Digital spaces where players interact, compete, collaborate, communicate, and form social identities through multiplayer games, forums, livestreaming platforms, and related gaming networks.

Online Radicalization: The process through which individuals may be exposed to, adopt, or spread extremist beliefs, exclusionary ideologies, or harmful group-based narratives in digital spaces.

Platform Governance: The rules, policies, moderation systems, reporting tools, sanctions, and accountability mechanisms used by gaming platforms to manage user behaviour.

Toxicity: Harmful or disruptive behaviour in gaming spaces, including abusive language, insults, trolling, griefing, hate speech, threats, and hostile communication.

Trolling: Deliberate provocative behaviour intended to upset, mislead, anger, or disrupt other players or community discussions.

Chapter 8
The Political Economy of Gaming Industries and Its Impact on Content Ecosystems

Tushar
http://orcid.org/0000-0001-7190-7687
United College of Engineering and Research, Prayagraj, India

Pooja Jaiswal
http://orcid.org/0009-0007-2507-1525
University of Allahabad, Prayagraj, India

Shyam Sundar
http://orcid.org/0009-0007-2507-1525
B.C.S. Prayagraj, India

ABSTRACT

The gaming industry in the world has expanded rapidly, and digital games are now complex socio- economic and cultural systems which affect communication, identity and political debate. This chapter looks at the political economy of gaming industries and its consequences for content ecologies in particular the financialization of the sector through venture capital investment and platform capitalism. It analyses the role of social platforms such as Discord, Twitch, Steam, Reddit, and Telegram that are closely connected to the gaming industry and that can serve as opportunities for social interaction and as a way to establish communities and/or radicalization pathways. The chapter discusses under self-determination theory perspectives, the

DOI: 10.4018/979-8-2600-1664-0.ch008

potential manipulation of psychological needs in the radicalization process of the recruitment of extremists. It focuses on problems with moderation, governance and digital infrastructure with regard to online play systems.

1. INTRODUCTION

The gaming industry has transformed into one of the most significant digital economies of the 21st century, impacting the world on a global scale. Today, with over three billion players globally and projected to earn over US$300 billion in revenue in coming years, the gaming industry plays a key role in the modern media, technology, and cultural industries (White et al., 2024; Lamphere-Englund, 2024). Its role in entertainment, gaming serves as a complex market with game developers, game publishers, platform operators, video streaming sites, sports organizations, advertisers, VC companies, and gaming communities. The economic, technological and cultural aspects have created a platform in which games are a powerful means of social engagement, identity building, political communication and content creation (Kim et al., 2008).

The past few years have seen a focus on the need to transcend the game texts and the players experience to consider the political economy of the game industry. Political economy approaches bring in the political aspect of the ownership, financing, governance and institutional arrangements behind the production and distribution of media. In the gaming industry, these factors are increasingly shaping the design of games as well as the construction, circulation and influence of content ecosystems on public conversation (Egliston, 2026). These trends have been exacerbated by the increasing financialization of the gaming sector, in which venture capital (VC), private equity and speculative investments have emerged as significant forces in the industrial landscape and technological innovation.

The venture capital market has become a major yet under studied player in the videogame industry, as noted by (Deterding et al., 2011). The venture capital investment is focused on scalable and high growth verticals like mobile gaming, digital distribution infrastructures, and blockchain gaming, AI and platform technologies. These investment trends are part of wider trends of financialization, in which finance institutions come to play a greater role in cultural production and technological development. Venture capital firms do not only invest money; they also influence what industries they invest in, the technologies they create, and the visions of the future they promote, both in material and narrative ways, legitimizing certain forms of innovation. This has made market logics increasingly prominent in gaming content ecosystems, focusing on fast growth and expansion, scalability, and the ability to extract data from platforms (Jones et al., 2014).

This growth also has introduced new social and political challenges. Modern games are not just about the experience of playing the game, but it also has a whole other set of platforms, including Discord, Twitch, Reddit, Steam, and other online communities where users connect, share, and form groups. (Gottfried & Sidoti, 2024) These are now significant areas in which to socialize and build communities, especially for younger people. Although the majority of interactions are positive, there have been concerns about the spread of toxic content, hate speech, harassment, misinformation and extremist messaging in these complex environments (Kim et al., 2015).

The connection between gaming and radicalization has thus increasingly been an area of study. As cited by (Grolnick et al., 1997), gaming communities can serve as identity creating spaces where marginalizing messages and attitudes may be reinforced through exposure to discriminatory, misogynistic and extremist content, and bring about a decrease in ability to resist being radicalized. Their research identifies the need to recognize the impact of gendered social identities, norms and social interactions on vulnerability to extreme messaging. Likewise, (Gottfried & Sidoti, 2024) maintain that it is not games themselves, but rather platforms affiliated with gaming which enable social relationships, recruitment networks, and ideological communities to develop that contribute to the process of radicalization in the gaming context. Such sites may serve as "radicalization funnels" that allow people to slip from a "safe" gaming environment to a less "safe" space with higher levels of extremist material (Kruglanski et al., 2014).

The political economy viewpoints of these developments force us to ask some key questions concerning the role of industry structure in content ecosystems. Business models that focus on engagement, retention and monetization of users can often inadvertently encourage controversial or emotional content. At the same time, strategies for investment based growth foster the development of digital infrastructures that allow for maximum participation and data production. This means that economics, technology and social interactions are tightly coupled and can affect the opportunities and risks in gaming contexts (Kowert & Newhouse, 2021).

This chapter explores the political economy of gaming industries shapes content ecosystems by focusing on intersections between financialization, platformization, digital governance and online socialization. It states that in the current context of games, it is necessary to consider the roles played by the economy in the creation of games, on the one hand, and in the shaping of communities and political and ideological statements, on the other. The chapter helps to fill gaps in the understanding of wider political, cultural and economic contexts of digital capitalism, platform power and online radicalization, and situates gaming within these wider processes (Jones et al., 2014; Lamphere-Englund, 2024).

2. POLITICAL ECONOMY OF CONTEMPORARY GAMING INDUSTRIES

2.1 Conceptual Foundations of Political Economy

The political economy of gaming industries is the analysis of economic structures, ownership relations, investment flows and power relations that influence the production, distribution and consumption of digital games. While the gameplay or player actions of games are studied by gameplay or player behavior, political economy examines the institutional and financial context surrounding the game. Today's gaming sector extends beyond just the code and software and into a complex web of gaming, gaming related communities, esports, streaming, investors, advertising, platform operators and publishers. Together, these actors decide on the creation of games, their monetization and the kinds of content that are visible in digital environments. The global nature of gaming as a cultural industry has made it crucial to comprehend the economic and political dynamics that drive growth, as this understanding is vital for grasping the social and ideological implications of the game (Grolnick et al., 1997).

2.2 Digital Capitalism and Platform Economies

The advent of digital capitalism has made gaming a platform based industry with data extraction, network effects and user engagement. Game ecosystems are not only related to games but also to other platforms that have the game as their core component: gaming adjacent platforms include Discord, Twitch, Reddit, Steam, and other social infrastructures where users interact, create content, and build communities (White et al., 2024). These platforms serve as intermediaries, enabling communication and also gathering useful user information that can be leveraged for advertising, subscription fees and targeted advertising.

Networks are a critical feature of platform economies, such that network size and participation lead to an increase in value. As a result, game developers focus on methods that can effectively engage, retain and encourage content production from their players. The model promotes building a large digital ecosystem that can be defined as a continuous cycle of participation, where gameplay, livestreaming, content sharing and social interaction are all combined. These environments foster opportunities for community and innovation, but they also bring about greater competition for user attention, and the exposure of emotionally charged, controversial, or polarizing content. Gaming adjacent platforms are important sites of ideological communication, which shape social norms, identity construction and political communication in gaming communities, according to researchers (Lamphere-Englund, 2024).

Figure 1. Financialization of the gaming industry

2.3 Financialization of the Gaming Sector

Financialization is a hallmark of the modern gaming industries, the increasing role of financial institutions and investment subjects in shaping the industrial development. Venture capital has become a pivotal force in the gaming industry, fueling innovation, growth, and technological advancements. (Gottfried & Sidoti, 2024) states that venture capital companies are focused on the high growth sectors of the industry, including mobile gaming, esports, AI, blockchain technologies, and digital platform infrastructures. These investments are not just economic ones they are investments in industrial priorities, through allocating resources to the creation of scalable and commercially viable business models as depicts in Figure 1.

Financialization can drive a business's focus on fast growth, market expansion and an increase in shareholder value, which can affect content production and platform design. Venture capitalists are intentional in building narratives around the future of gaming, creating visions of disruptions in technology, immersive virtual worlds, and dominance of platforms. Consequently, there is a strong linkage between the economy and cultural production. Beyond financing, financial actors have an impact on governance arrangements, innovation paths and the structuring of digital content systems. As a result, financial logics have come into play in gaming industries, focusing on profitability, scalability, and data-driven growth.

2.4 Market Concentration and Corporate Power

The rise of online gaming has also led to greater concentration and corporate power in the market. Today a relatively small number of multinational corporations own major game development, digital distribution and cloud services, advertising networks, and platform services. The concentration gives dominant companies a significant power to influence visibility, platform management and engagement of users. Large corporations consolidate their technological infrastructures and cultural production processes by making strategic investments, mergers and acquisitions.

Content moderation, algorithmic recommending system and community governance policies are some areas where corporate power is more visible. The circulation of information and cultural narratives is determined by platform operator's promotion, restriction, or removal of forms of content. The scholars have raised concerns about the potential for commercial interests to come into conflict with the actions aimed at combating toxicity, harassment, misinformation, and extremist content in gaming environments (White et al., 2024). This is a developing game ecosystem; questions around accountability of the companies, regulation and democratic governance are becoming more relevant as time goes on. It is important to have the dynamics understood to assess the economic power and its impact on digital culture and the broader politics of online play.

3. INVESTMENT, VENTURE CAPITAL, AND INDUSTRY GROWTH

3.1 Venture Capital in the Gaming Industry

The modern day gaming sector has grown to be vastly different from the traditional entertainment sector to a complex digital economy that has resulted in a massive amount of financial investment. One of the most powerful elements driving this change is venture capital (VC). It is a financial backer that, traditionally, was linked to tech startups, but now is becoming a key player in financing immersive digital technologies, artificial intelligence applications, platform services, esports organizations, and game development studios. (Grolnick et al., 1997) states that venture capitalists have been playing a growing role in the gaming industry, investing in areas that have a strong growth and scalability potential. Beyond just providing capital, their role is extended to influencing the priorities and technology of industry and expectations for future market conditions. Venture capital plays a role in shaping what new products, platforms and business models get the resources they need for expansion and commercialization, through its strategic funding decisions.

Venture capital is increasingly becoming a part of broader financialization trends of digital industries. For gaming companies, investment capital is becoming a critical resource for rapid growth, attracting more players, and navigating the fiercely competitive global gaming market. So, the economic factors have become part and parcel of the production and governance of gaming ecosystems.

3.2 Unicorn Startups and Platform Expansion

Venture capital investment is often manifested in the rise of startup companies referred to as "unicorns", those privately held businesses worth over one billion dollars. Unicorn companies are a symbol of innovation, disruption, and market growth in the gaming industry. VC firms are eager to exploit and invest in businesses that can scale at an exponential rate, leveraging a platform business model, digital technology, and user generated content ecosystems (Egliston, 2026). The growing number of gaming platforms has revolutionized the industry's framework. The modern gaming environment has now moved beyond the confines of a single game and instead is a large online network that will include communication, streaming, social interaction, and content creation. These platforms have emerged as integral parts of the wider gaming ecosystem (White et al., 2024), serving as hubs for community engagement, participation, and engagement within the gaming world. Network effects are an economic benefit that is often the reason venture-backed companies focus on platform expansion. The more people use the platform; it becomes more valuable, which in turn brings more people, content creators, advertisers and investors to it.

Unicorn startups have thus helped to further platformize gaming, by developing new, interconnected gaming environments that combine entertainment, socialization, and commerce. These developments bring with them economic opportunities, but they also allow operators of platforms more influence over content visibility, community governance, and community behaviors.

3.3 Investment Narratives and Future Gaming Markets

The financial calculations are not the only thing that affects investment decisions, but also narratives about the future. VCs are clearly creating and evangelizing visions of technology change that capture the investment opportunity and define the expectations of the industry. In his article, (Grolnick et al., 1997) highlights the critical role that investors have in shaping the future of gaming, focusing on the significant themes like artificial intelligence, cloud gaming, esports, blockchain technologies, virtual reality, and immersive digital worlds.

The stories have economic and cultural significance. From an economic perspective, they are worth investing in new technologies and promote entrepreneurship. Culturally, they influence and mold public perception on how gaming and digital entertainment should go forward. The anticipation of future video games that are more immersive and interconnected has led to a substantial investment in technologies that will help build large scale digital ecosystems. Investment stories that have a future oriented focus also shape platform development strategies. Companies want to position themselves in the expected growth areas and so there is more competition to dominate the new areas. Venture capital doesn't just react to the changes of industry, it's part of the evolution and growth of future markets.

3.4 Economic Drivers of Innovation and Content Production

Economic motives continue to play a crucial role in the innovation and content creation processes in the gaming sector. Companies are driven to innovate and continuously create new technologies, gameplay experiences, and digital services to achieve profitability, user engagement, and market expansion. Venture capital does this by supporting the experimentation and technological development required. Meanwhile, the overall shape of the content ecosystem is being influenced by economic factors. Content that is engaging and retains users is typically a top priority for platform operators as it can directly impact advertising revenue and platform growth. As mentioned by (White et al., 2024) gaming adjacent platforms serve as vital areas for community engagement and content sharing. They foster user generated content, live streaming, social networks and collaborative participation, leading to the creation of economic value.But issues are not without challenges when it comes to commercialization of content ecosystems.

The drive to share hot spots can expand contentious, sensational or polarizing material. The economic aims can impact moderation, governance, and content visibility as gaming platforms are more tied into a wider digital economy. This means it's crucial to comprehend the economic forces behind innovation in order to assess the opportunities and dangers in today's gaming context. Digital gaming in the twenty first century is the result of a combination of investment capital, platform growth, and market competition, all of which contribute to the technological, cultural, and political aspects.

4. PLATFORMIZATION OF GAMING ECOSYSTEMS

4.1 Digital Platforms and Network Effects

Platformization has been a radical shift in the gaming industry where digital platforms are now integral to content distribution, communication and community building. Gaming today is not limited to just a game-software package, but plays out in interconnected ecosystems that combine the fun of gaming, social networking, content production, livestreaming, and digital commerce. Platformization is a reflection of the general digital capitalism dynamics, where platforms are intermediaries between users, creators, advertisers, and businesses in a common technological setting.

Onc of the hallmarks of digital platforms is network effects. The more users that join, the more value the platform will add to them, which makes it even more appealing for others to join. They can get more value from the platform the more users there are, and they will become even more valuable to others to join. The more gaming communities grow, the more prevalent gaming platforms become to be attractive to players, content creators, advertisers, and investors. It has spurred gaming firms to focus on attracting and keeping players in their games, with the aim of increasing engagement and participation. (White et al., 2024) states that the rise in online gaming has created a very networked game environment where social interaction transcends gaming. These network effects further enhance the platform dominance and help to thrust power in the hands of a few number of platform operators.

4.2 Gaming Adjacent Platforms (Discord, Twitch, Reddit, Steam)

One of the key trends in the modern gaming industry is that of gaming adjacent platforms (GAPs), which host gaming related activities instead of being games. Discord, Twitch, Steam, and Reddit are all platforms that (White et al., 2024) consider being essential parts of the contemporary gaming scenario. They are places to communicate, share elements, build communities, livestream and participate. They can help players stay connected to others, share their experiences, plan games, and connect with other gaming cultures.

Studies have come to show that the more important part of the game experience is not only the game in itself, but the platforms it is played on, such as the games console. (Lamphere-Englund, 2024) states that much of social, political and ideological interactions take place outside of the game spaces. Moving from a gaming platform to a gaming adjacent platform affords some opportunities for communities to form and shape identity development, but also presents a risk of exposure to misinformation, toxic language and extremist content. Therefore, gaming infrastructures need to be comprehended as agglomerations of platforms and not as standalone entertainment products (Kim et al., 2008).

4.3 Datafication and User Engagement Models

One of the key aspects of platformize gaming ecosystems is datafication. Digital platforms are constantly gathering, analysing and manipulating data from users to maximize engagement, personalize experiences and enhance monetization opportunities. All interactions related to gameplay, communication, content preferences, viewing habits, social connections and more create data that can be turned into economic worth.

These recommendations are made using sophisticated algorithms that platform operators use to connect users with content, make user recommendations, and increase engagement. User engagement is now a critical measure since it has a direct impact on advertising revenue, subscription revenue, and platform growth. As a result, game makers create systems that foster more extended engagement with social components, reward frameworks, customized recommendations, and local area creation devices (Kim et al., 2015).

The notion of engagement extends beyond just individual games, and it is evident in the social dynamics of the gaming ecosystems as a whole. Online communities meet user's needs for social connection, competence, and belonging. These processes are good in that they benefit user experience, but can also result in user environments where they can become fully integrated into certain communities and information spaces. This can, in some instances, lead to more exposure to negative information or to feeding into ideological echo chambers.

4.4 Monetization Strategies and Platform Governance

A variety of monetization strategies are necessary to ensure the economic success of gaming platforms, turning user engagement into profit. These methods include digital advertising; subscription based content, micro transactions, virtual goods, livestream donations, sponsorship and marketing based on data. It is the desire of platform operators to maximize engagement as there is a greater economic opportunity available when there is more platform activity.

Meanwhile, there's been a significant governance challenge of platforms. Governance encompasses the policies, moderation regimes, algorithms and institutional practices that are employed to control the activities of platforms and their user behavior. The authors of (Grolnick et al., 1997) make a point of calling gaming environments "social environments", where social norms are created and challenged. Content moderation and supervision is needed for issues like Hate Speech, Harassment, Misogyny, Misinformation, and Extremist Content.

5. CONTENT ECOSYSTEMS IN ONLINE GAMING

5.1 User Generated Content and Participatory Cultures

The game culture has become a space in which user generated content (UGC) and participatory culture play an essential role in shaping content ecosystems. Modern gaming contexts allow game players to make a more active contribution to content creation, modification, and dissemination than do traditional media industries, in which the content is mostly created by professional creators. Players have become valuable contributors to the game through the use of game modifications, custom maps, fan communities, discussion forums, digital artwork and gaming videos. This participatory culture shifts consumers into becomes producers of digital content.

Gaming ecosystems are especially well suited for collaborative creativity, due to the technology and social environments they offer that promote participation. Contemporary gaming is not just about playing the game; it's a way of interacting with others within a larger network of information, experiences, and cultural references that are constantly exchanged. UGC contributes to increased player engagement, fostering stronger community connections, and prolonging the lifespan of video games. Participatory cultures also generate new challenges, in that negative content, misinformation, toxic discourse, and extremist narratives can be generated and spread in these cultures. As a result, user generated content is a vital element of the opportunities and risks of online gaming ecosystems.

5.2 Livestreaming, E-sports, and Influencer Economies

The advent of live streaming platforms and the development of e-sports have dramatically revolutionized gaming into a huge cultural and economic industry. YouTube Gaming and Twitch have allowed gamers to stream their gameplay online to reach audiences all over the world, establishing new forms of entertainment and social interaction. Livestreaming has opened up direct channels for content creators to interact with their audience, enabling them to build highly active communities with common interests in gaming.

Esports has also helped to expand the scope of the games content economies. The revenue that comes from competitive gaming tournaments is generated from sponsorships, advertising, media rights, and sales of the merchandise that is sold, and can reach millions of viewers. Esports development has helped to professionalize gaming and provide new job opportunities for gamers, commentators, analysts and event organizers.

Influencers are known to play a crucial role in these ecosystems. Whether via livestream or social media, influencers impact consumer behavior, social norms and culture in the gaming world. They are able to engage with a wide audience, which means they have significant influence over the flow of information and discussions within the public sphere. The gaming adjacent platforms serve as significant spaces where users engage with creators and forge identities together. This has led to the growth of the influencer economy in digital gaming, playing a key role in visibility, engagement, and commerce.

5.3 Algorithmic Amplification of Content

One of the hallmarks of today's content landscapes is the algorithmic curation, recommendation, and prioritization of content. Online platforms use algorithmic systems to show what content users will get, how long they will be able to stay on it and which communities they will be able to join. The algorithms look at user data, interests, interactions and viewing history to tailor content suggestions and ensure high user engagement.

Algorithmic amplification is a key factor in influencing information flows in gaming ecosystems. The posts with more engagement have a greater chance of being prioritized as they can help in retaining users and making the platform grows. This, in turn, has a major impact on user's ability to see live streams, videos, discussions, and other user-generated content. These systems are particularly useful for improving content discovery and personalization, but can also serve to amplify controversial, sensational or polarizing content.

Studies of gaming ecosystems indicate that algorithmic recommendation systems can inadvertently lead to access to harmful content in interconnected gaming communities and through platforms (Lamphere-Englund, 2024). Gaming platforms focus on engagement metrics, so over time, users could see more and more niche or ideologically driven content. This trend underscores the critical need to comprehend the impact of algorithms on digital experiences and their role in disseminating content across gaming platforms.

5.4 Community Formation and Digital Socialization

Community building is among the most crucial roles in today's video games landscapes. The online gaming context offers opportunities for people to create friendships, construct social identities, and engage in joint activities. Digital socialization takes place in the game, in communication, through the gaming live streams, gaming discussion forums, and through platforms that play near the game like Discord and Reddit.

(White et al., 2024) point out that gaming communities are key locations for the development of identity and social belonging. Often players form a deep relationship with a group of players and a common culture. Likewise, (Grolnick et al., 1997) state that gaming communities provide psychological services to their members that address needs for belongingness, competence, and social recognition. Such social benefits help to make online gaming ecosystems popular and long lasting.

Community development can also bring about vulnerabilities, however. In group and out group distinctions are often reinforced by strong group identities, sometimes leading to exclusionary behaviors, toxicity, and harassment or to an ideological polarization. When community norms are hostile or discriminatory, the same social processes that contribute to the sense of belonging and work together for the good of the community can also promote the transmission of harmful narratives. Thus, it is crucial to comprehend the digital socialization processes in order to assess the positive and negative effects of the content ecosystems in online gaming. The communities are still very much alive in the modern day and shape the social dynamics, content creation, and the politics of online gaming.

6. GAMING COMMUNITIES, IDENTITY, AND SOCIAL DYNAMICS

6.1 Gamer Identity and Identity Fusion

Nowadays, gaming communities can act as integral parts in the process of constructing identities within the digital society. Online games have advanced from a leisure activity into a social phenomenon and a number of people have come to adopt a gaming lifestyle. Gamer identity is the degree to which one identifies as a gamer through games, culture, community, and/or activities. This identity is sometimes strengthened by shared experiences, common interests, joint successes and involvement in gaming related social networks.

One of the most important concepts that come into mind when thinking about gaming communities is that of identity fusion, which occurs when a player feels a strong connection or sense of belonging to the gaming community as well as their own group within that community. According to (White et al., 2024), collective participation and social cohesion can be strengthened through a sense of belonging in gaming communities. If there is a sense of belonging at the heart of the gaming groups, it is possible that individuals will feel more attached to the norms, values, and behaviors of those groups. Identity fusion can improve the level of cooperation, trust and loyalty among members, but can also make them more susceptible to group influence and conformity. But in cohesive communities, high levels of identification can influence attitudes towards other groups and can aid in the development of rigid boundaries.

6.2 Online Belonging and Community Building

Social belonging and connection is one of the main advantages of playing games online. Today's gaming environment offers many ways to connect with others through multiplayer gaming, voice chat, discussion forums, livestreaming sites, and other gaming communities like Discord and Reddit. These areas allow people to make friends, work together toward shared goals, and engage in shared activities, all without needing to move to a different location.

(Grolnick et al., 1997) found that gaming communities are able to satisfy basic psychological needs related to belonging, competence and relatedness. The authors draw from Self Determination Theory to demonstrate that people want to connect with social environments that offer important social interaction and social recognition. These needs can often be met within gaming communities, where there are networks of support, opportunities for success, and a sense of belonging. This means that players often create an emotional bond with online communities and groups.

Gamers create a strong sense of community and belonging, which is beneficial to social well-being and social engagement. But robust relationships within communities can also help perpetuate community norms and shared worldviews. As such, a grasp of community building processes is key to assessing the advantages and potential hazards of digital socialization in games.

6.3 Gender, Race, and Cultural Representation

The importance of gender, race, and cultural representation has grown in significance in the field of gaming studies. Gaming communities are very diverse, but social inequalities and exclusion remain to affect participation and representation. In gaming contexts, social identities can play a significant role in shaping people's experience, as (White et al., 2024) indicate. Male and female relationships shape players views of, experiences of, and engagement in gaming communities.

The gaming culture has traditionally been encircled by masculine norms and practices, which can sometimes exclude women and other marginalized groups. Likewise, race and cultural stereotyping has an impact both in game and community. These dynamics can impact participation rates as well as perceptions of belonging and legitimacy of gaming spaces. The current gaming environments are more and more becoming spaces where a variety of representations and expressions of identity are possible. Web platforms empower marginalized communities to create supportive online communities, share experiences, and confront exclusion. However, there is still a significant debate around diversity, inclusion and representation that calls for further focus on social inequalities in gaming cultures.

6.4 Toxicity, Harassment, and Community Norms

Gaming communities are often troubled by the problems associated with toxic behavior, harassment and hostility. Toxicity is the communication and interactions that lead to negative and/or uninviting conditions for the participants. This can often involve discriminatory language, harassment, misogyny, racism, verbal abuse, and cyber bullying. In the modern gaming landscape, toxic behavior is recognized as one of the major challenges (White et al., 2024). Such behaviors are tolerated, challenged or normalized in the community depending on the community norms. Toxic practices can also, in some instances, get entrenched in community cultures, making it the norm to be toxic. These dynamics can make participation less likely, especially for marginalized groups, and enhance wider trends of exclusion.

There is also some research that suggests toxic environments make it more likely that individuals will be susceptible to extremist narratives and exclusionary ideologies. (Lamphere-Englund, 2024) state that people who want to belong and feel recognized are vulnerable to communities that support affirming their identity to a community while simultaneously fostering divisive and/or negative thinking. Hence, a good moderation, community standards (including inclusive) and proactive governance are key to successful gaming environments. Gaming communities provide strong social settings, affecting identity development, communication, and cultural involvement. They are not just about entertainment and their impact is reaching beyond that to social relations, political views, and digital engagement in today's society (Kowert & Newhouse, 2021).

7. RADICALIZATION PATHWAYS WITHIN GAMING ECOSYSTEMS

7.1 Extremist Exploitation of Gaming Spaces

The Internet has revolutionized the world of gaming, fostering highly interactive environments that bring together millions of users around the globe. These platforms are designed mainly to be used for recreation and social activities, but researchers have increasingly shown that these platforms can be used by extremist actors. Gaming Areas offer special opportunities for interaction, communication and community development, and are appealing environments for groups and individuals to convey ideological messages. Extremist groups understand that gaming communities tend to be composed of youth who are technologically savvy and spend long periods of time in online spaces (Kowert et al., 2022).

(Lamphere-Englund, 2024) state that there is little evidence of the direct effect of video games on radicalization. Rather, the exploitation of an extremist is usually through social relationships in the context of a gaming environment. These interactions can be through private chats, multiplayer communication channels, gaming forums, and platforms used for gaming that can have ideological content added over time. Extremist actors frequently do not use such explicit recruitment methods as recruitment centers, but rather adopt more covert engagement techniques which take advantage of existing social relations and community networks. As such, the gaming experience can turn into a territory where extremist stories are normalized and shared and reinforced without users initially understanding the extent of their ideological elements (Newhouse & Kowert, 2024).

7.2 Gaming-Adjacent Platforms as Radicalization Funnels

One common thread in the recent research is that of the role of gaming adjacent platforms (GAPs) in the process of radicalization. Communities like Discord, Reddit, Twitch, Telegram, and more communicate via messaging services and serve as an extension of the gaming community. Much of the social interaction surrounding gaming takes place outside of games, as per White et al. (2024). According to (Grolnick et al., 1997), these environments are opportunities for the potential "radicalization funnels." People may start to attend gaming groups for leisure, friendliness, or socialization but eventually come into contact with more ideological content with interactions with game community members. The shift can be gradual, starting with participating in online conversations about games and moving to more unregulated online environments with higher rates of extremist content (Newhouse & Kowert, 2024). Gaming adjacent platforms play a special role as they enable relationship building and engagement within the community over time. Members of these communities who form a strong connection with each other can be more open to information shared by their trusted community members. This can result in the transfer of the location of gaming spaces to external communication platforms, which can provide routes for radicalization processes to develop over time.

7.3 Gamification of Extremist Narratives

The other mechanism is important "the gamification of extremist narratives". Gamification is the use of game-based features (like badges, points, leader boards, and levels) in non-gaming environments. These tactics are now used by extremist actors more often to engage and appeal to digitally connected audiences through ideological content. (Lamphere-Englund, 2024) also points out those extremist groups have incorporated the aesthetics and mechanics of games in their propaganda. This can be seen in the use of first person shooter graphics, achievement-driven stories, competitive perspective, and engaging digital material similar to popular games. These tactics can help extremist messages to seem familiar and approachable to gaming viewers.

7.4 Recruitment, Propaganda, and Networked Communities

Decentralized and networked communities are employed as the medium of recruitment and propagation in gaming networks, rather than organizations. Digital platforms provide the ability for extremist actors to spread their message quickly, to create a social network, and to target audiences globally. According to (White et al., 2024), identity and social belonging are key aspects of gaming communities, which may make them appealing recruitment sites. Propaganda of the extreme is frequently built around the ideas of belonging, purpose, recognition and collective identity. Themes are similar to those of the psychological needs in Self-Determination Theory, including relatedness and social connection (Lamphere-Englund, 2024). People who feel socially isolated or who want to find more meaningful connections with others may thus be more susceptible to recruitment attempts offering them inclusion and identity affirmation.

Networked communities can easily spread a propaganda message through the sharing of content, affirmation of a message, and recruitment of members by peer to peer communication. Modern recruitment methods are often different to traditional propaganda, and usually utilise informal social networks over direct organizational channels. The delegated structure makes it harder to detect and intervene in extremist content, and facilitates its spread through interconnected gaming ecosystems. Radicalization in games is seen as a social and communicative process that takes place across interwoven online environments. Gaming is not a radicalizing environment in itself, but the wider one can provide the opportunity to radicalize, spread ideology, and recruit to extremist groups on a community basis. It is important to know these pathways in order to create effective prevention, moderation, and digital governance strategies.

8. ECONOMIC INCENTIVES AND THE CIRCULATION OF HARMFUL CONTENT

8.1 Attention Economy and Engagement Metrics

The current gaming environment is part of a larger digital attention economy, where the focus is on valuing user's attention as an economic commodity. The digital platforms are monetized by advertisement, subscriptions, sponsorships, and data based services, with user engagement being a key business goal. This has led to a growing trend in the design of systems that encourage more people to join, stay active, and engage with games, which involves maximizing participation, retention, and interaction. Additional metrics like watch time, clicks, comments, shares, reactions, session duration, and other indicators have emerged as the key markers of platform success (Przybylski et al., 2009).

In gaming ecosystems, engagement rates can impact content creation and content distribution. Content producers such as streamers, influencers, esports organisations and community managers are encouraged to produce content that will catch the attention of audiences for a long time. As a result of the financialization of gaming industries, (Egliston, 2026) noted an emphasis on growth oriented strategies that focus on scalability and user engagement. As a result, platform operators are incentivized to pay for content that evokes powerful emotions drives high engagement figures and encourages reengagement.

8.2 Algorithmic Visibility and Content Amplification

Algorithms are key in shaping contentable experience users have in games. These are implemented on modern platforms using a recommendation system which uses data about the user's behavior, interests, social networks, and interaction history to tailor the content that appears in their feed. The idea behind these systems is to bring content that users will watch, share, or talk about to maximize engagement. The organization of information by the algorithm has a significant impact on the visibility of the contents. As gaming ecosystems grow more complex, (White et al., 2024) point out, they are not just about games; they are about a range of media consumption and continuous networking among users. In such contexts, algorithms are potent gatekeepers that influence public discourse, cultural participation.

Recommendation algorithms improve the content discovery process but can also amplify problematic content. Engagement carries more weight than social consequences for content that has high levels of engagement. This means that misinformation, toxic discourse, false conspiracy theories and extremist narratives can appear to be more visible if they are successful in garnering attention of an audience. (Lamphere-

Englund, 2024) contend that gaming related platforms can serve as "pathways" for users to come across more and more niche ideological material. This algorithmic amplification can then help shape digital echo chambers, which tend to echo back existing ideas and minimize exposure to other viewpoints.

8.3 Commercial Pressures and Moderation Challenges

The challenges for platform operators to balance commercial issues with content moderation tasks are enormous. The investments in technological systems, human reviewers, policy development and community management are significant to achieve effective moderation. However, any stringent user's moderation policy can lead to decreased user engagement, community backlash, or even conflicts with the platform's growth targets.

This is a tension of politics and economics of the gaming platform. It is often the case that companies will encourage greater participation as the larger the number of users, the more economic value may be garnered from advertising and data collection. But the same platforms are increasingly being called upon to respond to offensive actions like harassment, hate speech, misinformation, and extremist activity. (White et al., 2024) highlight that gaming communities are intricate social spaces that are greatly affected by community norms, which shape user actions. The balancing of interests between users, content creators, advertisers, regulators and platform operators is therefore key to the implementation of moderation policies.

8.4 Misinformation, Hate Speech, and Extremist Content

One of the biggest problems of today's gaming era is the circulation of harmful content. The proliferation of misinformation, hate speech, discriminatory language and extremist content on platforms used by gamers for communication, content sharing and community-building has grown. While gaming is not a leading driver of radicalization, it is possible that exposure to harmful ideologies can be facilitated by a combination of digital environments (Lamphere-Englund, 2024). Networked communities are fast spreaders of misinformation because users are likely to turn to trusted peers and influencers for information. Likewise, the normalization of hate speech and discriminatory material can happen when there is a lack of norms that intersect exclusionary behavior. There are certain gaming communities that have reproduced social inequalities, as highlighted by (White et al., 2024) in their report on forms of hostility that occur in these groups, including gendered hostility and hostility toward individual's identity.

These ecosystems are increasingly being used by extremist actors to incite ideological messages within a larger cultural discussion and within online networks. They do not generally pursue direct recruitment but rather strategies for exposure that involve a gradual introduction of political narratives into the current social relations. Consequently, it is possible for negative content to be embedded in entertainment, community engagement and identity development.

9. GOVERNANCE, REGULATION, AND INDUSTRY RESPONSES

9.1 Content Moderation Frameworks

In the era of complex, digital environments, gaming content moderation has emerged as a key element in platform governance. Today's gaming platforms serve millions of people that play, talk, livestream and share content on linked electronic networks. These activities encourage creativity and social interaction but they can also lead to harassment, hate speech, misinformation and extremism. As a result, platform operators have established their own systems and processes for content moderation to ensure safe and inclusive platforms.

Content moderation is generally an amalgamation of automated systems and human control. AI and machine learning algorithms are becoming more prevalent for the detection of harmful language, violations of policy rules, and flagging of suspicious content for review. While automated moderation has many advantages, it also has many disadvantages since the context, cultural differences, and shifting ways of communicating online can make content difficult to evaluate. As (White et al., 2024) point out, gaming communities have their own distinct social norms and communication patterns, which can make it challenging to consistently identify and regulate harmful behavior. A good moderation framework thus needs to strike a balance between safeguarding user's rights and protecting freedom of expression. Content moderation is a key, and difficult, part of digital governance as the gaming ecosystems evolve.

9.2 Corporate Responsibility and Self-Regulation

The concept of Corporate Responsibility has become an important topic in the gaming sector. Online platform operators, online game developers, online game publishers and streaming services are becoming aware of their part in the creation of online environments and their impact on online experiences. As gaming companies are responsible for the technological infrastructure that facilitates social interaction, they have a major responsibility to deal with harmful behaviors and ensure positive community standards.

One of the key methods that the industry actors adopt is self regulation. Businesses develop community standards, policies, and procedures, including reporting procedures and enforcement policies that are designed to discourage and prevent negative behavior and abuse of users. (White et al., 2024) state that proactive measures are necessary to tackle harassment, discrimination, and exclusionary behaviors within gaming communities to build and sustain healthy gaming environments. In response, many have beefed up trust and safety teams and bolstered moderation technologies to enhance platform governance.

9.3 Government Policies and Regulatory Approaches

The world has seen governments taking a greater role in digital platforms and online content regulation. This is a challenge for policymakers to strike a balance between innovation and economic growth and the protection of freedom of expression and addressing online harms. In addition to the growing number of platforms that provide gaming related content, digital communities have attracted significant interest and concern about misinformation, cyber bullying, hate speech, and extremist content.

Studies on radicalization in gaming environments underline the need for regulation in tackling new threats. (Lamphere-Englund, 2024) suggest that online radicalization can happen across multi-layered digital spaces where content can spread across platforms. Consequently, there is a growing emphasis on content takedown provisions, risk assessment, and transparency obligations on platforms, as well as platform accountability (Theobald et al., 2026).

The way that governments have responded to the crisis has differed in many ways between jurisdictions. There are differences in focus between countries in terms of the co-regulatory models that foster partnerships between industry and regulators and the more interventionist approaches that include legal requirements and enforcement mechanisms. These disparities do not mean that there is no shared goal: to create governance frameworks that can effectively limit the extent of online harms and still allow for legitimate online participation. Technology is constantly evolving and is a continuing challenge to policymakers. Regulatory systems have a hard time keeping pace with new technologies, new business models and trans-border digital networks. As a result, governance systems have to be flexible and adaptable to the evolving digital context.

9.4 Multi-Stakeholder Governance Models

In complex environments like the modern gaming industry, the adoption of multi-stakeholder governance models is proposed and supported by many scholars, which require multiple industry stakeholders, governments, researchers, civil society organisations, educators and user communities to work together illustrated in Figure 3. They acknowledge that none of these institutions can claim the authority or expertise to solve all the governance issues related to online gaming. Multi-stakeholder governance places the importance of shared responsibility on creating safer and more inclusive digital environments. The industry brings technology and platforms, the government offers legal and regulatory frameworks, researchers provide evidence based insights and civil society brings the advocacy for user's rights and community well-being. (White et al., 2024) emphasize the need to consider multiple viewpoints when considering issues of identity, inclusion and problematic content in gaming communities.

Figure 2. Holistic governance frameworks

Co-governance frameworks are especially applicable to tackling radicalization and online extremism. (Lamphere-Englund, 2024) provide evidence that radicalization can occur across various platforms and social contexts, and that intervention singularly across one or a few of these spaces are not enough. Collaborating across sectors can foster better information exchange, bolster prevention measures, and build digital resilience.

A holistic strategy is necessary to ensure effective governance of gaming ecosystems, incorporating moderation measures, corporate responsibility, regulatory monitoring, and cooperative partnerships as illustrated in Figure 2. In an era where gaming is a core part of digital culture, governance frameworks need to adapt to the changing dynamics of gaming in increasingly interconnected online environments to manage innovation, user participation and social responsibility.

Figure 3. Multi-stakeholder governance models

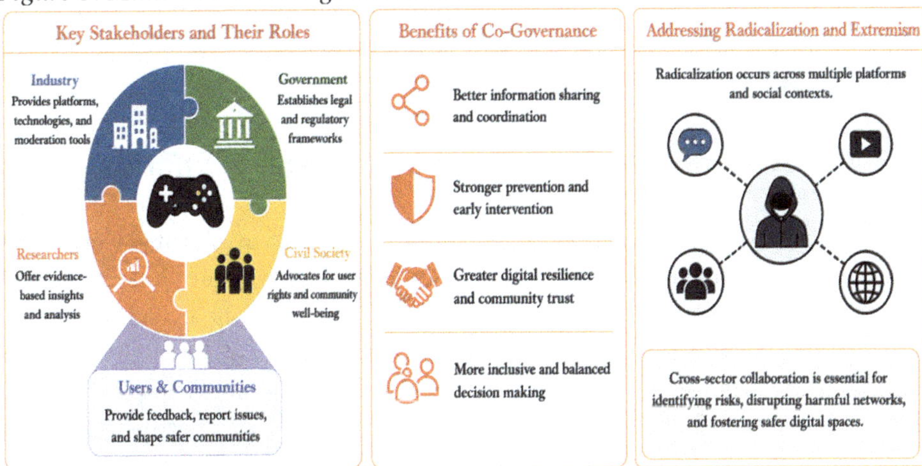

10. EMERGING TECHNOLOGIES AND FUTURE TRANSFORMATIONS

10.1 Artificial Intelligence in Gaming Ecosystems

The world of gaming is undergoing a transformational shift with the emergence of AI in the gaming industry, which is impacting game development, content creation, user engagement, and platform governance. Today, many gaming companies use AI-powered technologies to optimize the gaming experience, tailor content recommendations, boost gaming moderation, and improve user retention strategies. These algorithms leverage artificial intelligence to process significant amounts of data relating to user behavior, offering a personalized experience based on their interaction patterns and preferences.

AI is being used in game design, but it's also playing an important role in gaming adjacent platforms. Machine learning based recommendation systems on streaming and community platforms help to identify content that has the greatest potential to engage users, while automated moderation tools help to identify harmful actions, hate speech, and violations of the platform's policies. Other types of AI-generated content could also shape radicalization dynamics, such as the ability to create and share tailored ideologically driven messages quickly (Theobald et al., 2026). The emergence of such developments underscores the dual role of AI tools, both in enhancing efficiency and user experiences and in providing potential avenues for manipulation, misinformation, and dissemination of harmful content. The future of gaming ecosystems will be shaped by the ongoing growth of AI capabilities, bringing forth significant challenges and questions about transparency, accountability, and ethical governance.

10.2 Virtual Worlds, Metaverse, and Immersive Platforms

One of the emerging trends of digital gaming is the creation of virtual worlds and metaverse environments. The metaverse is an idea of a persistent, interconnected virtual world in which people can engage interact, socialize, collide, and participate in virtual experiences using avatars, or digital counterparts of themselves. These environments merge social networks, e-commerce, entertainment and virtual collaboration within a single technological framework, on top of already established game environments. Venture capital investments have been playing a key role in advancing innovations related to the metaverse. As investors continue to view immersive technologies as a crucial element in the future of gaming, (Egliston, 2026) believes that this will undoubtedly lead to further growth in the gaming sector.

As virtual worlds grow, so will the way people interact and create content in these environments. The growth of virtual worlds could have a significant impact on how people interact and create content within them. The gaming community may be better positioned to become more ingrained within the persistent digital environments where the entertainment and day to day lives blend together. These advancements not only provide opportunities for improved creativity, collaboration, and economic engagement but also pose governance challenges, such as privacy, identity management, content moderation, and platform accountability. As such, the rise of an immersive gaming platform is expected to alter the economy and society of gaming (Kowert et al., 2022).

10.3 Blockchain, Digital Assets, and New Economic Models

Blockchain technology is also another revolutionary technology that is transforming the gaming world. Blockchain creates new economic models by allowing for the establishment of decentralized systems of ownership and value exchange, which are alternative to traditional platform structures. Non-fungible tokens (NFTs), virtual currencies, and virtual rewards are digital assets that enable players to own, trade, and monetize virtual items within a virtual world.

Political economy-wise, blockchain is an effort to re-imagine the relationships between creators, players and platform operators. Proponents say that co-ownership models provide more autonomy and flexibility for users with opportunities for economic engagement. One of the main reasons venture capitalists have taken an interest in blockchain gaming is its scalability and its potential for creating new revenue streams (Egliston, 2026). But blockchain is still controversial. Some critics point to speculations, fluctuations in markets, regulatory uncertainty, environmental sustainability and disparities in wealth.

10.4 Opportunities and Risks for Content Ecosystems

The advantages and potential hazards of emerging technologies for content ecosystems are great. Innovations, like AI, immersive platforms, and decentralized technologies, have the potential to improve the creativity, economic opportunities, access to services, and engagement of communities. On the other hand, innovations, such as AI, immersive platforms, and decentralized technologies, can bolster creativity, expand economic opportunities, improve accessibility, and strengthen community engagement. New forms of content production, participation and digital entrepreneurship can be supported by these technologies, which will benefit both content producers and users. However, technological innovation brings with it new challenges. (White et al., 2024) highlight the existing problems of toxicity, harassment, and exclusion in online gaming communities. New technologies might be exacerbating these issues by making it easier to distribute content on a larger scale, faster, and more complex.

The governance structures that will shape the future of gaming will need to be strong and effective, ensuring that there is a balance between innovation and social responsibility. The process of technological change should be handled in a way that promotes inclusive, safe and sustainable digital environments, and a collaborative effort is needed between policymakers, platform operators, researchers and civil society. As gaming evolves and technology advances, it is important to grasp the opportunities and potential dangers of new technologies to determine the future trajectory of gaming, digital culture, and online communities.

Table 1. Integrated framework of gaming industries and digital content ecosystems

Dimension	Key Components	Impact on Content Ecosystems	Opportunities	Challenges
Political Economy	Ownership structures, market power, corporate control	Determines content production, distribution, and visibility	Industry growth and innovation	Market concentration and monopolistic practices
Digital Capitalism & Platformization	Digital platforms, network effects, data-driven business models	Expands user participation and content circulation	Global connectivity and content accessibility	Platform dependency and power asymmetries
Venture Capital & Investment	Venture funding, startups, unicorn companies	Shapes technological innovation and future market trends	Rapid development of gaming technologies	Profit-driven priorities may overshadow social concerns
Gaming-Adjacent Platforms	Discord, Twitch, Reddit, Steam	Facilitates community interaction and content sharing	Enhanced social engagement and collaboration	Exposure to harmful or extremist content
User-Generated Content (UGC)	Mods, fan content, streaming, forums	Increases creativity and participatory culture	Community-driven innovation	Difficulty in content moderation
Esports & Influencer Economy	Professional gaming, livestreaming, sponsorships	Expands audience reach and monetization opportunities	New career pathways and economic growth	Commercialization and influencer-driven misinformation
Identity & Community Formation	Gamer identity, social belonging, online communities	Strengthens social ties and cultural participation	Inclusive digital communities	Group polarization and exclusionary practices
Radicalization Pathways	Extremist exploitation, gaming-adjacent networks	Influences ideological exposure and narrative circulation	Improved understanding of prevention strategies	Recruitment and dissemination of extremist ideologies
Attention Economy & Algorithms	Recommendation systems, engagement metrics	Determines content visibility and amplification	Personalized user experiences	Amplification of toxic and sensational content
Governance & Regulation	Content moderation, corporate responsibility, policy frameworks	Regulates platform behavior and community standards	Safer and more inclusive environments	Balancing free expression and user protection
Emerging Technologies	AI, Metaverse, Blockchain, NFTs	Reshapes content creation and digital interaction	New economic and creative opportunities	Privacy, security, and governance challenges

Table 1 provides a comprehensive picture of political economy of games industry as well as its impact on the content ecosystem. It shows the major factors that influence the creation, dissemination and consumption of digital content: platformization, venture capital investment, user generated content, esports, community formation, governance mechanisms and new technologies. The framework emphasizes the interconnections between economic structures, technological innovations, social dynamics, and regulatory processes that shape today's gaming ecosystems and social impacts (Kruglanski et al., 2014).

11. APPLICATIONS

Policy makers, gaming companies, education and learning, researchers and digital governance institutions all benefit from the findings of this chapter. By comprehending the political economy of gaming ecosystems, platform operators can work out effective content moderation strategies, enhance community management, and minimise the dissemination of harmful content. The information from these platforms surrounding gaming can contribute to the development of interventions specific to online radicalization and digital literacy for users. Moreover, an understanding of VC investment behaviors and platform management can guide VC actors in creating viable business models that address innovation, profitability, and social responsibility. The findings can also be used in educational institutions and policy-making to create evidence based policies regarding online predatorism, misinformation and extremist exploitation of gaming communities.

12. FUTURE DIRECTIONS

The impact of AI, virtual environments and algorithmic content recommendation systems in gaming ecosystems and content distribution should be explored further. There is a need for increased awareness of the potential of new technologies like generative AI, metaverse platforms and blockchain games to change the dynamics of community interaction and radicalization routes. A longitudinal study examining the role of gamer identity, social belonging, and online behavior would be able to offer more insights into how digital participation and ideology is mediated. Furthermore, inter-cultural and inter-regulatory comparisons can help contribute to understanding of good governance frameworks. Future research on the topic should also consider multi-stakeholder perspectives that look at how industry, government, civil society and academic views can be incorporated into a strategy to support safer, more inclusive and socially responsible gaming ecosystems.

CONCLUSION

The modern gaming industry is a highly fractured digital economy that is characterized through platformization, financialization, technisation and intricate social dynamics. The chapter proves that gaming is not only entertainment but also a place to produce content, to develop identity and to interact with the community simultaneously. The gaming industry is still evolving, with its impact on society growing as a result of new technologies like artificial intelligence, blockchain, and virtual reality, alongside platform centric business models and venture capital investments. Concurrently, gaming platforms, and platforms associated with gaming space, are emerging as crucial spaces for socializing, sharing content, and in some instances, exposure to harmful narratives and extremist ideologies (White et al., 2024). The political economy and digital governance lenses show the importance of appropriate moderation, regulation, and multi-stakeholder partnerships in making future gaming ecosystems innovative, inclusive, and socially responsible.

REFERENCES

Deterding, S., Sicart, M., Nacke, L., O'Hara, K., & Dixon, D. (2011). Gamification: Using game-design elements in non-gaming contexts. In CHI EA '11: Proceedings of the SIGCHI Conference on Human Factors in Computing Systems Extended Abstracts (pp. 2425–2428). Association for Computing Machinery. DOI: 10.1145/1979742.1979575

Egliston, B. (2026). From hits to unicorns: Venture capital in the videogame industry. *New Media & Society*, 14614448251397398. Advance online publication. DOI: 10.1177/14614448251397398

Gottfried, J., & Sidoti, O. (2024, May 9). Teens and video games today. Pew Research Center. https://www.pewresearch.org/internet/2024/05/09/teens-and-video-games-today/

Grolnick, W. S., Deci, E. L., & Ryan, R. M. (1997). Internalization within the family: The self-determination theory perspective. In Grusec, J. E., & Kuczynski, L. (Eds.), *Parenting and children's internalization of values: A handbook of contemporary theory* (pp. 135–161). Wiley.

Jones, C. M., Scholes, L., Johnson, D., Katsikitis, M., & Carras, M. C. (2014). Gaming well: Links between videogames and flourishing mental health. *Frontiers in Psychology*, *5*, 260. Advance online publication. DOI: 10.3389/fpsyg.2014.00260 PMID: 24744743

Kim, E. J., Namkoong, K., Ku, T., & Kim, S. J. (2008). The relationship between online game addiction and aggression, self-control and narcissistic personality traits. *European Psychiatry : The Journal of the Association of European Psychiatrists*, *23*(3), 212–218. DOI: 10.1016/j.eurpsy.2007.10.010 PMID: 18166402

Kim, K., Schmierbach, M. G., Chung, M. Y., Fraustino, J. D., Dardis, F., & Ahern, L. (2015). Is it a sense of autonomy, control, or attachment? Exploring the effects of in-game customization on game enjoyment. *Computers in Human Behavior*, *48*, 695–705. DOI: 10.1016/j.chb.2015.02.011

Kowert, R., Martel, A., & Swann, W. B.Jr. (2022). Not just a game: Identity fusion and extremism in gaming cultures. *Frontiers in Communication*, *7*, 1007128. Advance online publication. DOI: 10.3389/fcomm.2022.1007128

Kowert, R., & Newhouse, A. (2021). Landscape of extremist behavior in games [Conference presentation]. Game Developers Conference 2021, San Francisco, CA, United States.

Kruglanski, A. W., Gelfand, M. J., Bélanger, J. J., Sheveland, A., Hetiarachchi, M., & Gunaratna, R. (2014). The psychology of radicalization and deradicalization: How significance quest impacts violent extremism. *Political Psychology, 35*(S1), 69–93. DOI: 10.1111/pops.12163

Lamphere-Englund, G. (2024). Theories of digital games and radicalization. In Schlegel, L., & Kowert, R. (Eds.), *Gaming and extremism: The radicalization of digital playgrounds* (pp. 32–56). Routledge., DOI: 10.4324/9781003388371-3

Newhouse, A., & Kowert, R. (2024). Digital games as vehicles for extremist recruitment and mobilization. In Schlegel, L., & Kowert, R. (Eds.), *Gaming and extremism: The radicalization of digital playgrounds* (pp. 72–94). Routledge., DOI: 10.4324/9781003388371-5

Przybylski, A. K., Ryan, R. M., & Rigby, C. S. (2009). The motivating role of violence in videogames. *Personality & Social Psychology Bulletin, 35*(2), 243–259. DOI: 10.1177/0146167208327216 PMID: 19141627

Schlegel, L., & Kowert, R. (2024). *Gaming and extremism: The radicalization of digital playgrounds*. Routledge. DOI: 10.4324/9781003388371

Theobald, E., d'Amato, A., Welles, J., Elson, J. S., & Hunter, S. (2026). Radicalization in the gaming ecosystem: The application of self-determination theory. *First Monday*. Advance online publication. DOI: 10.5210/fm.v31i1.14371

White, J., Wallner, C., Lamphere-Englund, G., Frankie, L., Kowert, R., Schlegel, L., Kingdon, A., Phelan, A., Newhouse, A., Saiz, G., & Regeni, P. (2024). *Radicalisation through gaming: The role of gendered social identity. Royal United Services Institute*. RUSI.

Chapter 9
Religious Radicalization in the Afghanistan–Pakistan Borderlands:
Historical Roots and Contemporary Challenges

Muhammad Asad Latif
http://orcid.org/0009-0006-9378-9953
Islamia University of Bahawalpur, Pakistan

ABSTRACT

This chapter examines the historical evolution of radicalization in the region, tracing its roots from the Soviet–Afghan War and the subsequent rise of militant organizations to the post-9/11 security landscape and the Taliban's return to power in Afghanistan. It argues that radicalization is not solely a religious phenomenon but is deeply intertwined with political instability, socioeconomic marginalization, external interventions, ethnic dynamics, and weak state institutions. The chapter further explores the role of religious seminaries, cross-border mobility, digital media, and extremist propaganda in facilitating recruitment and ideological dissemination across the porous Afghanistan–Pakistan border. It also assesses the contemporary security, humanitarian, and governance challenges arising from violent extremism, including terrorism, forced displacement, border insecurity, and regional instability.

INTRODUCTION

The Afghanistan–Pakistan borderlands constitute one of the most strategically significant and politically contested regions in contemporary international relations

DOI: 10.4018/979-8-2600-1664-0.ch009

(Abbas 2023). Stretching across the Durand Line, this mountainous and porous frontier has historically functioned as a corridor for trade, migration, cultural exchange, and religious interaction (Abbas 2023; 2020; Bacon & Byman 2021). At the same time, it has also served as a space where conflict, insurgency, and ideological extremism have evolved over successive decades (Abbasi 2020). Since the late twentieth century, the region has become synonymous with religious radicalization, militant mobilization, and transnational terrorism, attracting sustained attention from scholars, policymakers, and international organizations (Ahmed & Abbasi 2023). Understanding the historical origins and contemporary manifestations of radicalization in the Afghanistan–Pakistan borderlands is therefore essential for explaining broader patterns of insecurity and political instability in South Asia (Bacon & Byman 2021).

Religious radicalization in the Afghanistan–Pakistan region cannot be understood through religion alone (Barfield 2012). Rather, it is the outcome of a complex interaction between historical conflicts, geopolitical rivalries, economic deprivation, ethnic politics, weak governance, and foreign intervention (Barfield 2012; Matloob et al 2023; Naz & Shamsi 2022). While religious narratives have often been employed to legitimize militant movements, the structural conditions that facilitate radicalization extend far beyond theological interpretations (Farag et al. 2025). Decades of armed conflict, state fragility, refugee displacement, inadequate educational opportunities, and persistent socioeconomic inequalities have collectively created an environment in which extremist organizations have found fertile ground for recruitment and mobilization (Latif, 2025; 2025; 2025; 2024).

The origins of contemporary radicalization are closely linked to the Soviet invasion of Afghanistan in 1979. The invasion transformed Afghanistan into the center of an international proxy conflict involving regional and global powers (Gopal & Linschoten 2017). During this period, thousands of foreign fighters entered Afghanistan to participate in the anti-Soviet jihad, supported financially and militarily by external actors. Pakistan emerged as a critical logistical and strategic hub for these operations, while refugee camps and religious seminaries along the border expanded significantly (Gul 2023). Although these institutions initially served humanitarian and educational purposes, some later became associated with the dissemination of militant ideologies and the recruitment of combatants. The institutional and ideological networks established during this period continued to influence regional security long after the Soviet withdrawal (Haider et al. 2020).

The political vacuum that followed Afghanistan's civil war during the 1990s further accelerated processes of radicalization (Haq & Khan 2025). The emergence of the Taliban reflected not only ideological transformation but also the consequences of prolonged conflict, institutional collapse, and the absence of effective governance (Harpviken 1999). Simultaneously, militant organizations operating across the Afghanistan–Pakistan border strengthened their organizational capacity through cross-border mobility, tribal affiliations, and informal financial networks. The porous nature of the Durand Line enabled armed groups to exploit geographic and administrative limitations, complicating efforts by both governments to establish effective border management and security cooperation (Hussain et al. 2023).

The terrorist attacks of 11 September 2001 fundamentally reshaped regional and global security priorities (Latif, 2026; 2026; 2026; 2026; 2026; 2006; 2026; 2026). Afghanistan once again became the center of international military intervention, while Pakistan assumed a central role in global counterterrorism initiatives (Iqbal 2023). Despite extensive military operations and substantial international assistance, extremist violence persisted across the borderlands (Jamal & Maley 2023). Militant organizations adapted to changing security environments by decentralizing their operations, exploiting local grievances, and utilizing digital communication technologies for recruitment, propaganda, and fundraising. Rather than disappearing, radicalization evolved into increasingly sophisticated forms that combined traditional religious messaging with modern communication platforms (Johnson et al., 2017).

Contemporary patterns of radicalization are also closely connected to socioeconomic and governance challenges (Johnson et al., 2017). Border communities frequently experience poverty, unemployment, limited access to education, weak public services, and inadequate political representation. Such structural inequalities contribute to feelings of marginalization and social exclusion, conditions that extremist organizations often exploit by offering alternative sources of identity, belonging, and economic support (Juergensmeyer 2008). Young people facing limited educational and employment opportunities may become particularly vulnerable to recruitment through ideological narratives that promise dignity, purpose, and social recognition (Khan 2011).

Ethnic dynamics further complicate the security landscape of the Afghanistan–Pakistan borderlands. Pashtun communities residing on both sides of the Durand Line share historical, linguistic, cultural, and familial ties that transcend national boundaries (Khan 2021). While these cross-border relationships have historically facilitated legitimate social and economic interaction, they have also created opportunities for militant organizations to establish transnational networks that operate beyond conventional state control. Consequently, counter-radicalization strategies must recognize the complex social realities of border communities rather than relying exclusively on militarized approaches (Kiessling 2016).

The rapid expansion of digital media has introduced new dimensions to religious radicalization. Extremist organizations increasingly utilize social media platforms, encrypted messaging applications, online publications, and digital videos to disseminate ideological narratives, recruit supporters, and coordinate activities across national borders (Kilcullen 2016). Digital communication has significantly reduced geographical constraints, enabling radical ideologies to circulate beyond traditional religious institutions. This transformation demonstrates that contemporary radicalization is simultaneously a physical and virtual phenomenon, requiring comprehensive responses that integrate technological regulation, digital literacy, and community-based resilience initiatives (Kilcullen 2016).

The humanitarian consequences of prolonged radicalization remain profound. Afghanistan and Pakistan have experienced repeated cycles of violence, terrorism, internal displacement, refugee movements, destruction of infrastructure, and economic disruption (Leake 2022). Millions of Afghan refugees have sought protection in Pakistan over several decades, creating additional governance and humanitarian challenges for host communities (Lee, 2022). Protracted displacement, limited educational access, legal uncertainty, and social exclusion have generated vulnerabilities that, in some contexts, may contribute to the persistence of extremist recruitment. Addressing radicalization therefore requires not only security interventions but also long-term investments in humanitarian assistance, social development, and inclusive governance (Maley, 2018).

Although military operations have weakened several militant organizations, experience demonstrates that security-centered responses alone are insufficient to eliminate radicalization (Maley, 2020). Sustainable peace depends upon strengthening democratic institutions, promoting equitable economic development, improving educational systems, enhancing border governance, protecting human rights, and fostering cooperation between Afghanistan, Pakistan, and the broader international community. Community engagement, religious dialogue, youth empowerment, and locally grounded peacebuilding initiatives are equally important components of effective counter-extremism strategies (Maley, 2020).

This chapter examines the historical evolution and contemporary challenges of religious radicalization in the Afghanistan–Pakistan borderlands through an interdisciplinary perspective. It explores how historical conflicts, geopolitical competition, fragile governance, socioeconomic inequalities, cross-border networks, and digital technologies have shaped the emergence and transformation of extremist movements. By situating radicalization within its broader political, economic, and social contexts, the chapter moves beyond simplistic explanations that attribute violent extremism exclusively to religious ideology. Ultimately, it argues that durable solutions require integrated policies addressing both the structural drivers of radicalization and the immediate security threats posed by militant organizations. Such an approach contributes to a more comprehensive understanding of one of the world's most enduring and complex conflict zones while identifying pathways toward sustainable peace, regional stability, and human security in the Afghanistan–Pakistan borderlands.

LITERATURE REVIEW

Religious radicalization in the Afghanistan–Pakistan borderlands has attracted considerable scholarly attention (Marsden 2002) over the past four decades owing to its implications for regional security, international terrorism, migration, and state stability (Matloob et al. 2023). Existing literature generally agrees that radicalization is a multidimensional process shaped by historical experiences, political instability, socioeconomic inequalities, geopolitical competition, and ideological mobilization (Naz & Shamsi 2022). Rather than attributing violent extremism solely to religious beliefs, contemporary scholars emphasize the interaction of structural and contextual factors that create opportunities for extremist organizations to recruit supporters and sustain their operations (Naz 2021). Consequently, research on the Afghanistan–Pakistan borderlands has increasingly adopted interdisciplinary perspectives that integrate insights from political science, sociology, security studies, international relations, and religious studies (Naz 2021; Qureshi & Khalid 2024; Rubab 2024).

A substantial body of scholarship traces the origins of contemporary radicalization to the Soviet invasion of Afghanistan in 1979. Researchers argue that the Soviet–Afghan War fundamentally transformed the political landscape of the region by encouraging foreign intervention, proxy warfare, and the mobilization of transnational jihadist networks (Qureshi & Khalid 2024). During this period, financial and military assistance provided by external actors contributed to the expansion of militant organizations operating across the Afghanistan–Pakistan border (Rashid, 2010). Refugee settlements and religious seminaries also expanded rapidly, providing humanitarian support while simultaneously creating environments in which certain militant ideologies could develop. Studies consistently suggest that the institutional and ideological networks established during the anti-Soviet resistance continued to influence regional security long after the withdrawal of Soviet forces (Naz 2021; Qureshi & Khalid 2024; Rubab 2024).

The rise of the Taliban during the 1990s represents another major focus within the literature. Scholars generally interpret the Taliban's emergence as a consequence of prolonged civil war, institutional collapse, weak governance, and widespread insecurity rather than as a purely religious movement (Barfield 2012; Matloob et al 2023; Naz & Shamsi 2022). Research indicates that the absence of effective state institutions enabled armed groups to establish authority in many parts of Afghanistan, while cross-border tribal and ethnic relationships facilitated the movement of personnel and resources between Afghanistan and Pakistan (Rubin 2022). These studies emphasize that the porous nature of the Durand Line has historically complicated border governance and allowed militant organizations to exploit administrative weaknesses on both sides of the frontier (Rubab 2024).

Following the terrorist attacks of 11 September 2001 (2024; 2024; 2024), academic attention increasingly shifted toward the Global War on Terror and its consequences for Afghanistan and Pakistan. Numerous studies examine the effectiveness of military interventions, counterterrorism operations, and intelligence cooperation in reducing extremist violence (Ruttig 2012). While several researchers acknowledge that security operations disrupted major militant organizations, many conclude that military responses alone have produced only temporary successes (Semple 2014). Persistent governance deficits, corruption, political instability, and social exclusion have continued to provide opportunities for extremist organizations to regenerate despite sustained counterterrorism efforts. Consequently, contemporary scholarship increasingly advocates comprehensive strategies that integrate security policies with political reform, economic development, and social inclusion (Shah & Ehsan 2023).

Another important theme within the literature concerns the socioeconomic dimensions of radicalization. Numerous studies (Roberts & Browne 2021; Fàbregues et al. 2023) demonstrate that poverty, unemployment, inadequate education, and limited access to public services increase social vulnerability, particularly among young people living in conflict-affected border communities. Although scholars caution against simplistic assumptions that poverty directly causes terrorism, there is broad agreement that economic deprivation can reinforce political grievances and facilitate recruitment when combined with insecurity and weak governance (İNAÇ & Asefi 2021). Educational inequality has received particular attention, with researchers emphasizing the importance of expanding access to quality education while strengthening critical thinking and civic engagement to reduce susceptibility to extremist narratives (Zaman 2018).

The literature also highlights the significance of refugee displacement and migration in shaping the security environment of the Afghanistan–Pakistan borderlands (Waqas 2023). Decades of armed conflict have generated one of the world's largest and most protracted refugee populations. Scholars argue that prolonged displacement, legal uncertainty, and limited economic opportunities create humanitarian challenges that require careful policy responses (Theros 2023). At the same time, researchers emphasize that refugees should not be automatically associated with violent extremism, as the overwhelming majority seek safety rather than political violence. Instead, existing studies recommend policies promoting refugee integration, education, employment, and social inclusion to reduce long-term vulnerabilities (Sinno, 2015).

Recent scholarship (Barfield 2012; Matloob et al 2023; Naz & Shamsi 2022) increasingly focuses on digital radicalization and the growing influence of communication technologies. Extremist organizations have adapted to technological change by utilizing social media platforms, encrypted messaging applications, online publications, and digital videos to disseminate propaganda and recruit supporters.

Researchers (Hussain et al. 2023) argue that digital communication has significantly expanded the geographical reach of extremist narratives while reducing dependence on traditional organizational structures. Consequently, scholars recommend combining cybersecurity measures with digital literacy programs and credible online counter-narratives to reduce the effectiveness of extremist propaganda among younger audiences (Siddique 2014).

Despite the substantial growth of research on religious radicalization in the Afghanistan–Pakistan borderlands, several important gaps remain (Sharan, 2022). Much of the existing literature examines individual factors such as terrorism, military operations, refugee movements, or governance separately, while relatively fewer studies adopt integrated historical perspectives that explain how these factors interact over time (Shah & Ehsan 2023). Moreover, limited attention has been devoted to examining the combined influence of historical legacies, cross-border governance, digital transformation, and socioeconomic inequalities within a single analytical framework. This chapter addresses these gaps by synthesizing interdisciplinary scholarship to provide a comprehensive understanding of the historical roots and contemporary challenges of religious radicalization. Through this integrated perspective, the chapter contributes to ongoing debates regarding regional security, conflict prevention, governance reform, and sustainable peacebuilding in the Afghanistan–Pakistan borderlands.

METHODS

Research Design

This chapter adopts a qualitative research design (Creswell & Plano Clark, 2018; Tashakkori & Teddlie, 2010) based on documentary and historical analysis to examine the historical roots and contemporary challenges of religious radicalization in the Afghanistan–Pakistan borderlands. Given the complexity of radicalization as a multidimensional social and political phenomenon, a qualitative approach provides an appropriate framework for exploring the historical, ideological, geopolitical, and socioeconomic factors that have contributed to the emergence and evolution of extremist movements. Rather than relying on primary fieldwork, the chapter synthesizes existing academic scholarship, policy documents, and historical records to construct a comprehensive understanding of the region's security dynamics. This approach enables the integration of diverse perspectives from political science, sociology, security studies, religious studies, and international relations while identifying long-term patterns that cannot be captured through quantitative methods alone 9Denzin, 2012; Fetters et al., 2013).

Data Sources

The analysis is based entirely on secondary sources obtained from peer-reviewed journal articles, scholarly books, government publications, reports from international organizations, and policy papers produced by reputable research institutes. Additional historical evidence was gathered from official reports issued by the United Nations, the World Bank, the International Crisis Group, and regional security organizations addressing conflict, terrorism, governance, and refugee movements in Afghanistan and Pakistan. Relevant literature published over the past four decades was reviewed to capture both historical developments and contemporary transformations in radicalization. The selected sources provide evidence on the Soviet–Afghan War, the emergence of militant organizations, the impact of the post-9/11 security environment, border governance, digital radicalization, and recent political developments following the Taliban's return to power. Using multiple categories of evidence strengthens the credibility of the analysis through data triangulation and allows the chapter to present a balanced interpretation of competing scholarly perspectives (Kumar 2019).

Data Analysis

The collected literature was analyzed using thematic analysis, a widely recognized qualitative technique for identifying recurring concepts, relationships, and explanatory patterns within documentary evidence (Israel & Hay 2006). The analysis involved several stages. First, relevant publications were systematically reviewed to identify discussions related to the historical evolution of radicalization in the Afghanistan–Pakistan borderlands. Second, key themes were coded according to recurring topics, including geopolitical conflict, religious ideology, socioeconomic marginalization, cross-border militancy, refugee displacement, governance deficits, digital extremism, and counter-radicalization initiatives. Third, these themes were comparatively examined to identify similarities, differences, and changing patterns across different historical periods. Finally, the findings were synthesized into an integrated analytical framework that explains how structural, political, and ideological factors interact to sustain religious radicalization in the region (Etikan et al 2016). The thematic approach facilitates a nuanced understanding of radicalization by emphasizing the interconnected nature of historical events, institutional developments, and contemporary security challenges.

Reliability, Validity, and Ethical Considerations

To enhance the reliability of the study, only credible and authoritative sources were included in the review, with particular emphasis on peer-reviewed publications and internationally recognized institutional reports. Triangulation of multiple data sources was employed to minimize potential bias and ensure consistency across historical and contemporary interpretations. The chapter also critically evaluates conflicting viewpoints in the literature rather than relying on a single explanatory perspective, thereby improving analytical validity. As the research is based exclusively on publicly available secondary data, no human participants were involved, and institutional ethical approval was not required. Nevertheless, ethical research principles were maintained through accurate citation practices, careful representation of existing scholarship, and objective interpretation of evidence. Particular attention was given to avoiding the stigmatization of religious communities by recognizing that radicalization is shaped by complex political, economic, historical, and social processes rather than by religion alone. This methodological framework provides a rigorous and transparent basis for examining religious radicalization in the Afghanistan–Pakistan borderlands while supporting evidence-based conclusions regarding its historical development and contemporary policy implications.

RESULTS

Table 1 presents a chronological overview of the historical evolution of religious radicalization in the Afghanistan–Pakistan borderlands from the Soviet invasion of Afghanistan in 1979 to the contemporary security environment. The findings demonstrate that radicalization has developed through successive political and geopolitical transformations rather than emerging solely from religious motivations. The Soviet–Afghan War established the initial conditions for militant mobilization, supported by extensive foreign intervention, refugee displacement, and the expansion of religious institutions along the border. Following the Soviet withdrawal, Afghanistan's political instability and civil war created a governance vacuum that facilitated the emergence of the Taliban and other armed organizations. The events of 11 September 2001 further transformed the region into the center of the Global War on Terror, intensifying military operations while simultaneously encouraging militant groups to adopt more decentralized organizational structures. The Table also illustrates how border insecurity, weak governance, and recurring refugee movements have consistently reinforced opportunities for extremist recruitment and cross-border militancy. In recent years, digital communication technologies have become increasingly important for ideological dissemination and organizational coordination, complementing traditional recruitment methods. Despite numerous military campaigns and international counterterrorism initiatives, the persistence of fragile institutions, socioeconomic inequalities, and regional political rivalries continues to sustain conditions conducive to radicalization. Overall, the historical evidence suggests that religious radicalization in the Afghanistan–Pakistan borderlands represents a cumulative process shaped by interconnected political, economic, social, and security factors. These findings underscore the importance of adopting comprehensive policy responses that address structural vulnerabilities alongside immediate security concerns to promote long-term regional stability.

Table 2 summarizes the principal structural, political, socioeconomic, and ideological drivers of religious radicalization in the Afghanistan–Pakistan borderlands. The analysis demonstrates that radicalization is nt the product of a single factor but rather the outcome of multiple interconnected conditions that reinforce one another over time. Weak governance, political instability, border insecurity, and foreign intervention emerge as the most influential structural determinants, creating environments in which militant organizations can expand their influence. At the same time, poverty, unemployment, social exclusion, and inadequate educational opportunities contribute to widespread socioeconomic grievances that increase the vulnerability of marginalized populations, particularly young people, to extremist recruitment. The Table further highlights the significance of extremist ideology, sectarian divisions, and the misuse of certain religious institutions in facilitating ideological mobilization. While religion often provides the language through which militant groups justify their activities, the findings indicate that ideological narratives gain traction primarily when combined with political grievances and limited socioeconomic opportunities. Additionally, the increasing use of digital media has transformed the radicalization process by enabling extremist organizations to disseminate propaganda, recruit supporters, and coordinate activities across national boundaries with greater speed and anonymity. Organized crime and regional geopolitical rivalries further complicate the security environment by providing financial resources and strategic support to militant networks. Collectively, these findings suggest that effective counter-radicalization policies must extend beyond military operations and incorporate governance reforms, educational development, economic inclusion, community engagement, digital literacy, and regional cooperation. Addressing these structural drivers simultaneously is essential for reducing the long-term appeal and resilience of extremist movements in the Afghanistan–Pakistan borderlands.

Table 3 provides a comparative overview of the major militant organizations that have operated in the Afghanistan–Pakistan borderlands and examines their ideological orientation, operational areas, recruitment strategies, funding sources, and security implications. The comparison demonstrates that although these organizations differ in their historical origins, leadership structures, and strategic objectives, they share several common characteristics, including the exploitation of porous borders, weak governance, political instability, and local grievances. Groups such as the Taliban, Tehrik-i-Taliban Pakistan (TTP), Al-Qaeda, and ISIS-K have significantly influenced the regional security landscape by adopting adaptable organizational structures and expanding their activities through cross-border mobility and decentralized networks. The Table also illustrates that extremist organizations increasingly rely on multiple recruitment mechanisms, including religious narratives, ethnic affiliations, online propaganda, and local socioeconomic vulnerabilities. Financial sustainability is maintained through diverse sources, including illicit trade, external support, taxation in areas under their control, and criminal networks. Furthermore, digital media has emerged as a powerful instrument for ideological dissemination, recruitment, fundraising, and operational coordination, enabling militant groups to expand their influence beyond traditional geographical boundaries. Despite extensive military campaigns and counterterrorism initiatives undertaken by Afghanistan, Pakistan, and international partners, many organizations have demonstrated considerable resilience by adapting to changing political and security environments. These findings suggest that countering militant organizations requires an integrated strategy combining effective border management, intelligence cooperation, financial disruption, community engagement, educational reform, and regional diplomatic collaboration. Such a multidimensional approach is essential for weakening extremist networks and promoting sustainable peace and security across the Afghanistan–Pakistan borderlands.

Table 4 evaluates the principal counter-radicalization strategies implemented or proposed to address religious extremism in the Afghanistan–Pakistan borderlands. The analysis indicates that while military operations and intelligence-led counterterrorism measures have disrupted several militant organizations, these interventions have achieved only limited long-term success when implemented without complementary political, social, and economic reforms. Border management initiatives, including fencing, surveillance, and enhanced security cooperation, have contributed to reducing unauthorized cross-border movement; however, the region's complex geography and longstanding tribal connections continue to present significant implementation challenges. Consequently, security-oriented approaches alone are insufficient to eliminate the structural conditions that sustain radicalization. The Table further demonstrates that preventive strategies, including educational reform, community engagement, youth empowerment, madrasa curriculum modernization, digital counter-narratives, and employment generation, offer greater potential for addressing the underlying causes of violent extremism. Refugee integration policies, inclusive governance, judicial reform, and respect for human rights also emerge as critical components of sustainable peacebuilding, as they reduce social exclusion and strengthen public confidence in state institutions. Moreover, regional diplomacy and international cooperation remain essential for disrupting transnational militant networks, improving intelligence sharing, and coordinating border security policies between Afghanistan and Pakistan. The findings suggest that the most effective approach is a comprehensive strategy that integrates security measures with governance reforms, socioeconomic development, and community-based resilience. Such a multidimensional framework is more likely to reduce extremist recruitment, strengthen institutional capacity, and promote long-term stability in one of the world's most fragile and conflict-affected border regions.

Table 1. Historical evolution of religious radicalization in the Afghanistan–Pakistan borderlands

Period	Major Event	Political Context	External Actors	Religious Influence	Militant Organizations	Border Dynamics	Refugee Flow	Governance	Security Impact	Economic Impact	Social Impact	Media Role	Policy Response	Overall Significance
1979	Soviet invasion	Cold War	USSR, USA	High	Mujahideen	Open	Massive	Weak	High	Severe	Displacement	Limited	Military support	Beginning of jihad
1980	Proxy war	Regional conflict	USA, Pakistan	High	Mujahideen	Porous	Increasing	Weak	High	Decline	Instability	Print media	Foreign aid	Expansion
1984	Refugee expansion	Conflict	UN agencies	Moderate	Local groups	Open	Very high	Weak	Moderate	Poor	Camps	Limited	Humanitarian aid	Long-term effects
1988	Geneva Accords	Peace efforts	UN	Moderate	Fragmented groups	Open	High	Weak	Moderate	Recovery	Uncertain	Newspapers	Diplomacy	Transition
1989	Soviet withdrawal	Power vacuum	Regional powers	High	Armed factions	Porous	High	Fragile	High	Weak	Conflict	Radio	Limited	Civil war
1992	Civil war	Fragmentation	Neighbours	High	Warlords	Unstable	Continuing	Collapsed	Very high	Collapse	Violence	Local media	Minimal	Instability
1994	Taliban emergence	Institutional vacuum	Pakistan	Very high	Taliban	Cross-border	High	Weak	High	Limited	Religious mobilization	Religious networks	None	New phase
1996	Taliban rule	Islamic Emirate	Regional actors	Very high	Taliban	Flexible	Stable	Centralized	High	Weak	Restrictions	State media	Isolation	Consolidation
2001	9/11 attacks	Global War on Terror	NATO	High	Al-Qaeda	Militarized	Renewed	Transitional	Very high	Decline	Fear	Global media	Counter-terrorism	Major shift
2005	Insurgency	Reconstruction	NATO	High	Taliban	Active	Moderate	Weak	High	Limited	Polarization	Television	Security reforms	Intensification
2010	Cross-border militancy	Counterin-surgency	International coalition	High	TTP	Highly porous	Moderate	Weak	Very high	Weak	Extremism	Digital media	Joint operations	Expansion
2015	ISIS presence	Regional competition	Multiple actors	High	ISIS-K	Cross-border	Moderate	Weak	High	Weak	Radicalization	Social media	Counter-ISIS	Diversification
2021	Taliban return	Political transition	Regional powers	High	Taliban	Open	Increased	Fragile	High	Crisis	Uncertainty	Online platforms	Diplomacy	New reality
2023	Border tensions	Security disputes	Pakistan, Afghanistan	Moderate	TTP	Restricted	Moderate	Weak	High	Weak	Polarization	Digital media	Border control	Escalation
2026	Contemporary phase	Regional uncertainty	International community	Moderate	Multiple groups	Monitored	Moderate	Developing	Persistent	Recovery efforts	Resilience	AI & digital media	Integrated policies	Continuing challenge

Table 2. Major drivers of religious radicalization

Driver	Historical Role	Political Influence	Economic Effect	Social Effect	Religious Dimension	Border Effect	Recruitment	Propaganda	Violence	Governance Impact	Regional Impact	Digital Role	Counter-measure	Risk Level
Poverty	High	Medium	High	High	Low	Medium	High	Medium	Medium	Weak institutions	High	Low	Development	High
Unemploy-ment	Medium	Medium	High	High	Low	Medium	High	Medium	Medium	Weak governance	Medium	Low	Employment	High
Refugee crisis	High	Medium	Medium	High	Medium	High	Medium	Low	Medium	Pressure	High	Low	Integration	High
Weak governance	High	High	Medium	High	Medium	High	High	Medium	High	Major	High	Medium	Institutional reform	High
Foreign intervention	High	High	Medium	Medium	Medium	High	High	Medium	High	Destabilization	High	Low	Diplomacy	High
Sectarianism	Medium	Medium	Low	High	High	Medium	Medium	High	High	Polarization	Medium	High	Dialogue	High
Extremist ideology	Medium	High	Low	High	Very High	Medium	High	Very High	High	Weakens trust	High	Very High	Education	High
Madrasas misuse	Medium	Medium	Low	Medium	High	Medium	Medium	Medium	Medium	Moderate	Medium	Low	Curriculum reform	Medium
Border insecurity	High	High	Medium	Medium	Medium	Very High	High	Medium	High	Weak control	Very High	Medium	Border management	High
Ethnic grievances	Medium	Medium	Medium	High	Low	High	Medium	Low	Medium	Moderate	Medium	Low	Inclusion	Medium
Digital media	Low	Medium	Low	High	High	Low	High	Very High	Medium	Moderate	High	Very High	Digital literacy	High
Organized crime	Medium	High	High	Medium	Low	High	Medium	Low	High	Corruption	High	Medium	Law enforcement	High
Political instability	High	Very High	Medium	High	Medium	High	High	Medium	High	Severe	High	Medium	Governance	High
Regional rivalry	High	High	Medium	Medium	Low	High	Medium	Low	High	Diplomatic strain	Very High	Low	Cooperation	High
Social exclusion	Medium	Medium	Medium	High	Medium	Medium	High	Medium	Medium	Weak cohesion	Medium	Medium	Community engagement	High

Table 3. Major militant organizations

Organization	Origin	Ideology	Area	Leadership	Cross-border Activity	Recruitment	Funding	Media Use	Violence	International Links	Current Status	Primary Target	Counter-measures	Threat Level
Taliban	Afghanistan	Islamist	Afghanistan	Central	High	High	Mixed	High	High	Regional	Active	Government	Military	High
TTP	Pakistan	Islamist	Pakistan	Decentralized	High	High	Mixed	High	High	Regional	Active	State	Counter-terrorism	High
Al-Qaeda	Global	Jihadist	Regional	Network	High	Medium	External	High	High	Global	Limited	Western interests	Intelligence	High
ISIS-K	Afghanistan	Salafi	Afghanistan	Regional	Medium	High	External	Very High	High	Global	Active	Civilians	Security	High
Haqqani Network	Afghanistan	Islamist	Borderlands	Family	High	Medium	Mixed	Medium	High	Regional	Active	Military	Operations	High
IMU	Central Asia	Islamist	Border	Network	Medium	Medium	Mixed	Medium	Medium	Regional	Limited	Security forces	Cooperation	Medium
LeJ	Pakistan	Sectarian	Pakistan	Cells	Low	Medium	Local	Medium	High	Limited	Active	Minorities	Policing	Medium
JeM	Pakistan	Islamist	Pakistan	Central	Medium	Medium	Mixed	Medium	High	Regional	Active	India	Monitoring	High
LeT	Pakistan	Islamist	Pakistan	Central	Medium	Medium	Mixed	Medium	High	Regional	Active	India	Sanctions	High
Hizb-i-Islami	Afghanistan	Islamist	Afghanistan	Political	Low	Low	Mixed	Low	Medium	Regional	Political	Government	Dialogue	Medium
ETIM	Xinjiang	Islamist	Border	Network	Low	Low	External	Low	Medium	International	Limited	China	Intelligence	Low
Jundallah	Iran border	Sectarian	Border	Cells	Low	Medium	Mixed	Medium	Medium	Regional	Limited	Iran	Border security	Medium
Ansarullah	Regional	Islamist	Border	Network	Low	Medium	Local	Medium	Medium	Limited	Limited	State	Monitoring	Medium
Local Cells	Various	Mixed	Borderlands	Fragmented	Medium	Medium	Local	Medium	Medium	None	Active	Local institutions	Community policing	Medium
Emerging Groups	Various	Mixed	Regional	Unknown	Medium	Medium	Unknown	High	Medium	Uncertain	Emerging	Multiple	Prevention	Medium

Table 4. Counter-radicalization strategies

Strategy	Government	Community	Religious Leaders	Education	Security	Border Control	Digital Policy	International Support	Refugee Policy	Economic Development	Peace-building	Human Rights	Effectiveness	Sustain-ability	Priority
Military operations	High	Low	Low	Low	High	High	Low	High	Low	Low	Low	Medium	Medium	Medium	High
Intelligence sharing	High	Low	Low	Low	High	High	Medium	High	Low	Low	Low	Medium	High	High	High
Border fencing	High	Low	Low	Low	Medium	Very High	Low	Medium	Medium	Low	Low	Medium	Medium	High	High
Educational reform	Medium	High	High	Very High	Low	Low	Medium	Medium	Medium	Medium	High	High	High	High	High
Madrasa reform	Medium	High	High	High	Low	Low	Low	Medium	Low	Low	Medium	High	High	High	High
Employment programs	Medium	High	Low	Medium	Low	Low	Low	Medium	Medium	Very High	Medium	High	High	High	High
Community dialogue	Low	Very High	High	Medium	Low	Low	Low	Low	Medium	Medium	Very High	High	High	High	High
Counter-narratives	Medium	High	High	Medium	Low	Low	Very High	Medium	Low	Low	High	High	High	Medium	High
Digital monitoring	High	Low	Low	Low	Medium	Low	Very High	Medium	Low	Low	Low	Medium	Medium	Medium	High
Youth engagement	Medium	Very High	Medium	High	Low	Low	Medium	Low	Medium	High	High	High	High	High	High
Refugee integration	Medium	High	Medium	High	Low	Low	Low	High	Very High	High	High	High	High	High	High
Regional diplomacy	High	Low	Low	Low	Medium	High	Low	Very High	Medium	Medium	High	High	Medium	High	High
Judicial reform	High	Low	Low	Low	Medium	Medium	Low	Medium	Low	Medium	Medium	High	High	High	Medium
Good governance	Very High	High	Medium	Medium	Medium	Medium	Medium	Medium	Medium	High	High	Very High	Very High	High	Very High
Comprehen-sive approach	Very High	Very High	High	High	High	High	High	High	High	High	High	High	Very High	Very High	Very High

DISCUSSION

The findings of this chapter demonstrate that religious radicalization in the Afghanistan–Pakistan borderlands is a multidimensional phenomenon shaped by historical, political, socioeconomic, and geopolitical processes rather than by religion alone. The historical analysis reveals that the roots of contemporary extremism can be traced to the Soviet invasion of Afghanistan in 1979, which transformed the region into a major arena of proxy warfare during the Cold War. External military assistance, ideological mobilization, and the proliferation of armed groups established networks that continued to influence regional security long after the Soviet withdrawal. The subsequent collapse of state institutions and the Afghan civil war further intensified instability, creating conditions that enabled militant organizations to expand across the porous Afghanistan–Pakistan border. These historical developments suggest that radicalization has evolved cumulatively through successive conflicts instead of emerging as an isolated religious movement.

The results also indicate that weak governance remains one of the most significant structural drivers of radicalization. Fragile political institutions, ineffective public administration, limited access to justice, and inadequate service delivery have reduced public confidence in state authority across many border communities. In such environments, militant organizations frequently present themselves as alternative providers of security, justice, and social welfare. This institutional vacuum has enabled extremist groups to recruit individuals by exploiting local grievances and dissatisfaction with government performance. Consequently, strengthening governance should be viewed as an essential component of long-term counter-radicalization policies rather than merely a political objective.

Socioeconomic inequalities further contribute to the persistence of extremist recruitment. High levels of poverty, unemployment, inadequate educational opportunities, and social exclusion create conditions in which vulnerable populations become more susceptible to extremist narratives. Although economic hardship alone does not inevitably produce violent extremism, it often interacts with political marginalization and insecurity to increase recruitment opportunities for militant organizations. Border communities that experience prolonged deprivation and limited state investment frequently face greater exposure to extremist influence. These findings reinforce broader scholarly arguments that sustainable peace requires inclusive economic development alongside security interventions.

Another important finding concerns the role of cross-border dynamics in facilitating radicalization. The Durand Line has historically remained difficult to regulate because of its mountainous geography, extensive tribal networks, and longstanding cultural connections among Pashtun communities residing on both sides of the border. These cross-border relationships have traditionally supported legitimate trade, migration, and family interactions. However, militant organizations have also exploited these same networks to move personnel, resources, and weapons while avoiding state surveillance. Consequently, border management remains one of the most complex security challenges facing both Afghanistan and Pakistan. Improving border governance therefore requires not only enhanced security infrastructure but also greater bilateral cooperation and community participation.

The chapter also highlights the transformation of extremist recruitment through digital technologies. Contemporary militant organizations increasingly utilize social media platforms, encrypted communication applications, online videos, and digital publications to disseminate ideological narratives and recruit supporters. Unlike earlier forms of radicalization that depended heavily on face-to-face interaction within localized religious settings, digital communication enables extremist messages to reach broader audiences across national boundaries. This technological transformation has significantly expanded the operational capabilities of militant organizations while reducing their dependence on physical infrastructure. As a result, governments must complement conventional security measures with digital literacy programs, online counter-narratives, and improved cyber-monitoring mechanisms to reduce the spread of extremist propaganda.

The findings further demonstrate that refugee displacement has become both a humanitarian and security concern within the Afghanistan–Pakistan borderlands. Decades of conflict have displaced millions of Afghan citizens, many of whom have sought refuge in Pakistan. Although the overwhelming majority of refugees have no connection to violent extremism, prolonged displacement, restricted economic opportunities, legal uncertainty, and limited educational access may create vulnerabilities that extremist organizations attempt to exploit. This observation emphasizes the importance of distinguishing humanitarian protection from security concerns while ensuring that refugee policies promote social inclusion, educational access, and economic participation. Stigmatizing displaced populations may further exacerbate marginalization and undermine effective peacebuilding efforts.

The comparative assessment of militant organizations indicates that extremist groups differ considerably in organizational structure, ideological orientation, operational priorities, and geographical reach. Nevertheless, they share common strategies of exploiting governance weaknesses, local grievances, and cross-border mobility. Their adaptability has enabled them to survive repeated military operations by decentralizing command structures, diversifying funding mechanisms, and expanding digital communication capabilities. These characteristics explain why purely military approaches have often produced temporary tactical successes without eliminating the broader conditions that sustain violent extremism. Long-term security therefore depends on reducing both organizational capacity and societal vulnerability.

The evaluation of counter-radicalization strategies demonstrates that comprehensive approaches produce more sustainable outcomes than security-centered interventions alone. Military operations and intelligence cooperation remain necessary for disrupting immediate terrorist threats; however, they must be integrated with educational reform, employment generation, community engagement, judicial accountability, and institutional strengthening. Religious leaders, civil society organizations, educators, and local communities also play important roles in promoting moderate interpretations of religion and strengthening resilience against extremist narratives. Likewise, investments in education, healthcare, infrastructure, and youth employment contribute to reducing the structural inequalities that frequently facilitate extremist recruitment.

Regional cooperation represents another critical dimension of effective counter-radicalization. Afghanistan and Pakistan share interconnected security challenges that cannot be addressed independently. Intelligence sharing, coordinated border management, joint development initiatives, and diplomatic engagement are essential for disrupting transnational militant networks while reducing mutual distrust. International organizations and regional partners likewise have important responsibilities in supporting peacebuilding, humanitarian assistance, refugee protection, and institutional development. A coordinated regional framework is therefore more likely to produce durable security outcomes than fragmented national responses.

Overall, this chapter demonstrates that religious radicalization in the Afghanistan–Pakistan borderlands should be understood as the product of historical legacies, political instability, socioeconomic exclusion, geopolitical competition, and technological transformation rather than religious ideology alone. Addressing this challenge requires integrated policies that combine effective security measures with inclusive governance, economic development, educational reform, digital resilience, and regional cooperation. Such a multidimensional strategy offers the greatest potential for reducing violent extremism, strengthening state institutions, and promoting sustainable peace and human security across one of the world's most strategically important yet persistently unstable border regions.

CONCLUSION

Religious radicalization in the Afghanistan–Pakistan borderlands remains one of the most enduring and complex security challenges in South Asia. This chapter has demonstrated that the emergence and persistence of violent extremism cannot be explained solely through religious ideology. Instead, radicalization has evolved through the interaction of historical conflicts, geopolitical competition, weak governance, socioeconomic inequalities, cross-border mobility, refugee displacement, and technological transformation. These interconnected factors have collectively created an environment in which militant organizations have been able to recruit followers, sustain their operations, and adapt to changing political and security conditions.

The historical analysis reveals that the foundations of contemporary radicalization were established during the Soviet–Afghan War, when foreign intervention, proxy warfare, and the mobilization of militant networks reshaped the political landscape of the region. The subsequent Afghan civil war, the rise of the Taliban, and the post-9/11 Global War on Terror further intensified instability while transforming the Afghanistan–Pakistan borderlands into a focal point of international counter-terrorism efforts. Although military campaigns have weakened several extremist organizations, they have not eliminated the structural conditions that facilitate radicalization. Instead, militant groups have continuously adapted by decentralizing their organizational structures, exploiting porous borders, utilizing digital technologies, and capitalizing on local grievances.

The chapter further highlights that weak governance and socioeconomic marginalization remain central drivers of extremist recruitment. Communities experiencing persistent poverty, unemployment, inadequate education, limited healthcare, and political exclusion are generally more vulnerable to the influence of militant organizations. Likewise, fragile institutions and ineffective public administration reduce public trust in state authority, enabling extremist groups to portray themselves as alternative providers of justice, security, and social support. These findings reinforce the argument that sustainable peace cannot be achieved through military interventions alone but requires long-term investments in institutional capacity, inclusive governance, and equitable socioeconomic development.

Another important conclusion concerns the growing influence of digital technologies on contemporary radicalization. Social media platforms, encrypted communication applications, and online propaganda have significantly expanded the ability of extremist organizations to disseminate ideological narratives, recruit supporters, and coordinate activities across national boundaries. Consequently, governments must strengthen digital governance, promote media literacy, and develop credible counter-narrative strategies that reduce the appeal of extremist messaging among vulnerable populations, particularly youth.

The findings also emphasize the importance of regional cooperation between Afghanistan and Pakistan. Given the transnational nature of militant networks and the historical interconnectedness of border communities, unilateral security measures are unlikely to produce lasting stability. Effective responses require coordinated border management, intelligence sharing, judicial cooperation, humanitarian assistance, refugee protection, and sustained diplomatic engagement. International organizations and regional stakeholders should continue supporting peacebuilding initiatives that address both immediate security threats and the broader structural conditions contributing to violent extremism.

In conclusion, religious radicalization in the Afghanistan–Pakistan borderlands should be understood as a multidimensional phenomenon rooted in historical, political, economic, and social processes rather than in religion itself. Addressing this challenge requires an integrated policy framework that combines effective counterterrorism measures with governance reform, educational development, economic inclusion, community resilience, digital regulation, and regional collaboration. Such a comprehensive approach offers the greatest opportunity to reduce extremist violence, strengthen democratic institutions, improve human security, and foster sustainable peace across one of the world's most strategically significant and conflict-affected regions. Future research should continue examining the evolving relationship between digital radicalization, cross-border governance, and regional peacebuilding to inform evidence-based policymaking and long-term conflict prevention strategies.

REFERENCES

Abbas, H. (2023). *The Return of the Taliban: Afghanistan After the Americans Left.* Yale University Press.

Abbasi, A. (2020). Hybrid War Threats and Essence of Perception Management. *IPRI Journal, 20*(2), 1–25. DOI: 10.31945/iprij.200201

Ahmed, D., & Abbasi, M. (2023). *Democracy Under God: Constitutions, Islam, and Human Rights in the Muslim World.* Cambridge University Press. DOI: 10.1017/9781316662618

Bacon, T., & Byman, D. (2021). De-talibanization and the onset of insurgency in Afghanistan. *Studies in Conflict and Terrorism, 46*(10), 1840–1867. DOI: 10.1080/1057610X.2021.1872159

Barfield, T. (2012). *Afghanistan: A Cultural and Political History.* Princeton University Press.

Creswell, J. W., & Plano Clark, V. L. (2018). *Designing and conducting mixed methods research* (3rd ed.). SAGE Publications.

Denzin, N. K. (2012). riangulation 2.0. *Journal of Mixed Methods Research, 6*(2), 80–88. DOI: 10.1177/1558689812437186

Etikan, I., Musa, S. A., & Alkassim, R. S. (2016). Comparison of convenience sampling and purposive sampling. *American Journal of Theoretical and Applied Statistics, 5*(1), 1–4. DOI: 10.11648/j.ajtas.20160501.11

Fàbregues, S., et al. (2023). Use of mixed methods research in intervention studies to improve health outcomes: A review and practical guidance. *Journal of Mixed Methods / Applied Health Research.* DOI: 10.3389/fpsyg.2022.956300

Farag, T., Neuberger, C., Kretzschmar, S., Sehl, A., Wiethaus, L., & Gäng, J. (2025). Intrastate conflict and transformation of the media system: The case of Afghanistan. *Media, War & Conflict,* 17506352251362600. Advance online publication. DOI: 10.1177/17506352251362600

Fetters, M. D., Curry, L. A., & Creswell, J. W. (2013). Achieving integration in mixed methods designs—Principles and practices. *Health Services Research, 48*(6 Pt 2), 2134–2156. DOI: 10.1111/1475-6773.12117 PMID: 24279835

Gopal, A., & Linschoten, A. 2017. "Ideology in the Afghan Taleban." Berlin: Afghanistan Analysts Network. https://www.afghanistan-analysts.org/wp-content/uploads/2017/06/201705-AGopal-ASvLinschoten-TB-Ideology.pdf

Gul, S. (2023). India's Hybrid Warfare Against Pakistan: PPP and PML-N Governments. *Journal of Political Research & Social Science*, *10*(2). https://ojs.mul.edu.pk/index.php/JPRSS/article/download/385/233

Haider, M. W., Azad, T. M., & Warrich, H. (2020). A critical review of hybrid warfare: Challenges to Pakistan. *Global Mass Communication Review*, *5*(4), 72–90. DOI: 10.31703/gmcr.2020(V-IV).06

Haq, M. Z. U., & Khan, M. (2025). Digital Hybrid Warfare (7GW): Threats to Pakistan's Security and a Framework for Countermeasures. *Journal of Regional Studies Review*, *4*(2), 92–104. DOI: 10.62843/jrsr/2025.4b115

Harpviken, K. (1999). The Taliban Threat. *Third World Quarterly*, *20*(4), 861–870. DOI: 10.1080/01436599913604

Hussain, S., Roofi, Y., Faheem, F., & Qamar, M. T. R. (2023). Hybrid Warfare in Pakistan: How it's affecting CPEC. *Pakistan Journal of Humanities and Social Sciences*, *11*(2), 1733–1739. DOI: 10.52131/pjhss.2023.1102.0476

İNAÇ, H., & Asefi, J. (2021). The Discussion of Political Islam and Democracy in Afghanistan. *Turkish Journal of Policy Studies*, *1*(1), 1–12.

Iqbal, R. (2023). The Evolving Regional Strategic Environment and Hybrid Competition in South Asia. World Scientific, 9 (1): 93-106. DOI: 10.1142/S2377740023500057

Israel, M., & Hay, I. (2006). *Research ethics for social scientists*. SAGE Publications. DOI: 10.4135/9781849209779

Jamal, A. S., & Maley, W. (2023). *The decline and fall of republican Afghanistan*. Oxford University Press.

Johnson, T. H., DuPee, M., & Shaaker, W. (2017). *Taliban narratives: The use and power of stories in the Afghanistan conflict*. Oxford University Press.

Juergensmeyer, M. (2008). *Global rebellion: Religious challenges to the secular state, from Christian militias to Al Qaeda* (Vol. 16). Univ of California Press.

Khan, H. (2021). Critical Study of Propaganda & 5th-Generation War. Uniselinus Education Publication. https://www.uniselinus.education/sites/default/files/2021-11/hamid%20khan.pdf

Khan, R. M. (2011). *Afghanistan and Pakistan: Conflict, Extremism, and Resistance to Modernity*. Woodrow Wilson Center Press. DOI: 10.56021/9781421403847

Kiessling, H. (2016). *Faith, Unity, Discipline: The Inter-Service-Intelligence (ISI) of Pakistan*. Oxford University Press.

Kilcullen, D. (2016). *Blood year: The unraveling of Western counterterrorism.* Oxford University Press.

Kumar, R. (2019). *Research methodology: A step-by-step guide for beginners* (5th ed.). SAGE Publications.

Latif, M. A. (2024). Make America Hate Again? Before and After Trump there were Differences in How Muslim and Islam were Portrayed in American Media. *Social Identities, 30*(4), 287–305. DOI: 10.1080/13504630.2024.2382126

Latif, M. A. (2024). The Identity of Religion Always comes up: The War, The Mass Media and The Reproduction of Muslim Identity in the West. *Social Network Analysis and Mining, 14*(1), 1–18. DOI: 10.1007/s13278-024-01354-2

Latif, M. A. (2024). The Rise of Religious Authoritarianism: Muslims, Ethno-Politics, and Racial Identity in India. *National Identities, 27*(3), 15–41. DOI: 10.1080/14608944.2024.2442079

Latif, M. A. (2024). Qatar's Efforts to Change the Image of Muslims after 9/11. *Contemporary Arab Affairs, 17*(3), 416–441. DOI: 10.1163/17550920-bja00046

Latif, M. A. (2025). Indian Mass Media and Politics of Hindutvazation: A Contextualizing Islamophobia and Global War against Muslims. *Race and Social Problems, 18*(4), 1–18. DOI: 10.1007/s12552-025-09469-7

Latif, M. A. (2025). Race, Religion, Holy Wars and the Muslim "Other". *Nationalism & Ethnic Politics, 30*(4), 605–628. DOI: 10.1080/13537113.2025.2537492

Latif, M. A. (2025). Classifying Muslims in Contemporary Europe: Their identity religion and race in Germany and United Kingdom. *International Journal on Minority and Group Rights, 33*(1), 1–29. DOI: 10.1163/15718115-bja10201

Latif, M. A. (2026). Hybrid Conflict in the Afghanistan–Pakistan Context: Digital War Mechanisms, Media Geopolitics, and the Dynamics of Online Radicalization. *Journal of Information Technology & Politics*, 1–20. Advance online publication. DOI: 10.1080/19331681.2026.2697181

Latif, M. A. (2026). Supporting trans youth amid symbolic inclusion and material exclusion: Family control, lived marginalization, and resilience in Pakistan. *International Journal of Transgender Health*, 1–17. Advance online publication. DOI: 10.1080/26895269.2026.2661008

Latif, M. A. (2026). Racialized Vulnerability and Socioeconomic Determinants of Health Among Afghan Refugees in Pakistan. *Scientific Reports, 16*(1), 11434. Advance online publication. DOI: 10.1038/s41598-026-42144-4 PMID: 41764346

Latif, M. A. (2026). *Racialization, Gender, and Health: Afghan Women's Identity Formation and Belonging in Contemporary Pakistan*. Human Arenas., DOI: 10.1007/s42087-026-00639-6

Latif, M. A. (2026). Framing the Muslim 'Other': Mass Media and Islamophobic Practices Shaping Identity, Representation and Power in the West. *Studies in Ethnicity and Nationalism*, sena.70026. Advance online publication. DOI: 10.1111/sena.70026

Latif, M. A. (2026). The Politics of Digital "Othering": Online Hate Networks and the Marginalization of Muslim Communities in Europe. *Nationalism & Ethnic Politics*, 1–27. Advance online publication. DOI: 10.1080/13537113.2026.2696614

Latif, M. A. (2026). The Trouble Triangle: Islamophobia, Neoliberalism, and the Construction of Muslim Identity as "Other". *Insight Turkey*, *28*(1), 161–194. DOI: 10.25253/99.2026281.11

Latif, M. A. (2026). The Iran–Saudi Rapprochement and Religious Extremism: Implications for Pakistan's Foreign Policy and Regional Stability. *Contemporary Arab Affairs*, *19*(3), 70–90. DOI: 10.1163/17550920-bja00115

Leake, E. (2022). *Afghan crucible: The Soviet invasion and the making of modern Afghanistan*. Oxford University Press.

Lee, J. L. (2022). *Afghanistan: A History from 1260 to the Present*. Reaktion books.

Maley, W. (2018). *Transition in Afghanistan: Hope, despair and the limits of statebuilding*. Routledge. DOI: 10.4324/9781315143071

Maley, W. (2020). *The Afghanistan Wars*. Bloomsbury Publishing.

Marsden, P. (2002). *The Taliban: war and religion in Afghanistan*. New Africa Books.

Matloob, N., Matloob, N., & Ishaq, S. (2023). Hybrid Warfare: Strategies and Counterstrategies in the India-Pakistan Rivalry. *Journal of Peace and Diplomacy*, *4*(1), 78–99. DOI: 10.59111/JPD.004.01.043

Naz, F., & Shamsi, Z.-u.-H. (2022). Hybrid Warfare and its Nuances: A Case-Study from South Asia. IPRI Journal, 22 (1): 25-43. DOI: 10.31945/iprij.220102

Naz, I. H. (2021). Foreign Policy in Hybrid Warfare Environment – Way Forward for Pakistan. *Margalla Papers*, *25*(1), 1–11. DOI: 10.54690/margallapapers.25.1.46

Qureshi, H. I. A., & Khalid, I. (2024). Hybrid Warfare in the 21st Century: Implications for Pakistan. *Journal of Development and Social Sciences*, *5*(4), 459–468. DOI: 10.47205/jdss.2024(5-IV)39

Rashid, A. (2010). *Taliban: militant Islam, oil and fundamentalism in Central Asia*. Yale University Press.

Roberts, B., & Browne, J. (2021). Systematic review update: Factors influencing the psychological health of conflict-affected populations in low- and middle-income countries. *Global Public Health, 16*(3), 421–439.

Rubab, M. (2024). Security Dynamics of Pakistan: Hybrid Warfare & Media Threats. *Pakistan Social Sciences Review, 8*(2), 1–12. https://ojs.pssr.org.pk/journal/article/download/530/387/805

Rubin, B. R. (2022). Afghanistan under the Taliban: Findings on the current situation. *Stimson Center, 20.*

Ruttig, T. (2012). How Tribal Are the Taliban? In Bashir, S., & Crews, R. D. (Eds.), *Under the Drones: Modern Lives in the Afghanistan-Pakistan Borderlands* (pp. 102–135). Harvard University Press.

Semple, M. (2014). *Rhetoric, ideology, and organizational structure of the Taliban movement*. United States Institute of Peace.

Shah, H. J., & Ehsan, M. (2023). Hybrid Warfare: Emerging Challenges for Pakistan. *Journal of Contemporary Studies, 11*(2), 234. DOI: 10.54690/jcs.v11i2.234

Sharan, T. (2022). *Inside Afghanistan: political networks, informal order, and state disruption*. Routledge. DOI: 10.4324/9781315161617

Siddique, A. (2014). *The Pashtun question: The unresolved key to the future of Pakistan and Afghanistan.* Hurst.

Sinno, A. H. (2015). *Organizations at war in Afghanistan and beyond.* Cornell University Press.

Tashakkori, A., & Teddlie, C. (2010). *Mixed methods in social and behavioral research* (2nd ed.). SAGE Publications.

Theros, M. (2023). Knowledge, power and the failure of US peacemaking in Afghanistan 2018–21. *International Affairs, 99*(3), 1231–1252. DOI: 10.1093/ia/iiad092

Waqas, M. (2023). Hybrid Warfare in a Post-Truth Era: A Case Study of Pakistan. Discourse: An International Journal of Communication. https://discourse.org.pk/index.php/discourse/article/download/260/158

Zaman, M. Q. (2018). *Islam in Pakistan: A history* (Vol. 68). Princeton University Press.

ADDITIONAL READING

Latif, M. A. (2024). Terrorism New Wave and Online Radicalization. *Historical, 3*(2), 169–180. DOI: 10.58355/historical.v3i2.109

Latif, M. A. (2024). Composing violence: The limits of exposure and the making of minorities. *National Identities, 27*(3), 371–372. DOI: 10.1080/14608944.2024.2411897

Latif, M. A. (2024). Muslim, Minorities and the Media: Discourse on Islam in the West. *Social Identities, 30*(4), 445–447. Advance online publication. DOI: 10.1080/13504630.2024.2388128

Latif, M. A. (2025). Mapping Modern Islamophobia: A Contextualizing BJP's Hindutva Ideology and Muslim (Mis) Representation in Indian Media. In Hermann, J. (Ed.), *Minorities – New Challenges and Horizons* (pp. 1–19). IntechOpen., DOI: 10.5772/intechopen.1007744

Latif, M. A. (2025). A Review Essay on Muslim Victimization in New Crusade Wars. *Social Identities, 30*(5), 527–531. DOI: 10.1080/13504630.2024.2395282

Latif, M. A. (2025). Managing Religion and Religious Changes in Iran: A Socio-Legal Analysis. *British Journal of Middle Eastern Studies*, 1–2. Advance online publication. DOI: 10.1080/13530194.2025.2548142

Latif, M. A. (2025). Twelve Feminist Lessons of War. *Australian Feminist Studies, 40*(123), 124–125. Advance online publication. DOI: 10.1080/08164649.2025.2515535

Latif, M. A. (2025). The nation form in the global age. Ethnographic perspectives. *National Identities*. Advance online publication. DOI: 10.1080/14608944.2025.2515758

Latif, M. A. (2026). Islamophobia in European Digital Spaces: Disinformation, Algorithms, Online Hate Networks, and Their Impacts on Peacebuilding. In Jamil, (Eds.), *Digital Hate Speech, Disinformation, and Peace in Religiously Diverse Regions* (pp. 97–126). IGI Global., DOI: 10.4018/979-8-3373-6068-3.ch004

Latif, M. A. (2026). The Use of Religious Fantasy as a Means of Promoting Terror. In Lyle, P., & Kukreja, J. (Eds.), (pp. 317–340). IGI Global Publishers., DOI: 10.4018/979-8-3373-4903-9.ch011

Latif, M. A. (2026). A Review Essay on Racialization, Otherization and Muslim Identity in Contemporary World. *Social Identities, 32*(2), 198–202. Advance online publication. DOI: 10.1080/13504630.2025.2485072

Latif, M. A. (2026). Race, Ethnicity, Nationality and the Law: Legal Paradoxes in Conceptualization and Operationalization. *Griffith Law Review*, *35*(2), 188–190. Advance online publication. DOI: 10.1080/10383441.2026.2691667

Muhammad Asad Latif. (2025). *Fixing Gender: The Paradoxical Politics of Training Peacekeepers*. International Peacekeeping Peacekeeping., DOI: 10.1080/13533312.2025.2553106

Chapter 10
Gaming in the Modern Age: Digital Politics and Extremism in Gaming

Atharva Shrirkushna Joshi
http://orcid.org/0009-0009-5000-2753
Vishwakarma Institute of Technology, India

Nitish Mangesh Kulkarni
http://orcid.org/0009-0002-0977-4929
Vishwakarma Institute of Technology, India

Ananya Pankaj Jagtap
http://orcid.org/0009-0004-2463-9877
Vishwakarma Institute of Technology, India

ABSTRACT

In this chapter, we consider the dynamics of the interplay of the internet games community, gaming, and radicalization. We investigate whether internet gaming and the related discourse could be considered the environment of ideological indoctrination, community building, and mobilization of extremists. Our analysis of events includes such topics as GamerGate movement, the emergence of toxic behavior in online gaming, and the effects of irony culture, anonymity, and the algorithms of gaming sites on the political conduct of people. This chapter focuses not only on the problems posed by gaming but also on the positive phenomena of inclusive gaming communities.

DOI: 10.4018/979-8-2600-1664-0.ch010

1. INTRODUCTION

1.1 The Convergence of Gaming and Political Radicalization

The intersection of digital gaming and political radicalization represents one of the most consequential, yet underexamined, phenomena of the contemporary information age. Over the past two decades, online gaming environments have evolved from simple recreational spaces into richly complex social ecosystems, hosting hundreds of millions of simultaneous users across shared virtual worlds, competitive arenas, and community platforms. These spaces do not exist in a political vacuum. They are inhabited by real people, carrying real beliefs, embedded in real communities, and shaped by real ideological currents that flow both from and into the broader digital public sphere. What makes gaming environments distinctive is not simply their size, but the depth and persistence of the social bonds they generate. Unlike passive media consumption, gaming demands active participation, cooperative problem-solving, and sustained community engagement — conditions that make it a uniquely powerful context for identity formation and, by extension, for political socialization.

This report examines how online gaming platforms and communities have become sites of political identity formation, ideological contestation, and, in some cases, radicalization. It situates gaming within the broader literatures on online extremism, media studies, and digital sociology, arguing that the unique affordances of gaming environments — including anonymity, community belonging, persistent social interaction, and the normalization of transgressive humor — create conditions that are particularly susceptible to the infiltration and amplification of radical political ideas. At the same time, the report cautions against deterministic or panic-driven readings of gaming culture, emphasizing the importance of nuance, empirical grounding, and attention to the diverse political ecologies that exist across different gaming communities. Gaming is neither a radicalization machine nor an apolitical leisure activity; it is a complex social terrain on which political struggles of our age are being fought.

The report draws on a range of empirical sources, including ethnographic accounts, computational studies, journalistic investigations, survey data from organizations such as the Anti-Defamation League, and primary documentation from gaming communities themselves. Where possible, it distinguishes between communities and genres, resisting the temptation to treat 'gamers' as a homogeneous category. It is also attentive to the ways in which moral panics about gaming can themselves become politically mobilized, and it maintains a commitment to the kinds of methodological rigor and intellectual honesty that the subject demands.

1.2 Why Gaming Matters: Scale, Demographics, and Social Architecture

Understanding gaming and radicalization is not merely an academic exercise. With gaming representing the world's largest entertainment industry by revenue — surpassing film and music combined — and with hundreds of millions of young people spending significant portions of their social lives in gaming environments, the political dimensions of these spaces carry considerable real-world weight. According to industry estimates, the global gaming market generated approximately $184 billion in revenue in 2023, a figure that dwarfs the combined revenues of the global box office and recorded music industries (see Figure 1). More importantly, gaming is not simply a consumer product; it is a social infrastructure through which a substantial portion of the world's population maintains friendships, forms identities, and navigates the transition from adolescence to adulthood.

The demographic profile of gaming is itself politically significant. While gaming has become more diverse in recent years, the core communities most associated with political radicalization — particularly those organized around competitive first-person shooters, real-time strategy games, and gaming-adjacent platforms such as 4chan and certain Discord servers — remain disproportionately composed of young men between the ages of 15 and 30. This is precisely the demographic that political extremist movements, across the ideological spectrum but especially on the far right, have historically targeted for recruitment. The overlap between the demographics of gaming communities and the demographics of extremist recruitment is not coincidental; it reflects deliberate strategic choices by movements that have recognized gaming spaces as fertile ground for spreading their ideas.

Beyond demographics, the social architecture of gaming platforms — including voice chat, persistent community structures, reputation systems, and the intense emotional experiences of competitive and cooperative play — creates conditions for the kinds of deep social bonds that are, in other contexts, recognized as key prerequisites for ideological influence. When a young person's closest friends are the people they game with, when their sense of belonging and self-worth is tied to their standing in a gaming community, and when the social norms of that community include the casual expression of extreme political views, the conditions for radicalization are powerfully present, regardless of any individual platform's formal content policies.

Table 1. Entertainment Sector Comparison (2023 Estimates). Gaming commands the largest revenue of any entertainment industry globally

Entertainment Sector	Est. Global Revenue (USD)	Primary Demographic	Growth Trend (5yr)
Gaming	$184 Billion	Ages 18–34	↑ +68%
Streaming Services	$109 Billion	Ages 25–44	↑ +45%
Box Office (Film)	$43 Billion	Ages 18–49	↓ −12%
Sports Broadcasting	$54 Billion	Ages 25–54	↑ +18%
Recorded Music	$26 Billion	Ages 16–34	↑ +31%

1.3 Scope, Argument, and Organization of This Report

The report proceeds in eleven substantive chapters, each addressing a distinct dimension of the relationship between gaming, politics, and radicalization. The argument advanced is not that gaming causes radicalization in any simple or mechanistic sense, but rather that gaming environments constitute a distinctive set of social conditions — affordances, demographics, community architectures, and communicative norms — that interact with broader political forces to produce both risks of radicalization and opportunities for progressive political community-building. Understanding these interactions requires a multi-level analysis that moves between the micro-level dynamics of individual gaming relationships, the meso-level structures of gaming communities and platforms, and the macro-level political and cultural forces that shape the broader environment in which gaming takes place.

The report is intended to be useful to multiple audiences. For academic researchers, it offers an integrative theoretical framework and a synthesis of the available empirical literature, along with a detailed research agenda identifying priority areas for future investigation. For policymakers and platform operators, it provides an evidence-based assessment of the risks and dynamics of gaming-related radicalization, along with a critical evaluation of existing responses and recommendations for more effective approaches. For educators, community organizers, and concerned citizens, it offers a nuanced account of a phenomenon that is frequently either dismissed or sensationalized, and that deserves the kind of careful, empirically grounded attention this report seeks to provide.

2. THEORETICAL FRAMEWORK: RADICALIZATION IN DIGITAL ENVIRONMENTS

2.1 Evolution of Radicalization Scholarship

Scholarly understandings of radicalization have evolved considerably since the early security studies literature that dominated post-9/11 discourse. Early models, exemplified by frameworks such as Moghaddam's (2005) 'staircase to terrorism' and Wiktorowicz's (2004) process model, tended to emphasize individual psychological pathways toward violent extremism, focusing on grievance, identity crisis, and ideological adoption as the key variables driving individuals from mainstream political views toward extremist ones. While these frameworks remain influential in certain respects, they have been critiqued for their linearity, their focus on jihadist movements to the exclusion of other forms of extremism, their tendency to treat radicalization as a pathway with a definite endpoint, and their insufficient attention to the social and environmental contexts in which radicalization occurs (Schmid, 2013; Horgan, 2014). A growing body of research has demonstrated that radicalization is rarely the product of individual psychology alone but is instead deeply shaped by the social environments in which individuals are embedded.

More recent scholarship has shifted toward understanding radicalization as a fundamentally social process embedded in specific community structures and communicative environments (McCauley & Moskalenko, 2017; Moonshot CVE, 2020). This shift is particularly relevant to the study of online radicalization, where the architecture of digital platforms — recommendation algorithms, affordances for community formation, and the dynamics of virality — plays an active role in shaping the ideological trajectories of individual users. Researchers such as Benkler, Faris, and Roberts (2018), in their landmark study of the American media ecosystem, demonstrated that online information environments are not neutral conduits but active shapers of belief, with certain platforms and communities functioning as accelerants of political polarization and, in some cases, radicalization. This insight has profound implications for the study of gaming, which constitutes one of the most structurally distinctive and densely populated of all online social environments.

The question of what precisely counts as 'radicalization' is itself contested and consequential. A broad definition — the process of adopting increasingly extreme political views — risks pathologizing legitimate political engagement and dissent. A narrow definition — the process of moving toward violence — risks missing the broader landscape of cognitive and attitudinal changes that may predispose individuals to support or excuse political violence without personally engaging in it. For the purposes of this report, radicalization is understood as a process of belief-change in which individuals come to hold increasingly extreme political views, to perceive political opponents as fundamentally illegitimate or inhuman, and to endorse or normalize violence as a political tool. This definition is broad enough to capture the range of relevant phenomena in gaming spaces while remaining analytically distinct from mere political engagement or ideological commitment.

2.2 Key Theoretical Constructs and Their Relevance to Gaming

Several theoretical constructs are especially relevant to the gaming context and deserve extended consideration. Social identity theory (Tajfel & Turner, 1979) explains how group membership functions as a source of self-esteem and belonging, making individuals susceptible to in-group favoritism and out-group hostility — dynamics that are powerfully operative in competitive gaming environments where teams, guilds, and factions structure social life. When a player's sense of worth is tied to the performance and reputation of their gaming community, the psychological stakes of inter-group competition are elevated, and the social pressure to adopt the values and attitudes of the in-group intensifies. This dynamic creates fertile ground for the transmission of political attitudes within gaming communities, as the desire to belong and to maintain standing within a valued group can override critical evaluation of the ideas being shared.

The concept of 'cognitive radicalization' — which refers to the process by which individuals come to adopt increasingly extreme beliefs without necessarily engaging in violent action — is particularly useful for analyzing gaming environments (Neumann, 2013). Gaming communities can serve as spaces where radical ideas are first encountered, tested, and normalized through social interaction, without any clear or immediate path toward political violence. This distinction between cognitive and behavioral radicalization is important for avoiding both the overstatement of gaming's role in producing violent extremists and the understatement of its role in shaping political beliefs and attitudes. The evidence suggests that the more common outcome of gaming-related radicalization is cognitive rather than behavioral — individuals who come to hold extreme political views but do not act on them violently — though this does not diminish the significance of these changes or their potential long-term consequences.

Research on 'stochastic terrorism' (Hamm & Spaaij, 2017) highlights how the cumulative effect of radical rhetoric, even when not directed at specific targets or individuals, can increase the overall probability of politically motivated violence by energizing actors on the margins of extremist communities. This framework is relevant to gaming because it suggests that the normalization of extreme political rhetoric in gaming spaces — even when framed as humor or irony — can have real-world consequences that extend beyond the immediate social contexts in which the rhetoric is produced. The aggregate effect of millions of gaming interactions in which extremist ideas are treated as normal or entertaining may be to lower the threshold of political violence for a small subset of deeply radicalized individuals, even if the vast majority of participants in those interactions would never personally engage in violence.

Table 2. Key theoretical frameworks and their application to gaming-related radicalization

Theoretical Model	Core Claim	Relevance to Gaming	Key Scholar(s)
Social Identity Theory	Group membership drives in-group loyalty and out-group hostility	Clan/guild dynamics, gaming tribalism	Tajfel & Turner (1979)
Echo Chamber Model	Closed communities amplify shared beliefs unchallenged	Private Discord servers, gaming subreddits	Sunstein (2017)
Cognitive Radicalization	Belief adoption precedes and may not lead to violence	Normalization of extreme humor and views in gaming chat	Neumann (2013)
Stochastic Terrorism	Radical rhetoric statistically increases probability of violence	Extremist streamers and content creators	Hamm & Spaaij (2017)
Online Disinhibition	Anonymity reduces social constraints on behavior	Pseudonymous chat, anonymous matchmaking	Suler (2004)

3. THE POLITICAL ECOLOGY OF ONLINE GAMING

3.1 Diversity of Gaming Environments

Online gaming encompasses an enormous diversity of genres, platforms, communities, and demographics. First-person shooters (FPS) such as Counter-Strike and Call of Duty attract large, predominantly male audiences and are frequently associated with aggressive competitive cultures in which trash-talk, insult, and provocative speech are normalized as features of the game experience rather than deviations from it. Massively multiplayer online role-playing games (MMORPGs) such as World of Warcraft and Final Fantasy XIV support large, often more demographically diverse communities organized around cooperative play, shared narrative, and the development of persistent social relationships. These communities tend to develop stronger formal governance structures — including elected leadership, codes of conduct, and mechanisms for dispute resolution — that can provide meaningful resistance to extremist infiltration.

Battle royale games such as Fortnite, PUBG, and Apex Legends occupy a middle ground, combining the competitive intensity of FPS games with the massive player bases and cross-demographic appeal of more casual titles. Their enormous popularity among teenagers and young adults, combined with their integration with streaming platforms and social media, makes them particularly important vectors for the spread of political content — both progressive and reactionary — through gaming culture. Sandbox games such as Minecraft and Roblox, while often dismissed as children's entertainment, host complex political communities and have been the sites of politically significant events, including the construction of virtual monuments to protest events and the organization of community responses to real-world political developments.

Table 3. Genre-level political risk profiles in online gaming

Genre	Example Titles	Primary Demographic	Political Risk Profile
First-Person Shooter (FPS)	Counter-Strike, Call of Duty	Young males 16–30	Higher — male-dominated, competitive, anonymized voice chat
MMORPG	World of Warcraft, FFXIV	Broader demographic mix	Moderate — strong moderation culture in established communities
Real-Time Strategy (RTS)	StarCraft, Age of Empires	Males 18–35	Moderate — politically engaged but less toxic than FPS
Battle Royale	Fortnite, PUBG, Apex Legends	Ages 13–25, mixed gender	Variable — large young user base, mixed moderation
Casual/Mobile	Candy Crush, Among Us	Broad/family	Lower — less sustained community formation
Indie/Narrative	Celeste, Disco Elysium	Adults, progressive lean	Lower risk; often progressive political communities

3.2 Structural Features Relevant to Political Dynamics

Certain structural features cut across many gaming environments and are relevant to understanding their political dimensions. First, gaming communities are characterized by strong in-group identity formation. Players develop attachments to particular games, genres, and communities that function as markers of social belonging and cultural identity. These identities can become intensely defended, and perceived threats to them — whether from outside critics, game developers changing game features, or the entry of new demographic groups into gaming spaces — can generate powerful emotional responses that are easily channeled into political mobilization. The defense of 'gaming culture' against perceived outsiders, a dynamic made explosively visible during the GamerGate controversy of 2014, illustrates how gaming identity can become the vector through which broader reactionary political currents enter and take hold within gaming communities.

Second, online gaming environments are characterized by a distinctive communicative culture that places high value on provocation, transgression, and ironic detachment. What researchers have called 'irony culture' or 'shitposting culture' — the use of irony, absurdism, and deliberate offensiveness as modes of social bonding and cultural signaling — is particularly prevalent in gaming communities (Phillips, 2015; Nagle, 2017). This culture presents a significant analytical and policy challenge because it creates deliberate ambiguity about the sincerity of expressed views. When a user in a gaming chat channel posts a neo-Nazi meme, is this sincere expression of neo-Nazi ideology, ironic performance of transgression, or something in between that cannot be cleanly categorized? The answer matters enormously for understanding and responding to radicalization in gaming spaces, but it is often genuinely difficult to determine.

Third, the social architecture of gaming platforms — including voice chat, text chat, matchmaking systems, and guild or clan structures — creates conditions for sustained social interaction that go well beyond the consumption of political media. Radicalization in gaming environments often occurs through prolonged social relationships, where individuals are gradually introduced to more extreme ideas by trusted community members over weeks, months, or even years. This gradual, relationship-mediated process is substantially more effective at producing genuine ideological change than exposure to extremist content through impersonal media, because it connects ideological content to social bonds that matter to the individual. Breaking these bonds, or risking them by questioning the ideas being shared, carries real social costs that discourage critical engagement.

3.3 The Role of Humor, Irony, and 'Edgy' Culture

One of the most analytically challenging aspects of gaming culture's relationship to political radicalization is the central role of humor, irony, and deliberate transgression as mechanisms through which political ideas are introduced, normalized, and spread. The use of irony provides powerful protection against direct confrontation or criticism: anyone who objects to an ironic statement of extreme views can be accused of not understanding the joke, of being overly sensitive, or of applying inappropriate standards to obviously non-serious content. At the same time, research on the psychology of humor suggests that even ironic expressions of extreme views can shift attitudes and normalize the ideas they apparently mock, particularly when they are repeated frequently and in social contexts where group belonging is at stake.

The 'irony-to-sincerity pipeline' — a pattern in which ideas that begin as ironic provocations gradually become sincere commitments as individuals become more deeply embedded in extremist communities — has been documented by researchers studying the radicalization of far-right movements online (Nagle, 2017; Hawley, 2017). In gaming contexts, this pipeline often begins with the adoption of gaming community norms around transgressive humor, progresses through exposure to more explicitly political content framed as humor, and eventually arrives at sincere ideological commitment as the individual's social world becomes increasingly centered on communities where these views are taken seriously. Understanding this progression is essential for developing effective interventions, as approaches designed to address sincere ideological commitment are likely to be ineffective at the early stages of this process.

4. GAMERGATE, TROLLS, AND THE RISE OF THE ALT-RIGHT

4.1 Origins and Significance of GamerGate

No account of gaming and political radicalization can avoid engaging with Gamer-Gate, the controversy that erupted in August 2014 and came to function as a major inflection point in the relationship between gaming culture and right-wing politics. GamerGate began ostensibly as a controversy about 'ethics in games journalism' but rapidly evolved into a coordinated harassment campaign targeting women, feminists, and progressive voices in the gaming industry and media. Its targets included game developer Zoe Quinn, critic Anita Sarkeesian, and developer Brianna Wu, among many others, who received sustained campaigns of threats, doxxing, and abuse. The episode was not simply an outbreak of online harassment — though it was certainly that — but a political event that crystallized a set of tensions around gender, identity, and cultural change that had been building in gaming communities for years.

The significance of GamerGate for understanding gaming and radicalization lies less in its immediate content than in the organizational and ideological infrastructure it helped create. GamerGate brought together a loose coalition of gaming enthusiasts, men's rights activists, and nascent alt-right figures around a shared narrative of grievance: the claim that 'social justice warriors' were corrupting gaming culture with feminist and progressive ideology. This narrative proved highly effective at mobilizing young men who felt their cultural identity under threat, and it served as a gateway for many participants into broader right-wing political communities. The sense of cultural siege that GamerGate produced — the feeling that gaming, as a male-dominated space of belonging and status, was under attack by outsiders — provided a powerful emotional engine for political mobilization that extended well beyond the specific controversies about game journalism ethics that ostensibly triggered the event.

It is important to recognize that GamerGate was not simply a symptom of pre-existing political radicalization among gamers. It also functioned as a radicalizing event in its own right, politicizing individuals who had previously understood gaming as an apolitical leisure activity and providing them with a framework for understanding political conflict in terms of cultural siege and defensive identity. This politicization was not uniform in its direction — many participants in GamerGate-era debates were radicalized toward progressive political positions in reaction against the harassment — but the dominant vector of radicalization ran toward right-wing and reactionary politics, and it produced a significant cohort of young men whose political identities were fundamentally shaped by the experience.

4.2 GamerGate as Organizational Infrastructure and Alt-Right Incubator

GamerGate demonstrated the organizational capacity of gaming-adjacent online communities to an extent that surprised many observers. The coordination of harassment campaigns across platforms — including Reddit, 4chan, Twitter, and gaming forums — showcased the ability of decentralized online communities to conduct sustained and sophisticated political operations without any formal organizational structure. The techniques developed during GamerGate, including the use of sock puppet accounts to amplify messages, the coordinated targeting of advertisers to apply financial pressure to media outlets, and the strategic deployment of ostensibly neutral framing ('ethics in journalism') to provide cover for what was in practice a targeted harassment campaign, would later be refined and deployed by the broader alt-right movement.

Figures who would later become central to the alt-right movement used GamerGate as a platform to build audiences and hone rhetorical strategies. The controversy demonstrated that gaming communities could be effective recruitment grounds for right-wing politics, and it established a set of rhetorical and organizational templates — the framing of reactionary politics as cultural defense, the use of irony and humor to spread extreme ideas, the targeting of progressive critics for sustained harassment — that would shape the character of online right-wing politics for years to come. Angela Nagle's analysis (2017) traces direct lines of influence from GamerGate-era gaming communities to the broader online culture that produced the alt-right's distinctive style of political engagement.

Table 4. GamerGate timeline and political legacy (2014–present)

Period	Key Events	Political Significance
Aug 2014	GamerGate begins; harassment campaigns target Quinn, Sarkeesian, and Wu	First large-scale politicization of gaming identity around reactionary grievance
Sep–Oct 2014	Coordination via 4chan, Reddit, Twitter; "ethics in journalism" framing emerges	Demonstrates cross-platform extremist organizing capacity
Late 2014	Alt-right figures use GamerGate audience to build broader platforms	Gaming becomes recruitment pipeline for nascent alt-right
2015–2016	GamerGate tactics adapted for broader culture war battles	Establishes template for online right-wing political organizing
2017–Present	Legacy persists in continued harassment of women and minorities in gaming	Ongoing normalization of misogyny and harassment in gaming spaces

5. EXTREMIST RECRUITMENT AND RADICALIZATION PIPELINES IN GAMING SPACES

5.1 Deliberate Recruitment Strategies by Extremist Organizations

The deliberate use of gaming spaces for extremist recruitment is a well-documented phenomenon that has become increasingly sophisticated over time. Far-right organizations, including white nationalist groups, incel communities, and various accelerationist movements, have developed explicit strategic frameworks for using gaming platforms and communities as recruitment vectors (Moonshot CVE, 2020; Anti-Defamation League, 2019). These strategies are not improvised or opportunistic but reflect deliberate organizational planning, with some extremist groups producing formal guides and training materials for members on how to conduct effective recruitment in gaming environments. The strategies exploit the specific social dynamics of gaming communities — the high value placed on in-group loyalty, the normalization of transgressive humor, the dense social networks formed through cooperative play, and the relative youth and social isolation of many participants.

Recruitment tactics in gaming environments typically follow a graduated approach that researchers have described as a 'radicalization pipeline.' Initial contact is often made through ostensibly normal gaming interaction — playing together, discussing games, sharing humor — which establishes a baseline of social trust between the recruiter and the target. The recruiter's extremist commitments may not be visible at this stage; they present as an ordinary and entertaining gaming companion. Over subsequent interactions, the recruiter begins introducing more edgy or provocative content, often framed as humor or as 'red pills' — a term derived from the Matrix film franchise and adopted by online right-wing communities to describe information that supposedly reveals uncomfortable truths that the mainstream refuses to acknowledge. This framing positions extremist content as sophisticated and countercultural, appealing to young people's desire for insider knowledge and their resistance to perceived mainstream conformity (see Figure 2).

5.2 Platform-Specific Dynamics and Empirical Exposure Data

Discord, the voice and text chat platform originally designed for gaming communities, has been repeatedly implicated in extremist activity and deserves particular attention as a site of radicalization. Its combination of semi-private servers, persistent community structures, strong integration with gaming platforms, and gaming-adjacent cultural norms made it attractive to extremist groups seeking to build communities outside the reach of mainstream platform moderation. The platform's architecture — which allows any user to create a server, control its membership, and set its content norms — makes it structurally resistant to top-down content moderation in ways that more centralized platforms are not. Numerous Discord servers associated with extremist movements have been identified and shut down, but the ease of creating new servers means that enforcement actions typically result in community migration rather than genuine disruption.

Research by the Anti-Defamation League (2019) found that approximately 23% of online gamers had been exposed to white supremacist rhetoric in gaming spaces, with younger male gamers being disproportionately likely to report such exposure. Perhaps more troublingly, the 2020 ADL report found that exposure to extremist content in gaming spaces has become both more common and more sophisticated over time, with recruiters using psychological techniques derived from commercial marketing, behavioral science, and online community management to identify vulnerable targets and tailor their approaches accordingly (see Figure 3). These findings suggest that extremist use of gaming spaces is not an opportunistic or incidental phenomenon but a deliberate and increasingly professionalized strategy that is adapting to platform moderation in real time.

Table 5. Key empirical findings on extremism in gaming spaces and their policy implications

Finding	Source	Policy Implication
65% of gamers report exposure to racist slurs in online play	ADL (2020)	Platforms must strengthen real-time voice/text moderation
23% of gamers encountered white supremacist content	ADL (2019)	Targeted enforcement in high-risk game genres
Younger males (16–24) are primary recruitment targets	Moonshot CVE (2020)	Age-targeted digital literacy programs needed
Discord servers used in Charlottesville 2017 rally planning	Multiple journalistic sources	Platform accountability for semi-private server moderation
Incel ideology overlaps with gaming community metaphors	Multiple academic sources	Cross-community monitoring for misogynistic radicalization

5.3 The Incel-Gaming Overlap and Gender-Based Radicalization

The relationship between gaming communities and incel ideology deserves particular attention as a distinct radicalization pathway with its own dynamics and risk profile. Incel communities — online communities centered on the shared experience of 'involuntary celibacy' and frequently characterized by extreme misogyny, nihilism, and in some cases explicit advocacy of sexual violence and mass murder — have significant cultural and social overlaps with certain gaming communities. These overlaps are not incidental. Both incel communities and certain gaming communities are organized around young, predominantly male populations who feel marginalized, who use specialized vocabulary and in-group humor as mechanisms of community cohesion, and who have developed elaborate ideological frameworks for making sense of perceived social failure and exclusion.

Several individuals who have committed incel-motivated violence, including perpetrators of mass shootings in the United States and Canada, were reported to have been active in gaming communities, and the manifestos and online posts they left behind drew extensively on gaming metaphors and imagery. Incel rhetoric has developed a gaming-inflected vocabulary — concepts such as 'leveling up,' 'grinding,' 'game theory,' and the notion of a 'sexual marketplace' structured like a competitive game with winners and losers — that makes it particularly accessible to individuals already immersed in gaming culture. The appropriation of gaming language by incel ideology is not merely stylistic; it reflects a substantive overlap in the ways that both communities frame social life as a competitive, zero-sum struggle in which status and belonging are scarce resources to be fought over rather than goods that can be shared.

6. PLATFORM AFFORDANCES AND THE ARCHITECTURE OF RADICALIZATION

6.1 Anonymity, Pseudonymity, and the Online Disinhibition Effect

Understanding radicalization in gaming environments requires attention not only to the human actors involved but to the technical architectures of the platforms through which they interact. Platform affordances — the features and design choices that shape what users can do and how they interact — play an active role in enabling or constraining the social dynamics through which radicalization occurs, and no analysis of gaming and radicalization is complete without serious engagement with these structural dimensions. Anonymity and pseudonymity are among the most significant platform affordances relevant to radicalization in gaming environments. The ability to interact under a pseudonym, without real-world social accountability, reduces the social costs of expressing extreme views and engaging in harassment. Research consistently shows that anonymity is associated with increased antisocial behavior online — a phenomenon described as the 'online disinhibition effect' (Suler, 2004) — and that this effect is particularly pronounced in contexts of social exclusion or perceived threat.

In gaming environments, where pseudonymous interaction is the norm and real-world identities are rarely disclosed, the online disinhibition effect can create conditions in which extreme speech and behavior are normalized through repetition and social reinforcement. Importantly, this normalization is not simply a matter of individual psychological processes; it is a social phenomenon that is produced and maintained through collective interaction. When a gaming community's shared culture includes the casual expression of extreme views, new members are socialized into this culture in the same way they are socialized into any other community norm — through observation, imitation, and the social rewards of conformity. The barrier to expressing extreme views is progressively lowered for each individual as they observe others doing so without consequence, and may eventually disappear altogether.

6.2 Recommendation Algorithms, Matchmaking, and Community Architecture

Recommendation and matchmaking algorithms constitute another critical platform feature with significant implications for radicalization dynamics. In gaming contexts, these algorithms determine which players are matched together for play and which communities or content are recommended to users. Research on recommendation algorithms in other contexts — most notably YouTube — has documented so-called 'rabbit hole' effects in which users are gradually exposed to more extreme content through algorithmically generated recommendation chains (Ribeiro et al., 2020). While the specific dynamics of these effects remain contested in the academic literature, the basic mechanism is well-established: algorithms optimized for engagement tend to recommend increasingly stimulating and emotionally provocative content, and extremist political content is often highly engaging in ways that drive continued platform use.

The architecture of community spaces — including guilds, clans, Discord servers, and subreddits — shapes the social dynamics of gaming communities in ways that are directly relevant to radicalization. These structures create bounded social environments with their own norms, hierarchies, and identities, which can function either as moderating forces that enforce prosocial behavior or as incubators for increasingly extreme ideas. Research on online community dynamics (Kraut & Resnick, 2012) has shown that community moderation and norm-setting have significant effects on member behavior, with communities that actively enforce prosocial norms showing lower rates of harassment and extremism than those that do not. This finding has clear implications for gaming communities, suggesting that the presence or absence of active moderation and community governance is a key variable in determining whether a given community is more or less vulnerable to extremist infiltration.

Table 6. Platform-level radicalization risk and moderation approaches in gaming-adjacent spaces

Platform	Key Features	Radicalization Risk	Moderation Approach
Discord	Semi-private servers, voice/text, persistent community	High — difficult to moderate private servers	Trust & Safety team; server bans; limited proactive scanning
Twitch	Live streaming, real-time chat, parasocial relationships	Medium-High — incentivizes provocative content	Channel bans; hate speech policy enforcement (inconsistent)
Steam	Game distribution, community forums, group features	Medium — community forums can host extremist content	Content reporting; group removals; forum moderation
Reddit	Gaming subreddits, semi-public communities	Variable — depends on subreddit culture	Subreddit bans; quarantines; content policy enforcement
4chan /v/ board	Anonymous imageboard, gaming focus	Very High — near-zero moderation, anonymous	Minimal; relies on self-regulation only

6.3 The Streaming Economy and Content Creator Incentives

The economics of streaming and content creation platforms such as Twitch and YouTube Gaming add another layer of complexity to the relationship between gaming and radicalization. Streamers and content creators who discuss gaming often also engage with political content, and the attention economy dynamics of these platforms — which reward emotionally engaging, provocative, and controversial content with views, subscriptions, and advertising revenue — can create powerful incentives for the production and amplification of politically extreme material. The financial incentives that encourage content creators to be provocative and controversial are structurally misaligned with the interests of platform safety and community health, and this misalignment is particularly acute in gaming content, where aggressive and transgressive behavior has historically been rewarded rather than punished by audiences.

Several prominent gaming content creators have been implicated in the spread of extremist ideas, either through explicit advocacy or through the more subtle but perhaps equally consequential normalization of extremist rhetoric in the context of gaming commentary. The blurring of gaming content and political commentary on streaming platforms represents a particularly important area for further research and policy attention, as it suggests that the radicalization dynamics of gaming communities cannot be addressed solely through the moderation of in-game behavior and chat but must also encompass the broader ecosystem of gaming-adjacent content creation and consumption.

7. COUNTER-NARRATIVES: PROGRESSIVE POLITICS AND GAMING

7.1 Political Diversity in Gaming Communities

While much of the scholarly and journalistic attention to gaming and politics has focused on the right-wing and extremist dimensions of the relationship, it is essential to recognize that gaming communities are not uniformly or even predominantly politically radical. The political landscape of gaming is highly diverse, encompassing communities organized around progressive, feminist, LGBTQ+, anti-racist, and other left-leaning political orientations. Understanding gaming and politics requires engaging with this diversity rather than focusing exclusively on the most alarming manifestations of the phenomenon. Research that treats 'gaming culture' as synonymous with right-wing extremism or toxicity risks producing a distorted picture that ignores the majority of gaming activity, alienates the millions of gamers who do not share extremist views, and undermines the credibility of efforts to address the genuine problems that do exist.

Progressive gaming communities have emerged as significant sites of political organization, identity formation, and in some cases activism. Games such as Night in the Woods, Celeste, Disco Elysium, and Spiritfarer have attracted large communities of players who engage with the games' progressive political themes — including mental illness, economic precarity, labor exploitation, and leftist political philosophy — as central elements of their gaming identity. The communities that have formed around these games function as spaces for progressive political socialization and discussion, demonstrating that the relationship between gaming culture and political radicalization is not exclusively rightward in its direction and that games themselves can be vehicles for thoughtful political engagement.

7.2 Community-Based Counter-Radicalization Practices

Research on progressive gaming communities also reveals important dynamics of counter-radicalization that deserve greater attention from researchers, policymakers, and platform operators. Several gaming communities have developed sophisticated grassroots practices for identifying and excluding extremist recruiters, educating members about radicalization tactics, and creating inclusive social environments that provide genuine belonging without requiring ideological conformity or the acceptance of extreme views. These community-level interventions are in some respects more promising than top-down platform enforcement, because they are embedded in the social relationships and cultural norms that make gaming communities meaningful to their members.

The role of community moderation and community culture in shaping the political character of gaming spaces cannot be overstated. Communities with strong norms of inclusion, active moderation, and a clear sense of shared values tend to be more resistant to extremist infiltration than those without such structures, regardless of the formal policies of the platforms on which they are hosted. This suggests that interventions aimed at supporting the development of healthy community governance structures within gaming communities — including tools, training, and resources for community moderators — may be more effective at reducing radicalization risk than purely content-based approaches.

The streaming and content creation ecosystem has also produced significant progressive and left-wing gaming culture that functions as a visible counter-narrative to the association of gaming with right-wing extremism. Streamers and creators who engage explicitly with socialist, feminist, and anti-racist politics while playing games have built substantial and loyal audiences, demonstrating that there is genuine demand for politically progressive gaming content and that the attention economy does not exclusively reward right-wing provocation. These creators and their communities represent important resources for counter-extremism efforts and deserve recognition and support from researchers and civil society organizations working in this space.

8. INSTITUTIONAL RESPONSES: PLATFORMS, POLICYMAKERS, AND CIVIL SOCIETY

8.1 Platform Company Responses and Their Limitations

The recognition that gaming spaces can function as sites of political radicalization has prompted responses from a range of institutional actors, including platform companies, government agencies, civil society organizations, and game developers themselves. These responses have been uneven in their scope, effectiveness, and ideological orientation, reflecting both the genuine difficulty of moderating complex online environments at scale and the competing interests of the actors involved. Platform companies, in particular, face a structural tension between their commercial interest in maintaining large and engaged user bases — which argues for relatively permissive content policies — and the reputational and regulatory costs of being associated with extremist activity — which argues for more robust enforcement.

Discord has evolved from a platform with minimal content moderation in its early years to one that maintains a substantial trust and safety team and actively removes servers that violate its community guidelines. The platform's response to GamerGate-adjacent extremism and its later removal of servers associated with the Charlottesville rally and other extremist events represent genuine improvements in its approach to harmful content. However, the platform's decentralized architecture — which allows any user to create a server and control its membership and content — makes comprehensive moderation extremely difficult and structurally resistant to enforcement. Researchers have documented the persistence of extremist communities on Discord despite repeated enforcement actions, as communities migrate to new servers, use invite-only access to avoid detection, and develop sophisticated strategies for evading moderation.

Major game publishers and developers have also begun to engage more directly with extremism and harassment in their communities, implementing stronger reporting tools, investing in automated moderation systems, and in some cases making explicit public commitments to community health and inclusion. However, these efforts have been criticized as insufficient and inconsistent, and the commercial pressures that make aggressive enforcement of community standards difficult have not fundamentally changed. The gaming industry's self-regulatory track record on community health issues — including its long and largely failed history of addressing toxic behavior in competitive gaming — provides limited grounds for optimism that voluntary action will be sufficient without additional external pressure from regulators and civil society.

8.2 Government, Law Enforcement, and Civil Society

Government and law enforcement responses to gaming-related radicalization have been primarily focused on the most severe cases, particularly those involving violence or terrorism. Law enforcement agencies in several countries have developed specialized units focused on online extremism that monitor gaming platforms among other online environments, and there has been increased information-sharing between platforms and law enforcement following major incidents of gaming-adjacent extremism. Following the 2019 Christchurch attack, in which the perpetrator broadcast the attack on Facebook Live, referenced gaming culture in his manifesto, and addressed his audience using gaming-adjacent language ('subscribe to PewDiePie'), several governments introduced or accelerated new legislation aimed at regulating online content and holding platforms accountable for extremist material hosted on their services.

Civil society organizations have played an important and underappreciated role in documenting and responding to extremism in gaming spaces. The Anti-Defamation League's Center on Technology and Society has produced some of the most comprehensive empirical data on hate and harassment in gaming, providing the evidence base that has informed both platform policy and public debate. Organizations such as the Institute for Strategic Dialogue and Moonshot CVE have developed specific programs targeting gaming communities, including counter-narrative campaigns, training for streamers and community managers, and consultation with platform companies on their trust and safety approaches. These efforts represent a valuable complement to platform enforcement and government regulation, though they face significant resource constraints relative to the scale of the problem they address.

Table 7. Institutional actor assessment — strengths and limitations of responses to gaming-related radicalization

Actor Type	Key Interventions	Strengths	Limitations
Platform Companies	Policy enforcement, ban systems, trust & safety teams	Reach; technical capability; real-time access	Profit motives; reactive; inconsistent enforcement
Government / Law Enforcement	Legislation, online monitoring, prosecutions	Legal authority; cross-border cooperation	Slow; may threaten free speech; limited gaming expertise
Civil Society (NGOs)	Research, reports, training programs, advocacy	Independence; research depth; community trust	Resource-constrained; limited enforcement power
Game Developers	In-game reporting tools, community statements, design choices	Embedded in community; design-level interventions	Commercial conflicts; limited scope; post-hoc responses
Academic Researchers	Longitudinal studies, policy recommendations, public education	Rigor; independence; long-term insight	Slow publication cycles; limited platform data access

9. METHODOLOGICAL CHALLENGES IN STUDYING GAMING AND RADICALIZATION

9.1 Causality, Selection Effects, and the Limits of Correlation

The study of gaming and radicalization presents distinctive methodological challenges that have significantly limited the development of a rigorous empirical literature on this topic. These challenges reflect both the general difficulties of studying radicalization — a phenomenon that is inherently rare, covert, and difficult to observe directly — and the specific characteristics of gaming environments as research objects. The most fundamental methodological challenge is the problem of establishing causal relationships between gaming and radicalization. The vast majority of research in this area is correlational, documenting associations between participation in gaming communities and exposure to or adoption of extreme political views without being able to demonstrate that gaming community participation caused the radicalization rather than the reverse.

This problem of reverse causation — sometimes called the 'selection effect' — is particularly acute in the study of gaming and radicalization because there are strong a priori reasons to expect both causal directions. On one hand, participation in gaming communities characterized by extremist content and norms may genuinely shift individuals' political views in more extreme directions through the social processes described above. On the other hand, individuals who are already sympathetic to extreme political views may actively seek out gaming communities where such views are prevalent, because these communities provide social acceptance and belonging that they cannot find elsewhere. Disentangling these two causal pathways requires longitudinal data on individuals' political attitudes and gaming behavior measured over time, combined with statistical methods that can account for selection into different types of gaming communities.

9.2 Access, Observation, and the Ethics of Research in Closed Communities

The study of online gaming communities also raises significant challenges of access and observation. Many of the most relevant communities — Discord servers organized around extremist subcultures, private gaming guilds with extremist leadership, closed forums — are not publicly accessible, making systematic observation extremely difficult without either deceptive access (which raises serious ethical questions) or the cooperation of community members who are unlikely to be forthcoming. Researchers who have conducted ethnographic work in these communities have typically relied on participant observation over extended periods, a method that is both extremely time-intensive and that raises fundamental questions about the ethics of covert research. The tension between the scientific value of access to closed extremist communities and the ethical obligations of researchers to their subjects and to society has not been satisfactorily resolved in the literature and represents a significant ongoing challenge for the field.

The use of computational methods — including natural language processing of publicly accessible text data from gaming forums, subreddits, and social media platforms — provides an important complement to ethnographic approaches but has its own significant limitations. Computational methods are better suited to identifying patterns in large volumes of text than to capturing the situated meanings, social dynamics, and cultural contexts that give that text its political significance. The distinction between ironic and sincere expression of extreme views, which is central to understanding radicalization in gaming communities, is notoriously difficult for computational methods to detect reliably. Similarly, the specific vocabulary, in-jokes, and coded language of gaming communities creates significant challenges for standard approaches to hate speech detection and political content classification.

10. A RESEARCH AGENDA FOR GAMING, POLITICS, AND RADICALIZATION

10.1 Priority Research Directions

The foregoing analysis suggests a number of priority areas for future research that could substantially advance our understanding of the relationship between gaming, politics, and radicalization. First, longitudinal research on political socialization in gaming communities is urgently needed. While there is considerable cross-sectional evidence of associations between gaming community participation and political attitudes, the lack of longitudinal data makes it impossible to draw robust conclusions about causal relationships or developmental trajectories. Future research should track cohorts of gamers over time, measuring political attitudes, gaming behavior, and community participation at multiple time points, and should employ statistical methods capable of distinguishing selection effects from genuine causal effects of community participation on political attitudes.

Second, comparative research across gaming genres, communities, and platforms is needed to move beyond the tendency to treat 'gaming culture' as monolithic. As documented in Section 3 of this report, the political dynamics of first-person shooter communities, MMORPG communities, and casual gaming communities differ substantially, and research that can identify the community-level factors that moderate the relationship between gaming and radicalization — including community size, governance structure, demographic composition, and platform architecture — would have both significant theoretical value and direct practical implications for platform design and community management.

Third, research on the effectiveness of counter-extremism interventions in gaming spaces is needed to inform practical responses. Despite the proliferation of such interventions — from platform enforcement actions to community education programs to counter-narrative campaigns — there is very little rigorous evidence about what works, for whom, and under what conditions. Future research should include randomized or quasi-experimental evaluations of specific interventions, using outcome measures that capture both changes in individual political attitudes and changes in community-level norms and behavior.

10.2 Methodological and Structural Recommendations

Interdisciplinary collaboration is essential for making meaningful progress on these questions. The study of gaming and radicalization sits at the intersection of criminology, political science, communications, sociology, computer science, and game studies, and no single disciplinary framework is adequate to the complexity of the phenomena involved. Research teams that bring together expertise from multiple disciplines — combining computational analysis of large-scale platform data with qualitative ethnographic work, psychological survey research, and game studies perspectives — are likely to produce more complete and reliable knowledge than those working within single disciplinary traditions. Funding agencies and research institutions should create structural incentives for this kind of interdisciplinary collaboration.

Greater attention to the global dimensions of gaming and radicalization is also urgently needed. The majority of existing research has focused on English-language gaming communities and North American or European political contexts, but gaming is a genuinely global phenomenon and the relationship between gaming culture and radical politics takes significantly different forms in different national and cultural contexts. The political dynamics of gaming communities in South Korea, Brazil, India, and Indonesia — to name just a few major gaming markets — are shaped by very different political histories, cultural norms, and extremist movements than those of the United States or Western Europe, and research that attends to these differences would substantially enrich our theoretical understanding while also having direct practical relevance for the design of context-appropriate responses.

- Fund longitudinal cohort studies tracking political attitudes and gaming behavior over time.
- Establish platform data-sharing agreements that give researchers access to behavioral data needed for causal inference.
- Develop validated measurement instruments for gaming-related radicalization that can be applied consistently across studies.
- Create interdisciplinary research networks linking criminologists, game scholars, political scientists, and computational researchers.
- Conduct rigorous evaluations of existing counter-extremism interventions in gaming spaces.
- Extend research beyond English-language, Western contexts to cover major gaming markets globally.

11. CONCLUSION

This report has examined the complex, multidimensional relationship between online gaming, political identity formation, and radicalization. It has argued that gaming environments constitute distinctive sociotechnical spaces with specific affordances — including pseudonymity, strong in-group identity formation, transgressive humor culture, and sustained social interaction — that create conditions both for the infiltration and amplification of radical political ideas and for the development of diverse, including progressive, political communities. The relationship between gaming and radicalization is neither simple nor one-directional, and understanding it requires moving beyond both the 'gaming-is-harmless' and 'gaming-creates-terrorists' framings that have dominated popular discourse toward a more nuanced, empirically grounded, and theoretically sophisticated analysis.

The report has documented the historical significance of GamerGate as an event that crystallized and accelerated the relationship between gaming culture and right-wing politics, while also recognizing that gaming communities contain rich progressive traditions and that many gaming communities actively develop sophisticated practices of resistance to extremist infiltration. It has examined the deliberate recruitment strategies employed by extremist groups in gaming spaces, the role of platform affordances — particularly anonymity, recommendation algorithms, and community architecture — in enabling or constraining radicalization dynamics, and the varied and often inadequate responses of institutional actors including platform companies, policymakers, and civil society organizations. Throughout, it has emphasized the methodological challenges that complicate the development of a rigorous empirical literature on this topic and the importance of sustained, interdisciplinary research investment to address these challenges.

Several key conclusions emerge with sufficient force from the available evidence to warrant emphasis. First, gaming environments are genuinely important sites of political socialization and, in some cases, radicalization, and they deserve serious scholarly and policy attention that they have not consistently received. The tendency to dismiss gaming communities as politically insignificant — a tendency driven partly by condescending assumptions about gamers and partly by the genuine difficulty of taking gaming seriously as a political phenomenon — has contributed to a failure to develop adequate responses to real and growing problems. Second, the political dynamics of gaming communities are highly variable and cannot be understood through broad generalizations about 'gaming culture.' Effective responses must be tailored to the specific social, cultural, and technical contexts of particular gaming communities and platforms.

Third, effective responses to gaming-related radicalization require engagement with the specific social and technical features of gaming environments rather than the application of generic counter-extremism frameworks developed in other contexts. The irony culture, the specific social dynamics of community formation through cooperative play, the gaming-specific vocabulary and metaphors through which extremist ideas are expressed and transmitted, and the distinctive economics of gaming content creation all require approaches that are sensitive to gaming's particular characteristics. Finally, the voices and perspectives of gaming community members — including those who have been targeted by extremism and harassment, those who have been radicalized and subsequently stepped back from extremist communities, and those who have developed effective grassroots practices of counter-extremism — are essential resources for both research and policy that have been insufficiently engaged.

As gaming continues to expand as a social and cultural force, and as digital environments become increasingly central arenas for the formation of political identities and the conduct of political struggles, the questions raised in this report will only grow in significance. The challenge for researchers, policymakers, practitioners, and gaming communities themselves is to develop responses that are adequate to the genuine complexity of these phenomena — responses that neither dismiss the real risks of gaming-related radicalization nor stigmatize gaming communities as inherently dangerous, that engage seriously with the democratic possibilities as well as the authoritarian threats that powerful online social spaces contain, and that treat the protection of gaming communities from extremist infiltration as an integral part of the broader project of building healthy, inclusive, and resilient digital publics.

REFERENCES

Anti-Defamation League. (2019). *Free to play? Hate, harassment, and positive social experience in online games.* ADL Center on Technology and Society.

Anti-Defamation League. (2020). *Hate is no game: Hate and harassment in online games.* ADL Center on Technology and Society.

Benkler, Y., Faris, R., & Roberts, H. (2018). *Network propaganda: Manipulation, disinformation, and radicalization in American politics.* Oxford University Press. DOI: 10.1093/oso/9780190923624.001.0001

Hamm, M., & Spaaij, R. (2017). *The age of lone wolf terrorism.* Columbia University Press. DOI: 10.7312/hamm18174

Hawley, G. (2017). *Making sense of the alt-right.* Columbia University Press. DOI: 10.7312/hawl18512

Horgan, J. (2014). *The psychology of terrorism* (2nd ed.). Routledge. DOI: 10.4324/9781315882246

Kraut, R., & Resnick, P. (2012). *Building successful online communities: Evidence-based social design.* MIT Press. DOI: 10.7551/mitpress/8472.001.0001

Massanari, A. (2017). GamerGate and the fappening: How Reddit's algorithm, governance, and culture support toxic technocultures. *New Media & Society*, *19*(3), 329–346. DOI: 10.1177/1461444815608807

McCauley, C., & Moskalenko, S. (2017). Understanding political radicalization: The two-pyramids model. *The American Psychologist*, *72*(3), 205–216. DOI. 10.1037/amp0000062 PMID: 28383974

Moghaddam, F. M. (2005). The staircase to terrorism: A psychological exploration. *The American Psychologist*, *60*(2), 161–169. DOI: 10.1037/0003-066X.60.2.161 PMID: 15740448

Moonshot, C. V. E. (2020). *Online gaming and extremism.* Moonshot CVE.

Nagle, A. (2017). *Kill all normies: Online culture wars from 4chan and Tumblr to Trump and the alt-right.* Zero Books.

Neumann, P. R. (2013). The trouble with radicalization. *International Affairs*, *89*(4), 873–893. DOI: 10.1111/1468-2346.12049

Phillips, W. (2015). *This is why we can't have nice things: Mapping the relationship between online trolling and mainstream culture*. MIT Press. DOI: 10.7551/mitpress/10288.001.0001

Ribeiro, M. H., Ottoni, R., West, R., Almeida, V. A. F., & Meira, W. (2020). Auditing radicalization pathways on YouTube. *Proceedings of FAT, 2020*, 131–141.

Schmid, A. P. (2013). Radicalisation, de-radicalisation, counter-radicalisation: A conceptual discussion and literature review. ICCT Research Paper.

Suler, J. (2004). The online disinhibition effect. *Cyberpsychology & Behavior*, *7*(3), 321–326. DOI: 10.1089/1094931041291295 PMID: 15257832

Sunstein, C. R. (2017). *Republic: Divided democracy in the age of social media*. Princeton University Press. DOI: 10.1515/9781400884711

Tajfel, H., & Turner, J. C. (1979). An integrative theory of intergroup conflict. In Austin, W. G., & Worchel, S. (Eds.), *The social psychology of intergroup relations* (pp. 33–47). Brooks/Cole.

Wiktorowicz, Q. (2004). Joining the cause: Al-Muhajiroun and radical Islam. Paper presented at the Roots of Islamic Radicalism Conference, Yale University.

Chapter 11
Gaming, Radicalization, and the Politics of Online Play

Apeksha Mhaisdhune
http://orcid.org/0009-0006-1867-5622
Vishwakarma Institute of Technology, Pune, India

Meghana Mate
Vishwakarma Institute of Technology, Pune, India

Krushna Maske
http://orcid.org/0009-0009-0176-0064
Vishwakarma Institute of Technology, Pune, India

Dhananjay Bhagat
Vishwakarma Institute of Technology, Pune, India

ABSTRACT

The gaming industry has evolved from a niche form of entertainment into a major force within the global digital economy, influencing technology, culture, and commerce. This chapter examines the political economy of gaming by analyzing how corporate ownership, digital platforms, and market structures shape the production, distribution, and consumption of gaming content. It explores the growth of console, PC, mobile, and cloud gaming, highlighting the increasing concentration of power among large technology and gaming corporations. The chapter also investigates labor conditions, platformization, monetization strategies, esports, streaming, and user-generated content within contemporary gaming ecosystems. Particular attention is given to data collection, algorithmic governance, market competition, and consumer

DOI: 10.4018/979-8-2600-1664-0.ch011

engagement. By integrating political economy and digital media perspectives, the chapter provides a critical understanding of gaming as a platform-based industry and discusses emerging challenges related to artificial intelligence, sustainability, and digital governance.

1. INTRODUCTION

1.1 Background of the Global Gaming Industry

The gaming industry has evolved from a niche recreational activity into one of the most influential and economically powerful sectors within the global digital economy (*Video Game Cultures and the Construction of Identities in Contemporary Society | Request PDF*, n.d.). What began with arcade machines and early home consoles during the late twentieth century has grown into a multi-billion-dollar ecosystem that attracts diverse audiences across age groups, cultural backgrounds, and geographic regions. Rapid technological advancement, widespread internet connectivity, and the convergence of digital media have been central to this transformation (Lin, 2022). Today, gaming represents not only a dominant entertainment medium but also a major economic, technological, and cultural force actively reshaping digital communication and content ecosystems worldwide . The historical trajectory of gaming reflects broader transformations in digital capitalism, as the medium evolved from a specialized hobby associated with younger demographics into a mainstream cultural phenomenon with global reach and commercial significance.

The contemporary gaming market is characterized by several interconnected and mutually reinforcing sectors: console gaming, personal computer gaming, mobile gaming, and cloud gaming. Console gaming maintains a significant industry presence through advanced gaming systems providing immersive interactive experiences (SINGH & KUMAR CHANDOLA, 2026). PC gaming sustains influence through online multiplayer platforms, competitive esports communities, and digital distribution services. Mobile gaming, however, has emerged as the fastest-growing segment, propelled by widespread smartphone adoption across both developed and developing economies, affordable data services, and free-to-play business models that have expanded gaming audiences well beyond traditional demographics. The emergence of cloud gaming further transforms industry dynamics by enabling on-demand streaming without expensive hardware, centralizing control within dominant technology corporations and accelerating the shift of gaming toward subscription-based service economies similar to those established in music and video streaming (*Audience Labour in the Age of AI-Generated Comments: Insights from Reddit | Request PDF*, n.d.).

Economically, gaming revenues now surpass those of traditional entertainment industries including film and music in many regions of the world, demonstrating the extraordinary commercial scale of contemporary gaming industries. Gaming ecosystems have extended far beyond game development itself to encompass esports, live-streaming content creation, influencer economies, virtual marketplaces, digital advertising, merchandise, and interactive media production (Oltean et al., 2021). These developments confirm that gaming has become a broader digital ecosystem involving data production, social interaction, cultural participation, and economic exchange at a genuinely global scale, warranting serious scholarly attention through the lens of political economy.

Figure 1. Evolution of the global gaming industry

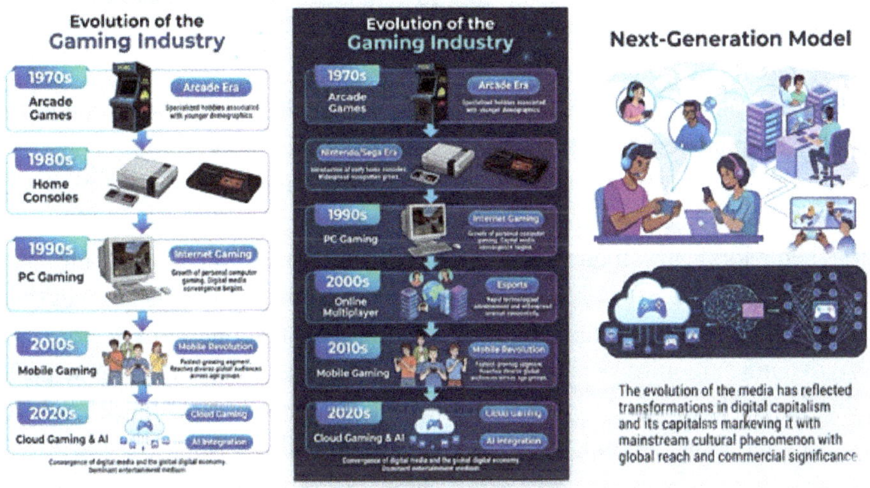

1.2 Political Economy Perspective on Gaming

Understanding the gaming industry requires an analytical approach that goes beyond purely technological or entertainment-centered perspectives. A political economy framework examines the relationships between power, ownership, labor, and capital within digital media systems, investigating how corporations, platforms, governments, and market forces shape gaming content, business models, labor practices, and audience engagement (Mosco, 2009). Rather than treating media industries as neutral technological systems, political economy analyzes them as institutions embedded within capitalist economic relations where profit generation, market expansion, and the accumulation of capital function as primary organizational objectives shaping all aspects of media production and consumption.

Within gaming, a political economy perspective reveals how a small number of multinational corporations exercise decisive influence over content production, distribution infrastructure, and user interaction. The concentration of ownership raises persistent concerns regarding monopoly power, diminished market competition, and the systematic marginalization of independent developers who lack the financial resources and platform access available to dominant corporations (Mirowski, 2008). Equally significant is the relationship between capital and labor within gaming industries: game development involves highly skilled creative and technical workers, yet industry labor conditions are frequently characterized by precarious employment arrangements, long working hours, wage stagnation, and the cultural normalization of exploitative crunch culture that prioritizes production deadlines over worker well-being (*A Playful Multitude? Mobilising and Counter-Mobilising Immaterial Game Labour*, n.d.).

Platform operators further reshape gaming ecosystems by functioning as powerful gatekeepers regulating visibility, monetization opportunities, and market accessibility for developers and content creators. Data-driven economic models transform gaming ecosystems into systems that prioritize continuous user interaction, behavioral surveillance, and platform loyalty over other values, integrating gaming into broader structures of surveillance capitalism where user attention and personal behavioral data constitute primary economic resources (Tortajada, 2020). These dynamics require systematic political economy analysis to understand how gaming industries generate value, distribute power, and shape cultural production within contemporary digital capitalism (Bonenfant, 2021).

1.3 Objectives and Scope of the Chapter

This chapter critically examines the political economy of gaming industries and their profound impact on contemporary digital content ecosystems. The primary objective is to analyze how economic structures, corporate power, digital platforms, and regulatory mechanisms collectively shape the production, distribution, and consumption of gaming content. Adopting an interdisciplinary perspective that integrates political economy with digital media studies and cultural industry analysis, the chapter provides a comprehensive understanding of gaming as both a cultural industry and a platform-based economic system embedded within global digital capitalism.

The chapter systematically investigates the commercialization and platformization of gaming, focusing on how live-service models, subscription platforms, and algorithmic governance mechanisms influence market competition, content discoverability, and developer autonomy. It analyzes advanced monetization strategies including microtransactions, loot boxes, and behavioral engagement systems, examining their ethical implications and the regulatory challenges they pose for consumer protection. The chapter explores participatory cultures encompassing streaming, esports industries, modding communities, and user-generated content, critically assessing tensions between democratized participation and corporate control over platform infrastructures. Finally, it addresses emerging challenges related to artificial intelligence integration, blockchain economies, environmental sustainability, and the governance frameworks necessary for equitable digital gaming ecosystems. Through this analysis, the chapter contributes to broader scholarly discussions on digital capitalism, media convergence, and the political economy of contemporary global gaming industries.

2. THEORETICAL FOUNDATIONS OF POLITICAL ECONOMY IN GAMING

2.1 Political Economy of Media and Communication

The political economy of media and communication provides an essential theoretical foundation for analyzing the structure, operation, and power relations that characterize gaming industries. Political economy scholars analyze media industries not as culturally neutral or technologically deterministic systems, but as institutions embedded within capitalist economic structures where profit generation, market control, and ideological influence operate as central forces shaping media production, distribution, and consumption (Sjøvaag et al., 2026). This perspective moves beyond descriptive accounts of technological change to examine how economic interests, ownership structures, and class relations determine the conditions under which gaming content is created, circulated, and experienced by audiences.

Classical political economy, particularly Marxist theory and its subsequent critical media theory extensions, offers foundational tools for gaming analysis. The concept of commodification is especially relevant to contemporary gaming ecosystems, where games function not simply as creative cultural expressions but as commodities engineered for continuous consumption, repeated monetization, and profit maximization within capitalist markets (Fuchs, 2014). Horkheimer et al. (2002) argued that mass cultural industries standardize production according to commercial logic to maintain consumer conformity and ensure market efficiency (Ramsauer, 2026). Although developed in a different historical context, this critique applies with considerable force to contemporary gaming, where franchise-based production, sequel dependency, live-service repetition, and algorithmically optimized design strategies dominate large-scale commercial content creation. The financial risks associated with major game development investments often lead corporations to prioritize commercially proven formulas over experimental or socially critical content.

The commodification of digital entertainment extends well beyond game products themselves. Online interactions, streaming performances, user-generated content, and social participation within gaming communities are increasingly monetized by digital platforms, transforming these activities into economic processes. Users simultaneously function as consumers, producers of content, and unpaid digital laborers who generate value for corporations through advertising exposure, data production, and platform engagement metrics (Terranova, 2000). Political economy frameworks therefore illuminate how gaming industries integrate economic exploitation, technological infrastructure, and cultural production into interconnected systems of power and profit that shape digital life in fundamental ways.

Figure 2. Political economy framework of the gaming industry

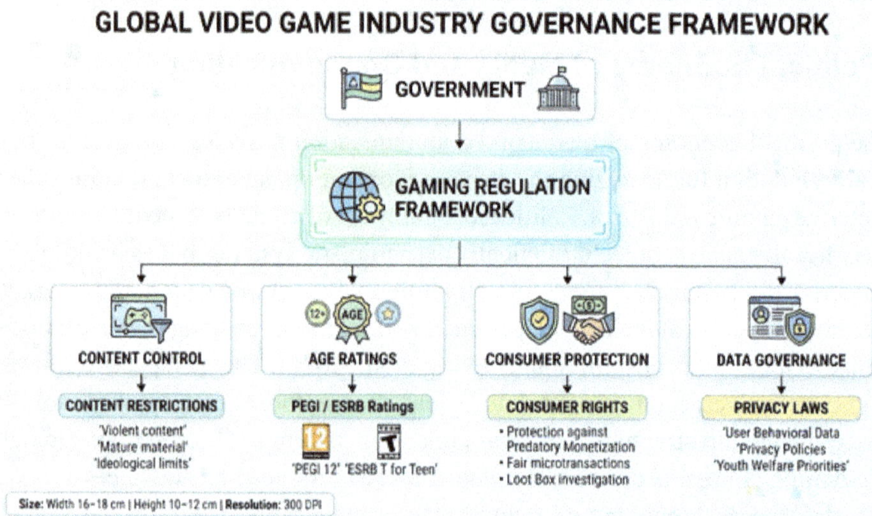

2.2 Digital Platform Capitalism

The rise of digital platform capitalism has fundamentally reorganized the structure, operation, and economic logic of gaming industries worldwide (De Minicis, 2026). Srnicek (2017) defines platform capitalism as an economic system in which digital platforms function as intermediaries facilitating interactions between producers, consumers, advertisers, and content creators while extracting economic value through data collection, algorithmic management, and market control over critical digital infrastructures. Gaming platforms have become dominant ecosystems governing content distribution, user engagement, and monetization practices through mechanisms that extend beyond traditional market competition into forms of structural dependency and algorithmic governance.

Surveillance capitalism, as theorized comprehensively by Zuboff (2019), provides a critical framework for understanding data extraction practices within gaming industries. Corporations systematically collect vast quantities of behavioral data generated through every interaction within gaming ecosystems, including player activity, movement patterns, purchase decisions, social communications, and competitive performance metrics (Smart, 2025). This data is analyzed through sophisticated algorithmic systems to predict consumer preferences, optimize monetization strategies, maximize user retention, and increase spending. Data has therefore become a strategic economic resource within gaming platform capitalism, with user participation continuously transformed into commercially valuable information assets that support targeted advertising, personalized engagement systems, and market forecasting capabilities.

Van Dijck, Poell, and de Waal (2018) further demonstrate how digital platforms exercise societal influence well beyond their immediate commercial functions through control over infrastructures, datafication practices, and algorithmic architectures that shape social participation (Lucchesi, 2026). Within gaming ecosystems, platform dependency creates structural inequalities between large technology corporations and smaller developers who rely on dominant storefronts, cloud marketplaces, and online services for economic sustainability and audience access. Independent developers must accept platform-defined revenue-sharing arrangements, technical requirements, and content governance systems that significantly constrain their autonomy and bargaining power within digital markets.

Figure 3. Platform capitalism and data flows in gaming ecosystems

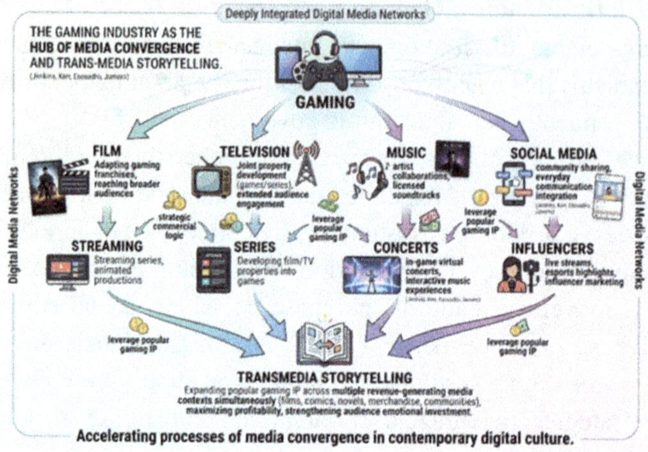

2.3 Cultural Industries and Creative Labor

Gaming is widely recognized as a central component of contemporary cultural and creative industries, combining technological innovation with narrative design, visual art, interactive gameplay, music composition, and immersive world-building to create distinctive cultural experiences (Kerr, 2017). However, despite its creative character and cultural significance, gaming reflects economic inequalities and labor challenges common to other capitalist cultural industries (Kerr, 2017). Game development requires collaboration among programmers, designers, writers, animators, sound engineers, and marketing specialists — a diverse creative workforce whose labor generates the cultural value that sustains gaming industries economically, yet whose working conditions frequently fail to reflect that value.

Creative labor within gaming industries is commonly idealized in cultural discourse as innovative, fulfilling, and passion-driven. Many workers enter game development because of genuine enthusiasm for games and digital creativity. Political economy scholars argue, however, that the idealization of creative passion can function as an ideological mechanism that obscures exploitative working conditions by framing overwork and economic precarity as acceptable expressions of professional dedication. Crunch culture represents the most visible manifestation of this dynamic: the normalization of excessive overtime during critical production stages results in physical exhaustion, mental health deterioration, burnout, and compromised personal well-being, with workers frequently unable to refuse without jeopardizing employment or professional reputation (Pembro, 2021).

Precarious employment through temporary contracts, freelance arrangements, and project-based labor instability further characterizes gaming labor markets. Studio closures following commercially unsuccessful releases, regular mass layoffs during corporate restructuring, and the outsourcing of development tasks to lower-wage international markets create conditions of persistent labor insecurity even within large corporations. The relative weakness of labor unions and collective bargaining within gaming industries across most jurisdictions further limits workers capacity to organize against these conditions, maintain higher wages, or secure improved working environments.

3. STRUCTURE OF THE GLOBAL GAMING INDUSTRY

3.1 Major Stakeholders in Gaming Ecosystems

The global gaming industry comprises a highly interconnected ecosystem of multiple stakeholder categories who contribute to the production, distribution, monetization, and consumption of gaming content in diverse and often asymmetric ways (*Digital Entertainment Gaming as a Site for (Informal) Historical Learning | Request PDF*, n.d.-a). These stakeholders include game developers, publishers, platform owners, streaming and esports companies, digital content creators, and consumers, each occupying distinct positions within gaming value chains while collectively shaping the economic and cultural dynamics of gaming industries. Understanding these stakeholder relationships is essential for analyzing how power is distributed across gaming ecosystems and how different actors benefit unevenly from the commercial success of digital entertainment.

Game developers form the creative and technological foundation of gaming industries (*(PDF) Study on the Use of Serious Games in Business Education*, n.d.). They range from independent creators and small studios to large multinational corporations employing thousands of specialized professionals across multiple departments. Independent developers often pursue experimental narrative approaches, artistic innovation, and niche audience engagement that larger studios typically avoid due to higher commercial risk. Publishers play central roles in financing, marketing, and distributing games globally, frequently shaping creative decisions by prioritizing commercially viable genres and monetization systems over developer preferences, particularly when significant investment capital is at stake. Platform owners have become among the most influential actors within contemporary gaming ecosystems, operating digital marketplaces, app stores, and console platforms that regulate how games are distributed, priced, discovered, and monetized across global markets (Novianto, 2025b). Streaming platforms and esports organizations represent rapidly expanding sectors that have transformed gaming into participatory media entertainment and professional spectator sport respectively. Consumers and content creators are no longer passive participants within these ecosystems; they actively contribute to gaming cultures through streaming, community building, user-generated content, and fan creativity that generates economic value corporations increasingly integrate into platform business models (Pivovarov, 2026a).

Figure 4. Key stakeholders in the global gaming industry ecosystem

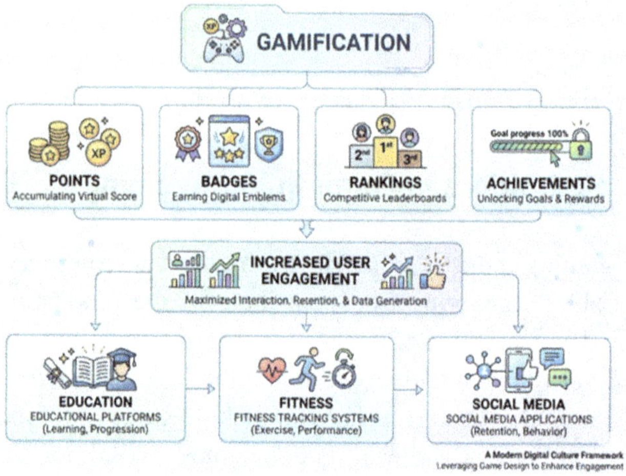

3.2 Market Concentration and Corporate Dominance

The global gaming industry has experienced profound market concentration over the past two decades, resulting in the dominance of a relatively small number of multinational corporations over major segments of game development, publishing, hardware manufacturing, digital distribution, and online platform services. This concentration reflects broader patterns within digital capitalism where economic power becomes increasingly centralized within platform-based technology corporations capable of leveraging network effects, data advantages, and infrastructure control to consolidate market position. Vertically integrated corporate ecosystems combine hardware production, software development, digital marketplaces, subscription services, and online infrastructure ownership, enabling corporations to maximize profits while maintaining significant control over consumer experiences, pricing systems, and industry standards.

Mergers and acquisitions have accelerated market concentration substantially. Large gaming corporations frequently acquire successful development studios, intellectual property portfolios, streaming platforms, and technology companies to strengthen competitive positioning and eliminate potential rivals before they reach scale. Industry consolidation affects both labor conditions and creative autonomy, as acquired studios face pressure to align their output with commercially successful franchise models and monetization systems rather than pursuing independent creative visions. Political economy scholars describe the resulting market structures as oligopolies controlled by a limited number of corporations wielding decisive influence over content production, distribution systems, and platform governance (Muttaqin, 2026). Corporate data ownership further extends economic power beyond content portfolios: companies leverage behavioral insights derived from vast user datasets to optimize monetization strategies, personalize advertising, and predict market trends, reinforcing the centrality of information control within contemporary gaming economies (C Dey, 2026).

The concentration of corporate power within gaming industries also carries significant implications for cultural production and public discourse (*(PDF) Modelling Data-Driven Marketing Adoption in Indian B2B IT/TES Service Providers*, n.d.-a). When a small number of corporations dominate content ecosystems, they acquire considerable influence over which narratives, representations, and cultural values receive amplification through globally distributed gaming experiences. Independent developers who might challenge dominant aesthetic conventions, explore politically complex themes, or serve underrepresented communities often struggle to achieve commercial visibility within markets structured by corporate oligopolies and algorithmic platform governance. Addressing these structural tendencies requires regulatory intervention targeting monopolistic market behavior alongside active support policies for independent game development that preserve creative diversity and cultural pluralism within gaming industries as vital components of democratic digital culture.

3.3 Globalization of Gaming Markets

Globalization has transformed gaming industries into highly interconnected transnational systems characterized by global distribution networks, cross-border investment flows, and the international circulation of gaming cultures (Oonk, 2000a). Advances in digital technologies, mobile infrastructure, and internet connectivity have enabled games to reach global audiences rapidly and at scale, creating transnational gaming communities that connect players across geographic, linguistic, and cultural boundaries. Regions including Asia, Latin America, Africa, and the Middle East have experienced substantial growth in gaming participation driven by expanding smartphone accessibility, more affordable mobile data services, and improvements in digital payment infrastructure that enable participation in digital gaming economies (Kerr, 2017).

Localization strategies have become essential components of global gaming market expansion. Companies adapt language, narrative content, cultural references, visual aesthetics, and marketing approaches to align with the expectations and sensitivities of different regional audiences. Effective localization enables corporations to maximize global market reach while increasing audience engagement across diverse cultural contexts. However, globalization also intensifies transnational cultural flows that critics argue may promote cultural homogenization by privileging commercially dominant entertainment models associated with large Western and East Asian multinational corporations, potentially marginalizing indigenous game development industries and local cultural expressions (*(PDF) Cultural Imperialism Revisited: Counselling and Globablisation*, n.d.). Cross-border investments, international outsourcing arrangements, and platform-based distribution networks further embed gaming economies within unequal global production systems shaped by the dynamics of digital capitalism and transnational corporate power (Dimic-Janjic et al., 2025).

4. MONETIZATION MODELS AND ECONOMIC STRATEGIES

4.1 Evolution of Gaming Revenue Models

The gaming industry has undergone a fundamental transformation in its revenue generation strategies across three major phases of development . Early gaming economies relied primarily on physical sales of hardware and software products distributed through retail networks, with consumer revenue generated through one-time purchases of complete game experiences. This model established gaming as commercially viable entertainment but limited revenue potential to discrete product release cycles. The transition to digital distribution, enabled by internet connectivity, online payment infrastructure, and cloud computing capacity, eliminated many logistical constraints and significantly altered competitive dynamics within gaming markets (Novianto, 2025c). Digital storefronts became powerful intermediaries regulating visibility, pricing, and revenue-sharing arrangements between developers, publishers, and consumers, enabling global content distribution at reduced marginal cost while generating new dependencies for developers.

Subscription-based gaming represents an important further evolution in gaming economies (*Digital Entertainment Gaming as a Site for (Informal) Historical Learning | Request PDF*, n.d.-b). Similar to subscription models established in film and music streaming industries, gaming subscription platforms provide users with access to extensive game libraries for recurring monthly fees, generating predictable revenue streams and stronger platform loyalty while reducing individual game purchase barriers. The most recent development involves cloud gaming services that transform gaming into a fully on-demand digital service, accessible through internet-connected devices without requiring expensive hardware ownership. This transition accelerates the shift within digital capitalism from product-based systems centered on discrete consumer purchases toward service-oriented ecosystems focused on continuous engagement, subscriber retention, and data-driven monetization across extended user relationships.

Figure 5. Evolution of revenue models in the gaming industry

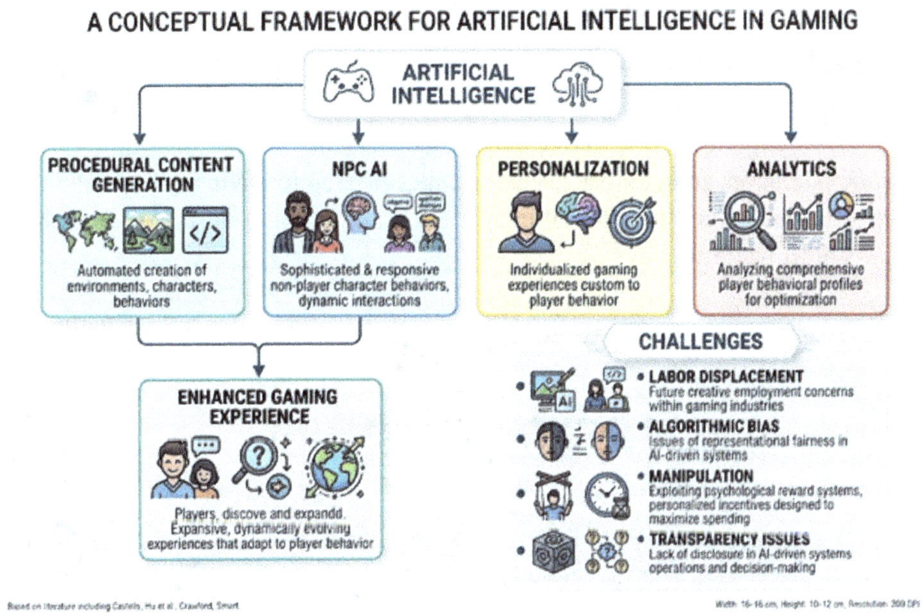

4.2 Microtransactions and In-Game Economies

Microtransactions have become among the most significant and extensively deployed monetization strategies within contemporary gaming industries (Merkulova & Bobrov, 2026). Unlike traditional full-game purchase models, microtransactions generate ongoing revenue through small in-game payments for cosmetic items, virtual currencies, character customization options, downloadable content expansions, or gameplay advantages designed to facilitate progression. These systems allow companies to generate continuous revenue from engaged players who have already purchased or downloaded games, extending commercial value well beyond the initial purchase transaction (Woodcock & Johnson, 2019). Cosmetic purchases including character skins, visual enhancements, and aesthetic modifications generate revenue without affecting competitive balance, while downloadable content and expansion passes extend game lifespans through post-launch gameplay additions.

Loot box systems and randomized reward mechanisms have generated substantial ethical and regulatory debate due to their structural resemblance to gambling products (MacDougall, 2020). Players spend real or virtual currency to receive random digital items without guaranteed specific rewards, creating patterns of repetitive and risk-based spending behavior that critics argue exploit psychological reward systems and may encourage compulsive spending (Li et al., 2019a). Several national governments and regulatory agencies have investigated whether loot boxes should be legally classified as gambling products subject to consumer protection regulations, with some jurisdictions imposing mandatory disclosure requirements or outright restrictions. Freemium and pay-to-win models further illustrate the commercialization of gameplay experiences, with free-to-play games generating profitability through in-game purchases and competitive advantages offered to paying users that create functional inequalities within multiplayer environments and raise concerns about fairness in game design.

Figure 6. Types of microtransactions in contemporary games

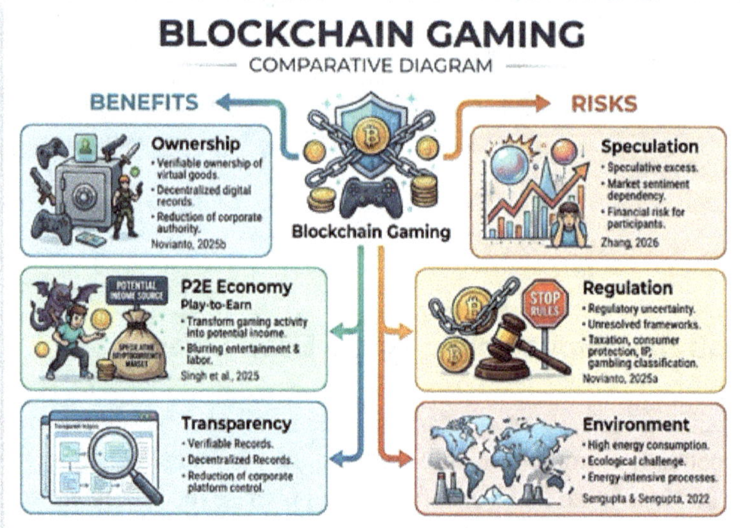

4.3 Live-Service and Engagement Economies

The rise of live-service gaming has fundamentally changed how games are conceptualized, produced, and monetized within contemporary gaming industries. Unlike traditional games released as finished products with discrete commercial lifecycles, live-service games operate as continuously evolving platforms receiving regular content updates, seasonal events, competitive rotations, and ongoing feature additions designed to sustain player engagement and monetization over extended periods measured in years rather than months (Pivovarov, 2026b). This model transforms gaming development into perpetual maintenance and content production operations requiring sustained resource commitments from developers and continuous investment of time and money from players.

Seasonal passes, battle pass systems, and engagement loop mechanics have become ubiquitous monetization mechanisms within live-service environments. These systems create progression-based incentives tied to ongoing gameplay activity, rewarding continued engagement with cosmetic items, exclusive content, and digital status markers available only within specific time-limited windows. Limited availability and expiration dates generate urgency that motivates spending and extensive time investment from players. Data analytics and behavioral targeting play essential roles in optimizing these engagement economies: gaming companies collect comprehensive behavioral data and analyze it through machine learning systems to personalize monetization approaches, identify at-risk churning users, and design reward systems that maximize retention rates and spending frequency (Nefedchenko et al., 2025). This integration of data-driven systems into core gameplay design reflects broader surveillance capitalism dynamics where user participation continuously generates commercially exploitable behavioral information (Zuboff, 2019).

4.4 Advertising and Brand Integration

Advertising and brand integration have grown into increasingly important revenue components within gaming economies as gaming audiences expand in scale and demographic diversity (*(PDF) Modelling Data-Driven Marketing Adoption in Indian B2B IT/TES Service Providers*, n.d.-b). In-game advertising integrates branded content directly within gameplay environments through virtual billboards, sponsored events, product placements within game worlds, and branded digital items embedded in play experiences. Mobile gaming industries rely particularly heavily on advertising-based revenue because free-to-play titles generate income primarily through advertisements displayed during gameplay sessions, making advertising one of the primary revenue mechanisms for mobile game publishers targeting casual gaming demographics.

Influencer marketing partnerships and esports sponsorship agreements have become major economic drivers as gaming personalities attract large, highly engaged audiences that brands seek to reach through authentic promotional relationships (Sahaya Raj J, 2025). Gaming influencers and streamers function as cultural intermediaries shaping consumer preferences and purchase decisions within online communities in ways that conventional advertising often cannot achieve. Cross-media promotional ecosystems further demonstrate the convergence of gaming with digital marketing industries, with gaming franchises collaborating with film studios, music labels, fashion brands, and consumer goods companies to create integrated transmedia marketing campaigns that extend gaming brands into broader digital consumer culture and leverage gaming audiences for commercial purposes beyond gaming itself (Jenkins & Plasencia, 2017a).

5. PLATFORMIZATION AND CONTENT CONTROL

5.1 Digital Distribution Platforms

Digital distribution platforms have fundamentally transformed the organizational structure and operational logic of the global gaming industry (Shipra, 2019). Online storefronts now serve as the primary infrastructure through which gaming content reaches global consumers, providing centralized systems for purchasing, downloading, updating, and managing digital games across console, personal computer, and mobile ecosystems. While platformization initially appeared to democratize content production by significantly reducing barriers associated with physical distribution for independent developers, it has increasingly produced platform dependency as a defining structural characteristic of contemporary gaming industries (Van Dijck et al., 2018). Developers and publishers of all scales must negotiate access to these centralized platform infrastructures to reach the audiences necessary for commercial viability.

Platform owners function as powerful gatekeepers determining market access and commercial success through multiple regulatory mechanisms operating simultaneously (Novianto, 2025a). They establish content approval requirements, advertising standards, monetization system specifications, and revenue-sharing arrangements that extract significant commissions from game sales and in-game transactions, typically ranging from fifteen to thirty percent of all revenue generated through their infrastructure. Developers must comply with platform-specific technical requirements and content standards to maintain visibility within digital marketplaces.

This structural dependency creates pronounced power asymmetries between large platform corporations and smaller studios relying on these infrastructures for economic survival and audience reach. Political economy analysis emphasizes that platformization centralizes economic and cultural power within limited corporate infrastructures while transforming games from standalone entertainment products into services perpetually dependent on platform-controlled ecosystems for delivery, updates, and community features (&   , 2026).

Figure 7. Platformization and gatekeeping in the gaming industry

5.2 Algorithmic Visibility and Discoverability

One of the most consequential effects of platformization is the increasingly dominant role of algorithmic recommendation systems in determining content visibility and commercial discoverability within gaming markets (Zobel, 2019). Digital marketplaces contain thousands of available titles competing for limited user attention, making algorithmic discoverability a critical determinant of commercial success or obscurity. Recommendation systems employ machine learning and data analytics to personalize content suggestions based on user behavior patterns, purchase histories, engagement metrics, and predicted preferences, aiming to maximize platform retention and consumer spending. These systems shape not only what individual users encounter but also which games achieve cultural visibility and commercial momentum within gaming ecosystems (Srnicek, 2017).

Algorithmic visibility systems produce structural power asymmetries within gaming markets that systematically advantage commercially successful franchises supported by large publishers over smaller independent productions. Popular games associated with major publishers receive disproportionate promotional exposure through featured placements, recommendation priority, and advertising amplification, reinforcing existing commercial hierarchies through mechanisms that appear technologically neutral but reflect underlying economic relationships between platform operators and powerful publishing partners. Independent creators and small developers are particularly disadvantaged by these systems, frequently lacking financial resources for sponsored promotional campaigns or algorithmic optimization strategies that larger corporations deploy systematically. Questions of transparency and democratic accountability are also significant: recommendation algorithms operate through proprietary technologies rarely disclosed to developers or consumers, concentrating decision-making power over cultural visibility within private corporate systems with limited public accountability (*(PDF) [Book Review] Custodians of the Internet: Platforms, Content Moderation, and the Hidden Decisions That Shape Social Media*, n.d.).

5.3 Datafication and User Surveillance

Datafication within gaming industries transforms every dimension of player interaction into quantifiable behavioral data that corporations collect, analyze, and monetize through increasingly sophisticated technological systems (Schmidt, 2022). Player activities including movement through game environments, purchase decisions, social communications, competitive performance, time investment patterns, and emotional responses indicated through engagement metrics continuously generate behavioral data profiles that gaming companies treat as strategic commercial assets (Paganoni & Becerra, 2026). Personalization algorithms and predictive analytics systems analyze these comprehensive behavioral datasets to optimize monetization approaches for individual users, increasing the probability of additional purchases and extended platform engagement through targeted offers, customized content recommendations, and algorithmically calibrated reward timing.

Ethical and privacy implications of extensive player datafication are substantial and insufficiently addressed by existing regulatory frameworks in many jurisdictions (Lane et al., 2013). Many players remain substantially unaware of the comprehensiveness of behavioral data collection occurring through gaming platforms, the commercial uses to which this data is applied, and the third-party relationships through which gaming companies share or sell data insights. Privacy policies governing data collection are frequently written in technical language inaccessible to ordinary users, limiting the meaningfulness of formal consent mechanisms. Concerns are especially acute regarding younger users who constitute significant gaming demographic segments: children and adolescents may be particularly susceptible to targeted monetization systems designed using behavioral psychology principles, raising serious questions about ethical responsibilities of gaming corporations toward vulnerable audience segments and the adequacy of existing child data protection regulations (Anna Krzysztofik et al., 2026).

6. PARTICIPATORY CULTURES AND USER-GENERATED CONTENT

6.1 Streaming and Gaming Influencers

The emergence of participatory digital cultures has profoundly transformed gaming industries by dramatically expanding the role of audiences from passive content consumers to active cultural creators, community builders, and economic participants within digital entertainment ecosystems (Jenkins & Plasencia, 2017b). Live-streaming technologies have enabled gamers to broadcast gameplay experiences in real time to global audiences numbering in the millions, transforming gaming performance into a major genre of digital entertainment that blurs boundaries between gameplay, media production, and community interaction. Streaming platforms dedicated to gaming content have become central components of gaming industry economics, generating substantial advertising revenue, subscription income, and creator economy employment while simultaneously amplifying game visibility and consumer interest (Jenkins, 2020).

Gaming influencers and content creators have emerged as economically significant actors within digital entertainment industries, building loyal audience communities through authentic gameplay performances, humor, commentary, and social interaction that complement or sometimes surpass the marketing effectiveness of traditional advertising (Taylor, 2018). Successful influencers develop recognizable personal brands and generate revenue through platform-administered advertising programs, direct brand sponsorship agreements, merchandise sales, audience subscription systems, and community donation mechanisms. Monetization through audience engagement has become central to streaming economies, with platform algorithms rewarding creators whose content maintains high engagement metrics through recommendations and featured placement. However, creator economies exist within conditions of significant platform dependency and economic precarity: content creators rely heavily on algorithmic visibility, platform monetization policies, and advertising market conditions controlled by corporations, creating vulnerability to policy changes, algorithmic updates, or market shifts that can substantially and suddenly alter creator income (*Alienation of Labors and Fans in Digital Economy - From Digital Labor to Emotional Labor | Request PDF*, n.d.).

Figure 8. Participatory culture in gaming ecosystems

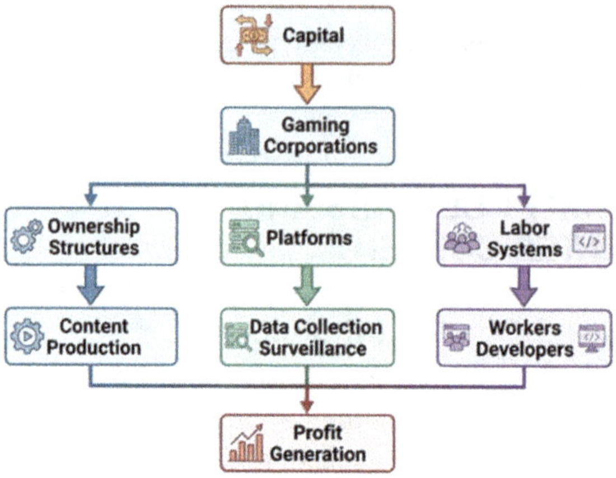

6.2 Esports and Competitive Gaming

Esports has evolved from informal competitive gaming communities into a highly professionalized entertainment industry involving international tournament circuits, major corporate sponsorships, professionally managed team organizations, and large-scale media production for global audiences (Taylor, 2012). Professional gaming careers now attract talented players, coaches, analysts, and support staff to organized competitive ecosystems with substantial prize pools, corporate team ownership, and dedicated training facilities comparable to those supporting traditional athletic programs. The institutionalization of competitive gaming has contributed to mainstream recognition of esports as legitimate professional activity, though questions regarding player welfare, career sustainability, and fair compensation remain significant ongoing concerns (Taylor, 2012).

Media rights negotiations, broadcasting agreements, and sponsorship contracts with corporations from technology, automotive, consumer goods, and financial services industries generate substantial revenue flows that sustain esports organization operations, tournament infrastructure, and media production (Macedo et al., 2024). Esports events attract millions of concurrent online viewers and significant physical live audiences, generating media value that legitimizes gaming as mainstream entertainment. However, the rapid commercialization of competitive gaming has also generated concerns regarding player exploitation, intense training demands, short career spans resulting from physical and mental burnout, and structural dependency on game publishers who control intellectual property rights, tournament licensing, and competitive format specifications that determine how professional esports ecosystems operate.

Figure 9. Organizational structure of the esports industry

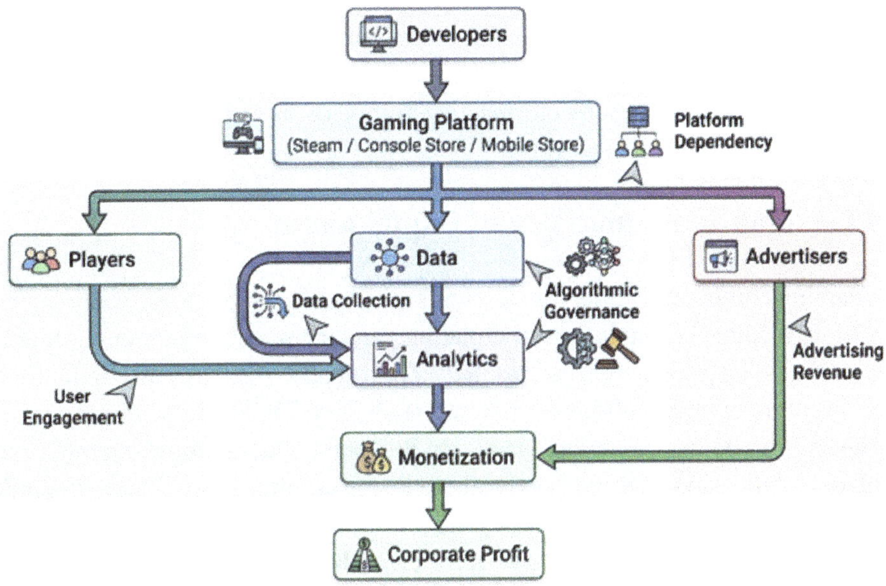

6.3 Modding and User-Generated Content

User-generated content and modding communities represent important dimensions of participatory creativity within gaming ecosystems that generate cultural and commercial value while raising significant questions about labor, ownership, and the boundaries of corporate and community relationships (*Precarious Playbour: Modders and the Digital Games Industry*, n.d.). Modding practices, through which players create new game content including additional levels, characters, mechanics, visual modifications, and gameplay systems, extend the cultural lifespan of games and drive community engagement in ways that complement official development activities. Some of the most commercially significant gaming franchises and genres emerged originally from modding communities that transformed existing commercial games into innovative new gameplay experiences, demonstrating the creative potential of participatory production within gaming cultures.

Despite the apparent democratization of content creation that modding communities represent, platform ownership of user-created content and corporate control over intellectual property assets remain persistent structural tensions. Gaming companies typically maintain comprehensive legal authority over modifications and derivative content through licensing agreements and terms of service, commercially benefiting from community-generated creative labor while limiting creators ownership rights and economic autonomy over their contributions (Dajer & de, 2020). These dynamics illustrate what political economy scholars describe as the integration of user-generated content into systems of digital labor and platform-based value extraction, where community creativity serves corporate commercial interests without corresponding compensation or formal recognition of the economic value generated through unpaid participatory work.

6.4 Gaming Communities and Digital Labor

Gaming communities function as vital organizational structures sustaining participatory cultures, maintaining active platform engagement, and generating ongoing cultural value for gaming ecosystems (Ritzer & Jurgenson, 2010). Fan communities, multiplayer networks, online discussion forums, and social media gaming groups enable players to exchange knowledge, build social relationships, organize competitive events, and collectively contribute to the cultural significance of gaming through activities that extend well beyond individual gameplay experiences. These community structures generate direct economic value for corporations and platforms through advertising exposure, platform retention metrics, and data production while operating largely through voluntary participation motivated by social interest and cultural enthusiasm rather than economic compensation (Ritzer & Jurgenson, 2010).

Community moderation represents a particularly significant but frequently underrecognized form of digital labor within gaming ecosystems (Gillespie, 2019). Online gaming communities depend on volunteer moderators and community managers who regulate member behavior, resolve interpersonal conflicts, enforce platform guidelines, remove harmful content, and create welcoming environments that sustain active participation. This moderation work is essential for maintaining healthy communities that attract and retain users, yet it typically occurs without financial compensation and with limited recognition of its economic significance for platform commercial performance. Gaming communities also confront persistent challenges including online harassment, gender discrimination, racial hostility, and toxic behavioral patterns that create hostile environments, disproportionately affecting women, LGBTQ+ players, and members of minority communities and requiring more effective governance responses from both corporations and community members (Salter & Blodgett, 2017).

The political economy of gaming communities reveals deeper tensions between the genuine social value these communities create and the extractive commercial relationships through which platforms and corporations benefit from community vitality. Community-generated cultural content, social norms, and collective identities constitute significant assets for gaming platforms whose commercial valuations depend substantially on active engaged user bases. Yet the governance structures through which platform corporations make decisions affecting community welfare — including monetization system changes, content moderation policy updates, and platform feature modifications — typically exclude meaningful community participation or voice. Developing more democratic and accountable governance frameworks for gaming communities represents an important challenge for researchers and policymakers committed to digital ecosystems that genuinely serve both commercial and community interests.

7. REGULATION, ETHICS, AND GOVERNANCE

7.1 Government Regulation of Gaming Industries

As gaming has grown into a major component of the global digital economy with significant cultural and social influence, governments and regulatory institutions have increasingly intervened to address issues of content control, consumer protection, data governance, and digital rights management (Garima Dhaka, 2024). Gaming industries now reach and influence hundreds of millions of users worldwide across demographic groups, making regulation an important dimension of contemporary media policy and digital governance. Content regulation frameworks vary significantly across national contexts, with different governments imposing restrictions based on cultural, political, religious, or moral considerations regarding violent content, gambling mechanics, political themes, and mature material (Ayewoh-Odiase, 2025). Some states require publishers to modify or remove content before games can be distributed within national markets, demonstrating how gaming industries are shaped by political systems and ideological frameworks as well as economic forces.

Age-rating classification systems represent important regulatory mechanisms implemented across multiple major gaming markets. Regulatory organizations classify games by age appropriateness according to criteria including violence intensity, sexual content, language, gambling elements, and thematic maturity, providing guidance for parents and consumers while establishing minimum standards for retail access. However, enforcement of age-rating systems remains inconsistent across digital platforms and online marketplaces, particularly regarding underage access to age-restricted content and monetization systems. National gaming policy approaches differ markedly depending on economic priorities and political contexts: some governments actively support gaming industries through investment programs, tax incentives, esports development initiatives, and digital innovation funding, while others impose participation restrictions due to addiction concerns, youth welfare priorities, or political control over digital media content.

Figure 10. Regulatory frameworks governing the gaming industry

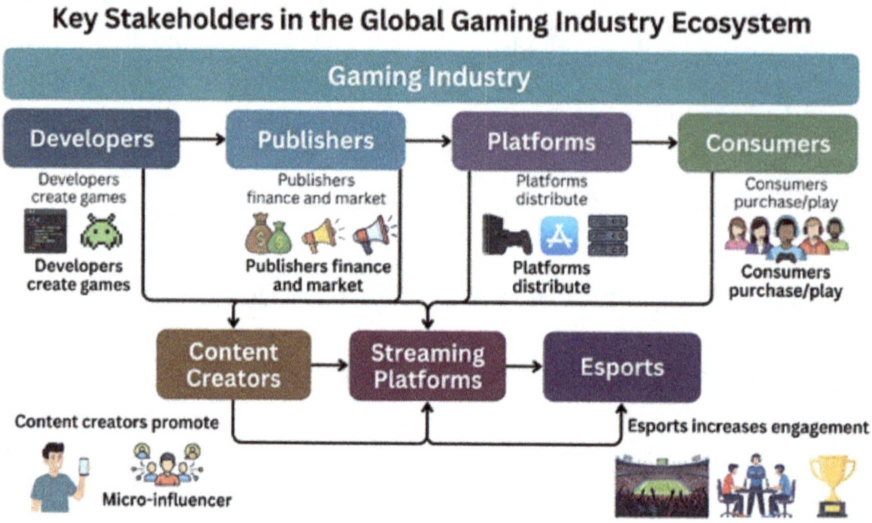

7.2 Ethical Concerns in Monetization

The commercialization of gaming has generated substantial and growing ethical concerns regarding monetization practices and their effects on player welfare across demographic groups. Contemporary games increasingly deploy engagement-driven economic systems employing psychological reward mechanisms, personalized incentive systems, and behavioral nudging techniques to encourage continuous user engagement and ongoing financial spending (von Schomberg, 2025). Political economy scholars argue that these systems frequently prioritize corporate profitability over ethical considerations of consumer well-being, with design choices systematically calibrated to maximize spending rather than enhance genuine player satisfaction or enjoyment (*(PDF) Zackariasson, P. & Wilson, T. L. (2012) (Eds). The Video Game Industry. Formation, Present State and Future. London: Routledge.*, n.d.).

Loot box controversies have become focal points of policy debate regarding the ethical dimensions of gaming monetization (Li et al., 2019b). Randomized reward systems structurally parallel gambling mechanisms in their combination of monetary expenditure with uncertain outcomes, creating patterns of repetitive risk-based spending that critics argue exploit psychological reward systems and may encourage compulsive behavior. Consumer protection concerns are particularly acute regarding younger players who may be especially vulnerable to these monetization mechanisms and unable to evaluate the financial implications of repeated small purchases that accumulate into substantial expenditure. Several governments have responded with investigative proceedings, mandatory disclosure requirements, or direct restrictions on loot box systems. Digital purchases generally, including virtual currencies, subscription systems, and hidden microtransaction costs, create financial transparency challenges that existing consumer protection frameworks designed for physical retail environments are frequently inadequate to address effectively.

7.3 Intellectual Property and Platform Governance

Intellectual property rights form a central axis of governance within gaming ecosystems because games incorporate diverse creative assets including software systems, narrative content, visual art, music, and character designs whose ownership determines significant economic relationships (*(PDF) Academic Publishing in the Digital Era: The Role of Cross-Media Publishing in Expanding the Scope and Accessibility of Research*, n.d.). Copyright issues have grown more complex and contested with the expansion of streaming, modding, esports broadcasting, and user-generated content that involves copyrighted gaming material in diverse contexts and for varied commercial and non-commercial purposes. Content creators streaming gameplay footage, modding communities creating derivative content, and esports organizations broadcasting competitive events all navigate intellectual property relationships with game publishers that vary considerably in their clarity, fairness, and commercial implications (Coyle, 2017)

Ownership of digital assets and virtual goods presents an emerging governance frontier generating significant tension between consumer expectations and corporate legal authority. Players purchase substantial quantities of virtual items including cosmetic skins, in-game currencies, collectible characters, and digital equipment, often investing significant financial resources with reasonable expectations of persistent value and continued access. However, corporations typically retain comprehensive legal control over digital assets through licensing agreements and terms of service that preserve platform authority to modify, restrict, or terminate access to purchased digital goods. Platform governance additionally shapes creator and user rights through terms of service enforcement, content moderation decisions, and monetization policy changes, with platform operators possessing significant authority to remove content, suspend accounts, or eliminate monetization access affecting creator livelihoods without recourse mechanisms proportionate to economic impact (Nurik, 2019)

7.4 Diversity, Inclusion, and Representation

Diversity, inclusion, and representation have emerged as significant governance and cultural quality dimensions within gaming industries, receiving growing attention from researchers, developers, advocacy organizations, and regulatory bodies. Historically, gaming industries have faced substantial criticism for systematic underrepresentation of women, racial minorities, LGBTQ+ individuals, people with disabilities, and other marginalized identity groups in both gaming content and gaming workforces (Takru, 2025). Contemporary developers increasingly recognize diversity and representation as both ethical obligations and commercial imperatives, as gaming audiences themselves reflect substantial demographic diversity across gender, age, cultural background, and identity.

Accessibility and inclusive design have gained considerable professional attention within game development communities (*The Promotion of Diversity and Inclusion in Olympic Games: An Intersection Between Future Opportunities and Career Experiences for HBCU Student-Athletes | Request PDF*, n.d.). Developers increasingly implement customizable control schemes, comprehensive subtitle systems, colorblind accessibility modes, adjustable difficulty parameters, and adaptive technology compatibility that enable players with physical or cognitive differences to participate more fully in gaming experiences. Despite these positive developments, online harassment, gender discrimination, racial hostility, and discriminatory community behavior remain pervasive challenges within many gaming environments, disproportionately affecting women, LGBTQ+ players, and members of minority communities who report significantly higher rates of targeted harassment within competitive and social gaming spaces. Effective governance frameworks addressing these challenges require coordinated responses from platform operators, game developers, and regulatory institutions.

8. IMPACT OF GAMING INDUSTRIES ON BROADER CONTENT ECOSYSTEMS

8.1 Convergence of Gaming and Media Industries

Gaming industries have become deeply integrated with broader media and entertainment industries, contributing substantially to accelerating processes of media convergence that characterize contemporary digital culture (Jenkins, 2020). Gaming no longer functions as an isolated entertainment medium confined to consoles or personal computers; it operates as a component of larger digital media networks interconnecting film, television, music, social media platforms, streaming services, digital advertising, and online communication systems in increasingly dense and commercially significant ways (Escuadro & Jamero, 2026). This convergence reflects both the growing cultural centrality of gaming and the strategic commercial logic of large entertainment corporations seeking to leverage popular gaming intellectual property across multiple revenue-generating media contexts simultaneously (Jenkins, 2020).

The integration of gaming with film and television industries has become commercially significant and culturally prominent (Kerr, 2017). Popular gaming franchises are adapted into streaming series, theatrical films, and animated productions that reach audiences beyond dedicated gaming communities, while successful film and television properties are developed into games that extend audience engagement and generate additional revenue. Music industries have established creative and commercial connections with gaming through artist collaborations for in-game virtual concerts, licensed soundtrack partnerships, and interactive music experiences that transform games into cultural spaces hosting musical events alongside gameplay. Social media platforms amplify gaming content through live streams, esports highlights, influencer marketing, and community sharing, integrating gaming into everyday digital communication and increasing its cultural reach (Jenkins et al., 2013). Transmedia storytelling strategies allow major entertainment corporations to extend intellectual property across games, films, comics, novels, merchandise, and community platforms, maximizing profitability while strengthening audience emotional investment.

Figure 11. Media convergence and cross-platform integration of gaming industries

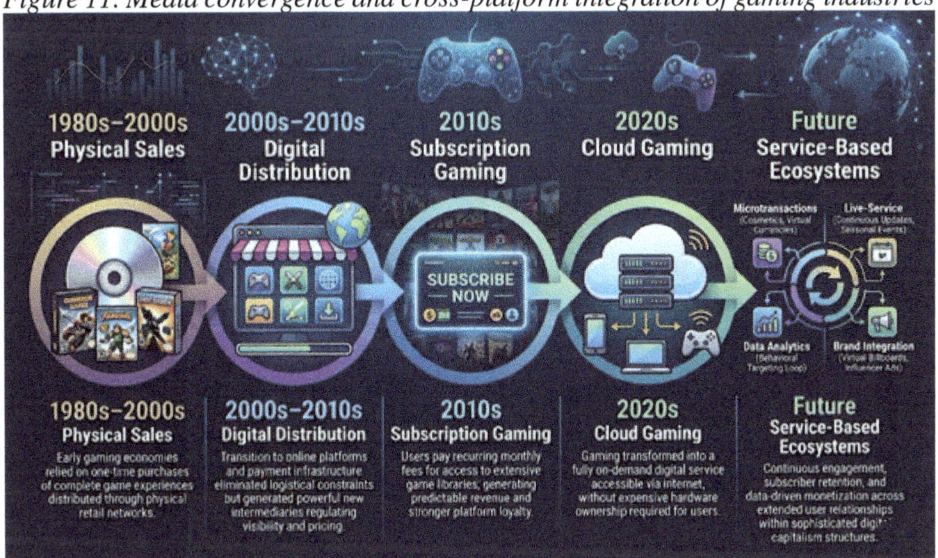

8.2 Influence on Digital Content Production

Gaming industries have exerted significant influence on broader digital content production practices, aesthetic conventions, and platform design logics that now extend across numerous non-gaming digital environments. Gaming-inspired visual styles including immersive interface design, animated achievement systems, progress indicators, and interactive graphic elements have migrated into mainstream digital platforms, applications, and media products. Gaming communication practices, terminology, humor, and cultural references have become widely integrated into digital youth culture and online social interaction, demonstrating gaming's substantial influence on digital language and communication norms across demographic groups who may not identify primarily as dedicated gamers.

Gamification represents one of gaming's most far-reaching and commercially significant influences on broader digital culture and platform design (Menz & McLinton, 2026). The deliberate application of game design mechanics including points, badges, rankings, progress visualization, achievement recognition, and competitive comparison to non-gaming digital environments has become a widespread strategy for maximizing user engagement, behavioral compliance, and platform retention across social media applications, educational platforms, fitness tracking systems, professional software, and consumer loyalty programs (*Reality Is Broken: Why Games Make Us Better and How They Can Change the World*, n.d.). These gaming-inspired engagement mechanics maximize user retention and generate behavioral data while creating psychological engagement dynamics that prioritize platform time and activity over other user values. Gaming industries have simultaneously contributed to normalizing user-generated content and participatory creativity as expected features of digital platforms, influencing platform design philosophy across the digital economy toward greater community customization, user expression, and collaborative content production.

Figure 12. Application of gamification elements across digital platforms

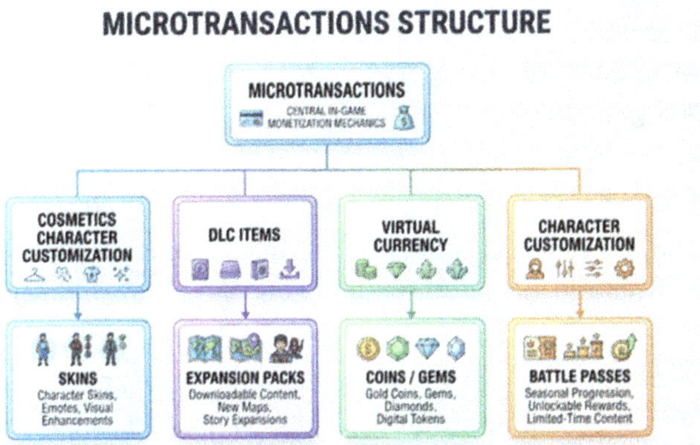

8.3 Economic and Cultural Impacts

The gaming industry generates substantial and diverse economic impacts across multiple industrial sectors and geographic regions (Spiller, 2026). Direct employment in game development requires collaboration among programmers, designers, writers, animators, sound engineers, quality assurance specialists, and marketing professionals, while gaming ecosystems generate additional employment in esports management, streaming production, digital advertising, content creation, event organization, and merchandise production. Gaming technologies drive innovation in graphics processing, artificial intelligence systems, cloud computing infrastructure, virtual reality development, and online networking, with gaming-driven technological advances generating applications and commercial value across digital industries well beyond entertainment (Castells, 2010).

Culturally, gaming contributes significantly to globalization dynamics and soft power relationships between national entertainment industries (*(PDF) Soft Power: The Means to Success in World Politics, and: America the Virtuous: The Crisis of Democracy and the Quest for Empire (Review)*, n.d.). Successful gaming franchises reach international audiences and facilitate global circulation of cultural symbols, narratives, and representational frameworks that influence how different societies understand and relate to gaming-producing cultures (Oonk, 2000b). Governments increasingly recognize gaming as a domain of cultural diplomacy and national soft power, with strong gaming industries contributing to national digital reputation and international cultural influence. At the community level, gaming environments provide younger generations with important spaces for social connection, collaborative problem-solving, identity expression, and cross-cultural interaction that shape digital social competencies with implications extending well beyond gaming contexts. However, gaming cultures also generate concerns regarding addiction vulnerability, online harassment impacts, and the psychological effects of engagement-optimized platform design, requiring balanced assessment of gaming's complex cultural and social impacts.

The relationship between gaming and broader cultural and social systems must be understood through a political economy lens that recognizes both the genuine value created and the structural inequalities reproduced by gaming industries. Employment generation, technological innovation, and cultural globalization represent real and significant contributions. However, these benefits are distributed unequally across geographic regions, demographic groups, and stakeholder categories within gaming value chains. Workers in lower-wage production regions, independent developers navigating monopolistic platform ecosystems, and communities underrepresented in mainstream gaming content all experience gaming industries differently from the major corporate beneficiaries of platform capitalism (Novianto, 2025b). Governance frameworks committed to more equitable distribution of gaming industry benefits must address these structural inequalities explicitly, rather than assuming that aggregate industry growth automatically translates into broadly shared social welfare.

9. EMERGING TRENDS AND FUTURE CHALLENGES

9.1 Artificial Intelligence and Procedural Content

Artificial intelligence has become one of the most transformative technological forces shaping the present and future trajectory of gaming industries and digital entertainment ecosystems more broadly (Castells, 2010). AI-driven procedural content generation enables automated creation of game environments, character behaviors, narrative branching, and gameplay system variations through algorithmic processes, allowing developers to create expansive, dynamically evolving gaming experiences that adapt to player behavior while managing certain production constraints (Hu et al., 2024). AI personalization systems analyze comprehensive player behavioral profiles to customize difficulty parameters, content recommendations, and engagement incentive timing, creating individualized gaming experiences designed to maximize retention and spending for each specific user. Machine learning advances enable more sophisticated and responsive non-player character behaviors, more convincing synthetic dialogue, and more adaptive game world reactions to player decisions.

Despite substantial technological opportunities, AI integration raises significant concerns regarding creative labor displacement, algorithmic governance, and behavioral manipulation within gaming economies. As AI systems become increasingly capable of generating visual artwork, narrative dialogue, programming code, and gameplay design elements, concerns grow regarding the future of creative employment within gaming industries and the potential for AI deployment to intensify cost-reduction pressures at the expense of human creative workers (Crawford, 2021). AI-driven engagement optimization systems may effectively manipulate player behavior through precisely calibrated reward timing and personalized psychological incentives designed to maximize spending and platform time, raising ethical questions about the boundaries between personalization and manipulation (Smart, 2025). Questions of algorithmic bias, representational fairness, and transparency in AI-driven systems require sustained governance attention as AI becomes more central to gaming experience design.

Figure 13. Applications and challenges of artificial intelligence in gaming

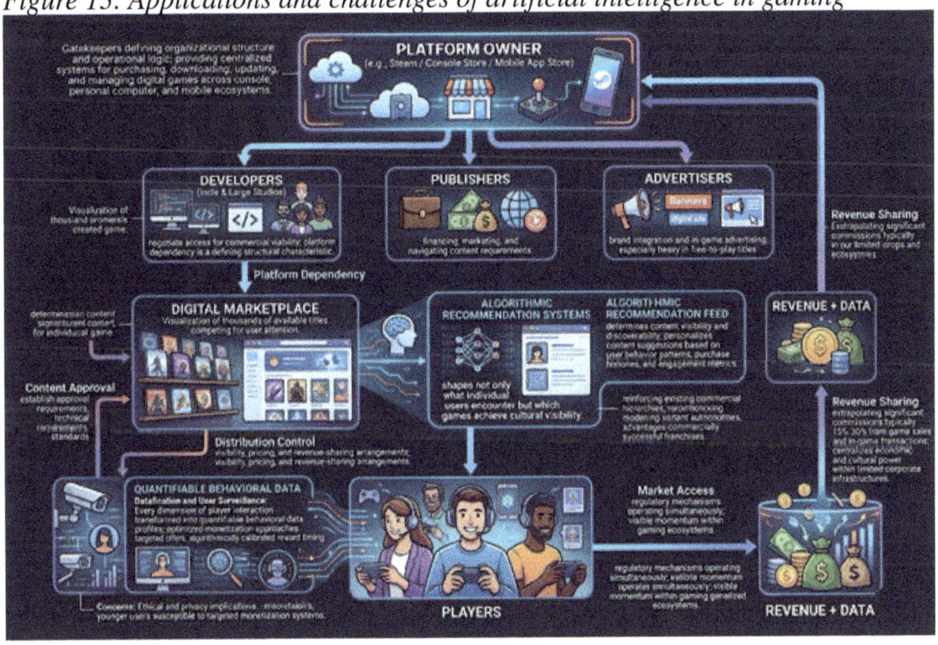

9.2 Blockchain, NFTs, and Virtual Economies

Blockchain technologies and non-fungible tokens have introduced proposed new economic and ownership models within gaming industries that generate significant commercial interest alongside substantial controversy (Zhang, 2026). Proponents argue that blockchain-based gaming systems can provide players verifiable ownership of virtual goods through decentralized digital records that exist independently of centralized corporate platform control, potentially reducing corporate authority over digital asset permanence and transferability. NFT-based gaming ecosystems promote play-to-earn economic models in which gameplay participation connects to speculative cryptocurrency markets, transforming gaming activity into a potential income source for players in ways that blur distinctions between entertainment, labor, and financial investment (Singh et al., 2025).

Critical assessments of blockchain gaming highlight substantial concerns regarding speculative excess, environmental impact, and regulatory uncertainty (*Forging Blockchains: Spatial Production and Political Economy of Decentralized Cryptocurrency Code/Spaces*, n.d.). NFT markets frequently function as speculative financial vehicles where asset value depends primarily on market sentiment and artificial scarcity rather than underlying cultural or gameplay significance, creating financial risk for participants. Environmental costs of energy-intensive blockchain computational processes conflict with broader digital sustainability commitments. Regulatory frameworks for cryptocurrency gaming assets remain unresolved across most jurisdictions, creating legal uncertainty regarding taxation, consumer protection, intellectual property, and potential gambling classification. Political economy analysis reveals that corporate interest in blockchain gaming often reflects opportunities to expand platform-controlled revenue extraction rather than genuine commitment to player economic empowerment, as large companies seek to integrate new monetization layers into existing commercial infrastructures.

Figure 14. Blockchain-based gaming ecosystem and associated risks

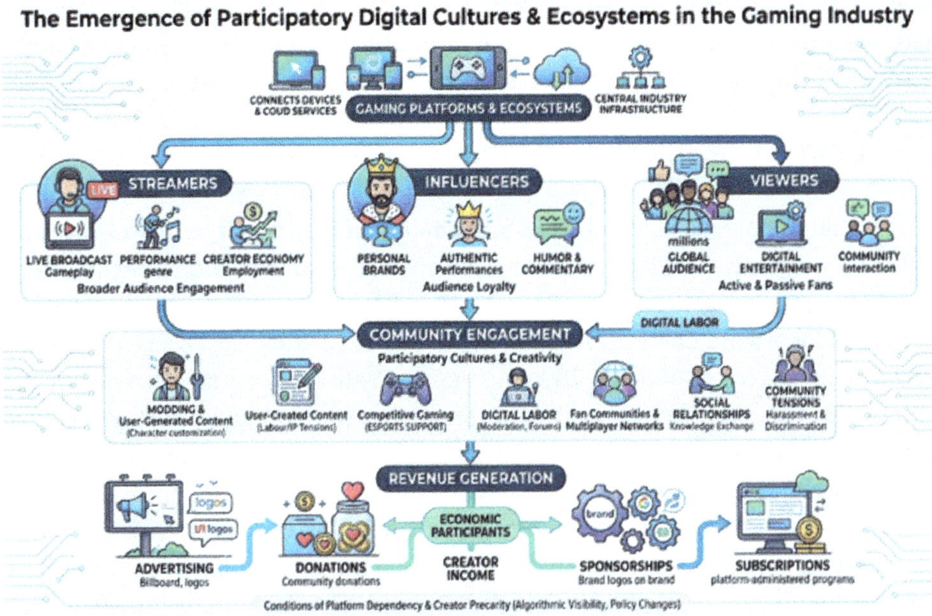

9.3 Sustainability of Gaming Ecosystems

Long-term sustainability concerns encompass environmental, economic, labor, and cultural dimensions of gaming industry development that require integrated governance responses. The energy consumption associated with modern gaming infrastructure including data centers, cloud computing systems, streaming servers, and high-performance gaming hardware contributes to digital industries' growing environmental footprint (Sengupta & Sengupta, 2022). Hardware production cycles, planned obsolescence dynamics, and electronic waste generated by frequent device replacements create ecological challenges that gaming industries have been slow to systematically address. Cryptocurrency-integrated gaming systems potentially intensify environmental concerns through additional computational energy demands.

Labor sustainability requires sustained attention to crunch culture normalization, precarious employment conditions, inadequate mental health support systems, and barriers to collective bargaining that affect diverse categories of gaming workers from development studio employees to esports athletes and digital content creators. Cultural sustainability involves maintaining sufficient diversity in gaming content, accessible entry points for independent developers, and equitable community conditions that welcome players from all demographic backgrounds. Sustainable gaming ecosystems require balancing legitimate commercial profitability with ecological responsibility, fair labor standards, creative autonomy, competitive market diversity, and democratic participation in gaming culture governance—dimensions that purely market-driven approaches to gaming industry organization consistently undervalue.

9.4 Future of Regulation and Platform Governance

The future governance landscape for gaming industries will be shaped by how effectively societies develop regulatory frameworks capable of addressing platform capitalism dynamics, digital labor conditions, datafication practices, and transnational media system characteristics that existing regulatory approaches were not designed to govern (Novianto, 2025a). Gaming platforms operate across national boundaries while regulatory institutions remain primarily organized at national or regional levels, creating persistent jurisdictional gaps in data privacy enforcement, intellectual property protection, taxation of digital services, content moderation standards, and digital labor rights. International regulatory coordination mechanisms may become increasingly necessary to address global gaming platform operations effectively, though achieving meaningful coordination among governments with different political systems and economic interests presents substantial practical challenges (van Dijck et al., 2018).

Governance frameworks require careful balancing of multiple competing objectives: protecting users from exploitative monetization, invasive surveillance, and manipulative behavioral design while preserving technological innovation and genuine creative freedom; ensuring market competition while recognizing legitimate economies of scale in platform services; and enforcing platform accountability while avoiding governance approaches that create new barriers to participation or expression. Political economy perspectives emphasize the importance of algorithmic transparency requirements, platform data governance standards, digital labor rights protections, and antitrust policy reforms capable of addressing the structural market concentration that characterizes contemporary gaming ecosystems. Civil society organizations and gaming communities play important roles as advocacy voices for more equitable and democratic governance frameworks, complementing regulatory action by governments and supranational institutions in shaping the norms and standards governing gaming industries. The governance architecture required for sustainable gaming industries will need to address the fundamental power asymmetry between large platform corporations and the diverse communities of developers, creators, workers, and players whose collective contributions generate the cultural and economic value that makes gaming commercially and socially significant.

Figure 15. Future governance framework for digital gaming platforms

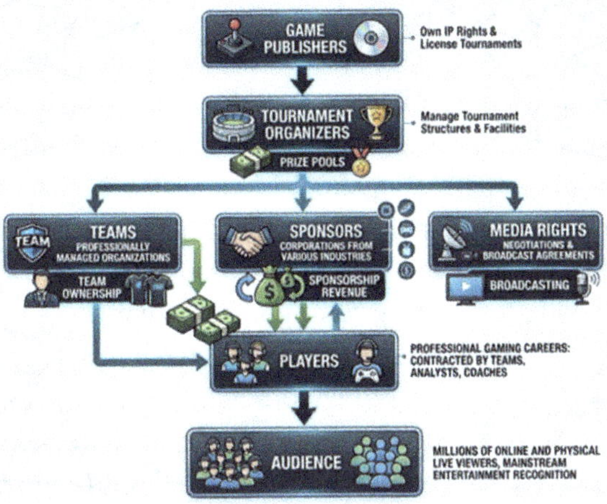

10. CONCLUSION

10.1 Summary of Key Arguments

This chapter has systematically examined the political economy of gaming industries through analysis of the relationships between corporate power structures, digital platform organizations, monetization systems, labor dynamics, participatory cultures, and regulatory frameworks that together constitute contemporary gaming ecosystems (Sjøvaag et al., 2026). A central and recurring argument is that gaming operates within broader structures of political economy where ownership concentration, capital accumulation imperatives, and market control mechanisms strongly determine the conditions under which gaming content is produced, distributed, consumed, and monetized. Large multinational corporations increasingly dominate gaming ecosystems through acquisitions, platform ownership, and intellectual property concentration, with economic power organized among a limited number of global technology and entertainment corporations exercising decisive influence over industry standards, creative priorities, and market accessibility (Kerr, 2017).

Platform capitalism has emerged as the dominant organizational logic governing contemporary gaming industries (Novianto, 2025a). Digital distribution platforms, streaming infrastructures, cloud gaming services, and subscription ecosystems function as central intermediaries controlling market access, audience reach, and monetization mechanisms for developers and content creators of all scales. Algorithmic governance shapes cultural visibility and consumption patterns in ways that systematically advantage commercially powerful incumbents over smaller and independent producers. Advanced monetization strategies encompassing microtransactions, live-service engagement loops, behavioral targeting systems, and data-driven personalization generate extraordinary profits while raising persistent ethical concerns regarding consumer manipulation, addiction facilitation, and the commodification of player psychological vulnerabilities (Menz & McLinton, 2026).

Participatory cultures have simultaneously transformed gaming industries and broader digital media environments while remaining structurally embedded within corporate-controlled platform ecosystems that capture most of the economic value generated through community creativity and engagement (Andrews, 2025). Streaming economies, esports industries, modding communities, and user-generated content have expanded creative participation opportunities while reinforcing digital labor dynamics where user activity generates commercial value for platforms without commensurate compensation (*Digital Labor: The Internet as Playground and Factory | Request PDF*, n.d.). Labor conditions throughout gaming industries — characterized by crunch culture normalization, precarious employment patterns, and limited collective bargaining — represent persistent political economy concerns demanding greater regulatory and scholarly attention (Bonenfant, 2021).

10.2 Major Challenges and Opportunities

Contemporary gaming industries present a complex interplay of significant challenges and genuine opportunities that require nuanced governance responses capable of addressing structural problems without foreclosing the cultural and economic potential of digital gaming ecosystems. Ethical monetization governance represents perhaps the most pressing near-term challenge, with microtransaction systems, loot box mechanics, and behavioral engagement design raising consumer welfare concerns that existing regulatory frameworks inadequately address, particularly regarding younger users. Market concentration and oligopolistic corporate power threaten competitive diversity, limit creative experimentation, create barriers for independent developers, and concentrate cultural influence over gaming narratives within a small number of corporate decision-making centers that may not reflect the diversity of gaming communities.

Significant opportunities for positive development coexist with these structural challenges. Digital platforms have expanded access to game development tools and global distribution infrastructure, enabling independent creators and small studios to reach audiences that would have been inaccessible in physical distribution eras. Esports industries create professional opportunities and cultural spaces for competitive excellence recognized increasingly by mainstream media and educational institutions. Streaming and content creation economies generate entrepreneurial pathways, community connection, and new forms of digital cultural labor that engage creative talent across diverse geographic and demographic contexts. Gaming technologies continue advancing capabilities in artificial intelligence, virtual reality, accessibility design, and interactive storytelling that benefit both entertainment and broader application domains including education, healthcare simulation, and professional training. User-generated content communities demonstrate the creative potential of participatory digital culture when supported by adequate platform infrastructure and equitable governance frameworks. Realizing these substantial opportunities while effectively addressing structural challenges requires coordinated and sustained action from policymakers, corporations, developers, researchers, and gaming communities committed to gaming ecosystems that balance commercial viability with cultural diversity, labor dignity, ethical monetization practices, and genuinely democratic governance structures.

10.3 Future Directions for Research and Policy

The rapid and continuing transformation of gaming industries highlights pressing needs for expanded academic research programs and regularly updated policy frameworks capable of responding to the evolving complexities of platform-based digital media ecosystems. Future political economy research should continue examining how corporate ownership structures, platform governance mechanisms, labor relations dynamics, and algorithmic systems interact to shape the conditions of digital participation and cultural production within gaming industries (van Dijck et al., 2018). Research specifically addressing data capitalism in gaming contexts should investigate how behavioral analytics systems, AI-driven personalization, and predictive modeling govern user experience and commercial relationships with implications for autonomy, privacy, and consumer rights (Smart, 2025).

Labor research within gaming industries requires greater attention to working conditions across the full spectrum of gaming labor including formal development employment, esports professional careers, streaming creator economies, and participatory digital labor performed by community members. Research on diversity, representation, accessibility, and online safety should continue examining structural barriers and governance responses with potential to make gaming environments more equitable for players across demographic groups (*(PDF) [Book Review] Custodians of the Internet: Platforms, Content Moderation, and the Hidden Decisions That Shape Social Media*, n.d.). Policy development priorities should include antitrust frameworks addressing platform market concentration, consumer protection standards governing digital monetization practices, data rights regulations ensuring meaningful user control over behavioral data, and labor standards capable of protecting workers across diverse gaming employment contexts. International cooperation mechanisms will become increasingly important as gaming platform governance challenges require coordination across jurisdictional boundaries that national regulatory approaches alone cannot effectively address. Sustainable, inclusive, and democratically accountable gaming ecosystems represent an achievable goal, but one requiring sustained commitment from researchers, policymakers, industry actors, and gaming communities working collectively to realize the positive potential of digital gaming while effectively addressing the structural challenges that platform capitalism, corporate concentration, and datafication pose for the future of equitable digital culture.

REFERENCES

, . ., & , . (2026). Policy Mobilities and the Global Exchange of Ideas, Authority, and Development Frameworks. , *3*, 635–656. https://doi.org/ DOI: 10.21608/abs.2025.422076.1070

A Playful Multitude? Mobilising and Counter-Mobilising Immaterial Game Labour. (n.d.). Https://Www.Researchgate.Net/Publication/26490723_A_Playful_Multitude_Mobilising_and_Counter-Mobilising_Immaterial_Game_Labour

Alienation of Labors and Fans in Digital Economy - From Digital Labor to Emotional Labor | Request PDF. (n.d.). Https://Www.Researchgate.Net/Publication/382598104_Alienation_of_Labors_and_Fans_in_Digital_Economy_-_From_Digital_Labor_to_Emotional_Labor

Andrews, C. (2025). Production, consumption, prosumption: How George Ritzer shifted the conversation in sociology from work to consumption and beyond. *Thesis Eleven, 191*, 120–128. DOI: 10.1177/07255136251395769

Audience labour in the age of AI-generated comments: Insights from Reddit | Request PDF. (n.d.). Https://Www.Researchgate.Net/Publication/399796174_Audience_labour_in_the_age_of_AI-Generated_comments_Insights_from_Reddit

Ayewoh-Odiase, P. E. (2025). Politics of Human Rights Protection in An Era of Global Terrorism.

Bonenfant, M. (2021). Hypermodern Video Games as Emblems of Empire or How the Gaming Multitude Adapts to Hypermodernity. *Games and Culture*, *16*(3), 357–370. DOI: 10.1177/1555412020961849

Castells, M. (2010). The Rise of the Network Society, Second Edition, With a New Preface. In *The Rise of the Network Society, Second Edition, With a New Preface*. Wiley-Liss Inc. DOI: 10.1002/9781444319514

Coyle, K. (2017). Book Review: Free Culture: How Big Media Uses Technology and the Law to Lock Down Culture and Control Creativity. *Information Technology and Libraries*, *23*(4), 198–199. DOI: 10.6017/ital.v23i4.9665

Crawford, K. (2021). Atlas of AI: Power, Politics, and the Planetary Costs of Artificial Intelligence. In *Atlas of AI: Power, Politics, and the Planetary Costs of Artificial Intelligence*. Yale University Press., DOI: 10.56315/PSCF3-22Crawford

Dajer, V., & de, P. (2020). Games in the age of empire. *Kultura*, 224–245. DOI: 10.5937/kultura2068224D

De Minicis, M. (2026). *Uncovering platforms: investigating and visualizing the variety of platform capitalism in Italy and Spain*. Cambio. Rivista Sulle Trasformazioni Sociali., DOI: 10.36253/cambio-17339

C Dey, D. N. (2026). <b>Book Review - THE AGE OF SURVEILLANCE CAPITALISM BY SHOSHANA ZUBOFF</b> *Global E-Journal of Social Scientific Research, 2*. DOI: 10.64706/h7bntw21

Dhaka, G. (2024). An Ellustrative Research on Challenges and Opportunities Faced Due To Evolving Legal Landscape of Online Gaming in India. *Communications on Applied Nonlinear Analysis, 32*(4s), 332–343. DOI: 10.52783/cana.v32.2824

Digital entertainment gaming as a site for (informal) historical learning | Request PDF. (n.d.-a). Https://Www.Researchgate.Net/Publication/336496091_Digital_entertainment_gaming_as_a_site_for_informal_historical_learning

Digital entertainment gaming as a site for (informal) historical learning | Request PDF. (n.d.-b). Https://Www.Researchgate.Net/Publication/336496091_Digital_entertainment_gaming_as_a_site_for_informal_historical_learning

Digital Labor: The Internet as Playground and Factory | Request PDF. (n.d.). Https://Www.Researchgate.Net/Publication/283985861_Digital_Labor_The_Internet_as_Playground_and_Factory

Dimic-Janjic, S., Stjepanovic, M., Belic, S., Vukosavljevic, D., Milivojevic, I., Trboljevac, N., Nikolic, N., Stamenic, S., Stojanovic, M., Stosic, K., Vasakova, M. K., Stevic, R., Colic, N., Lukic, K., Ilic, M., Isovic, L., Maric, N., Popevic, S., Vucinic-Mihailović, V., & Jovanovic, D. (2025). Clinical Characteristics and Survival of Patients with Idiopathic Pulmonary Fibrosis: Analysis of the Serbian Cohort from the EMPIRE Registry. *Diagnostics (Basel), 15*(17), 2121. Advance online publication. DOI: 10.3390/diagnostics15172121 PMID: 40941610

Escuadro, M. C. O., & Jamero, R. M. (2026). The Effectiveness of Meme Marketing in Brand Awareness Among KCC Mall of Marbel Customers. *International Journal of Innovative Science and Research Technology, 3044*, 3044. Advance online publication. DOI: 10.38124/ijisrt/26feb1400

Forging Blockchains: Spatial Production and Political Economy of Decentralized Cryptocurrency Code/Spaces. (n.d.). Https://Www.Researchgate.Net/Publication/317057295_Forging_Blockchains_Spatial_Production_and_Political_Economy_of_Decentralized_Cryptocurrency_CodeSpaces

Fuchs, C. (2014). Digital labour and Karl Marx. In *Digital Labour and Karl Marx*. Taylor and Francis., DOI: 10.4324/9781315880075

Gillespie, T. (2019). Custodians of the Internet. In *Custodians of the Internet*. Yale University Press., DOI: 10.12987/9780300235029

Horkheimer, M., Adorno, T. W., & Noeri, G. (2002). *Dialectic of enlightenment*. Stanford University Press. *(PDF) Zackariasson, P. & Wilson, T. L. (2012) (Eds). The Video game industry. Formation, present state and future. London: Routledge.* (n.d.). Https://Www.Researchgate.Net/Publication/266571389_Zackariasson_P_Wilson_T_L_2012_Eds_The_Video_game_industry_Formation_present_state_and_future_London_Routledge

Hu, C., Zhao, Y., Wang, Z., Du, H., & Liu, J. (2024). Games for Artificial Intelligence Research: A Review and Perspectives. *IEEE Transactions on Artificial Intelligence*, *5*(12), 5949–5968. DOI: 10.1109/TAI.2024.3410935

Jenkins, H. (2020). Convergence Culture. In *Convergence Culture*. New York University Press., DOI: 10.18574/nyu/9780814743683.001.0001

Jenkins, H., Ford, S., & Green, J. (2013). Spreadable media: Creating value and meaning in a networked culture. In *Spreadable Media: Creating Value and Meaning in a Networked Culture*. New York University Press., DOI: 10.3983/twc.2014.0633

Jenkins, H., & Plasencia, A. (2017a). Convergence Culture: Where Old and New Media Collide. In *Is the Universe a Hologram?* The MIT Press., DOI: 10.7551/mitpress/10428.003.0018

Jenkins, H., & Plasencia, A. (2017b). Convergence Culture: Where Old and New Media Collide. In *Is the Universe a Hologram?* The MIT Press., DOI: 10.7551/mitpress/10428.003.0018

Kerr, A. (2017). Global games: Production, circulation and policy in the networked era. In *Global Games: Production, Circulation and Policy in the Networked Era*. Taylor and Francis., DOI: 10.4324/9780203704028

Krzysztofik, A., Napierała, W., Hak, K. J., Jasiński, J. L., Leszczyńska, K. M., Mitan, A. M., Kańska, K. T., Krawczyk, K., Wieczorek, M. T., & Tomaszewska, A. M. (2026). DIGITAL SCREEN EXPOSURE AND MENTAL HEALTH OUTCOMES IN CHILDREN AND ADOLESCENTS: A NARRATIVE REVIEW. *International Journal of Innovative Technologies in Social Science*, *3*(1(49)). Advance online publication. DOI: 10.31435/ijitss.1(49).2026.5220

Lane, J., Stodden, V., Bender, S., & Nissenbaum, H. (2013). Privacy, big data, and the public good: Frameworks for engagement. In *Privacy, Big Data, and the Public Good: Frameworks for Engagement*. Cambridge University Press., DOI: 10.1017/CBO9781107590205

Li, W., Mills, D., & Nower, L. (2019a). The relationship of loot box purchases to problem video gaming and problem gambling. *Addictive Behaviors, 97*, 27–34. DOI: 10.1016/j.addbeh.2019.05.016 PMID: 31129456

Li, W., Mills, D., & Nower, L. (2019b). The relationship of loot box purchases to problem video gaming and problem gambling. *Addictive Behaviors, 97*, 27–34. DOI: 10.1016/j.addbeh.2019.05.016 PMID: 31129456

Lin, L. (2022). *Convergent Production Strategies: CCTV and HBS* (pp. 51–74). DOI: 10.1007/978-3-030-91756-2_3

Lucchesi, D. (2026). *Logics, Functioning, and Evolution of the Web: From Networked Society to Platform Society* (pp. 33–51). DOI: 10.1007/978-3-032-21265-8_3

MacDougall, R. (2020). Marx at the Arcade: Consoles, Controllers, and Class Struggle by Jamie Woodcock. *Labour (Halifax), 86*(1), 218–219. DOI: 10.1353/llt.2020.0059

Macedo, T., Kurtz, G. B., & Becka, L. (2024). Esports culture in South America. In *Routledge Handbook of Esports* (pp. 643–654). Taylor and Francis., DOI: 10.4324/9781003410591-68

Menz, S. N., & McLinton, S. S. (2026). Exploring the Experiences of Women Working in the Male-Dominated Video Game Industry. In *Gendered Marginalities* (pp. 231–261). Springer Nature Singapore., DOI: 10.1007/978-981-95-1557-8_11

Merkulova, T., & Bobrov, V. (2026). ARTIFICIAL INTELLIGENCE AS A DRIVER OF ECONOMIC TRANSFORMATION IN THE VIDEO GAME INDUSTRY. *Електронний Журнал "Ефективна Економіка."* DOI: 10.32702/2307-2105.2026.1.36

Mirowski, P. (2008). A Brief History of Neoliberalism, David Harvey. Oxford University Press, 2005, vii + 247 pages. *Economics and Philosophy, 24*(1), 111–117. DOI: 10.1017/S0266267108001715

Mosco, V. (2009). The Political Economy of Communication: A Living Tradition. *Media Asia, 36*(3), 146–155. DOI: 10.1080/23776277.2009.12224389

Muttaqin, M. Z. (2026). *Bourdieu's Ideas on Education.*, DOI: 10.1007/978-981-92-0600-1_1

Nefedchenko, O., Hladchenko, O., & Hlushakova, O. (2025). UKRAINIAN MEDIA IN THE AGE OF SURVEILLANCE CAPITALISM: FROM COMMUNICATION TO BEHAVIORAL PREDICTION. *Fìlologìčnì Traktati, 17*(2), 97. DOI: 10.21272/Ftrk.2025.17(2)-10

Novianto, A. (2025a). Introduction: Platformization of Work and Platform Capitalism. In *Cheap Labour Regime in Platform Capitalism* (pp. 1–10). Springer Nature Singapore. DOI: 10.1007/978-981-95-1841-8_1

Novianto, A. (2025b). Labour Regime Theory and the Problem of Platform Capitalism. In *Cheap Labour Regime in Platform Capitalism* (pp. 11–40). Springer Nature Singapore., DOI: 10.1007/978-981-95-1841-8_2

Novianto, A. (2025c). Labour Regime Theory and the Problem of Platform Capitalism. In *Cheap Labour Regime in Platform Capitalism* (pp. 11–40). Springer Nature Singapore., DOI: 10.1007/978-981-95-1841-8_2

Nurik, C. (2019). Book review: Custodians of the Internet: Platforms, content moderation, and the hidden decisions that shape social media. *Communication and the Public*, *4*(2), 182–184. DOI: 10.1177/2057047319851200

Oltean, O., Angi, D., Pavel, A., & Bogdan, R. (2021). *Culturepreneurs: Competitivitatea industriilor culturale i creative din Cluj-Napoca i zona metropolitană în context european: 5/2021*. Presa Universitară Clujeană., DOI: 10.52257/9786063710810

Oonk, G. (2000a). Modernity at Large: Cultural Dimensions of Globalization [review]. *Journal of World History*, *11*(1), 157–159. DOI: 10.1353/jwh.2000.0021

Oonk, G. (2000b). Modernity at Large: Cultural Dimensions of Globalization [review]. *Journal of World History*, *11*(1), 157–159. DOI: 10.1353/jwh.2000.0021

Paganoni, M. C., & Becerra, G. (2026). Big Data Discourses| Reframing Datafication: News Media Discourses on Big Data and AI. *International Journal of Communication*, *20*, 21. DOI: 10.65476/75d24f96

(PDF) Academic Publishing in the Digital Era: The Role of Cross-Media Publishing in Expanding the Scope and Accessibility of Research. (n.d.). Https://Www.Researchgate.Net/Publication/391867468_Academic_Publishing_in_the_Digital_Era_The_Role_of_Cross-Media_Publishing_in_Expanding_the_Scope_and_Accessibility_of_Research

(PDF) [Book Review] Custodians of the Internet: Platforms, Content Moderation, and the Hidden Decisions that Shape Social Media. (n.d.). Https://Www.Researchgate.Net/Publication/332633724_Book_Review_Custodians_of_the_Internet_Platforms_Content_Moderation_and_the_Hidden_Decisions_that_Shape_Social_Media

(PDF) Cultural imperialism revisited: counselling and globablisation. (n.d.). Https://Www.Researchgate.Net/Publication/272564478_Cultural_imperialism_revisited_counselling_and_globablisation

(PDF) Modelling Data-Driven Marketing Adoption in Indian B2B IT/TES Service Providers. (n.d.-a). Https://Www.Researchgate.Net/Publication/404804351_Modelling_Data-Driven_Marketing_Adoption_in_Indian_B2B_ITTES_Service_Providers

(PDF) Modelling Data-Driven Marketing Adoption in Indian B2B IT/TES Service Providers. (n.d.-b). Https://Www.Researchgate.Net/Publication/404804351_Modelling_Data-Driven_Marketing_Adoption_in_Indian_B2B_ITTES_Service_Providers

(PDF) Soft Power: The Means to Success in World Politics, and: America the Virtuous: The Crisis of Democracy and the Quest for Empire (review). (n.d.). Https://Www.Researchgate.Net/Publication/236795827_Soft_Power_The_Means_to_Success_in_World_Politics_and_America_the_Virtuous_The_Crisis_of_Democracy_and_the_Quest_for_Empire_review

(PDF) Study on the Use of Serious Games in Business Education. (n.d.). Https://Www.Researchgate.Net/Publication/304999644_Study_on_the_Use_of_Serious_Games_in_Business_Education

Pembro, K. (2021). Book Review: Marx at the Arcade: Consoles, Controllers, and Class Struggle Marx at the Arcade: Consoles, Controllers, and Class Struggle By WoodcockJamie. Chicago: Haymarket Books, 2019. 208 pages. Cloth $40.00 [or Paper $12.60]. ISBN: 9781642590142. *The Review of Radical Political Economics*, *53*(2), 361–364. DOI: 10.1177/0486613420967200

Pivovarov, A. M. (2026a). Mass Society: Evolution from the Industrial to the Platform Era. *Discourse*, *12*(1), 83–104. DOI: 10.32603/2412-8562-2026-12-1-83-104

Pivovarov, A. M. (2026b). Mass Society: Evolution from the Industrial to the Platform Era. *Discourse*, *12*(1), 83–104. DOI: 10.32603/2412-8562-2026-12-1-83-104

Precarious Playbour: Modders and the Digital Games Industry. (n.d.). Https://Www.Researchgate.Net/Publication/26490724_Precarious_Playbour_Modders_and_the_Digital_Games_Industry

Ramsauer, L. (2026). Kant's Dialectic of Enlightenment. *European Journal of Philosophy*, *34*(2), 639–655. Advance online publication. DOI: 10.1111/ejop.70056

Reality is Broken: Why Games Make Us Better and How They Can Change the World. (n.d.). Https://Www.Researchgate.Net/Publication/244486521_Reality_is_Broken_Why_Games_Make_Us_Better_and_How_They_Can_Change_the_World

Ritzer, G., & Jurgenson, N. (2010). Production, Consumption, Prosumption: The nature of capitalism in the age of the digital "prosumer.". *Journal of Consumer Culture*, *10*(1), 13–36. DOI: 10.1177/1469540509354673

Sahaya Raj, J., & Dr, A. (2025). Effectiveness of Social Media Marketing: Influencer Marketing and the Role of Online Communities in Customer Engagement and Brand Loyalty. *International Journal of Research and Innovation in Social Science, IX*(VIII), 5356–5361. DOI: 10.47772/IJRISS.2025.908000432

Salter, A., & Blodgett, B. (2017). Toxic geek masculinity in media: Sexism, trolling, and identity policing. In *Toxic Geek Masculinity in Media: Sexism, Trolling, and Identity Policing*. Springer International Publishing., DOI: 10.1007/978-3-319-66077-6

Schmidt, D. C. (2022). Data Collection in the Age of Surveillance Capitalism. In *Collecting in the Twenty-First Century* (pp. 200–220). Boydell and Brewer Limited., DOI: 10.1017/9781800103382.013

Sengupta, U., & Sengupta, U. (2022). SDG-11 and smart cities: Contradictions and overlaps between social and environmental justice research agendas. In *Frontiers in Sociology* (Vol. 7). Frontiers Media S.A. DOI: 10.3389/fsoc.2022.995603

Shipra. (2019). Book review: José Van Dijck, Thomas Poell and Martijn De Waal, The Platform Society: Public Values in a Connective World. *Indian Journal of Human Development, 13*, 235–238. DOI: 10.1177/0973703019870883

Singh, B., Wongmahesak, K., & Chandra, S. (2025). Transforming digital ownership and assessing role of blockchain technology and NFTs in future economy. In *Practical Strategies and Case Studies for Online Marketing 6.0* (pp. 343–368). IGI Global., DOI: 10.4018/979-8-3373-2058-8.ch015

Singh, I., & Kumar Chandola, T.SINGH. (2026). SPORTS BETTING: JUDICIAL INTERPRETATION AND LEGAL CHALLENGES IN INDIA. *Indian Journal of Legal Review, 6*(3). Advance online publication. DOI: 10.65393/OKXM4852

Sjøvaag, H., Falch, M., Tadayoni, R., Grönlund, M., & Lindberg, T. (2026). The political economy of networked media: The revenue and concentration of communication markets in the Nordics. *Nordicom Review, 47*(1), 98–125. DOI: 10.2478/nor-2026-0006

Smart, S. (2025). Introduction: Transitional Justice in the Age of Surveillance Capitalism. In *St Antony's Series: Part F870* (pp. 13–51). Palgrave Macmillan. DOI: 10.1007/978-3-031-89828-0_2

Spiller, R. (2026). Network Society Theory: The Rise of the Network Society – by Manuel Castells (1996). In *Key works: Theories in communication studies* (pp. 379–387). Springer Fachmedien Wiesbaden. DOI: 10.1007/978-3-658-50422-9_27

Takru, S. (2025). Gender Stereotyping and Female Representation in Video Games: A Contemporary Review and Reassessment. *International Journal For Multidisciplinary Research*, 7(6), 62888. Advance online publication. DOI: 10.36948/ijfmr.2025.v07i06.62888

Taylor, T. L. (2012). *Raising the Stakes*. The MIT Press., DOI: 10.7551/mitpress/8624.001.0001

Taylor, T. L. (2018). Watch Me Play: Twitch and the Rise of Game Live Streaming. In *Watch Me Play: Twitch and the Rise of Game Live Streaming*. Princeton University Press., DOI: 10.2307/j.ctvc77jqw

Terranova, T. (2000). Free Labor. *Social Text*, *18*(2), 33–58. DOI: 10.1215/01642472-18-2_63-33

The Promotion of Diversity and Inclusion in Olympic Games: An Intersection Between Future Opportunities and Career Experiences for HBCU Student-Athletes | Request PDF. (n.d.). Https://Www.Researchgate.Net/Publication/404037629_The_Promotion_of_Diversity_and_Inclusion_in_Olympic_Games_An_Intersection_Between_Future_Opportunities_and_Career_Experiences_for_HBCU_Student-Athletes

Tortajada, I. (2020). The Age of Surveillance Capitalism: The Fight for a Human Future at the New Frontier of Power, S. Zuboff (2019). *Catalan Journal of Communication & Cultural Studies*, *12*(1), 153–154. DOI: 10.1386/cjcs_00020_5

van Dijck, J., Poell, T., & de Waal, M. (2018). The Platform Society. In *The Platform Society*. Oxford University PressNew York. DOI: 10.1093/oso/9780190889760.001.0001

Video game cultures and the construction of identities in contemporary society | Request PDF. (n.d.). Https://Www.Researchgate.Net/Publication/275343809_Video_game_cultures_and_the_construction_of_identities_in_contemporary_society

von Schomberg, L. (2025). Towards a Constructive Ethics of Artificial Intelligence in the Age of Surveillance Capitalism. In *Integrated Science* (Vol. 35, pp. 205–221). Springer Nature., DOI: 10.1007/978-3-031-87023-1_16

Woodcock, J., & Johnson, M. R. (2019). The affective labor and performance of live streaming on Twitch. tv. *Television & New Media*, *20*(8), 813–823. DOI: 10.1177/1527476419851077

Zhang, Y. (2026). Monetary Integration and the Coordination of Cryptocurrency and Fiat Money in the Digital Asset Era. *Advances in Economics and Management Research*, *16*(1), 297. DOI: 10.56028/aemr.16.1.297.2026

Zobel, G. (2019). Review of "Algorithms of oppression: how search engines reinforce racism," by Noble, S. U. (2018). New York, New York: NYU Press. *Communication Design Quarterly Review*, *7*(3), 30–31. DOI: 10.1145/3321388.3321392

Compilation of References

(PDF) [Book Review] Custodians of the Internet: Platforms, Content Moderation, and the Hidden Decisions that Shape Social Media. (n.d.). Https://Www.Researchgate.Net/Publication/332633724_Book_Review_Custodians_of_the_Internet_Platforms_Content_Moderation_and_the_Hidden_Decisions_that_Shape_Social_Media

(PDF) Academic Publishing in the Digital Era: The Role of Cross-Media Publishing in Expanding the Scope and Accessibility of Research. (n.d.). Https://Www.Researchgate.Net/Publication/391867468_Academic_Publishing_in_the_Digital_Era_The_Role_of_Cross-Media_Publishing_in_Expanding_the_Scope_and_Accessibility_of_Research

(PDF) Cultural imperialism revisited: counselling and globablisation. (n.d.). Https://Www.Researchgate.Net/Publication/272564478_Cultural_imperialism_revisited_counselling_and_globablisation

(PDF) Modelling Data-Driven Marketing Adoption in Indian B2B IT/TES Service Providers. (n.d.-a). Https://Www.Researchgate.Net/Publication/404804351_Modelling_Data-Driven_Marketing_Adoption_in_Indian_B2B_ITTES_Service_Providers

(PDF) Modelling Data-Driven Marketing Adoption in Indian B2B IT/TES Service Providers. (n.d.-b). Https://Www.Researchgate.Net/Publication/404804351_Modelling_Data-Driven_Marketing_Adoption_in_Indian_B2B_ITTES_Service_Providers

(PDF) Soft Power: The Means to Success in World Politics, and: America the Virtuous: The Crisis of Democracy and the Quest for Empire (review). (n.d.). Https://Www.Researchgate.Net/Publication/236795827_Soft_Power_The_Means_to_Success_in_World_Politics_and_America_the_Virtuous_The_Crisis_of_Democracy_and_the_Quest_for_Empire_review

(PDF) Study on the Use of Serious Games in Business Education. (n.d.). Https://Www.Researchgate.Net/Publication/304999644_Study_on_the_Use_of_Serious_Games_in_Business_Education

A Playful Multitude? Mobilising and Counter-Mobilising Immaterial Game Labour. (n.d.). Https://Www.Researchgate.Net/Publication/26490723_A_Playful_Multitude_Mobilising_and_Counter-Mobilising_Immaterial_Game_Labour

Aarthi, S. Ravikumar, Sapayev Odilbek Uglu, V., Sottarov, A., & Singh, A. (2025). The privacy paradox. In *User-Centric Cybersecurity Implications for Sustainable Digital Transformation* (pp. 223–256). IGI Global Scientific Publishing. DOI: 10.4018/979-8-3373-3171-3.ch007

Aarthi, S., Ravikumar, R. N., & Pardaev, J. (2025). Synergizing multimodal generative AI and blockchain for the future of digital media. In *Advances in Computational Intelligence and Robotics* (pp. 1–34). IGI Global Scientific Publishing. DOI: 10.4018/979-8-3373-1504-1.ch001

Abbas, H. (2023). *The Return of the Taliban: Afghanistan After the Americans Left.* Yale University Press.

Abbasi, A. (2020). Hybrid War Threats and Essence of Perception Management. *IPRI Journal, 20*(2), 1–25. DOI: 10.31945/iprij.200201

Adiga, P. G., & Padmakumar, K. (2025). Exploring online masculinity in the Indian meme culture: A case of video Doge memes. *Journal of Creative Communications*, 09732586251344024. Advance online publication. DOI: 10.1177/09732586251344024

Ahmed, D., & Abbasi, M. (2023). *Democracy Under God: Constitutions, Islam, and Human Rights in the Muslim World.* Cambridge University Press. DOI: 10.1017/9781316662618

Åkerlund, M. (2025). Politics of deliberate inaction: The disconnect between platform justifications and user imaginaries on content moderation in a "free speech" online forum. *New Media & Society, 27*(3), 1235–1255. Advance online publication. DOI: 10.1177/14614448231190905

Akram, M., & Nasar, A. (2023). A bibliometric analysis of radicalization through social media. [Ege Academic Review]. *Ege Akademik Bakış*. Advance online publication. DOI: 10.21121/eab.1166627

Al-Bukhārī, M. ibn Ismāʿīl. (1997). a ī al-Bukhārī. Dār al-Salām.

Alienation of Labors and Fans in Digital Economy - From Digital Labor to Emotional Labor | Request PDF. (n.d.). Https://Www.Researchgate.Net/Publication/382598104_Alienation_of_Labors_and_Fans_in_Digital_Economy_-_From_Digital_Labor_to_Emotional_Labor

Ali, R., & Zaidi, H. (2024). Algorithmic radicalization and the feedback loop of outrage on South Asian digital forums. *Media and Communication Studies Quarterly, 11*(3), 145–167.

Allchorn, W., & Orofino, E. (2025). Policing extremism on gaming-adjacent platforms: Awful but lawful? *Frontiers in Psychology, 16*, 1537460. DOI: 10.3389/fpsyg.2025.1537460 PMID: 40823404

Al-Rawi, A. (2024). The Development of Video Game Representations of the Middle East. *Games and Culture, 15554120241255425*. Advance online publication. DOI: 10.1177/15554120241255425

Al-Tirmidhī, M. ibn ʿĪsā. (2007). *Jāmi al-Tirmidhī* (N. al-Albānī, Ed.). Dār al-Salām.

Alvarez-Melis, D., & Jaakkola, T. S. (2018). On the robustness of interpretability methods. In *Proceedings of the 2018 ICML Workshop on Human Interpretability in Machine Learning*.

American Psychological Association. (2020). *Publication manual of the American Psychological Association* (7th ed.). APA.

Anderson, C. A., & Bushman, B. J. (2001). Effects of violent video games on aggressive behavior, aggressive cognition, aggressive affect, physiological arousal, and prosocial behavior: A meta-analytic review of the scientific literature. *Psychological Science, 12*(5), 353–359. DOI: 10.1111/1467-9280.00366 PMID: 11554666

Anderson, C. A., & Jiang, J. (2018). *Teens, social media & technology 2018*. Pew Research Center.

Anderson, S. L., & Schrier, K. (2022). Disability and video games journalism: A discourse analysis of accessibility and gaming culture. *Games and Culture, 17*(2), 179–197. DOI: 10.1177/15554120211021005

Andrews, C. (2025). Production, consumption, prosumption: How George Ritzer shifted the conversation in sociology from work to consumption and beyond. *Thesis Eleven, 191*, 120–128. DOI: 10.1177/07255136251395769

Andrews, S., & Skoczylis, J. (2022, February 17). Understanding Attitudes to Extremism in Gaming Communities. GNET. https://gnet-research.org/2022/02/17/understanding-attitudes-to-extremism-in-gaming-communities/

Ansari, G., Kaur, P., & Saxena, C. (2024). Data augmentation for improving explainability of hate speech detection. *Arabian Journal for Science and Engineering, 49*(3), 3609–3621. DOI: 10.1007/s13369-023-08100-4

Anti-Defamation League. (2019). *Free to play? Hate, harassment, and positive social experience in online games*. ADL Center on Technology and Society.

Anti-Defamation League. (2020). *Hate is no game: Hate and harassment in online games*. ADL Center on Technology and Society.

Anti-Defamation League. (2024). *Hate is No Game: Hate and Harassment in Online Games 2023*.

Anykey. (2021). Diversity and inclusion in esports. Anykey Organization. https://www.anykey.org

Attanasio, G., Nozza, D., Pastor, E., & Hovy, D. (2022). Benchmarking post-hoc interpretability approaches for transformer-based misogyny detection. In *Proceedings of NLP Power! The First Workshop on Efficient Benchmarking in NLP* (pp. 100–112). Association for Computational Linguistics. DOI: 10.18653/v1/2022.nlppower-1.11

Audience labour in the age of AI-generated comments: Insights from Reddit | Request PDF. (n.d.). Https://Www.Researchgate.Net/Publication/399796174_Audience_labour_in_the_age_of_AI-Generated_comments_Insights_from_Reddit

Ayewoh-Odiase, P. E. (2025). Politics of Human Rights Protection in An Era of Global Terrorism.

Babaeianjelodar, M., Poorna Prudhvi, G., Lorenz, S., Chen, K., Mondal, S., Dey, S., & Kumar, N. (2022). Interpretable and high-performance hate and offensive speech detection. In *HCI International 2022—Late breaking papers: Interacting with extended reality and artificial intelligence* (pp. 233–244). Springer. DOI: 10.1007/978-3-031-21707-4_18

Bacon, T., & Byman, D. (2021). De-talibanization and the onset of insurgency in Afghanistan. *Studies in Conflict and Terrorism*, *46*(10), 1840–1867. DOI: 10.1080/1057610X.2021.1872159

Balkir, E., Nejadgholi, I., Fraser, K. C., & Kiritchenko, S. (2022). Necessity and sufficiency for explaining text classifiers: A case study in hate speech detection. In *Proceedings of the 2022 Conference of the North American Chapter of the Association for Computational Linguistics: Human Language Technologies* (pp. 2672–2686). Association for Computational Linguistics. DOI: 10.18653/v1/2022.naacl-main.192

Bandura, A. (1977). *Social learning theory*. Prentice Hall.

Bányai, F., Griffiths, M. D., Demetrovics, Z., & Király, O. (2019). The psychology of esports: A systematic literature review. *Journal of Gambling Studies*, *35*(2), 351–365. DOI: 10.1007/s10899-018-9763-1 PMID: 29508260

Barfield, T. (2012). *Afghanistan: A Cultural and Political History*. Princeton University Press.

Benkler, Y., Faris, R., & Roberts, H. (2018). *Network propaganda: Manipulation, disinformation, and radicalization in American politics*. Oxford University Press. DOI: 10.1093/oso/9780190923624.001.0001

Bensalem, I., Rosso, P., & Zitouni, H. (2024). Toxic language detection: A systematic review of Arabic datasets. *Expert Systems: International Journal of Knowledge Engineering and Neural Networks*, *41*(8), e13551. DOI: 10.1111/exsy.13551

Bogost, I. (2008). The rhetoric of video games. Ecology of Games: Connecting Youth, Games, and Learning, 117–140.

Bogost, I. (2007). *Persuasive Games: The Expressive Power of Videogames*. MIT Press. DOI: 10.7551/mitpress/5334.001.0001

Bonenfant, M. (2021). Hypermodern Video Games as Emblems of Empire or How the Gaming Multitude Adapts to Hypermodernity. *Games and Culture*, *16*(3), 357–370. DOI: 10.1177/1555412020961849

Bowen, G. A. (2009). Document analysis as a qualitative research method. *Qualitative Research Journal*, *9*(2), 27–40. DOI: 10.3316/QRJ0902027

Bowman, N. D., Bowen, D. A., Mercado, M. C., Resignato, L. J., & de Villemor Chauveau, P. (2024). "I did it without hesitation. Am I the bad guy?": Online conversations in response to controversial in-game violence. *New Media & Society*, *26*(4), 2315–2335. DOI: 10.1177/14614448221078865 PMID: 37441356

Braun, V., & Clarke, V. (2022). Thematic analysis: A practical guide. *Sage (Atlanta, Ga.)*.

Brenner-Levoy, J. (2023). Virtually masculine: Queer men's experiences with harassment in online video games. *Sociology of Sport Journal*, *40*(4), 385–398. DOI: 10.1123/ssj.2022-0170

British Esports. (2022). *Esports in education: A guide for schools*. British Esports Association.

Bronfenbrenner, U. (1979). *The ecology of human development: Experiments by nature and design*. Harvard University Press. DOI: 10.4159/9780674028845

Bunde, E. (2021). AI-assisted and explainable hate speech detection for social media moderators: A design science approach. In *Proceedings of the 54th Hawaii International Conference on System Sciences*. DOI: 10.24251/HICSS.2021.154

Bunt, G. R. (2018). *Hashtag Islam: How cyber-Islamic environments are transforming religious authority*. University of North Carolina Press. DOI: 10.5149/northcarolina/9781469643168.001.0001

Burgess, J., & Jones, C. (2020). Exploring the forced closure of a brand community that is also a participatory culture. *European Journal of Marketing*, *54*(5), 957–978. DOI: 10.1108/EJM-01-2019-0075

Butt, N. A. (2024). Gaming as a coping mechanism: Psychological distress, loneliness, and virtual guilds in urban Lahore. *Clinical Psychology Digest Pakistan*, *6*(2), 89–103.

C Dey, D. N. (2026). <b>Book Review - THE AGE OF SURVEILLANCE CAPITALISM BY SHOSHANA ZUBOFF</b> *Global E-Journal of Social Scientific Research, 2*. DOI: 10.64706/h7bntw21

Campbell, H. (Ed.). (2013). *Digital religion: Understanding religious practice in new media worlds*. Routledge.

Castells, M. (2010). The Rise of the Network Society, Second Edition, With a New Preface. In *The Rise of the Network Society, Second Edition, With a New Preface*. Wiley-Liss Inc. DOI: 10.1002/9781444319514

Chang, A. (2025). Safe spaces for feminist activists online: Chinese networked feminists' self-censorship strategies in response to online misogyny and government censorship. *Humanities & Social Sciences Communications*, *12*(1), 495. Advance online publication. DOI: 10.1057/s41599-025-04802-2

Chui, R. (2014). A multi-faceted approach to anonymity online: Examining the relations between anonymity and antisocial behaviour. *Journal of Virtual Worlds Research*, *7*(2). Advance online publication. DOI: 10.4101/jvwr.v7i2.7073

CIA. (2024). *The CIA World Factbook 2024-2025*. Central Intelligence Agency. https://www.cia.gov/the-world-factbook/

Coanda, I., & Aupers, S. (2020). Mechanisms of disclosure: A Socio-technical perspective on sociality in Massively Multiplayer Online Role-playing Games. *Television & New Media*, *21*(3), 315–333. DOI: 10.1177/1527476418824557

Condis, M. (2020). Hateful Games – Why White Supremacist Recruiters Target Gamers. In J. Reyman & E.M. Sparby, *Digital Ethics – Rhetoric and Responsibility in Online Aggression* (pp. 143–159). Routledge.

Corliss, V. I. (2011). *GAMING WITH GOD: A CASE FOR THE STUDY OF RELIGION IN VIDEO GAMES*. https://about.jstor.org/terms

Cote, A. C., Wilson, A., Hansen, J., Harris, B. C., Rahman, M. W. U., Can, O., Fickle, T., & Foxman, M. (2023). Taking care of toxicity: Challenges and strategies for inclusion in U.s. collegiate esports programs. *Journal of Electronic Gaming and Esports*, *1*(1). Advance online publication. DOI: 10.1123/jege.2022-0031

Coyle, K. (2017). Book Review: Free Culture: How Big Media Uses Technology and the Law to Lock Down Culture and Control Creativity. *Information Technology and Libraries*, *23*(4), 198–199. DOI: 10.6017/ital.v23i4.9665

Crawford, K. (2021). Atlas of AI: Power, Politics, and the Planetary Costs of Artificial Intelligence. In *Atlas of AI: Power, Politics, and the Planetary Costs of Artificial Intelligence*. Yale University Press., DOI: 10.56315/PSCF3-22Crawford

Creswell, J. W., & Plano Clark, V. L. (2018). *Designing and conducting mixed methods research* (3rd ed.). SAGE Publications.

Cyber Security Authority of Pakistan (CSAP). (2025). *Emerging Digital Threats: Gamified Recruiting, Extremist Servers, and Networked Radicalization in the Domestic Ecosystem*. CSAP Annual Intelligence Review.

Dajer, V., & de, P. (2020). Games in the age of empire. *Kultura*, 224–245. DOI: 10.5937/kultura2068224D

Dauber, C., Robinson, M., Basilous, J., & Blair, A. (2019). Call of Duty: Jihad – How the Video Game Motif Has Migrated Downstream from Islamic State Propaganda Videos. *Perspectives on Terrorism*, *13*(3), 17–31.

Davey, J. (2021). Gamers Who Hate: An Introduction to ISD's Gaming and Extremism Series. https://www.isdglobal.org/isd-publications/gamers-who-hatean - introduction-to-isds-gamingand-extremism-series/

Davey, J. (2021, August). Gamers Who Hate: An Introduction to ISD's Gaming and Extremism Series. Institute for Strategic Dialogue. https://www.isdglobal.org/isd-publications/gamers-who-hate-an-introduction-to-isds-gaming-andextremism -series/

Davidson, T., Warmsley, D., Macy, M., & Weber, I. (2017). Automated hate speech detection and the problem of offensive language. *Proceedings of the International AAAI Conference on Web and Social Media*, *11*(1), 512–515. DOI: 10.1609/icwsm.v11i1.14955

De Cleen, B., Bauwens, J., Joris, W., Shroufi, O., & Smets, K. (2025). Fictional frontlines: A mapping review and research agenda for the study of far-right engagement with films, television and video games. *Javnost (Ljubljana)*, *32*(3), 301–324. Advance online publication. DOI: 10.1080/13183222.2025.2547519

De Minicis, M. (2026). *Uncovering platforms: investigating and visualizing the variety of platform capitalism in Italy and Spain*. Cambio. Rivista Sulle Trasformazioni Sociali., DOI: 10.36253/cambio-17339

Dean, B. (2021). *Gamers who hate: An introduction to ISD's gaming and extremism series*. Institute for Strategic Dialogue. https://www.isdglobal.org/isd-publications/gamers-who-hate-an-introduction-to-isds-gaming-and-extremism-series/

DeCook, J. R., Cotter, K., Kanthawala, S., & Foyle, K. (2022). Safe from "harm": The governance of violence by platforms. *Policy and Internet*, *14*(1), 63–78. DOI: 10.1002/poi3.290

Denzin, N. K. (2012). riangulation 2.0. *Journal of Mixed Methods Research*, *6*(2), 80–88. DOI: 10.1177/1558689812437186

Department of Education Philippines. (2012). DepEd Child Protection Policy (DepEd Order No. 40, s. 2012). DepEd.

Department of Education Philippines. (2023). *Revised K to 10 Physical Education and Health Curriculum Guide*. DepEd.

Department of Information and Communications Technology. (2023). *Philippine digital infrastructure assessment 2023*. DICT.

Deterding, S., Sicart, M., Nacke, L., O'Hara, K., & Dixon, D. (2011). Gamification: Using game-design elements in non-gaming contexts. In CHI EA '11: Proceedings of the SIGCHI Conference on Human Factors in Computing Systems Extended Abstracts (pp. 2425–2428). Association for Computing Machinery. DOI: 10.1145/1979742.1979575

DeYoung, J., Jain, S., Rajani, N. F., Lehman, E., Xiong, C., Socher, R., & Wallace, B. C. (2020). ERASER: A benchmark to evaluate rationalized NLP models. In *Proceedings of the 58th Annual Meeting of the Association for Computational Linguistics* (pp. 4443–4458). Association for Computational Linguistics. DOI: 10.18653/v1/2020.acl-main.408

Dhaka, G. (2024). An Ellustrative Research on Challenges and Opportunities Faced Due To Evolving Legal Landscape of Online Gaming in India. *Communications on Applied Nonlinear Analysis*, *32*(4s), 332–343. DOI: 10.52783/cana.v32.2824

Digital entertainment gaming as a site for (informal) historical learning | Request PDF. (n.d.-a). Https://Www.Researchgate.Net/Publication/336496091_Digital_entertainment_gaming_as_a_site_for_informal_historical_learning

Digital entertainment gaming as a site for (informal) historical learning | Request PDF. (n.d.-b). Https://Www.Researchgate.Net/Publication/336496091_Digital_entertainment_gaming_as_a_site_for_informal_historical_learning

Digital Labor: The Internet as Playground and Factory | Request PDF. (n.d.). Https://Www.Researchgate.Net/Publication/283985861_Digital_Labor_The_Internet_as_Playground_and_Factory

Dimic-Janjic, S., Stjepanovic, M., Belic, S., Vukosavljevic, D., Milivojevic, I., Trboljevac, N., Nikolic, N., Stamenic, S., Stojanovic, M., Stosic, K., Vasakova, M. K., Stevic, R., Colic, N., Lukic, K., Ilic, M., Isovic, L., Maric, N., Popevic, S., Vucinic-Mihailović, V., & Jovanovic, D. (2025). Clinical Characteristics and Survival of Patients with Idiopathic Pulmonary Fibrosis: Analysis of the Serbian Cohort from the EMPIRE Registry. *Diagnostics (Basel)*, *15*(17), 2121. Advance online publication. DOI: 10.3390/diagnostics15172121 PMID: 40941610

Dodds, K. (2019). *Geopolitics: A very short introduction* (3rd ed.). Oxford University Press. DOI: 10.1093/actrade/9780198830764.001.0001

Donner, F. (2025). Structures that tilt: Understanding "toxic" behaviors in online gaming. *New Media & Society*, *27*(12), 6551–6568. DOI: 10.1177/14614448241270446

Dorris, W., Hu, R., Vishwamitra, N., Luo, F., & Costello, M. (2020). Towards automatic detection and explanation of hate speech and offensive language. In *Proceedings of the Sixth International Workshop on Security and Privacy Analytics* (pp. 23–29). Association for Computing Machinery. DOI: 10.1145/3375708.3380312

Doshi-Velez, F., & Kim, B. (2017). *Towards a rigorous science of interpretable machine learning* [Preprint]. arXiv.

Dwivedi, Y. K., Kshetri, N., Hughes, L., Rana, N. P., Baabdullah, A. M., Kar, A. K., Koohang, A., Ribeiro-Navarrete, S., Belei, N., Balakrishnan, J., Basu, S., Behl, A., Davies, G. H., Dutot, V., Dwivedi, R., Evans, L., Felix, R., Foster-Fletcher, R., Giannakis, M., … Yan, M. (2023). Exploring the darkverse: A multi-perspective analysis of the negative societal impacts of the metaverse. *Information Systems Frontiers: A Journal of Research and Innovation*, 1–44. DOI: 10.1007/s10796-023-10400-x

Egliston, B. (2026). From hits to unicorns: Venture capital in the videogame industry. *New Media & Society*, 14614448251397398. Advance online publication. DOI: 10.1177/14614448251397398

Ehsan, U., Liao, Q. V., Muller, M., Riedl, M. O., & Weisz, J. D. (2021). Expanding explainability: Towards social transparency in AI systems. In *Proceedings of the 2021 CHI Conference on Human Factors in Computing Systems* (pp. 1–19). Association for Computing Machinery. DOI: 10.1145/3411764.3445188

Eklund, L., von Essen, E., Jonsson, F., & Johansson, M. (2022). Beyond a dichotomous understanding of online anonymity: Bridging the macro and micro level. *Sociological Research Online*, *27*(2), 486–503. DOI: 10.1177/13607804211019760

ElSherief, M., Ziems, C., Muchlinski, D., Anupindi, V., Seybolt, J., De Choudhury, M., & Yang, D. (2021). Latent hatred: A benchmark for understanding implicit hate speech. In *Proceedings of the 2021 Conference on Empirical Methods in Natural Language Processing* (pp. 345–363). Association for Computational Linguistics. DOI: 10.18653/v1/2021.emnlp-main.29

English, F. W. (2010). *Deciding what to teach and test: Developing, aligning, and auditing the curriculum* (3rd ed.). Corwin Press.

Escuadro, M. C. O., & Jamero, R. M. (2026). The Effectiveness of Meme Marketing in Brand Awareness Among KCC Mall of Marbel Customers. *International Journal of Innovative Science and Research Technology, 3044*, 3044. Advance online publication. DOI: 10.38124/ijisrt/26feb1400

Esfahani, H. M. R. (1991). *Beijrut: Dar al-Elm* (1st ed.). Dar Al-Shamiah. [Mu'jam mufradat alfaz al-Qur'an]

Etikan, I., Musa, S. A., & Alkassim, R. S. (2016). Comparison of convenience sampling and purposive sampling. *American Journal of Theoretical and Applied Statistics*, *5*(1), 1–4. DOI: 10.11648/j.ajtas.20160501.11

Fàbregues, S., et al. (2023). Use of mixed methods research in intervention studies to improve health outcomes: A review and practical guidance. *Journal of Mixed Methods / Applied Health Research*. DOI: 10.3389/fpsyg.2022.956300

Farag, T., Neuberger, C., Kretzschmar, S., Sehl, A., Wiethaus, L., & Gäng, J. (2025). Intrastate conflict and transformation of the media system: The case of Afghanistan. *Media, War & Conflict*, 17506352251362600. Advance online publication. DOI: 10.1177/17506352251362600

FATF. (2025). *Comprehensive update on terrorist financing risks*. Financial Action Task Force. https://www.fatf-gafi.org/content/dam/fatf-gafi/publications/Comprehensive-Update-on-Terrorist-Financing-Risks-2025.pdf.coredownload.inline.pdf

Fatima, A., Ambreen, F., & Amin, R. (2024). Internet Gaming Disorder and Mental Health of Pakistani Adolescents: A Cross-Sectional Study. *Qlantic Journal of Social Sciences, 5*(2), 13–25. DOI: 10.55737/qjss.119114325

Fetters, M. D., Curry, L. A., & Creswell, J. W. (2013). Achieving integration in mixed methods designs—Principles and practices. *Health Services Research, 48*(6 Pt 2), 2134–2156. DOI: 10.1111/1475-6773.12117 PMID: 24279835

Fiadotava, A., Laineste, L., Castañar Rubio, G., & Chłopicki, W. (2025). *When the transnational rules: Humorous reactions to the Wagner Group rebellion in Estonia, Poland and Belarus*. Folklore., DOI: 10.7592/FEJF2025.97.transnational

Flanagan, M. (2009). *Critical Play: Radical Game Design*. MIT Press. DOI: 10.7551/mitpress/7678.001.0001

Forging Blockchains: Spatial Production and Political Economy of Decentralized Cryptocurrency Code/Spaces. (n.d.). Https://Www.Researchgate.Net/Publication/317057295_Forging_Blockchains_Spatial_Production_and_Political_Economy_of_Decentralized_Cryptocurrency_CodeSpaces

Fortuna, P., & Nunes, S. (2018). A survey on automatic detection of hate speech in text. *ACM Computing Surveys, 51*(4), 1–30. DOI: 10.1145/3232676

Fossberg, H., & Fangen, K. (2025). Weaponized humor and militarized masculinity: The role of memes in far-right discourse on the Russo-Ukrainian war. *Journal of Gender Studies*, 1–22. Advance online publication. DOI: 10.1080/09589236.2025.2545905

Fox, J., & Tang, W. Y. (2017). Women's experiences with general and sexual harassment in online video games: Rumination, organizational responsiveness, withdrawal, and coping strategies. *New Media & Society, 19*(8), 1290–1307. DOI. 10.1177/1461444816635778

Freeman, G., & Wohn, D. Y. (2020). Understanding esports team formation and how teams coordinate online during esports competitions. *Proceedings of the Annual Symposium on Computer-Human Interaction in Play*, 193–205. DOI: 10.1145/3410404.3414252

Frommel, J., Johnson, D., & Mandryk, R. L. (2023). How perceived toxicity of gaming communities is associated with social capital, satisfaction of relatedness, and loneliness. *Computers in Human Behavior Reports, 10*, 100302. DOI: 10.1016/j.chbr.2023.100302

Fuchs, C. (2014). Digital labour and Karl Marx. In *Digital Labour and Karl Marx*. Taylor and Francis., DOI: 10.4324/9781315880075

Galip, I., & Maragkou, E. (2026). Chatbox sociality: Extreme personae, speculative communities, and the affordances of alt-tech livestreaming. *First Monday*, *31*(5). Advance online publication. DOI: 10.5210/fm.v31i5.15437

Gazia, I., Hubbard, T., Scalona, T., Kang, Y., & Zuckerman, E. (2024). Proactive blocking through the automated identification of likely harassers. *Journal of Online Trust & Safety*, *2*(3). Advance online publication. DOI: 10.54501/jots.v2i3.175

Gee, J. P. (2007). *What video games have to teach us about learning and literacy* (2nd ed.). Palgrave Macmillan.

GIFCT. (2024). *Annual transparency report 2024.* Global Internet Forum to Counter Terrorism. https://gifct.org/wp-content/uploads/2025/07/GIFCT-Annual-and-Transparency-Report-2024.pdf

Gillespie, T. (2019). Custodians of the Internet. In *Custodians of the Internet.* Yale University Press., DOI: 10.12987/9780300235029

Gongane, V. U., Munot, M. V., & Anuse, A. D. (2022). Detection and moderation of detrimental content on social media platforms: Current status and future directions. *Social Network Analysis and Mining*, *12*(1), 129. DOI: 10.1007/s13278-022-00951-3 PMID: 36090695

Gongane, V. U., Munot, M. V., & Anuse, A. D. (2024). A survey of explainable AI techniques for detection of fake news and hate speech on social media platforms. *Journal of Computational Social Science*, *7*(1), 587–623. DOI: 10.1007/s42001-024-00248-9

Gonzalez, C., & Czlonka, L. (2010). Games for Peace. In Cannon-BowersJ.BowersC. (Eds.), Serious Game Design and Development: Technologies for Training and Learning (pp. 134–149)., DOI: 10.4018/978-1-61520-739-8.ch008

González-Calvo, G., Ospina-Betancurt, J., & Hortigüela-Alcalá, D. (2026). Doing gender online: Memetic performances and the digital construction of femininity. *Gender Issues*, *43*(1), 23. Advance online publication. DOI: 10.1007/s12147-026-09402-1

Gopal, A., & Linschoten, A. 2017. “Ideology in the Afghan Taleban.” Berlin: Afghanistan Analysts Network. https://www.afghanistan-analysts.org/wp-content/uploads/2017/06/201705-AGopal-ASvLinschoten-TB-Ideology.pdf

Gorwa, R., Binns, R., & Katzenbach, C. (2020). Algorithmic content moderation: Technical and political challenges in the automation of platform governance. *Big Data & Society*, *7*(1), 205395171989794. DOI: 10.1177/2053951719897945

Gotterbarn, D. (2010). The ethics of video games: Mayhem, death, and the training of the next generation. *Information Systems Frontiers, 12*(4), 369–377. DOI: 10.1007/s10796-009-9204-x

Gottfried, J., & Sidoti, O. (2024, May 9). Teens and video games today. Pew Research Center. https://www.pewresearch.org/internet/2024/05/09/teens-and-video-games-today/

Granic, I., & Lobel A. Engels, R. C. M. E. (2014a). The benefits of playing video games. *The American Psychologist, 69*(1), 66–78. DOI: 10.1037/a0034857 PMID: 24295515

Greipl, S., Lechner, M., Fischer, J., Schulze, H., Hohner, J., & Rieger, D. (2025). Tracking down the Candy Crush Terrorist: The fragile relation between gaming motives and radical attitudes. *Frontiers in Psychology, 16*(1585576), 1585576. DOI: 10.3389/fpsyg.2025.1585576 PMID: 41164730

Grolnick, W. S., Deci, E. L., & Ryan, R. M. (1997). Internalization within the family: The self-determination theory perspective. In Grusec, J. E., & Kuczynski, L. (Eds.), *Parenting and children's internalization of values: A handbook of contemporary theory* (pp. 135–161). Wiley.

Groves, C. L., & Anderson, C. A. (2017). Negative Effects of Video Game Play. In Handbook of Digital Games and Entertainment Technologies (pp. 1297–1322). Springer Singapore., DOI: 10.1007/978-981-4560-50-4_13

Gul, S. (2023). India's Hybrid Warfare Against Pakistan: PPP and PML-N Governments. *Journal of Political Research & Social Science, 10*(2). https://ojs.mul.edu.pk/index.php/JPRSS/article/download/385/233

Haider, M. W., Azad, T. M., & Warrich, H. (2020). A critical review of hybrid warfare: Challenges to Pakistan. *Global Mass Communication Review, 5*(4), 72–90. DOI: 10.31703/gmcr.2020(V-IV).06

Hamm, M., & Spaaij, R. (2017). *The age of lone wolf terrorism*. Columbia University Press. DOI: 10.7312/hamm18174

Haq, M. Z. U., & Khan, M. (2025). Digital Hybrid Warfare (7GW): Threats to Pakistan's Security and a Framework for Countermeasures. *Journal of Regional Studies Review, 4*(2), 92–104. DOI: 10.62843/jrsr/2025.4b115

Harpviken, K. (1999). The Taliban Threat. *Third World Quarterly, 20*(4), 861–870. DOI: 10.1080/01436599913604

Hashmi, S. (2025). The erosion of vertical authority: How peer networks on Discord reshape political and moral beliefs among Pakistani teenagers. *Digital Policy & Governance Review*, *4*(2), 75–93.

Hassan, S. (2016). *Turkey's "counter-strike" against Islamophobia in video games.* TRT WORLD. https://www.trtworld.com/americas/turkeys-counter-strike-against-islamophobia-in-video-games-225921

Hawley, G. (2017). *Making sense of the alt-right.* Columbia University Press. DOI: 10.7312/hawl18512

Hayday, E. J., & Collison, H. (2020). Exploring the contested notion of social inclusion and gender inclusivity within eSport spaces. *Social Inclusion (Lisboa)*, *8*(3), 197–208. DOI: 10.17645/si.v8i3.2755

Horgan, J. (2014). *The psychology of terrorism* (2nd ed.). Routledge. DOI: 10.4324/9781315882246

Horkheimer, M., Adorno, T. W., & Noeri, G. (2002). *Dialectic of enlightenment.* Stanford University Press. *(PDF) Zackariasson, P. & Wilson, T. L. (2012) (Eds). The Video game industry. Formation, present state and future. London: Routledge.* (n.d.). Https://Www.Researchgate.Net/Publication/266571389_Zackariasson_P_Wilson_T_L_2012_Eds_The_Video_game_industry_Formation_present_state_and_future_London_Routledge

Huang, F., Kwak, H., & An, J. (2023). Chain of explanation: New prompting method to generate quality natural language explanation for implicit hate speech. In *Companion proceedings of the ACM Web Conference 2023* (pp. 90–93). Association for Computing Machinery. DOI: 10.1145/3543873.3587320

Hu, C., Zhao, Y., Wang, Z., Du, H., & Liu, J. (2024). Games for Artificial Intelligence Research: A Review and Perspectives. *IEEE Transactions on Artificial Intelligence*, *5*(12), 5949–5968. DOI: 10.1109/TAI.2024.3410935

Hussain, S., Roofi, Y., Faheem, F., & Qamar, M. T. R. (2023). Hybrid Warfare in Pakistan: How it's affecting CPEC. *Pakistan Journal of Humanities and Social Sciences*, *11*(2), 1733–1739. DOI: 10.52131/pjhss.2023.1102.0476

Ibn Kathir, I. (2003). *Tafsir al-Qur'an al-Azim.* Dar al-Kutub al-Ilmiyah.

Ibrahim, M. A., Arifin, S., Yudistira, I. G. A. A., Nariswari, R., Abdillah, A. A., Murnaka, N. P., & Prasetyo, P. W. (2022). An explainable AI model for hate speech detection on Indonesian Twitter. *CommIT (Communication and Information Technology). Journal*, *16*(2), 175–182.

İNAÇ, H., & Asefi, J. (2021). The Discussion of Political Islam and Democracy in Afghanistan. *Turkish Journal of Policy Studies, 1*(1), 1–12.

Intelligence, G. S. M. A. (2025). *Mobile connectivity index 2025.* GSMA. https://www.mobileconnectivityindex.com/index.html

International Telecommunication Union. (2025). *World telecommunication/ICT indicators database.* ITU. https://www.itu.int/en/ITU-D/Statistics/pages/publications/wtid.aspx

Iqbal, R. (2023). The Evolving Regional Strategic Environment and Hybrid Competition in South Asia. World Scientific, 9 (1): 93-106. DOI: 10.1142/S2377740023500057

Iranzo-Cabrera, M., Castro-Bleda, M. J., Simón-Astudillo, I., & Hurtado, L.-F. (2025). Journalists' ethical responsibility: Tackling hate speech against women politicians in social media through natural language processing techniques. *Social Science Computer Review, 43*(3), 475–502. Advance online publication. DOI: 10.1177/08944393241269417

Israel, M., & Hay, I. (2006). *Research ethics for social scientists.* SAGE Publications. DOI: 10.4135/9781849209779

Jacovi, A., & Goldberg, Y. (2020). Towards faithfully interpretable NLP systems: How should we define and evaluate faithfulness? In *Proceedings of the 58th Annual Meeting of the Association for Computational Linguistics* (pp. 4198–4205). Association for Computational Linguistics. DOI: 10.18653/v1/2020.acl-main.386

Jahan, M. S., & Oussalah, M. (2023). A systematic review of hate speech automatic detection using natural language processing. *Neurocomputing, 546*, 126232. DOI: 10.1016/j.neucom.2023.126232

Jain, S., & Wallace, B. C. (2019). Attention is not explanation. In *Proceedings of the 2019 Conference of the North American Chapter of the Association for Computational Linguistics: Human Language Technologies* (pp. 3543–3556). Association for Computational Linguistics.

Jamal, A. S., & Maley, W. (2023). *The decline and fall of republican Afghanistan.* Oxford University Press.

Jenkins, H. (2009). *Confronting the challenges of participatory culture: Media education for the 21st century.* MIT Press. DOI: 10.7551/mitpress/8435.001.0001

Jenkins, H. (2020). Convergence Culture. In *Convergence Culture.* New York University Press., DOI: 10.18574/nyu/9780814743683.001.0001

Jenkins, H., Ford, S., & Green, J. (2013). Spreadable media: Creating value and meaning in a networked culture. In *Spreadable Media: Creating Value and Meaning in a Networked Culture*. New York University Press., DOI: 10.3983/twc.2014.0633

Jenkins, H., & Plasencia, A. (2017a). Convergence Culture: Where Old and New Media Collide. In *Is the Universe a Hologram?* The MIT Press., DOI: 10.7551/mitpress/10428.003.0018

Johnson, T. H., DuPee, M., & Shaaker, W. (2017). *Taliban narratives: The use and power of stories in the Afghanistan conflict*. Oxford University Press.

Jones, C. M., Scholes, L., Johnson, D., Katsikitis, M., & Carras, M. C. (2014). Gaming well: Links between videogames and flourishing mental health. *Frontiers in Psychology*, *5*, 260. Advance online publication. DOI: 10.3389/fpsyg.2014.00260 PMID: 24744743

Jonnalagadda, R., Singh, P., Seth, G., Khanna, A., Khanna, A., & Gogineni, A. (2023). Analysis of cross-functional stakeholder collaboration in online safety of children. *International Journal of Research Publication and Reviews*, *4*(11), 645–651. DOI: 10.55248/gengpi.4.1123.113201

Joshi, N., Ravikumar, R. N., Kishore, S., Pandit, S., Pandit, S., & Aarthi, S. (2026). Unmasking threat vectors in large language models. In *Advances in Computational Intelligence and Robotics* (pp. 1–34). IGI Global Scientific Publishing. DOI: 10.4018/979-8-3373-8252-4.ch001

Jovic, D., Butt, M.-A., Stanton, R., & Willma, T. (2023). Why play when you can watch or listen? Multi-modal engagements in digital gaming. *AoIR Selected Papers of Internet Research*. DOI: 10.5210/spir.v2022i0.12958

JPPS. (2026). Mental health community to brace for a newer gaming addiction. *Journal of Pakistan Psychiatric Society*, *23*(1). https://jpps.pk/index.php/journal/article/view/759

Juergensmeyer, M. (2008). *Global rebellion: Religious challenges to the secular state, from Christian militias to Al Qaeda* (Vol. 16). Univ of California Press.

Karas, T. (2025). Cultural criminology, counter-extremism and the contemporary far right. *Crime, Media, Culture*, *21*(3), 267–293. Advance online publication. DOI: 10.1177/17416590241279413

Karim, M. R., Dey, S. K., Islam, T., Sarker, S., Menon, M. H., Hossain, K., Chakravarthi, B. R., Hossain, M. A., & Decker, S. (2021). DeepHateExplainer: Explainable hate speech detection in under-resourced Bengali language. In *2021 IEEE 8th International Conference on Data Science and Advanced Analytics* (pp. 1–10). IEEE.

Kasianenko, K. (2025). Boosting the distant Other: Visibility practices on Japanese Twitter during Russia's war on Ukraine. *Convergence (London)*, *31*(3), 1056–1078. DOI: 10.1177/13548565251328776

Kaye, L. K., & Bryce, J. (2012). Putting the "fun" in video games: A qualitative focus group study of the social and psychological benefits of multiplayer gaming. *International Journal of Cyber Behavior, Psychology and Learning*, 2(4), 23–37.

Kerr, A. (2017). Global games: Production, circulation and policy in the networked era. In *Global Games: Production, Circulation and Policy in the Networked Era*. Taylor and Francis., DOI: 10.4324/9780203704028

Khan, H. (2021). Critical Study of Propaganda & 5th-Generation War. Uniselinus Education Publication. https://www.uniselinus.education/sites/default/files/2021-11/hamid%20khan.pdf

Khan, F., & Rahman, U. (2024). Socioeconomic marginalization and the digital escape: A study of competitive mobile gaming in South Punjab. *Pakistan Economic and Social Review*, *62*(1), 112–135.

Khan, R. M. (2011). *Afghanistan and Pakistan: Conflict, Extremism, and Resistance to Modernity*. Woodrow Wilson Center Press. DOI: 10.56021/9781421403847

Khan, S. A., & Qureshi, M. L. (2025). Virtual tribalism: The reframing of Ummah as an exclusionary gaming clan identity among South Asian youth. *Journal of Global Media and Communication*, *21*(1), 88–105.

Kiessling, H. (2016). *Faith, Unity, Discipline: The Inter-Service-Intelligence (ISI) of Pakistan*. Oxford University Press.

Kilcullen, D. (2016). *Blood year: The unraveling of Western counterterrorism*. Oxford University Press.

Kim, E. J., Namkoong, K., Ku, T., & Kim, S. J. (2008). The relationship between online game addiction and aggression, self-control and narcissistic personality traits. *European Psychiatry : The Journal of the Association of European Psychiatrists*, *23*(3), 212–218. DOI: 10.1016/j.eurpsy.2007.10.010 PMID: 18166402

Kim, K., Schmierbach, M. G., Chung, M. Y., Fraustino, J. D., Dardis, F., & Ahern, L. (2015). Is it a sense of autonomy, control, or attachment? Exploring the effects of in-game customization on game enjoyment. *Computers in Human Behavior*, *48*, 695–705. DOI: 10.1016/j.chb.2015.02.011

Kiritchenko, S., Nejadgholi, I., & Fraser, K. C. (2021). Confronting abusive language online: A survey from the ethical and human rights perspective. *Journal of Artificial Intelligence Research, 71*, 431–478. DOI: 10.1613/jair.1.12590

Koehler, D., Fiebig, V., & Jugl, I. (2022). From gaming to hating: Extreme-right ideological indoctrination and mobilization for violence of children on online gaming platforms. *Political Psychology*. Advance online publication. DOI: 10.1111/pops.12855

Kolb, D. A. (2015). *Experiential learning: Experience as the source of learning and development* (2nd ed.). Pearson Education.

Konikoff, D. (2021). Gatekeepers of toxicity: Reconceptualizing Twitter's abuse and hate speech policies. *Policy & Internet*, (poi3.265). DOI: 10.1002/poi3.265

Kordyaka, B., & Kruse, B. (2021). Curing toxicity – developing design principles to buffer toxic behaviour in massive multiplayer online games. *Safer Communities, 20*(3), 133–149. DOI: 10.1108/SC-10-2020-0037

Kosonen, H., & Löf, R. (2025). Pansy asses and terrorists: Sensibilities of anti-environmentalist toxic speech against Extinction Rebellion Finland. *European Journal of Cultural Studies, 28*(3), 883–903. Advance online publication. DOI: 10.1177/13675494241278931

Kou, Y. (2021). Punishment and its discontents: An analysis of permanent ban in an online game community. *Proceedings of the ACM on Human-Computer Interaction, 5*(CSCW2), 1–21. DOI: 10.1145/3476075

Kou, Y., & Gui, X. (2020). Mediating community-AI interaction through situated explanation. *Proceedings of the ACM on Human-Computer Interaction, 4*(CSCW2), 1–27. DOI: 10.1145/3415173

Kowert, R., & Newhouse, A. (2021). Landscape of extremist behavior in games [Conference presentation]. Game Developers Conference 2021, San Francisco, CA, United States.

Kowert, R., & Crevoshay, E. (2022). Harassment of game makers: Prevalence and impact. *F1000 Research, 11*, 1518. DOI: 10.12688/f1000research.126998.1

Kowert, R., Martel, A., & Swann, B. (2022). Not Just a Game: Identity usion and Extremism in Gaming Cultures. *Frontiers in Communication, 7*, 1007128. Advance online publication. DOI: 10.3389/fcomm.2022.1007128

Kowert, R., & Quandt, T. (2016). *The Video Game Debate: Unraveling the physical, social, and psychological effects of digital games*. Routledge.

Kowert, R., & Quandt, T. (2020). *Video games and social competence*. Routledge.

Kraut, R., & Resnick, P. (2012). *Building successful online communities: Evidence-based social design*. MIT Press. DOI: 10.7551/mitpress/8472.001.0001

Krippendorff, K. (2019). *Content analysis: An introduction to its methodology* (4th ed.). SAGE.

Krogh, S. C., Jensen, S. Q., & Larsen, M. C. (2026). Girl culture, unspectacular resistance and social media: A study of how adolescent girls undo emphasized femininity through shitposting. *Journal of Youth Studies*, *29*(1), 19–35. Advance online publication. DOI: 10.1080/13676261.2024.2392631

Kruglanski, A. W., Gelfand, M. J., Bélanger, J. J., Sheveland, A., Hetiarachchi, M., & Gunaratna, R. (2014). The psychology of radicalization and deradicalization: How significance quest impacts violent extremism. *Political Psychology*, *35*(S1), 69–93. DOI: 10.1111/pops.12163

Krzysztofik, A., Napierała, W., Hak, K. J., Jasiński, J. L., Leszczyńska, K. M., Mitan, A. M., Kańska, K. T., Krawczyk, K., Wieczorek, M. T., & Tomaszewska, A. M. (2026). DIGITAL SCREEN EXPOSURE AND MENTAL HEALTH OUTCOMES IN CHILDREN AND ADOLESCENTS: A NARRATIVE REVIEW. *International Journal of Innovative Technologies in Social Science*, *3*(1(49)). Advance online publication. DOI: 10.31435/ijitss.1(49).2026.5220

Kumar, R. (2019). *Research methodology: A step-by-step guide for beginners* (5th ed.). SAGE Publications.

Kuttymartin, N. (2025, October 1). Far-right extremism and gaming: How hate hijacks play. *RSIS Commentary*. https://rsis.edu.sg/rsis-publication/rsis/far-right-extremism-and-gaming-how-hate-hijacks-play/

Lakhani, S., & Wiedlitzka, S. (2022). *"Press F to Pay Respects": An Empirical Exploration of the Mechanics of Gamification in Relation to the Christchurch Attack. Terrorism and Political Violence*. Online First., DOI: 10.1080/09546553.2022.2064746

Lakomy, M. (2019). Let's Play a Video Game: Jihadi Propaganda in the World of Electronic Entertainment. *Studies in Conflict and Terrorism*, *42*(4), 383–406. DOI: 10.1080/1057610X.2017.1385903

Lane, J., Stodden, V., Bender, S., & Nissenbaum, H. (2013). Privacy, big data, and the public good: Frameworks for engagement. In *Privacy, Big Data, and the Public Good: Frameworks for Engagement*. Cambridge University Press., DOI: 10.1017/CBO9781107590205

Latif, M. A. (2024). Make America Hate Again? Before and After Trump there were Differences in How Muslim and Islam were Portrayed in American Media. *Social Identities*, *30*(4), 287–305. DOI: 10.1080/13504630.2024.2382126

Latif, M. A. (2024). Qatar's Efforts to Change the Image of Muslims after 9/11. *Contemporary Arab Affairs*, *17*(3), 416–441. DOI: 10.1163/17550920-bja00046

Latif, M. A. (2024). The Identity of Religion Always comes up: The War, The Mass Media and The Reproduction of Muslim Identity in the West. *Social Network Analysis and Mining*, *14*(1), 1–18. DOI: 10.1007/s13278-024-01354-2

Latif, M. A. (2024). The Rise of Religious Authoritarianism: Muslims, Ethno-Politics, and Racial Identity in India. *National Identities*, *27*(3), 15–41. DOI: 10.1080/14608944.2024.2442079

Latif, M. A. (2025). Classifying Muslims in Contemporary Europe: Their identity religion and race in Germany and United Kingdom. *International Journal on Minority and Group Rights*, *33*(1), 1–29. DOI: 10.1163/15718115-bja10201

Latif, M. A. (2025). Indian Mass Media and Politics of Hindutvazation: A Contextualizing Islamophobia and Global War against Muslims. *Race and Social Problems*, *18*(4), 1–18. DOI: 10.1007/s12552-025-09469-7

Latif, M. A. (2025). Race, Religion, Holy Wars and the Muslim "Other". *Nationalism & Ethnic Politics*, *30*(4), 605–628. DOI: 10.1080/13537113.2025.2537492

Latif, M. A. (2025b). The impact of American cinema on culture and creation of world view among society about Muslims: A sociological analysis of Hollywood movies (2012–2024). *Social Identities*, *31*(6), 754–776. DOI: 10.1080/13504630.2025.2518115

Latif, M. A. (2026). Framing the Muslim 'Other': Mass Media and Islamophobic Practices Shaping Identity, Representation and Power in the West. *Studies in Ethnicity and Nationalism*, sena.70026. Advance online publication. DOI: 10.1111/sena.70026

Latif, M. A. (2026). Hybrid Conflict in the Afghanistan–Pakistan Context: Digital War Mechanisms, Media Geopolitics, and the Dynamics of Online Radicalization. *Journal of Information Technology & Politics*, 1–20. Advance online publication. DOI: 10.1080/19331681.2026.2697181

Latif, M. A. (2026). *Hybrid Conflict, Migration, and Health Inequities in the Afghanistan–Pakistan Region: Digital Geopolitics, Structural Violence, and Refugee Lives*. Springer Nature.

Latif, M. A. (2026). *Racialization, Gender, and Health: Afghan Women's Identity Formation and Belonging in Contemporary Pakistan*. Human Arenas., DOI: 10.1007/s42087-026-00639-6

Latif, M. A. (2026). Racialized Vulnerability and Socioeconomic Determinants of Health Among Afghan Refugees in Pakistan. *Scientific Reports*, *16*(1), 11434. Advance online publication. DOI: 10.1038/s41598-026-42144-4 PMID: 41764346

Latif, M. A. (2026). Supporting trans youth amid symbolic inclusion and material exclusion: Family control, lived marginalization, and resilience in Pakistan. *International Journal of Transgender Health*, 1–17. Advance online publication. DOI: 10.1080/26895269.2026.2661008

Latif, M. A. (2026). The Iran–Saudi Rapprochement and Religious Extremism: Implications for Pakistan's Foreign Policy and Regional Stability. *Contemporary Arab Affairs*, *19*(3), 70–90. DOI: 10.1163/17550920-bja00115

Latif, M. A. (2026). The Politics of Digital "Othering": Online Hate Networks and the Marginalization of Muslim Communities in Europe. *Nationalism & Ethnic Politics*, 1–27. Advance online publication. DOI: 10.1080/13537113.2026.2696614

Latif, M. A. (2026). The Trouble Triangle: Islamophobia, Neoliberalism, and the Construction of Muslim Identity as "Other". *Insight Turkey*, *28*(1), 161–194. DOI: 10.25253/99.2026281.11

Latif, M. A.Muhammad Asad Latif. (2024). Terrorism New Wave: The Same Style but New Ways in the Context of Online Radicalization. *HISTORICAL: Journal of History and Social Sciences*, *3*(2), 169–180. DOI: 10.58355/historical.v3i2.109

Leake, E. (2022). *Afghan crucible: The Soviet invasion and the making of modern Afghanistan*. Oxford University Press.

Lee, J. L. (2022). *Afghanistan: A History from 1260 to the Present*. Reaktion books.

Lin, L. (2022). *Convergent Production Strategies: CCTV and HBS* (pp. 51–74). DOI: 10.1007/978-3-030-91756-2_3

Liu, M., Sun, Q., & Williams, D. (2025). With great power comes great accountability: Network positions, victimization, perpetration, and victim-perpetrator overlap in an online multiplayer game. *New Media & Society*, *27*(12), 6569–6590. DOI: 10.1177/14614448241268995

Livingstone, S., Stoilova, M., & Kelly, A. (2021). *Digital skills and competence, and digital and media literacy*. UNESCO., DOI: 10.54675/BBUM8498

Li, W., Mills, D., & Nower, L. (2019a). The relationship of loot box purchases to problem video gaming and problem gambling. *Addictive Behaviors, 97*, 27–34. DOI: 10.1016/j.addbeh.2019.05.016 PMID: 31129456

Lombardi, L. (2025). *Toxic talk: Structural toxicity on a Japanese anonymous textboard.* Emerging Media., DOI: 10.1177/27523543251376848

Lopez Naranjo, F., Maldonado, M. A., Cuadrado, E., & Moyano, M. (2025). Video games interventions to reduce radicalization and violent extremism in young people: A systematic review. *Games and Culture, 20*(6), 787–812. DOI: 10.1177/15554120231223067

Lucchesi, D. (2026). *Logics, Functioning, and Evolution of the Web: From Networked Society to Platform Society* (pp. 33–51). DOI: 10.1007/978-3-032-21265-8_3

Lundberg, S. M., & Lee, S.-I. (2017). A unified approach to interpreting model predictions. *Advances in Neural Information Processing Systems, 30*, 4765–4774.

MacAvaney, S., Yao, H.-R., Yang, E., Russell, K., Goharian, N., & Frieder, O. (2019). Hate speech detection: Challenges and solutions. *PLoS One, 14*(8), e0221152. DOI: 10.1371/journal.pone.0221152 PMID: 31430308

MacDougall, R. (2020). Marx at the Arcade: Consoles, Controllers, and Class Struggle by Jamie Woodcock. *Labour (Halifax), 86*(1), 218–219. DOI: 10.1353/llt.2020.0059

MacDowell, J. (2025). Breaking and making the fourth wall on YouTube: Direct address and audiovisual narration in online video. *Quarterly Review of Film and Video, 42*(6), 1399–1434. Advance online publication. DOI: 10.1080/10509208.2024.2444051

Macedo, T., Kurtz, G. B., & Becka, L. (2024). Esports culture in South America. In *Routledge Handbook of Esports* (pp. 643–654). Taylor and Francis., DOI: 10.4324/9781003410591-68

Mackintosh, E., & Mezzofiore, G. (2019). How the Extreme-Right Gamified Terror. *CNN* (October 10, 2019). https://edition.cnn.com/2019/10/10/europe/germany-synagogueattack-extremism-gamified-grm-intl/index.html

Madaminov, B., Ravikumar, R. N., & Aarthi, S. (2026). Forensic intelligence and cyber resilience for smart tourism ecosystems. In *Cybersecurity and Digital Trust in Smart and Sustainable Tourism* (pp. 161–194). IGI Global Scientific Publishing., DOI: 10.4018/979-8-2600-1850-7.ch006

Mahmoud, F. (2022). *The gamification of jihad: Playing with religion.*

Maley, W. (2018). *Transition in Afghanistan: Hope, despair and the limits of statebuilding*. Routledge. DOI: 10.4324/9781315143071

Maley, W. (2020). *The Afghanistan Wars*. Bloomsbury Publishing.

Malik, M. A., Rashid, M., & Ejaz, M. A. (2024). How Mainstream Video Games Are Unethically Targeting a Specific Religion. SSRN *Electronic Journal*, 25. DOI: 10.2139/ssrn.4831865

Mamadiyarov, Z., Ravikumar, R. N., & Aarthi, S. (2026). Cybercrime investigations and forensic readiness in tourism Ecosystems. In *Applications of Cybersecurity and Digital Forensics in Modern Tourism Systems* (pp. 59–94). IGI Global Scientific Publishing., DOI: 10.4018/979-8-3373-5826-0.ch003

Mandaville, P. (2010). *Global political Islam*. Routledge. DOI: 10.4324/9780203358511

Mansikka, J. (2014). *"Anti-religious" narratives in Japanese videogames: How institutional religion is depicted in two JRPG titles from the Final Fantasy series*. Abo Akademi university.

Marinett, M. (2021). The new frontier of platform policy. *Internet Policy Review*, *10*(3). Advance online publication. DOI: 10.14763/2021.3.1570

Marques, T. G., Schumann, S., & Mariconti, E. (2024). Positive behaviour interventions in online gaming: A systematic review of strategies applied in other environments. *Crime Science*, *13*(1), 14. Advance online publication. DOI: 10.1186/s40163-024-00208-8

Marsden, P. (2002). *The Taliban: war and religion in Afghanistan*. New Africa Books.

Martindale, S., Kennedy, H. W., Piskopani, A.-M., Ramchurn, R., & Gomez Bergin, A. (2026). Worlding otherwise: Virtual production as a participatory method for imagining safer digital futures. *Convergence (London)*, *32*(2), 331–351. DOI: 10.1177/13548565261427993

Massanari, A. (2017). #Gamergate and The Fappening: How Reddit's algorithm, governance, and culture support toxic technocultures. *New Media & Society*, *19*(3), 329–346. DOI: 10.1177/1461444815608807

Matloob, N., Matloob, N., & Ishaq, S. (2023). Hybrid Warfare: Strategies and Counterstrategies in the India-Pakistan Rivalry. *Journal of Peace and Diplomacy*, *4*(1), 78–99. DOI: 10.59111/JPD.004.01.043

Mazumdar, S. (2025). Politics as fun: Countering Indian digital nationalism with viral videos. *Television & New Media*, *26*(3), 373–389. Advance online publication. DOI: 10.1177/15274764241280635

McCauley, C., & Moskalenko, S. (2008). Mechanisms of political radicalization: Pathways toward terrorism. *Terrorism and Political Violence*, *20*(3), 415–433. DOI: 10.1080/09546550802073367

McCauley, C., & Moskalenko, S. (2017). Understanding political radicalization: The two-pyramids model. *The American Psychologist*, *72*(3), 205–216. DOI: 10.1037/amp0000062 PMID: 28383974

McGuckin, M. E., Turnnidge, J., Bruner, M. W., Lefebvre, J. S., & Côté, J. (2022). Exploring youth sport coaches' perceptions of intended outcomes of leadership behaviours. *International Journal of Sports Science & Coaching*, *17*(3), 463–476. DOI: 10.1177/17479541221076247 PMID: 41908295

McLean, L., & Griffiths, M. D. (2019). Female Gamers' Experience of Online Harassment and Social Support in Online Gaming: A Qualitative Study. *International Journal of Mental Health and Addiction*, *17*(4), 970–994. DOI: 10.1007/s11469-018-9962-0

Mehta, H., & Passi, K. (2022). Social media hate speech detection using explainable artificial intelligence (XAI). *Algorithms*, *15*(8), 291. DOI: 10.3390/a15080291

Meisner, C. (2023). Networked responses to networked harassment? Creators' coordinated management of "hate raids" on Twitch. *Social Media + Society*, *9*(2), 20563051231179696. Advance online publication. DOI: 10.1177/20563051231179696

Menz, S. N., & McLinton, S. S. (2026). Exploring the Experiences of Women Working in the Male-Dominated Video Game Industry. In *Gendered Marginalities* (pp. 231–261). Springer Nature Singapore., DOI: 10.1007/978-981-95-1557-8_11

Merkulova, T., & Bobrov, V. (2026). ARTIFICIAL INTELLIGENCE AS A DRIVER OF ECONOMIC TRANSFORMATION IN THE VIDEO GAME INDUSTRY. *Електронний Журнал "Ефективна Економіка."* DOI: 10.32702/2307-2105.2026.1.36

Merrill, S., Gardell, M., & Lindgren, S. (2025). How "the left" meme: Analyzing taboo in the Internet memes of r/DankLeft. *New Media & Society*, *27*(7), 3950–3972. Advance online publication. DOI: 10.1177/14614448241232144

Meske, C., & Bunde, E. (2023). Design principles for user interfaces in AI-based decision support systems: The case of explainable hate speech detection. *Information Systems Frontiers*, *25*(2), 743–773.

Miller-Idriss, C. (2025a). Misogyny incubators: How gaming helps channel everyday sexism into violent extremism. *Frontiers in Psychology*, *16*(1537477), 1537477. DOI: 10.3389/fpsyg.2025.1537477 PMID: 40735183

Mirowski, P. (2008). A Brief History of Neoliberalism, David Harvey. Oxford University Press, 2005, vii + 247 pages. *Economics and Philosophy, 24*(1), 111–117. DOI: 10.1017/S0266267108001715

Moghaddam, F. M. (2005). The staircase to terrorism: A psychological exploration. *The American Psychologist, 60*(2), 161–169. DOI: 10.1037/0003-066X.60.2.161 PMID: 15740448

Moonshot, C. V. E. (2021). *Gaming and extremism: Intervention strategies for the digital battlefield*. Moonshot CVE. https://moonshotcve.com

Moonshot, C. V. E. (2020). *Online gaming and extremism*. Moonshot CVE.

Mortensen, T. E. (2018). Anger, fear, and games: The long event of #GamerGate. *Games and Culture, 13*(8), 787–806. DOI: 10.1177/1555412016640408

Mosco, V. (2009). The Political Economy of Communication: A Living Tradition. *Media Asia, 36*(3), 146–155. DOI: 10.1080/23776277.2009.12224389

Munk, T. (2025). Digital defiance: Memetic warfare and civic resistance. *European Journal on Criminal Policy and Research, 31*(3), 501–528. Advance online publication. DOI: 10.1007/s10610-025-09613-4

Munn, L. (2023). Toxic play: Examining the issue of hate within gaming. *First Monday*. Advance online publication. DOI: 10.5210/fm.v28i9.12508

Murthy, D., Shermak, J., Pathania, S., Vinton, K., Whipple, K., Willard, L., & Madison, R. (2026). Rage against the AI machine: Can generative AI understand Donald Trump-related posts as well as humans? *Convergence (London)*, 13548565261459202. Advance online publication. DOI: 10.1177/13548565261459202

Musih, N., Trillò, T., & Hallinan, B. (2026). Resisting climate imaginaries: Future compass memes as combinatory mechanisms for imagining otherwise. *Information Communication and Society*, 1–20. Advance online publication. DOI: 10.1080/1369118X.2026.2616761

Muttaqin, M. Z. (2026). *Bourdieu's Ideas on Education*., DOI: 10.1007/978-981-92-0600-1_1

Nagle, A. (2017). *Kill all normies: Online culture wars from 4chan and Tumblr to Trump and the alt-right*. Zero Books.

National Alliance for Collegiate Esports. (2024). *State of collegiate esports 2024*. NACE.

Naz, F., & Shamsi, Z.-u.-H. (2022). Hybrid Warfare and its Nuances: A Case-Study from South Asia. IPRI Journal, 22 (1): 25-43. DOI: 10.31945/iprij.220102

Naz, I. H. (2021). Foreign Policy in Hybrid Warfare Environment – Way Forward for Pakistan. *Margalla Papers*, *25*(1), 1–11. DOI: 10.54690/margallapapers.25.1.46

Nefedchenko, O., Hladchenko, O., & Hlushakova, O. (2025). UKRAINIAN MEDIA IN THE AGE OF SURVEILLANCE CAPITALISM: FROM COMMUNICATION TO BEHAVIORAL PREDICTION. *Fìlologìčnì Traktati*, *17*(2), 97. DOI: 10.21272/Ftrk.2025.17(2)-10

Neumann, P. R. (2013). The trouble with radicalization. *International Affairs*, *89*(4), 873–893. DOI: 10.1111/1468-2346.12049

Newhouse, A., & Kowert, R. (2024). Radicalization in the gaming ecosystem: The application of self-determination theory. *Journal of Digital Social Research*, *6*(1), 78–99.

Newzoo. (2024). Global esports and live-streaming market report. Newzoo.

Newzoo. (2025). *Global games market report 2025*. Newzoo. https://newzoo.com

Nisar, M. (2024). Modding conflict: An analysis of user-generated nationalist and sectarian content in popular tactical shooters in Pakistan. *Journal of Digital Warfare and Security*, *3*(4), 312–330.

North America Scholastic Esports Federation. (2023). *Esports in education: NASEF impact report 2023*. NASEF.

Novianto, A. (2025a). Introduction: Platformization of Work and Platform Capitalism. In *Cheap Labour Regime in Platform Capitalism* (pp. 1–10). Springer Nature Singapore. DOI: 10.1007/978-981-95-1841-8_1

Novianto, A. (2025b). Labour Regime Theory and the Problem of Platform Capitalism. In *Cheap Labour Regime in Platform Capitalism* (pp. 11–40). Springer Nature Singapore., DOI: 10.1007/978-981-95-1841-8_2

Nurik, C. (2019). Book review: Custodians of the Internet: Platforms, content moderation, and the hidden decisions that shape social media. *Communication and the Public*, *4*(2), 182–184. DOI: 10.1177/2057047319851200

Oltean, O., Angi, D., Pavel, A., & Bogdan, R. (2021). *Culturepreneurs: Competitivitatea industriilor culturale i creative din Cluj-Napoca i zona metropolitană în context european: 5/2021*. Presa Universitară Clujeană., DOI: 10.52257/9786063710810

Oonk, G. (2000a). Modernity at Large: Cultural Dimensions of Globalization [review]. *Journal of World History, 11*(1), 157–159. DOI: 10.1353/jwh.2000.0021

Othman, A. (2025). The need for a Halal mode in video games: Ethical and cultural considerations. *ResearchGate*. https://www.researchgate.net/publication/389490207

Ozanne, M., Bhandari, A., Bazarova, N. N., & DiFranzo, D. (2022). Shall AI moderators be made visible? Perception of accountability and trust in moderation systems on social media platforms. *Big Data & Society, 9*(2), 205395172211156. DOI: 10.1177/20539517221115666

Paganoni, M. C., & Becerra, G. (2026). Big Data Discourses| Reframing Datafication: News Media Discourses on Big Data and AI. *International Journal of Communication, 20*, 21. DOI: 10.65476/75d24f96

Pakistan Software Export Board. (2024). Economic Potential of Online Gaming Industry in Pakistan. PSEB Industry Briefs.

Pantoliano, C. (2025). Playing doomsday: Video games and the politics of nuclear weapons. *Review of International Studies, 51*(4), 1–22. DOI: 10.1017/S0260210525000087

Parlak, C., & Kaygusuz, E. (2025). Neocolonialism in video games: The social discourse of Call of Duty 4: Modern Warfare (2007). *DiGRA Conference Proceedings*. https://doi.org/DOI: 10.26503/dl.v2025i2.2480

Patton, M. Q. (2015). *Qualitative research & evaluation methods* (4th ed.). SAGE.

Pembro, K. (2021). Book Review: Marx at the Arcade: Consoles, Controllers, and Class Struggle Marx at the Arcade: Consoles, Controllers, and Class Struggle By WoodcockJamie. Chicago: Haymarket Books, 2019. 208 pages. Cloth $40.00 [or Paper $12.60]. ISBN: 9781642590142. *The Review of Radical Political Economics, 53*(2), 361–364. DOI: 10.1177/0486613420967200

Pérez de la Fuente, O. (2023). Online Misogyny and the Law: Are Human Rights Protected on the Net? *The Age of Human Rights Journal*, (21). Advance online publication. DOI: 10.17561/tahrj.v21.8270

Petersen, L. N., & Johansen, M. B. (2025). Spaces of hybridized prefatory extremism (HYPE) on social media. *Social Media + Society, 11*(2), 20563051251340145. Advance online publication. DOI: 10.1177/20563051251340145

Pew Research Center. (2022). *Religious composition by country, 2010–2050*. Pew Research Center. https://www.pewresearch.org/religion/2015/04/02/religious-projection-table/

Phillips, W. (2015). *This is why we can't have nice things: Mapping the relationship between online trolling and mainstream culture.* MIT Press. DOI: 10.7551/mitpress/10288.001.0001

Pierson, J., Kerr, A., Robinson, S. C., Fanni, R., Steinkogler, V. E., Milan, S., & Zampedri, G. (2023). Governing artificial intelligence in the media and communications sector. *Internet Policy Review, 12*(1). Advance online publication. DOI: 10.14763/2023.1.1683

Pivovarov, A. M. (2026a). Mass Society: Evolution from the Industrial to the Platform Era. *Discourse, 12*(1), 83–104. DOI: 10.32603/2412-8562-2026-12-1-83-104

Politopoulos, A., et al. (2019). "History is our playground": Action and pedagogy in the Assassin's Creed series. *Journal of Interactive Technology and Pedagogy, 15.*

Postigo, H. (2007). Of mods and modders: Chasing down the value of gamer modification. *Games and Culture, 2*(4), 300–313. DOI: 10.1177/1555412007307955

Pötzsch, H. (2017). Selective realism: Filtering war in military shooters. *Games and Culture, 12*(2), 156–178. DOI: 10.1177/1555412015587802

Precarious Playbour: Modders and the Digital Games Industry. (n.d.). Https://Www.Researchgate.Net/Publication/26490724_Precarious_Playbour_Modders_and_the_Digital_Games_Industry

Prensky, M. (2010). *Teaching digital natives: Partnering for real learning.* Corwin Press.

Price, C. W. (2025). Ketchup is the whitest sauce: Memes as silly/serious bordered spaces in international relations. *International Political Sociology, 19*(3), olaf026. Advance online publication. DOI: 10.1093/ips/olaf026

Przybylski, A. K., Rigby, C. S., & Ryan, R. M. (2010). A motivational model of video game engagement. *Review of General Psychology, 14*(2), 154–166. DOI: 10.1037/a0019440

Przybylski, A. K., Ryan, R. M., & Rigby, C. S. (2009). The motivating role of violence in videogames. *Personality & Social Psychology Bulletin, 35*(2), 243–259. DOI: 10.1177/0146167208327216 PMID: 19141627

Pulos, A. (2013). Confronting Heteronormativity in Online Games. *Games and Culture, 8*(2), 77–97. DOI: 10.1177/1555412013478688

Qureshi, H. I. A., & Khalid, I. (2024). Hybrid Warfare in the 21st Century: Implications for Pakistan. *Journal of Development and Social Sciences, 5*(4), 459–468. DOI: 10.47205/jdss.2024(5-IV)39

Qureshi, S. A., & Bukhari, M. (2025). Peer bonds and psychological grooming: A network analysis of extremist Discord servers in Pakistan. *Strategic Intelligence Review, 7*(1), 112–134.

Quwaider, M., Alabed, A., & Duwairi, R. (2019). The Impact of Video Games on the Players Behaviors: A Survey. *Procedia Computer Science, 151*, 575–582. DOI: 10.1016/j.procs.2019.04.077

Ramsauer, L. (2026). Kant's Dialectic of Enlightenment. *European Journal of Philosophy, 34*(2), 639–655. Advance online publication. DOI: 10.1111/ejop.70056

Rashid, A. (2010). *Taliban: militant Islam, oil and fundamentalism in Central Asia.* Yale University Press.

Ravikumar, A. S., Kurbanova, N., Sevdim, K. E., Zaynitdinovna, B. D., & Jumaniyazova, N. (2026). Bridging knowledge and policy. In *Advances in Computational Intelligence and Robotics* (pp. 119–150). IGI Global Scientific Publishing. DOI: 10.4018/979-8-3373-7620-2.ch005

Ravikumar, R. S., Manujakshi, Aarthi, S., Urazbaeva, Y., & Tamilselvi, S. (2025). Navigating data privacy, security, and regulatory challenges in healthcare AI ensuring fairness, bias mitigation, interpretability, and trust. In *Transformative Role of Transformer Models in Healthcare* (pp. 25–54). IGI Global Scientific Publishing. DOI: 10.4018/979-8-3373-2038-0.ch002

Ravikumar, R. N., & Aarthi, S. (2025). Web-based cybersecurity architectures. In *Impact of Web Technologies on Digital Transformation* (pp. 187–216). IGI Global Scientific Publishing., DOI: 10.4018/979-8-3373-5167-4.ch007

Reality is Broken: Why Games Make Us Better and How They Can Change the World. (n.d.). Https://Www.Researchgate.Net/Publication/244486521_Reality_is_Broken_Why_Games_Make_Us_Better_and_How_They_Can_Change_the_World

Republic of the Philippines. (2012). *Data Privacy Act of 2012 (Republic Act No. 10173).* Official Gazette of the Philippines.

Ribble, M. (2015). *Digital citizenship in schools* (3rd ed.). International Society for Technology in Education.

Ribeiro, M. T., Singh, S., & Guestrin, C. (2016). "Why should I trust you?": Explaining the predictions of any classifier. In *Proceedings of the 22nd ACM SIGKDD International Conference on Knowledge Discovery and Data Mining* (pp. 1135–1144). Association for Computing Machinery.

Ribeiro, M. H., Ottoni, R., West, R., Almeida, V. A. F., & Meira, W. (2020). Auditing radicalization pathways on YouTube. *Proceedings of FAT, 2020*, 131–141.

Ritzer, G., & Jurgenson, N. (2010). Production, Consumption, Prosumption: The nature of capitalism in the age of the digital "prosumer.". *Journal of Consumer Culture, 10*(1), 13–36. DOI: 10.1177/1469540509354673

Rizvi, T. (2025). Beyond Laghw: Educating Pakistani parents on the psychological and social architecture of multiplayer video games. *Family and Child Studies Journal, 14*(2), 99–115.

Roberts, B., & Browne, J. (2021). Systematic review update: Factors influencing the psychological health of conflict-affected populations in low- and middle-income countries. *Global Public Health, 16*(3), 421–439.

Robinson, N. (2012). Videogames, militarism and relations of power in the global space. *International Political Sociology, 6*(2), 109–124.

Roy, O. (2004). *Globalised Islam: The search for a new ummah.* Hurst.

Rubab, M. (2024). Security Dynamics of Pakistan: Hybrid Warfare & Media Threats. *Pakistan Social Sciences Review, 8*(2), 1–12. https://ojs.pssr.org.pk/journal/article/download/530/387/805

Rubin, B. R. (2022). Afghanistan under the Taliban: Findings on the current situation. *Stimson Center, 20.*

Ruttig, T. (2012). How Tribal Are the Taliban? In Bashir, S., & Crews, R. D. (Eds.), *Under the Drones: Modern Lives in the Afghanistan-Pakistan Borderlands* (pp. 102–135). Harvard University Press.

Ryder, C. (2026). Despicable digital banter: Racist black and brown politicians in the U.K. *First Monday, 31*(5). Advance online publication. DOI: 10.5210/fm.v31i5.15438

Sageman, M. (2004). *Understanding terror networks.* University of Pennsylvania Press. DOI: 10.9783/9780812206791

Sahaya Raj, J., & Dr, A. (2025). Effectiveness of Social Media Marketing: Influencer Marketing and the Role of Online Communities in Customer Engagement and Brand Loyalty. *International Journal of Research and Innovation in Social Science, IX*(VIII), 5356–5361. DOI: 10.47772/IJRISS.2025.908000432

Saleem, M., & Anderson, C. A. (2013). Arabs as terrorists: Effects of stereotypes within violent contexts on attitudes, perceptions, and affect. *Psychology of Violence, 3*(1), 84–99. DOI: 10.1037/a0030038

Salter, A., & Blodgett, B. (2017). Toxic geek masculinity in media: Sexism, trolling, and identity policing. In *Toxic Geek Masculinity in Media: Sexism, Trolling, and Identity Policing*. Springer International Publishing., DOI: 10.1007/978-3-319-66077-6

Scacchi, W. (2010). Computer game mods, modders, modding, and the mod scene. *First Monday, 15*(5). Advance online publication. DOI: 10.5210/fm.v15i5.2965

Schlegel, L. (2020). Jumanji extremism? How games and gamification could facilitate radicalization processes. *Journal for Deradicalization, 23*(2), 112–144.

Schlegel, L., & Kowert, R. (2024). *Gaming and extremism: The radicalization of digital playgrounds*. Routledge. DOI: 10.4324/9781003388371

Schmid, A. P. (2013). Radicalisation, de-radicalisation, counter-radicalisation: A conceptual discussion and literature review. ICCT Research Paper.

Schmidt, D. C. (2022). Data Collection in the Age of Surveillance Capitalism. In *Collecting in the Twenty-First Century* (pp. 200–220). Boydell and Brewer Limited., DOI: 10.1017/9781800103382.013

Scholl, B. (2025). Playing on hard: Algorithmic border objects and inequality among esports student-athletes. *New Media & Society, 27*(8), 4891–4907. DOI: 10.1177/14614448241243097

Schut, K. (2013). *Of Games and God: A Christian Exploration of Video Games*. Brazos Press.

Semple, M. (2014). *Rhetoric, ideology, and organizational structure of the Taliban movement*. United States Institute of Peace.

Sengupta, U., & Sengupta, U. (2022). SDG-11 and smart cities: Contradictions and overlaps between social and environmental justice research agendas. In *Frontiers in Sociology* (Vol. 7). Frontiers Media S.A. DOI: 10.3389/fsoc.2022.995603

Shah, H. J., & Ehsan, M. (2023). Hybrid Warfare: Emerging Challenges for Pakistan. *Journal of Contemporary Studies, 11*(2), 234. DOI: 10.54690/jcs.v11i2.234

Sharan, T. (2022). *Inside Afghanistan: political networks, informal order, and state disruption*. Routledge. DOI: 10.4324/9781315161617

Sharma, S., Singh, J., Gupta, A., Ali, F., Khan, F., & Kwak, D. (2024). User safety and security in the metaverse: A critical review. *IEEE Open Journal of the Communications Society, 5*, 5467–5487. DOI: 10.1109/OJCOMS.2024.3397044

Shipra. (2019). Book review: José Van Dijck, Thomas Poell and Martijn De Waal, The Platform Society: Public Values in a Connective World. *Indian Journal of Human Development, 13*, 235–238. DOI: 10.1177/0973703019870883

Shou, S. (2023). Psychology behind aggressive language used in Honor of Kings. *Communications in Humanities Research*, *7*(1), 193–200. DOI: 10.54254/2753-7064/7/20230883

Shreha, S. A., Ravikumar, R. N., & Aarthi, S. (2025). Neuro-symbolic AI and Behavioral Intelligence. In *Advances in Computational Intelligence and Robotics* (pp. 121–152). IGI Global Scientific Publishing. DOI: 10.4018/979-8-3373-5012-7.ch005

Siddique, A. (2014). *The Pashtun question: The unresolved key to the future of Pakistan and Afghanistan.* Hurst.

Sinclair, B. (2017, September 8). *Religious fighting game gets Steam banned in Malaysia*. Gamesindustry.Biz.

Singh, B., Wongmahesak, K., & Chandra, S. (2025). Transforming digital ownership and assessing role of blockchain technology and NFTs in future economy. In *Practical Strategies and Case Studies for Online Marketing 6.0* (pp. 343–368). IGI Global., DOI: 10.4018/979-8-3373-2058-8.ch015

Singh, I., & Kumar Chandola, T.SINGH. (2026). SPORTS BETTING: JUDICIAL INTERPRETATION AND LEGAL CHALLENGES IN INDIA. *Indian Journal of Legal Review*, *6*(3). Advance online publication. DOI: 10.65393/OKXM4852

Sinno, A. H. (2015). *Organizations at war in Afghanistan and beyond.* Cornell University Press.

Sisler, V. (2008). Digital Arabs: Representation in video games and portrayal of the Middle East. *European Journal of Cultural Studies, 11*(2), 203–220.

Šisler, V. (2008). Digital Arabs: Representation in video games. *European Journal of Cultural Studies, 11*(2), 203–220. DOI: 10.1177/1367549407088333

Sjøvaag, H., Falch, M., Tadayoni, R., Grönlund, M., & Lindberg, T. (2026). The political economy of networked media: The revenue and concentration of communication markets in the Nordics. *Nordicom Review*, *47*(1), 98–125. DOI: 10.2478/nor-2026-0006

Smart, S. (2025). Introduction: Transitional Justice in the Age of Surveillance Capitalism. In *St Antony's Series: Part F870* (pp. 13–51). Palgrave Macmillan. DOI: 10.1007/978-3-031-89828-0_2

Snodgrass, J. G. (2023). *The avatar faculty: Ecstatic transformations in religion and videogames*. University of California Press.

Snyder, H. (2019). Literature review as a research methodology: An overview and guidelines. *Journal of Business Research, 104*, 333–339. DOI: 10.1016/j.jbusres.2019.07.039

Söğüt, F. (2022). Digital Games and Orientalism. In *Research Anthology on Game Design, Development, Usage, and Social Impact* (pp. 1457–1469). IGI Global. DOI: 10.4018/978-1-6684-7589-8.ch070

South Asia Terrorism Portal. (2026, May 16). Gaming terror. *Second Sight, 3*(41). https://www.satp.org/second-sight-volume-3-no-41

Spiller, R. (2026). Network Society Theory: The Rise of the Network Society – by Manuel Castells (1996). In *Key works: Theories in communication studies* (pp. 379–387). Springer Fachmedien Wiesbaden. DOI: 10.1007/978-3-658-50422-9_27

Squire, K. (2011). *Video games and learning: Teaching and participatory culture in the digital age*. Teachers College Press.

Squires, D. (2012). Curriculum alignment research suggests that alignment can improve student achievement. *The Clearing House: A Journal of Educational Strategies, Issues and Ideas, 85*(4), 129–135. DOI: 10.1080/00098655.2012.657723

Statista. (2024). Global esports audience overview. Statista Research Department.

Suler, J. (2004). The online disinhibition effect. *Cyberpsychology & Behavior, 7*(3), 321–326. DOI: 10.1089/1094931041291295 PMID: 15257832

Sunstein, C. R. (2017). *Republic: Divided democracy in the age of social media*. Princeton University Press. DOI: 10.1515/9781400884711

TaeHyuk Keum, B., & Hearns, M.TaeHyuk Keum. (2022). Online gaming and racism: Impact on psychological distress among Black, Asian, and Latinx emerging adults. *Games and Culture, 17*(3), 445–460. DOI: 10.1177/15554120211039082

Tajfel, H., & Turner, J. C. (1979). An integrative theory of intergroup conflict. In W. G. Austin & S. Worchel (Eds.), *The social psychology of intergroup relations* (pp. 33–47). file:///C:/Users/Hp/Downloads/tajfel-turner-1979-compressed.pdf

Tajfel, H., & Turner, J. C. (1979). An integrative theory of intergroup conflict. In Austin, W. G., & Worchel, S. (Eds.), *The social psychology of intergroup relations* (pp. 33–47). Brooks/Cole.

Takru, S. (2025). Gender Stereotyping and Female Representation in Video Games: A Contemporary Review and Reassessment. *International Journal For Multidisciplinary Research*, *7*(6), 62888. Advance online publication. DOI: 10.36948/ijfmr.2025.v07i06.62888

Tang, W. Y., & Fox, J. (2016). Men's harassment behavior in online video games: Personality traits and game factors. *Aggressive Behavior*, *42*(6), 513–521. DOI: 10.1002/ab.21646 PMID: 26880037

Tashakkori, A., & Teddlie, C. (2010). *Mixed methods in social and behavioral research* (2nd ed.). SAGE Publications.

Taylor, T. L. (2012). *Raising the Stakes*. The MIT Press., DOI: 10.7551/mitpress/8624.001.0001

Taylor, T. L. (2018). *Watch me play: Twitch and the rise of game live streaming*. Princeton University Press. DOI: 10.2307/j.ctvc77jqw

Telecom Regulatory Authority of India. (2025). *Telecom subscription data Q4 2025*. TRAI. https://www.ofcom.org.uk/siteassets/resources/documents/research-and-data/telecoms-research/telecoms-data-updates/telecommunications-market-data/telecommunications-market-data-update-q4-2025.pdf?v=415936

Terranova, T. (2000). Free Labor. *Social Text*, *18*(2), 33–58. DOI: 10.1215/01642472-18-2_63-33

The Promotion of Diversity and Inclusion in Olympic Games: An Intersection Between Future Opportunities and Career Experiences for HBCU Student-Athletes | Request PDF. (n.d.). Https://Www.Researchgate.Net/Publication/404037629_The_Promotion_of_Diversity_and_Inclusion_in_Olympic_Games_An_Intersection_Between_Future_Opportunities_and_Career_Experiences_for_HBCU_Student-Athletes

Theobald, E., d'Amato, A., Welles, J., Elson, J. S., & Hunter, S. (2026). Radicalization in the gaming ecosystem: The application of self-determination theory. *First Monday*. Advance online publication. DOI: 10.5210/fm.v31i1.14371

Theros, M. (2023). Knowledge, power and the failure of US peacemaking in Afghanistan 2018–21. *International Affairs*, *99*(3), 1231–1252. DOI: 10.1093/ia/iiad092

Thompson, J., & Lamphere-Englund, G. (2024). *Lethal Play: Modding, Extremism, and the Virtualization of Conflict*. SAGE Publications.

Topinka, R., Osborne-Carey, C., & Finlayson, A. (2024). Playing with the news on Reddit: The politics game on r/the_Donald. *International Political Sociology, 18*(2), olae015. Advance online publication. DOI: 10.1093/ips/olae015

Tortajada, I. (2020). The Age of Surveillance Capitalism: The Fight for a Human Future at the New Frontier of Power, S. Zuboff (2019). *Catalan Journal of Communication & Cultural Studies, 12*(1), 153–154. DOI: 10.1386/cjcs_00020_5

Tripathi, S. (2022). Women and online harassment. *Feminist Dissent*, (6), 133–158. DOI: 10.31273/fd.n6.2022.1265

Turabi, R. F., Rozi, S., Sawani, S., Kazi, M., & Asad, N. (2025). Internet gaming disorder and violent video gameplay among higher secondary school-going adolescents in Karachi, Pakistan—A cross-sectional study. *PLOS Mental Health, 2*(1), e0000179. DOI: 10.1371/journal.pmen.0000179 PMID: 41661772

Ubaradka, A., Ferguson, C. J., & Khanganba, S. P. (2026). Video games as conduits for radicalization: Impact of exposure to extremist recruitment and authoritarianism on sexist attitudes and aggression. *Psychology of Popular Media.* https://doi.org/ DOI: 10.1037/ppm0000642

UN Counter-Terrorism Committee Executive Directorate. (2020). *The use of the internet and information and communications technologies for terrorist purposes.* United Nations.

UN Counter-Terrorism Committee Executive Directorate. (2022). *Terrorist and violent extremist use of the internet and social media.* United Nations.

UNESCO. (2023). *Digital literacy framework for preventing violent extremism.* UNESCO. https://www.unesco.org

UNESCO. (2023). *Global framework for digital literacy skills.* UNESCO Publishing.

UNICRI. (2026). *Checkpoint Reached: Preventing Violent Extremism and Online Gaming.* United Nations Interregional Crime and Justice Research Institute. https://unicri.org/News-Checkpoint-Reached-Preventing-Violent-Extremism-and-Online-Gaming

van Dijck, J., Poell, T., & de Waal, M. (2018). The Platform Society. In *The Platform Society.* Oxford University PressNew York. DOI: 10.1093/oso/9780190889760.001.0001

Vaux, A.. (2021). Extremist networking on digital marketplaces: From gaming environments to encrypted chat apps. *International Journal of Cybersecurity, 9*(3), 201–218.

Vergel, P., La Parra-Casado, D., & Vives-Cases, C. (2024). Examining cybersexism in online gaming communities: A scoping review. *Trauma, Violence & Abuse*, *25*(2), 1201–1218. DOI: 10.1177/15248380231176059 PMID: 37243440

Video game cultures and the construction of identities in contemporary society | Request PDF. (n.d.). Https://Www.Researchgate.Net/Publication/275343809_Video_game_cultures_and_the_construction_of_identities_in_contemporary_society

von Schomberg, L. (2025). Towards a Constructive Ethics of Artificial Intelligence in the Age of Surveillance Capitalism. In *Integrated Science* (Vol. 35, pp. 205–221). Springer Nature., DOI: 10.1007/978-3-031-87023-1_16

Waldron, D. (2005). Role-Playing Games and the Christian Right: Community Formation in Response to a Moral Panic. *Journal of Religion and Popular Culture*, *9*(1), 3–3. DOI: 10.3138/jrpc.9.1.003

Wang, H., Hee, M. S., Awal, M. R., Choo, K. T. W., & Lee, R. K.-W. (2023). Evaluating GPT-3 generated explanations for hateful content moderation. In *Proceedings of the Thirty-Second International Joint Conference on Artificial Intelligence* (pp. 6255–6263). International Joint Conferences on Artificial Intelligence Organization. DOI: 10.24963/ijcai.2023/694

Waqas, M. (2023). Hybrid Warfare in a Post-Truth Era: A Case Study of Pakistan. Discourse: An International Journal of Communication. https://discourse.org.pk/index.php/discourse/article/download/260/158

Weidhase, N., & Wilde, P. (2026). "Gone too soon": Zombie humour on social media as cultural critique of the British monarchy. *Information Communication and Society*, *29*(1), 113–130. Advance online publication. DOI: 10.1080/1369118X.2025.2497945

Wells, G., Romhanyi, A., Reitman, J. G., Gardner, R., Squire, K., & Steinkuehler, C. (2024). Right-wing extremism in mainstream games: A review of the literature. *Games and Culture*, *19*(4), 469–492. DOI: 10.1177/15554120231167214

Wells, G., Romhányi, Á., & Steinkuehler, C. (2024). Hate speech and hate-based harassment in online games. *Frontiers in Psychology*, *15*, 1422422. DOI: 10.3389/fpsyg.2024.1422422 PMID: 40046807

White, J., Wallner, C., Lamphere-Englund, G., Frankie, L., Kowert, R., Schlegel, L., Kingdon, A., Phelan, A., Newhouse, A., Saiz, G., & Regeni, P. (2024). *Radicalisation through gaming: The role of gendered social identity. Royal United Services Institute*. RUSI.

Widyaningsih, R., & Megia, F. V. (2026). Intersection of the metaverse, Muslim identity, and radicalization risks: A global systematic review of digital religious communication. *Komunika: Jurnal Komunikasi Islam, 20*(1), 1–24. https://ejournal.uinsaizu.ac.id/index.php/komunika/article/view/15013

Wiktorowicz, Q. (2004). Joining the cause: Al-Muhajiroun and radical Islam. Paper presented at the Roots of Islamic Radicalism Conference, Yale University.

Wiktorowicz, Q. (2004). *Islamic activism: A social movement theory approach.* Indiana University Press.

Williams, D., Ducheneaut, N., Xiong, L., Zhang, Y., Yee, N., & Nickell, E. (2006). From tree house to barracks: The social life of guilds in World of Warcraft. *Games and Culture, 1*(4), 338–361. DOI: 10.1177/1555412006292616

Wolfowicz, M., Hasisi, B., & Weisburd, D. (2022). What are the effects of different elements of media on radicalization outcomes? A systematic review. *Campbell Systematic Reviews, 18*(2), e1244. DOI: 10.1002/cl2.1244 PMID: 36913204

Woodcock, J., & Johnson, M. R. (2019). The affective labor and performance of live streaming on Twitch. tv. *Television & New Media, 20*(8), 813–823. DOI: 10.1177/1527476419851077

Wood, J. (2026). Invitations to fascism: Mediated nostalgia in far-right Discord servers. *Crime, Media, Culture*, 17416590261446319. Advance online publication. DOI: 10.1177/17416590261446319

World Bank. (2025). [World Bank Group. https://databank.worldbank.org/source/world-development-indicators]. *World Development Indicators, 2025,* •••.

World Health Organization. (2022). *Public health implications of excessive gaming and digital engagement.* WHO Press.

Yodovich, N., & Kim, J. (2022). Exploring the feminization of backseat gaming through Girlfriend Reviews YouTube channel. *Games and Culture, 17*(5), 795–815. DOI: 10.1177/15554120211056124

Yousaf, M., & Anwar, S. (2024). Online gaming subcultures in Karachi: Class dynamics, social validation, and the transition of play. *Journal of Sociology and Social Anthropology, 12*(3), 210–229.

Yunhao, H., Sophie, E., Elizabeth, M. C., & Bianca, K. (2025). Player versus Player: A systematic review of cyberbullying in multiplayer online games. *Computers in Human Behavior Reports, 18,* 100675. DOI: 10.1016/j.chbr.2025.100675

Zaman, M. Q. (2018). *Islam in Pakistan: A history* (Vol. 68). Princeton University Press.

Zhang, X., & Davis, M. (2024). E-extremism: A conceptual framework for studying the online far right. *New Media & Society*, *26*(5), 2954–2970. DOI: 10.1177/14614448221098360

Zhang, Y. (2026). Monetary Integration and the Coordination of Cryptocurrency and Fiat Money in the Digital Asset Era. *Advances in Economics and Management Research*, *16*(1), 297. DOI: 10.56028/aemr.16.1.297.2026

Zobel, G. (2019). Review of "Algorithms of oppression: how search engines reinforce racism," by Noble, S. U. (2018). New York, New York: NYU Press. *Communication Design Quarterly Review*, *7*(3), 30–31. DOI: 10.1145/3321388.3321392

Zsila, Á., Shabahang, R., Aruguete, M. S., & Orosz, G. (2022). Toxic behaviors in online multiplayer games: Prevalence, perception, risk factors of victimization, and psychological consequences. *Aggressive Behavior*, *48*(3), 356–364. DOI: 10.1002/ab.22023 PMID: 35112713

, . ., & , . (2026). Policy Mobilities and the Global Exchange of Ideas, Authority, and Development Frameworks. , *3*, 635–656. https://doi.org/ DOI: 10.21608/abs.2025.422076.1070

About the Contributors

Muhammad Asad Latif is an interdisciplinary scholar specializing in sociology of religion, inequality, migration, and media studies. He holds a PhD from the School of Humanities and Social Sciences and has developed a strong research profile examining Islamophobia, racialization, and the construction of Muslim identities across global contexts, particularly in South Asia and the West. His work employs both qualitative and quantitative approaches to explore issues of social justice, minority rights, and political transformation. He has published extensively in internationally recognized, peer-reviewed journals and serves as a reviewer for leading academic outlets. His current research focuses on the intersections of migration, media representation, and social inequality in shaping contemporary forms of conflict and belonging. His work appears in journals such as Scientific Reports, Social Network Analysis and Mining, and Race and Social Problems, and he is an active reviewer for journals including Human Relations, Gender Issues, and Humanities and Social Sciences Communications.

***

Tushar received a B.Tech degree in electronics and communication from U.P.T.U., Lucknow (U.P.), in 2007. He received the M.B.A. degree in R.T.M. from Jiwaji University, Gwalior (M.P.), in 2009. He is a "gold medalist" in M.E. in Communication Control and Networking from M.P.C.T. Gwalior, M.P. The research interests include antenna and microwave communication, QCA design, and deep learning and their applications. Presently He is pursuing a Ph.D. and acting as an assistant professor at the United College of Engineering & Research, Prayagraj, India.

Mahmood Ahmad is an Assistant Professor of Islamic Studies with expertise in Islamic thought, theology, and contemporary religious issues. He is actively engaged in teaching, research, and academic mentorship, contributing to the advancement of Islamic scholarship through publications, conference presentations, and interdisciplinary research. His academic interests include Qur'anic studies, Islamic jurisprudence, ethics, and the role of religion in modern society. Dr. Ahmad is committed to promoting critical inquiry, intellectual development, and meaningful dialogue within the field of Islamic Studies.

Jamil Akhtar currently holds the esteemed position of an Assistant Professor of Islamic Studies at the University of Punjab in Lahore, Pakistan. His academic journey, from matriculation to his post-doctorate research at the University of Oxford, UK, has been characterized by an unwavering commitment to excellence. In recognition of his exceptional scholarly contributions, he was honored with the prestigious research award "International Postdoctoral Scholarship" from PHEC in Pakistan in 2021. This esteemed award facilitated his tenure at the Oxford Centre for Religion and Culture, RPC at the University of Oxford, UK. During his tenure, he collaborated closely with the distinguished Professor Dr. Paul Weller. Dr. Jamil achieved the remarkable feat of securing the first position in the Seerah research writing competition, held by the Ministry of Religious Affairs, Pakistan. His scholarly research pursuits have also taken him across borders, as he was selected to participate in two renowned Religious Summer Schools in 2022. These esteemed institutions include the Harvard Divinity School, USA and the Oxford Centre for Muslim-Christian Studies in Oxford, UK. He has authored several books

Duggirala Aravind is an academic professional associated with the Department of Aviation at ASET Institute of Science and Technology, Chennai, India. His academic interests are closely connected with aviation studies, airport operations, airline management, aviation safety, and the development of industry-oriented skills among students. He is committed to supporting learners in understanding the technical, managerial, and operational dimensions of the aviation sector. Through his teaching and academic engagement, he contributes to building student awareness of aviation standards, safety practices, communication skills, and professional discipline required in the global aviation industry. His role also reflects a strong focus on practical learning, career readiness, and the integration of classroom knowledge with real-world aviation practices. Mr. Aravind continues to contribute to aviation education by encouraging students to develop confidence, professionalism, ethical responsibility, and the necessary competencies for successful careers in aviation and allied sectors.

Rosalie Dela Cruz is an accomplished educator with 11 years of teaching experience. She currently serves as the Program Chair of the Bachelor of Science in

Exercise and Sports Science (BSESS) at the College of Human Kinetics in the University of Makati. Dedicated to the advancement of sports education, she is also a module writer in sports and a passionate dance specialist, inspiring students to excel in both academic and athletic pursuits. Her commitment to holistic learning and her expertise in physical education continue to contribute significantly to the university's mission of nurturing well-rounded individuals.

Ervin Echague is a Senior Education Program Specialist at the Bureau of Curriculum Development, Department of Education (DepEd) Central Office, where he plays a pivotal role in shaping national educational policies and curriculum frameworks. He is one of the specialists who crafted the MATATAG Physical Education and Health Curriculum and contributed to strengthening the Senior High School curriculum for Sports, Health, and Wellness. Prior to his tenure at DepEd, he served as an Assistant Professorial Lecturer III at the Polytechnic University of the Philippines (PUP) in Manila, where he advanced instruction and scholarship in physical education and movement sciences. Mr. Echague earned his Bachelor's degree in Physical Education from PUP Manila and a Master of Science in Human Movement Science from the University of the Philippines Diliman. He is currently pursuing a Doctor of Philosophy in Curriculum and Instruction at the Philippine Normal University, further solidifying his expertise in program development and pedagogical innovation.

Yonis Gulzar is an Associate Professor of Management Information Systems at King Faisal University, Saudi Arabia. His research lies at the intersection of artificial intelligence, computer vision, and intelligent information systems, with applications in healthcare analytics and smart agriculture. His recent work focuses on deep learning architectures for agricultural imaging, disease detection, seed classification, and AI-enabled decision support systems aimed at improving sustainability and productivity in precision agriculture. He also contributes to research on AI-driven knowledge systems and emerging technologies in digital transformation.

Jerome Hilario is an educational leader, researcher, and literacy advocate with over a decade of service in the Department of Education. He is currently pursuing his PhD in Reading Education at the University of the Philippines Diliman, with research focused on literacy development and assessment to inform system-level improvement. A multi-awarded educator, he has been recognized as Huwarang Guro Most Outstanding Secondary Teacher in 2017, HAMAKA Awardee as the Most Outstanding Teacher in Antipolo City in 2019, and Guronasyon Most Outstanding Secondary Teacher in the entire Rizal Province, reflecting his commitment to instructional excellence and teacher leadership. He has presented research on literacy and assessment in international conferences in Singapore and the Netherlands and completed leadership training in classroom assessment under the Japan International Cooperation Agency (JICA) in Japan. Currently, he serves as Supervising Education Program Specialist for Reading at the Bureau of Learning Delivery, where he leads national initiatives to strengthen reading instruction, assessment practices, and teacher development nationwide.

Pooja Jaiswal received the B.Sc. degree in Science from J.K. Institute of Applied Physics & Technology, University of Allahabad, Allahabad (U.P.) in 2007. She received the B.Tech degree in Electronics and communication from J.K. Institute of Applied Physics & Technology, University of Allahabad, Allahabad (U.P.) in 2010. She received the M.Tech degree in Electronics and communication from J.K. Institute of Applied Physics & Technology, University of Allahabad, Allahabad (U.P.) in 2012. Her research interest includes Antenna and Microwave communication and their applications. Presently she is pursuing PhD and acting as an Assistant professor in United college of Engineering & Research, Prayagraj.

Ilmira Jumaniyazova is an academician in the Department of Pedagogy and Psychology at Mamun University, Khiva, Uzbekistan. Her academic interests are closely associated with educational theory, pedagogical practice, developmental psychology, learner motivation, classroom interaction, and student-centered teaching approaches. She contributes to the field of pedagogy and psychology by supporting the development of effective teaching strategies that enhance learning outcomes, emotional well-being, and holistic student growth. Her work emphasizes the importance of integrating psychological principles into educational practice to create inclusive, supportive, and engaging learning environments. Dr. Jumaniyazova is actively involved in teaching, academic mentoring, curriculum-related activities, and scholarly development within the university context. She promotes reflective teaching, learner engagement, professional ethics, and the application of modern pedagogical methods in higher education. Through her academic and educational contributions, she supports the preparation of competent educators and socially responsible graduates. Her professional commitment reflects a strong dedication to quality education, psychological awareness, and the continuous improvement of teaching and learning practices in Uzbekistan.

Atham Jurayev is an academician in the Department of Pedagogy and Psychology at Termez University of Economics and Service, Termez, Uzbekistan. His academic interests are closely connected with pedagogical theory, educational psychology, learner development, teaching methodology, and the improvement of educational practices in contemporary learning environments. He contributes to the advancement of pedagogy by exploring effective instructional strategies, student motivation, psychological support in education, and the role of teachers in shaping holistic learner growth. His work emphasizes the importance of combining pedagogical knowledge with psychological understanding to enhance teaching effectiveness, classroom interaction, and student-centered learning. Dr. Jurayev is actively involved in academic, research, and educational development activities that support quality education and professional growth. Through his contributions, he promotes innovative teaching approaches, inclusive learning practices, and the integration of psychological principles into educational systems, thereby supporting the development of competent and socially responsible learners.

Odilbek Kosimov is working in the Department of Information Technology and Exact Sciences at Termez University of Economics and Service, Termez, Uzbekistan.

Nitish Kulkarni is a student of Vishwakarma Institute of Technology, Pune, with a strong interest in Artificial Intelligence and Machine Learning. I love researching new concepts, technologies, and applications in the field of AI/ML. I am always eager to learn, explore innovative ideas, and improve my technical knowledge. Apart from academics, I enjoy playing cricket, which helps me develop teamwork, discipline, and leadership skills. My goal is to grow as a skilled learner and contribute meaningfully to the field of technology.

Supratim Mukherjee is an academician and media education professional with expertise in communication studies, journalism, animation, VFX, media research, and academic administration. He is actively engaged in teaching, curriculum development, student mentoring, and research, focusing on digital media, creative technologies, industry-oriented education, and innovative learning practices in higher education.

Muhammad Nasar-u-Minallah is an Associate Professor of Geography at the Institute of Geography, University of the Punjab, Lahore, Pakistan. He holds a PhD in Geography from the University of the Punjab and completed a postdoctoral fellowship in Urban Landscape Ecology at Humboldt University of Berlin, Germany (2022). With over 16 years of teaching and research experience, his work focuses on urban climate change, land use/land cover changes, Urban Heat Islands, GIS, and remote sensing. He is the author of more than 80 research papers and serves as the Managing Editor of the Pakistan Geographical Review. Dr. Nasar-u-Minallah is also a YESI International Fellow at the University of York, UK, and has been elected Joint Secretary of the Pakistan Geographical Association.

Norov Omonovich is an academician in the Department of Philosophy at Tashkent State University of Economics, Tashkent, Uzbekistan. His academic and scholarly interests are closely related to philosophy, social thought, ethics, logic, cultural studies, and the philosophical foundations of human and economic development. He contributes to the study and teaching of philosophical concepts that help students develop critical thinking, analytical reasoning, moral awareness, and a deeper understanding of society and human values. Dr. Norov's work emphasizes the importance of philosophy in shaping responsible citizenship, ethical decision-making, and intellectual culture in modern educational and professional contexts. He is actively involved in academic and educational activities that support interdisciplinary learning and the development of reflective thinking among students. Through his teaching and scholarly contributions, Dr. Norov promotes the relevance of philosophical inquiry in addressing contemporary social, cultural, and institutional challenges.

Ravikumar R N is currently a Postdoctoral researcher at Universiti Malaysia Perlis, Malaysia. Also, working as an Assistant Professor (Sr. Grade) in the Department of Computer Science and Engineering at Jain (Deemed-to-be University), Bangalore, Karnataka. He has 13+ years of national and international teaching experience. He completed his PhD at Amity University, Rajasthan, M.E at VMRF Deemed University, B.E at Anna University, Chennai. He also holds a MiniMBA certificate from Swiss eLearning Institute, Switzerland. He has published numerous research articles in Scopus, SCI journals, Book chapters, and Conference papers. Also, he hold several patents and authored books. His specialization is ML, DL, Federated Learning, Recommendation Systems, and Optimization Techniques.

Aarthi S is a dedicated Assistant Professor in Computer Science with over six years of teaching experience. She is currently pursuing her Ph.D. at Marwadi University, Gujarat, and holds an M.Phil. and MCA from Bharathiar University, Tamil Nadu. Throughout her academic career, Aarthi has specialized in programming languages such as C++, Java, and C, and contributed to research in recommender systems and AI-related data privacy. She has published journal articles, contributed to book chapters, and actively participated in technical workshops. Known for her student mentorship and engagement in academic events, Aarthi remains committed to fostering innovation and excellence in computer science education.

Index

A

B

C

D

E

F

G

H

I

M

O

P

R

S

T

V

Y

www.ingramcontent.com/pod-product-compliance
Lightning Source LLC
LaVergne TN
LVHW062321300926
849161LV00007B/1520